SEARCHLIGHTS, SQUADRONS AND SUBMARINES 1939-1945

HALIFAX

at War

WILLIAM D. NAFTEL

FORMAC PUBLISHING COMPANY LIMITED
HALIFAX

Acknowledgements

Although there is only one name on the cover, a work such as this has many, many authors as a glance at the bibliography will show. I want to thank them all for their contributions, many published as scholarly histories or personal memoirs in the decades after the War, others recorded privately for family and friends, yet others passed on to me in person. I thank you all and I am in your debt.

Research for a project such as this is massive in scope, but it is made so much simpler by the high quality of the staff of the research institutions on which one necessarily depends. Unstinted thanks are due to the ever helpful and proactive staff of the Nova Scotia Archives and Records Management who are always there for you. Equally supportive was the Library/Archives of the Halifax Defence Complex, and the staffs of the Pier 21 Research Centre, and the Dalhousie University Archives. Although I passed like a ship in the night amongst the crowds, the University of King's College Library and the Killam Library of Dalhousie University provided quiet retreats when the time came to organize and compose.

My particular thanks go to Barrie Cahill, Hon. David Chipman, Charlotte Jeffries, Charlotte Mhyre, Joan Payzant, Dorothy Purchase, Joyce and Don Purchase, Gerald Smith, Miriam Walls. But these are just the tip of the iceberg. To all who should have been named but were not, my sincerest gratitude for helping to bring to life again this six years in the long life of An East Coast Port.

Formac Publishing Company Limited acknowledges the support of the Cultural Affairs Section, Nova Scotia Department of Tourism, Culture and Heritage. We acknowledge the financial support of the Government of Canada through the Book Publishing Industry Development Program (BPIDP) for our publishing activities.

NOVA SCOTIA
Tourism, Culture and Heritage

The Canada Council | Le Conseil des Arts
for the Arts | du Canada

Library and Archives Canada Cataloguing in Publication

Naftel, William D
Halifax at war : searchlights, squadrons and submarines, 1939-1945 / William D. Naftel.

ISBN 978-0-88780-739-8

1. World War, 1939-1945 — Nova Scotia — Halifax. 2. Halifax (N.S.) — History — 20th century. I. Title.

FC2346.4.N35 2008   971.6'22503   C2008-903851-7

Formac Publishing Company Limited
5502 Atlantic Street
Halifax, Nova Scotia B3H 1G4
www.formac.ca

Printed in Canada

Contents

PRELUDE 7

CHAPTER ONE: A DECLARATION OF WAR 15

CHAPTER TWO: THE MILITARY PRESENCE 35

CHAPTER THREE: IN TRANSIT 84

CHAPTER FOUR: A HARD-WORKING CITY 119

CHAPTER FIVE: DAY BY DAY 139

CHAPTER SIX: SCARCITY AMONGST PLENTY 184

CHAPTER SEVEN: THE END AND THE BEGINNING 226

BIBLIOGRAPHY 252

ENDNOTES 257

INDEX 277

Maps

figure 1.0

This post-war vision of the new City of Halifax would make it fit for the returning heroes by filling in the peninsulas vacant lands with new, planned neighbourhoods linked with the old, revitalized city by fine new roads for fine new cars.

figure 2.0

This 1934 map, intended for the pre-war tourist trade, presents the public face of what will become "An East Coast Port" from Africville Church to the North, to Point Pleasant Park on the South, and Dartmouth Common on the East to the vacant lands around the Chebucto Road Airport in the West end of the peninsula.

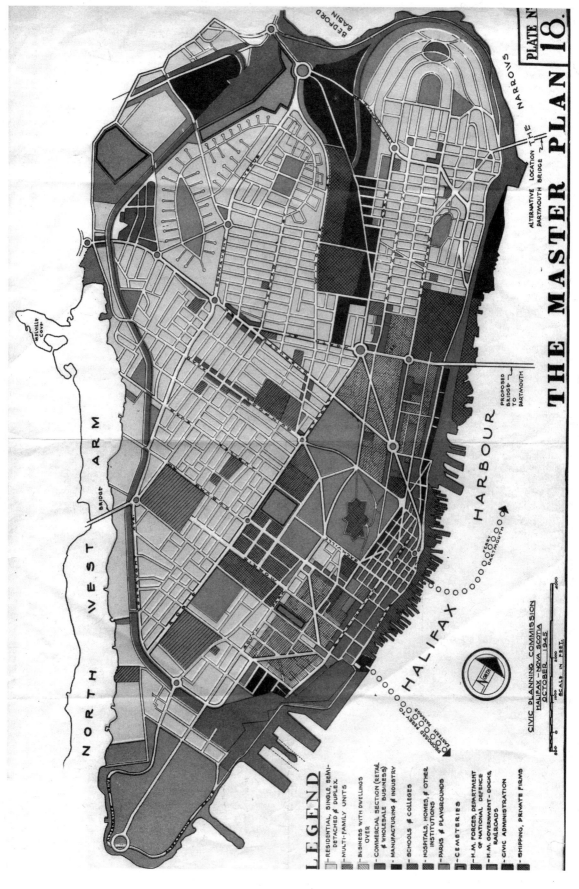

figure 1.0

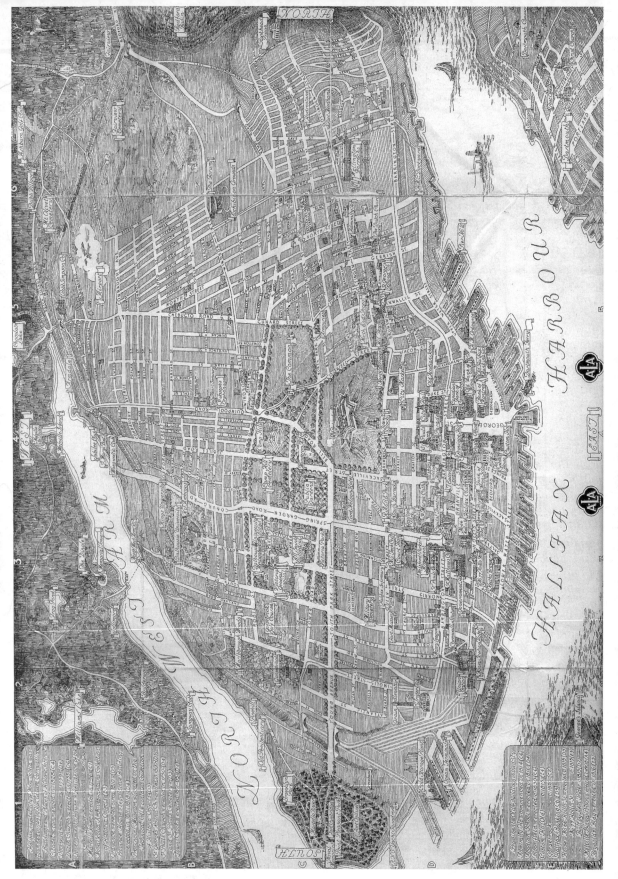

figure 2.0

Prelude

As dawn broke over Shelburne, Nova Scotia, on Saturday, 4 July 1936, the usual morning sounds of birds, motor boats and the first automobiles of the day were underscored by a deep, penetrating throb. Low on the western horizon the breaking dawn flashed on the silver hull of an enormous apparition floating in from the ocean, the German Zeppelin, *Hindenburg*, making landfall after departing the day before from its American terminus, Lakehurst, New Jersey, with a full complement of passengers. The early risers among them were getting ready for breakfast in the airship's sleek dining room; others, it has been speculated, were readying their cameras on behalf of the Third Reich's Air Ministry.

Even at this early hour Shelburne had its share of upturned faces, a phenomenon which followed the *Hindenburg* wherever it went; shops emptied, empty streets filled, cars stopped, whether in Rio de Janeiro, London, New York, or Nova Scotia. The airship cruised in from the ocean at about 1,000 feet, but if it followed normal procedure when over land in good weather, it would drop down to about 360 feet, giving passengers a good view. This procedure also created maximum impact on the earthbound audience, at 802 feet long the *Hindenburg* was about the size of a modern container ship. The *Hindenburg* and its smaller sister ship, the *Graf Zeppelin*, were an astonishing sight any time or place; but, more significantly, they embodied the concept of scheduled international air travel, scarcely more than a Buck Rogers fantasy a few years earlier.

The four big Mercedes-Benz engines pushed the Zeppelin along at about 80 miles an hour in favourable weather, so Shelburne soon slipped behind and the jagged coastline slid by underneath. The airship slowed down slightly to give a good view of the pretty resort town of Chester. Shortly after 8:00 a.m., Haligonians heard the first distant drone and, fore-warned by radio and word-of-mouth, like their contemporaries everywhere, they poured into the streets, onto roofs, climbed hills and rushed to windows. The huge shape loomed out of the west, moved slowly and irregularly over Melville Cove, followed the line of Quinpool Road, and passed over the Commons, the Citadel and HMC Dockyard. Continuing eastward, its steady drone faded, the silver shape gliding out over Cole Harbour, the Imperial Oil Refinery and Lawrencetown Beach and skirting a vast fog bank just offshore. As the day wore on, it followed the Nova Scotia coast-line, then headed out over the North Atlantic, towards home base at Friedrichshafen, the thousand year Reich of Adolf Hitler and destiny.

As the *Hindenburg* glided out of sight, it left behind not only thousands of excited citizens who would talk about the apparition for days, but also furrowed brows and pointed questions. By 1936 the "best behaviour" of the Berlin Olympics notwithstanding, suspicion was growing that Adolf Hitler and his Nazi party were not going to be good corporate citizens; that behind the fine new roads and rosy employment statistics there lurked another, more sinister agenda. The magnificent new *Hindenburg*, launched exactly four months before its Halifax début, carried on its enormous tail fin the Nazi swastika. Was there some subversive reason why the *Hindenburg* took that swing over the Citadel and HMC Dockyard? Was there some nefarious reason, other than a convenient fog bank, why it had swung inland over Nova Scotia without notifying Canadian authorities, as its captain was required to do? Well no harm done, said Ottawa, we have nothing to hide, unfortunately an all too accurate statement as the Halifax dockyard facilities reflected the kind of threat posed by Bismarck and Kaiser Wilhelm, not by Hitler's burgeoning Luftwaffe and Wehrmacht. Still, for Halifax in 1936, drowsing in the genteel poverty of Depression-era Canada, the appearance of the *Hindenburg* was a reminder, wake-up call, if you will, that while the rest of Canada might not be interested in its defences, others might be.[1]

A year later, in 1937, the German naval training ship KMS *Schleisen* (Kreigs Marine Schiff: commissioned in 1908 and a veteran of World War I's Battle of Jutland) visited Halifax, arriving and departing with many protestations of friendship and goodwill. Under the genial and charming command of its Captain, Thile Seebach, the officers dined at Government House, visited Lunenburg amidst a flurry of Union Jacks and Swastikas and the cadets cut a considerable swath amongst the Halifax girls invited to the parties and dances which accompanied the visit. Charlotte Myrhe (nee Akerlund) recalls a friend so badly smitten by one that the ship's inevitable departure left her desolate and depressed for weeks.[2] Who knew what the motive was then? Certainly the *Schleisen* was quick to shed its sheep's clothing in September 1939 when, with its sister ship, KMS *Schleswig-Holstein*, it fired the opening salvos of World War II when they bombarded the Polish coast on 1 September.[3]

Two years later, the future was much clearer: the Spanish Civil War; the invasion of the Saar; Anschluss with Austria; Munich; the rapprochement with Benito Mussolini's Fascist Italy, whose seizure of Abyssinia underlined his own ambitions; along with growing, if reluctant, realization that life for German Jews was seriously compromised. On 10 October 1938, Prime Minister Neville Chamberlain had snatched peace from the jaws of war by conceding that the German-speaking areas of Czechoslovakia might as well be incorporated into Hitler's Reich. With the Munich Accord it was sadly assumed that Hitler's goal was now accomplished and everyone could relax.

For the average Haligonian these events were but distant rumblings. The summer of 1939 was a rare treasure in Halifax, warm and sunny. The city still basked in the excitement of the visit that June of King George VI and that most winning of consorts, "the most dangerous woman in Europe" Hitler called her, Queen Elizabeth, along with the reassuring presence in the harbour of HMS *Southampton* and *Glasgow*, and the Royal Canadian Navy destroyers *Skeena* and *Saguenay* (virtually half of the R.C.N.'s fleet). As the *Empress of Britain* with an aerial escort of three big Stranraer flying boats, a substantial proportion of the resources of the tiny Royal Canadian Air Force, bore Their Majesties away, the tens of thousands waving goodbye from Citadel Hill and waterfront piers were confident that the Royal Navy still commanded the seas and all was right with the world. Alas, the *Empress of Britain* would be an early casualty of the coming war, sent to the bottom by a combined U-boat and Luftwaffe attack in October 1940.

Much more quietly, but in the long run perhaps just as significantly, on 15 August USS *Tuscaloosa* slipped into port at noon carrying on board U.S. President Franklin D. Roosevelt. The harbour batteries, in the middle of gun practice, ceased fire as the heavy cruiser glided by York Redoubt, but although the President remained on board, the niceties of protocol were followed including a 21 gun salute and the passing of official compliments. The President was on his way again, en route to a vacation along the coast of Labrador. But, it was not to be. Within the week, the *Tuscaloosa* was back, hurriedly and without ceremony of any kind this time, "to pick up mail" it was said, but clearly the splendour of the Labrador coastline had to be foregone in view of the rapidly deteriorating international situation.[4]

The Depression, while still a nasty reality for many, was easing and life was getting a little better. In 1934 the Dominion Government had started upgrading the old U.S. Navy seaplane base in Eastern Passage, turning it into a proper airport for the Royal Canadian Air Force; and it appeared that the long projected piers of the Ocean Terminals might actually be completed. Halifax was not large, about 62,000 people, with another 8,000 across the harbour in Dartmouth, a 10 minute ferry ride away. If you had a regular income, even a modest one, life was pretty good, and even more so if you came from long-established roots, because you were sure to have friends in high places within the city's stable, some might say static, social and political framework. Halifax was not such a great place to live if you had no job, no money and no friends, conditions that 20 years of Depression in the Maritimes had created.

For the fortunate, Halifax's residential areas were leafy and lovely, with generous boulevards and pleasant houses, the equal of any place in Canada. For those with little or nothing, later generations labelled their existence in dilapidated slums "third world," their only "safety net" the well intentioned but fitful and conditional charity of the municipality and the city churches.

Still, on those fine summer days in the late 1930s, even the poor could find the nickel to board a yellow tram bobbing toward the south end, the trolley snapping and crackling through the overhead at every route intersection, flanges screeching around the curves, to arrive at Point Pleasant Park. Its cool dark woods, beckoning beach, derelict forts and batteries were a child's paradise, and for the adult, a civilized wilderness to amble through or doze in, the city and all cares a world away. If money was less of an issue, there was the big ticket trip on the # 6 tram down Coburg, with a left at Oxford to "the Dingle" stop, thundering down the long wooden staircase to the Arm ferry, parting with a dime to cross the water to the more remote, and hence more exotic, charms of Fleming Park. Here were boats and canoes for hire, secluded beaches and the challenge of the long, echoing, nerve-wracking climb up the skinny iron staircase through the hollow interior of the Memorial Tower for the spectacular view of land and sky and sea, and one's tiny friends far below.

In those days Halifax was a service centre, its main industry the administrative machinery of a provincial capital, and to a lesser extent the regional operations of the Dominion Government. Schools, except for the Sacred Heart Convent and the Halifax Ladies College, were public, and in a unique and informal arrangement, were divided into those attended and taught by Roman Catholics and those attended and taught by Protestants, including those honorary Protestants, the Jews, who, except for the occasional Asian and the carefully segregated Black community in Africville, were as exotic as Halifax's multicultural makeup got.

High school matriculation was pretty much as far as most people, even the ambitious, felt the need to go and was entry level for almost all respectable jobs except the professions. For Roman Catholics high school was Saint Patrick's for boys and Saint Mary's for girls; and for Protestants and others, Bloomfield in the north end and the Halifax Academy in the south end, which would soon merge as Queen Elizabeth High School.

For the few who wished, and could afford to go on, Dalhousie University, joined by Anglican King's College in 1923, provided humanities degrees in the Protestant tradition, with small but high-quality faculties of law and medicine; while the Jesuits at Saint Mary's and the Sisters of Charity at Mount Saint Vincent in suburban Rockingham provided degrees for Roman Catholic boys and girls respectively. It was taken for granted that a university degree meant that the recipient was not only educated, but was also a gentleman or lady.

Church going, although not mandatory, was expected and common. It was a rare child who did not go to Sunday School and a rare family that did not appear in church with some regularity. Membership in fraternal organizations, such as the Masons, was equally important as much for business as social reasons; but as everywhere else it was accepted that a Roman Catholic or a Protestant would apply only to this or that organization or club. Similar rules applied in business and social life, and Jews, Blacks and other ethnic groups as well as women simply had to create their own organizations.

Health care was a private matter and, except in extreme cases, treatment just as likely occurred at home as in the hospitals, of which there were two, the Roman Catholic Infirmary and the Victoria General for everybody else. Across the harbour in Woodside was the provincially funded, non-denominational Nova Scotia Hospital for the mentally ill across the harbour in Woodside. The poor had access to the Carnegie-funded Public Health Clinic associated with Dalhousie University and its medical school, and a good thing too, because the City Medical Officer of Health did not believe in, and fought tooth and nail against vaccination, asserting it to be a dangerous innovation.

The Halifax labour force meant, by and large, the male population, because it was still generally accepted that, while a single girl might work in a shop, teach or nurse, once married, women stayed at home. To continue working, which often was not permitted anyway, was a reflection on a husband's ability to provide and led to suspicions that he was a drinker or shiftless or both. These attitudes persisted despite years of economic hardship, when many men struggled with the shame of unemployment.

Downtown, which for the most part meant Barrington, Hollis and Granville Streets between Spring Garden and Duke, was the retail and business district, while the labouring man's territory encompassed HMC Dockyard, the Halifax Shipyards to the north, the piers and marshalling yards of the Ocean Terminals to the south, the distant Canadian National Railway shops and engine terminals in Windsor Park, and across the harbour in Dartmouth, the rope works, sugar refinery, marine slips and Starr

Manufacturing. On the far periphery, a separate entity really, was the Imperial Oil Refinery, Imperoyal, near Eastern Passage.

Horse drawn "slovens" or low-slung delivery wagons still clattered over cobblestone streets, but the motor car and truck had asserted their presence and dominated, even though it would be years before traffic lights displaced the artistry of an accomplished traffic policeman. Many Haligonians depended on the city's canary-yellow tram cars for their transportation. These vehicles were unique in that the entire fleet of 59 were all one type, the "Birney Safety Car," so named because in the event that the driver became unconscious or lost control, the tram automatically came to a stop. Apart from safety considerations, the Birney Car had been selected because its small size made it ideal for navigating the tight curves of the downtown trackage imposed by the city's eighteenth-century street plan. The trams were adequate for the city's need, but while "cute" and well maintained, most residents had a love-hate relationship with them. As motor cars became more comfortable the tram's wooden seats appeared rudimentary; their unsophisticated suspension coupled with a short, one-truck wheelbase, which made them so good for those downtown curves, gave them a characteristic bobbing motion, the "Birney bob."

The whole system was under the jurisdiction of Nova Scotia Light and Power (N.S.L.&P.), which had taken over and upgraded it in 1919, along with the general power distribution and supply network. The garage or "barn" was located at the south end of Lower Water Street, a component of the N.S.L.&P. complex, which included the steam generating plant. A few bus lines serviced Dartmouth and suburban areas, such as the Bay Road, Dutch Village Road and the Bedford Highway; while the C.N.R. ran a train from Windsor Junction, morning in and late afternoon out, for those adventurous enough to live off the Peninsula.

The same investment that saw the rehabilitation of the street railway under the aegis of N.S.L.&P., also saw a much-needed upgrading of the electrical supply and generating system. Initially dependent upon steam-generated electricity from the Lower Water Street plant, the power company's capacity was upgraded by the addition, beginning in 1919, of hydroelectric power from a series of dams and plants at French Village and in the Gaspereau Valley, inaugurating long-distance, high-voltage power transmission. These plants were sufficient to relegate the company's downtown steam generating plant to stand-by status. By the 1930s electric lighting was ubiquitous, but many homes still cooked with coal gas generated by the N.S.L.&P. at its Lower Water Street complex.

The city's water supply was adequate, drawn from a chain of lakes in the highlands west of the Northwest Arm. Since the construction of a reservoir on the height of land at Robie and Lady Hammond, which for a time bore the designation "largest unsupported concrete dome in the British Empire," water pressure problems, which for years had plagued both householders and firemen, had been overcome.

Thus a snapshot of Halifax in the summer of 1939: A small city, adequately supplied and structured dangling at the end of a long transcontinental railway line. Not exactly forgotten, but made painfully aware, when Ottawa bureaucrats inquired if the Harbour was big enough for the *Empress of Britain* to turn around in, of just how peripheral they were. Halifax was a little shabby, but its infrastructure was sufficient for its needs and would do until a few years of post-Depression prosperity gave the city a chance to catch up with the rest of the country.

Then came 3 September 1939.

CHAPTER ONE:

A Declaration of War

On 3 September 1939, Haligonians knew Canada was at war, no matter if the Canadian Prime Minister for a week maintained the political fiction that the country was not, until Parliament had spoken. Although the Prime Minister was privy to the behind-the-scenes manoeuvering of the Canadian military during recent months, the average citizen was not aware. They might have noticed that since a quiet February meeting between the R.C.M.P. and the executives of Nova Scotia Light and Power, the city's generating plants and tram car barns on Lower Water Street had seen the erection of fencing and men could be seen setting up what looked like an elaborate lighting system. By early September, the N.S.L.&P. was ready. Water Street, like Downing Street, was waiting for Adolf Hitler to make his move. On 1 September he made it. At the power plant staff kept one ear on a specially installed radio while management sat by the telephone. These preparations were not unwarranted in light of the conventional wisdom that the ocean-borne threat from Germany lay not as it later developed, with the submarine but with fast, heavily armed raiders such as the *Bismarck*, *Graf Spee* and *Scharnhorst*. One of these ships could easily shell Halifax and amid the confusion, land a shore party at the power plant's coal wharf, seize the generating station, commandeer trams from the car barn to fan out across the city and overpower key installations. Another scenario had aircraft launched from a catapult on the deck of a German ship or from the cavernous hull of a Zeppelin hovering silently out at sea, to bomb the city into rubble, the way tens of thousands had seen in newsreels of the Spanish Civil War. At this distant remove, it was all very Buck Rogers and it did not happen; but these were popular perceptions of how war might develop,[5] threats regarded as serious well into the war. Admiral Stuart Bonham-Carter of the Royal Navy, in charge of naval operations in Halifax until late 1941, fully expected an air raid at any time. Given the key role Halifax played in the convoy system, he always considered that the Germans over-looked a major opportunity: "They can fit up an old freighter to carry any number of seaplanes from 8 up, wait for a calm day to hoist them out by derrick, fly over here, drop bombs and incendiaries on the Dockyard, the oil tanks, the docks and wooden sections of the city, then land in Bedford Basin, get into their rubber boats, blow up their planes and paddle ashore crying 'Kamarad!' and be well fed by the Mounted Police for the duration of the war."[6]

Around 5:00 a.m., 3 September, probably the first Haligonians to hear that a state of war existed between Germany and Great Britain was the night shift at the generating station. By the time the morning shift arrived three hours later, Nova Scotia Light and Power, if not the Dominion of Canada, was also at war. All their facilities, extending to the Annapolis Valley and Cumberland County, were now under guard. On Water Street, the new fencing was extended to the coal-gas plant and the car barn, and the whole designated a "Restricted Zone." Tram cars returning after the morning rush hour, as well as all motor cars, were stopped before they entered the property and searched for incendiaries. Over the next few days the vital substations at Armdale, Ochterloney Street and Tufts Cove, which dropped power into the city from hydro-plants at French Village and Gaspereau, were also fenced in and guarded 24 hours a day, and their main transformers were encased in steel armour plate.[7]

None of this came as much of a surprise to Haligonians, unlike Torontonians, whose pacifist *Toronto Star* had for months ignored the grow-ing tensions in Europe and fed readers an escapist diet of news about babies, local crime and agricultural fairs. Haligonians, on the other hand, had active preparation. On 4 June, for example, hundreds of Haligonians flocked to the municipal airport on Bayer's Road, across from the Industrial School farm and just east of the big Robert Simpson department store and catalogue warehouse, where the newly formed First Anti-Aircraft Battery, the first such in Canada,[8] strutted its stuff. Granted, there was no Royal Canadian Air Force to speak of, so the boys organized their own targets, two planes belonging to the Halifax Aero Club. One plane was piloted by a Battery officer, Captain Ira B. McCallum, the other by Henry Gates, a flying instructor.[9]

Since the agreement to partition Czechoslovakia at Munich in 1938 the Royal Canadian Navy had been quietly clearing its decks for action. Richard Oland, a Halifax reservist, was called in to command a newly created Naval Control Service, the ghost structure of which (complete with furnished office space) had been awaiting since the beginning of 1939 the signal to begin organizing escorts for convoys of merchant ships. In mid-August the signal had come.[10] A week later, on the 26th day of that sunny August, mobilization orders came down to the R.C.N. and the Halifax militia regiments, the Princess Louise Fusiliers (Machine Gunner) and the Halifax Rifles. At 2:30 p.m the 23 officers and 179 other ranks of the First (Halifax) Coast Brigade (later Regiment) paraded, and by 6:30 that evening they were garrisoning the three functioning harbour batteries, Sandwich, McNab and Ogilvie.[11] The lives of citizen soldiers all over Halifax and Dartmouth slipped out of their control as they sat in the back of hastily assembled Ford and Chevy trucks that rumbled and bounced over dirt roads to the half-abandoned batteries that ringed the harbour entrance.[12]

The identity of the enemy was no secret. The theatres had been featuring Edward G. Robinson in *Confessions of a Nazi Spy*: "... the first film that dares call a swastika a swastika ... because it will open the eyes of 130,000,000 people ... because it will forever blast the Nazis out of the America they betray!"[13]

THE NOT-SO-PHONEY WAR AT HOME

For Halifax the anticipated war had begun. There was no fanfare, no bands, but rather a silent gathering of people along the waterfront to watch the tiny east coast fleet of the Royal Canadian Navy put out to sea. There was none of the hysteria that marked the beginning of the World War I. No

German Shepherds or Dachshunds were put down by patriotic owners. But there would be rumours of captured spies and firing squads within the Citadel, and stories that the raw, edgy militia at York Redoubt had been hard on local cows not quick enough with the password.[14] Down at the Ocean Terminals though, on that first day, crowds big enough to be held back by special guards watched as hundreds of nervous American tourists scrambled to get back on board their cruise ships. The Swedish *Gripsholm* and the Dutch *Rotterdam* were headed back to the safety of New York, but their passengers were half convinced that a lurking threat was waiting just off Sambro to fix them in its sights.[15] A week later, when Canada officially entered the war on 10 September, it was "old news" for a city already more involved than any other in the country was or would be over the next six years.

There were some immediate effects. Donald Purchase, then a 12-year-old living on north Robie Street, recalls that the neighbours' three sons, long unemployed, disappeared quickly into the first recruiting drives. One of these sons, he recalls, reappeared six years later transformed from feckless youth to crisp veteran. As a harbinger of things to come, the R.C.N.'s hard-pressed Atlantic fleet practically doubled in size when HMC ships *Fraser* and *St. Laurent* arrived from the Pacific to join *Saguenay* and *Skeena*, a voyage so hotly pressed that the firebrick linings of their boilers had burnt out and had to be replaced.

Also by the end of September the Royal Navy took over jurisdiction of HMC Dockyard with the arrival of Admiral Stuart Bonham-Carter (1889 -1972), who headed the Third Battle Squadron, a force of elderly battleships and light cruisers intended to provide convoy support and a credible defence of Canada's east coast, which the much-neglected R.C.N. clearly could not yet do.[16] Owing to scarcity of space in the Dockyard, and to avoid jurisdictional grey areas with his Canadian colleagues, Admiral Bonham-Carter directed his command from the cramped and seedy elegance of the former motor yacht HMS *Seaborne*.

Seemingly overnight, the streets of the city, so tranquil and orderly just weeks before, were flooded with thousands of servicemen with little money and nothing to do. Everywhere were the uniforms of the Royal Navy, and increasingly the R.C.N.; and soldiers, many of whom were kitted out in leftover uniforms from World War I, along with the new blue of the R.C.A.F. fresh from their new Station, still under construction, across the harbour in Eastern Passage. As Archibald MacMechan, a well-known Nova Scotia writer, so pithily remarked, "When a sailor makes port after a voyage, two things he must have. One is a drink."[17] Patriotic euphoria ruled in the autumn of 1939, and the Royal Navy was welcomed back "home" with open arms; but Halifax had forgotten that regiments and fleets of single men did not mean only band concerts and smart parades, balls and parties. A half-century earlier, Halifax could have absorbed the men of a British regiment and a Royal Naval squadron at one and the same time, with no more than the occasional belch. To the Haligonians of 1939 that was another time and place and they were in for a severe case of indigestion.

Early on Halifax was given a sober reminder of what might be in store with the arrival at the Ocean Terminals on 13 September of the American freighter *City of Flint*. On board were the 221 dazed survivors of the British liner *Athenia*, torpedoed the very day war was declared by the German U-30 with the loss of 112 lives. It did not matter that the German government was almost as upset about the incident as Britain and the Dominions. Crowded with Americans fleeing Europe, it caused a hardening of attitudes in the U.S.A. that the Nazis, surprised by the reaction to the invasion of Poland, were still hoping to avoid. Six weeks later, on 14 October, U-47 sank HMS *Ark Royal* lying at anchor in the shelter of Scapa Flow. The future role of the submarine began to become clear to both layman and naval strategist.

All these events were unpleasant enough, but the man in the Halifax street can hardly be blamed for silently rejoicing. For the first time in decades government agencies and the Halifax Shipyards were actually hiring; wages were on the rise for local workers, and the newcomers who had begun to flood into town brought supply and demand with them. Thomas Raddall recalled that first Christmas of the war as one of confidence and good cheer. Food, drink, clothing, everything was cheap and abundant. City residents invited young servicemen into their homes and did their best to make them feel welcome. Skating parties flocked to the lakes or the Egg Pond on the South Commons, and the theatres were jammed. The only fly in the ointment was that, despite Hitler's statement to the Reichstag in October that all he wanted was peace, some spoilsport had banned out-door Christmas lights.[18]

HERALDS AND HARBINGERS

It was now easier for Haligonians to keep informed because radio, which had materialized over the last 10 years, rapidly increased in significance with the outbreak of the war. Anyone with a radio now knew up to the minute if anything was going on. John Fisher, whose programme Noontime Melodies was broadcast over CHNS during the early years of the war, rec-ognized this medium as a great source of social change. Compared with even a few years before, his listeners could now "... flick a radio dial and spend several minutes in the swankiest and most cosmopolitan club in New York City ... or they can snap the dial and hear what the smart people are doing in Florida. Or if they want excitement they can tune in to London."

One change brought by the war, perhaps unrecognized at this stage, was the growing opportunity for women in the workforce. For the single girl looking to earn a living, opportunities opened up for clerks and stenogra-phers which paid a living wage. The working girl might make $14.50 a week, out of which she budgeted for board, $5.00; lunches, $1.25; transit, 75¢; clothes, $4.00; makeup, $1.10; entertainment, $1.00; and War Stamps, 50¢. To keep within her salary, be patriotic and pay the tax increase, which jumped from 80¢ a week to $1.54, she was advised to adopt a "Victory Budget," which reduced her lunch money to $1.00, clothes allowance to $3.70, makeup to 90¢ and entertainment to 76¢. This economy meant not only that she could pay taxes but also put aside an extra quarter for another War Savings Stamp.[20]

These early days of World War II also heralded, again yet unrecog-nized, the end of the domestic servant. Middle class households intending to keep up appearances aspired to at least one maid; even new flats had a room for the maid in the attic and a button in the dining room to summon her from the kitchen to clear the table. The single girl in Musquodoboit, looking to get away from home without having to get married in to the bar-gain, had no option but to "go into service." But, as opportunities opened up for clerks and stenographers and as war work provided even more unusual jobs, so went the necessity of living in the garret of someone else's house being watched like a hawk even on your one day off. For the next six years more and more options presented, and the working girl never looked back. By 1945 domestic service was dead.

This was the period of the "phoney war" and these last months of 1939 and the first few of 1940 were good. The city bustled with activity, there was no bad news and no nasty telegrams yet. The province called upon farmers to increase their grain acreage by 50 percent — "This Is The Empire's Call To You, Mr. Farmer"[21] — and to support them the government called upon the clergy to use their pulpits on Sunday, 15 October, to explain the food situation to their congregations and "invoke the blessing of Almighty God on the efforts of our Farmers."

THE EAST COAST PORT BEGINS TO FILL UP: CONVOYS

Barely two weeks after the war began, convoy HX1, 18 ships, slipped out of Halifax Harbour. It was the first convoy of the war and if there had been early debate in some circles that convoys were overkill, the loss of the *Athenia* silenced it. On a pragmatic level, for longshoremen and railway men, HX1 had meant welcome employment. Little did they realize how much it would dominate their futures. It did not take long for the Germans to catch on and by November their short-wave radio was confidently announcing the size and departure of convoys leaving Halifax.[22] Word of a convoy's departure invariably leaked back to Berlin, often, as naval intelligence believed, by way of Venezuela.

Fortunately, right up to May 1945, the Germans might know when it left, but never its route or the kind of protection it had once Chebucto Head had faded into the mist behind it.[23] Such knowledge was the job of crack U-Boat commanders, who rapidly turned the "nuisance" of early strategists into the dreaded "wolf packs" of the Battle of the Atlantic, which nearly strangled Britain in 1942 and 1943 and brought World War II to the doorstep of Haligonians. That it did not happen earlier in the war — and Admiral Bonham-Carter expected it every day — reflects Hitler's veto of a 1940 proposal by Grand Admiral Raeder to station two submarines off Halifax. The pickings would have been rich, but the Führer judged that the carnage would alarm neutral America.[24]

Keeping a convoy secret was, of course, impossible. Anyone could see the vast anchorage of Bedford Basin filling up day by day with ships; family hosts knew when their naval guests would not be around; taxi drivers, summoned to the waterfront to pick up a ship's captain, knew by the briefcase and the Naval HQ destination that a pre-departure briefing was being held.[25] Don Purchase and his buddies watched in fascination countless times as the parade passed through the Narrows in front of their vantage point at Fort Needham just up the hill from their classrooms at Richmond School. Every eight days, more or less, the Basin and Harbour emptied out in a matter of hours, sometimes unseen during the night, and then slowly began to fill up again. And residents of Halifax and Dartmouth who had fond memories of swimming around the Basin or at Point Pleasant, looked with dismay at the shoreline now turned into a yeasty stew of garbage and oil.

THE REAL THING BEGINS

On 9 April 1940, the residents of Copenhagen, Denmark, awoke to the sound of Wehrmacht soldiers goose-stepping resolutely and unannounced towards the Royal Palace. On the same day in Norway, Vidkun Quisling opened the doors of his mineral-rich country to the Germans and made his name forever a byword for treachery. A month later the Luftwaffe exploded the vaunted neutrality of Belgium and the Netherlands, and annihilated central Rotterdam in a terror bombing that heralded what became the "Blitzkreig." Belgium and the Netherlands capitulated on 28 and 14 May, respectively. "The war," wrote Dartmouth resident Bobbie Johnston in her diary, "just gets worse and worse .... Where it will stop no one knows."[26]

The only bright spot that dark spring came on 10 May when Winston Churchill succeeded Neville Chamberlain as Prime Minister, and three days later galvanized and electrified the free world with his iconic speech: "I have nothing to offer but blood, toil, tears and sweat [in the pursuit of] victory at all costs, victory in spite of all terror, victory, however long and hard the road may be; for without victory, there is no survival."[27] Two weeks later, on 26 May, the whole British Empire united in a prayer for peace. "I am going to go to church too and do my small bit," wrote Bobbie Johnston, "I hope it will soon all be over but it certainly doesn't look that way now."[28]

For the next two and a half years the radio in the livingroom became a conduit to the world, each time the stentorian voice of Lorne Greene spoke, "bringing us news of fresh disasters" (to quote the popular 1960's revue "Beyond the Fringe").

The first of these disasters, Dunkirk, followed on the German sweep across northern France and the collapse of French resistance, which left British troops stranded on the continent. That astounding rescue of some 340,000 men, between 27 May and 4 June, from the enclave of Dunkirk, rife with stories of hastily recruited Edwardian paddle steamers and private yachts laden to the gunwales with much of the British Army steaming across the channel to safety, was a sustaining miracle which gave consolation to the now stand-alone British Empire. It had to do for a while, because on 11 June 1940, Italy entered the war, forming with Germany, and later Japan, what became known as the Axis Powers. Three days later the Germans entered Paris. A new French government exiled to the resort town of Vichy, with the elderly Marshal Henri Petain at its head, sued for peace, and on 22 June signed an armistice which left but half the country in its hands and left Britain and the Dominions, in the eyes of the Nazis and many in the United States, up the creek without a paddle.

THE FIRST STRAINS APPEAR

Halifax began early in the game to struggle with the impact of the war. With the arrival of the Royal Navy's Third Squadron at the end of September 1939, and frequent visits until June 1940 by the French Navy (Marine Nationale), it became immediately clear that there were problems. Pay for a British rating was about $1.00 a day, and for the French about fifty cents. Even if the city had an abundance of entertainment venues, good restaurants, taverns and bars, which it certainly did not, anything other than an occasional visit would have been out of the question for these men. While in port, there was little for them to do but wander aimlessly up and down the main streets of a city quite at a loss about how to cope with them.

Recognizing a need, a group of naval officers' wives and their friends approached Saint Mark's Church on Gottingen Street, close to Wellington Barracks and HMC Dockyard, and persuaded the Vestry to turn over the church hall. They established the North End Servicemen's Canteen, the first of many. This canteen and others, such as the Ajax Club and the many lunch and coffee hours sponsored by church groups, were of local inspiration;

others were sponsored by national organizations: the Y.M.C.A., the Knights of Columbus, the I.O.D.E., the Canadian Legion, the Red Cross, etc., which set up what became known as "huts" or "hostels" in the downtown close to the harbour. Their aim was to provide servicemen and women and merchant seamen with a clean, decent place to go for a meal, a cup of coffee or a place to relax and read a magazine outside their crowded and smelly fo'c'sles and barracks.

The smaller officer class had other resources open to them, partly because they had more money and partly because they had more private and family connections. Naval wardrooms afloat and ashore provided resources, while Halifax's private clubs opened their doors to the officers of the merchant navy. Although the national organizations were somewhat better bankrolled than the local groups, all of them performed miracles of organization, cadging, wheedling and borrowing, all of which became more necessary as the war dragged on.

Initially, this hospitality exacted a small price, because until the spring of 1942 there were few restrictions, other than price or availability, on what one could purchase. But after that, quotas and rationing began to erode supply and demand, and the ability to scrounge became an asset. The spirit of hospitality was not limited to Halifax, but certainly flourished in the city, and as need and effort became more apparent across the country the Department of National War Services was established in June 1940 to co-ordinate all voluntary war services. On an individual level, once it became clear that the war was no flash in the pan, middle class families began to donate their cottages and summer camps and open their homes, initially to the sons and daughters of friends, and then to strangers as the need became more urgent. Jessie Coade would recall going to a party where she danced with a young man: "He seemed so nice, so I invited him to bring a few of his friends to dinner at my house. Well, the next day there were 16 of them at my door. I don't know how we fed them.[29]

REGISTRATION IS INTRODUCED

The Liberal government of Mackenzie King was much strengthened by a solid victory in the Dominion election on 26 March 1940, and on 20 June Parliament passed the National Resources Mobilization Act, which required "persons to place themselves, their services and their property at the disposal of His Majesty in the right of Canada, as may be deemed necessary or expedient" for the assistance of Britain and the defence of Canada. National Registration, which took place 19 to 21 August 1940, listed every man and woman over the age of 16 in a country-wide registry. Used initially for military service, the registry eventually expanded to labour, those men and women who for one reason or another did not qualify for the military.

This initial registration focused on men with a series of 18 questions about military and agricultural experience. Women were part of this process, but were quizzed only on agricultural experience,[30] until a year later, when between 14 and 19 September 1941 women were re-registered,[31] a reflection of manpower shortages and the growing potential of women as a part of the workforce.

Registration was serious stuff. Newspaper advertisements continually reminded 16-year-olds that with their birthday came the obligation to register, and just because, for some reason or other, you did not qualify for the military, you were not off the hook. A worker was frozen in his occupation and could not move without permission, easy enough to get if you were a stenographer or clerk, but almost impossible if your job was classed as essential, such as a coal miner, stevedore, shipyard worker, railway employee or any of the new war industries that sprang up.

Originally under the jurisdiction of the Department of National War Services, registration was transferred to the Department of Labour in 1942, where it became known as the National Selective Service (NSS), "to direct civilian labour supply in order to meet the requirements of war and essential services." NSS incorporated not only the National Registration but also other labour mobilization programmes initiated since September 1939.[32]

The Halifax office, responsible for all of Nova Scotia, was set up in the basement of the Bank of Nova Scotia on Bedford Row in September 1940, under the assumption that it would initiate the military call-up of unmarried men from 20 to 25 years of age, and then the office would then be closed. After the end of the "Phoney War" and Dunkirk, those assumptions died. As the war expanded and the responsibilities of Selective Service extended to include recruitment of women and, then, the assignment of civilians to war industries, the operation grew and moved to the fourth floor of the bank in September of 1942.[33]

For women, the registration requirement was new and startling, but John Fisher assured them that it was okay and, indeed, necessary and patriotic to leave the house and children to go down and register. It was actually simple if they accepted a radical departure from the norm: "Put your husband to work. He's always talking about how easy it is to run the house. So when he comes home tonight you slip out and register and let him look after the house. You see the registration booths are open until ten o'clock."[34]

A variation on this "conscription" of labour was the Manning Pool for merchant seamen. Being of various nationalities seamen were not subject to Canadian law, but with the institution of the convoy system, casually picking up crew at the local shipping office was no longer good enough. Accordingly, in the summer of 1941, all British merchant seamen "on the beach" in eastern Canada were required, and others encouraged, to register at a central Manning Pool in Halifax. From a base in Mulgrave Park in the north end of the city, they could be drawn upon as required by ships in port.[35]

CONTROLS APPEAR

Even before registration began playing a role in people's lives, on 3 September 1939, under the War Measures Act and while still pretending Canada was not at war, the King government created the Wartime Prices and Trade Board (W.T.P.B.). Under its Chairman, Donald Gordon, the Board had a huge impact upon the lives of those who served on the home front. Eventually, its army of administrators, controllers and clerks, which grew to number 6,000, reduced the lives of all Canadians to fundamentals. Initially empowered to ensure that the prices of food, fuel and other necessities remained reasonable, its jurisdiction gradually expanded to include investigating prices and profits; licensing producers, distributors and sellers; fixing prices, regulating sales, seizing goods, controlling imports and exports, regulating rentals and housing; in October 1941, controlling wages and prices based strictly on the cost of living; and culminating in the spring of 1942 with the gradual introduction of rationing.

Closely integrated with the W.P.T.B. with an equal if less obvious impact upon civilian life was the Wartime Industries Control Board (W.I.C.B.), an agency of the Department of Munitions and Supply under whose jurisdiction fell every industry in the country considered vital to the war effort, a definition which became so broad as to affect even umbrella manufacturers.

The point of all of this regulation and control was to shift manufacturing from civilian goods to military hardware and direct the consumer from consuming to saving. The aim of the Dominion Government was to finance the war within Canada, using Canadian resources, which meant persuading people to fork over as much as possible to the wartime economy with the promise of future repayment. The process began on 24 June 1940, with the introduction of hefty war taxes. Nova Scotia's J.L. Ilsley, then Finance Minister, issued the first of many admonitions: "Common sense will ask them what will become of their property or their income if Germany and Italy should conquer the British Empire. Idealism will teach them that money and material things are as nothing compared with the freedom and the dignity which it alone can bring as a benediction to the life of man."[36] It took two years before the screw tightened hard, because it took that long for government to realize just how tough the fight with Nazi Germany was going to be.

The first intimation that the free market was on shaky ground came in October 1941, when the Wartime Prices and Trade Board, after two years of busying itself with industrial supplies, announced, "Every Person Or Firm Manufacturing, Handling, or Dealing in Food, Feeds, Livestock, Poultry, Yarn, Cloth, Clothing or Footwear Must Have A License by December 1, 1941." Radios and appliances were already facing serious restrictions, and this announcement meant that the sale of just about everything that was not immoral or illegal fell under the control of the central government. No doubt to the astonishment of later bureaucrats, no license fee was extracted; but to continue in business a License Identification Card was required and a blue and gold Window Certificate displayed at the store entrance.[37]

Concurrently, under the aegis of both the Wartime Prices and Trade Board and the National War Labour Board, two new controls were introduced as "Canada's wartime design for living," otherwise known as wage and price controls. The Dominion Bureau of Statistics had triggered the move when it predicted a potential annual rate of inflation of 6 percent. Prices of goods and services were frozen as of 17 November 1941, as were basic wages, subject to consideration by local boards, with the proviso that cost of living bonuses could be awarded every three months after 15 February 1942. These regulations were not popular. Labour unions hated them; merchants and farmers, who for the first time in a generation were about to profit from the increased demand, were often disgruntled; and black marketeers did a thriving business, often simply in ration coupons rather than actual commodities. The regulations seem to have worked, however, for most individuals, particularly in a place such as Halifax where there were extremes in the availability of necessities, but fewer extremes in terms of wealth. With wage and price controls, for the remainder of the war prices rose across the country by a total of only 3.8 percent, the best performance of any allied economy.[38]

The war had to be paid for, so that "temporary" World War I innovation, income tax, was tightened up in 1942. Gone were the easy-going days when the dutiful citizen filed and paid on his or her own initiative. Not only had rates climbed to the highest in Canadian history (an average of $350.00 for every man, woman and child in the country), but as of September 1942, employers deducted at source every pay day, and remitted it directly to Ottawa,[39] a wartime innovation with us still.

Of equal impact was the rationing of necessities made scarce by the increasing demands of the war effort, the necessity of keeping Britain fed, and the eventual realization that the manufacturing sector had to shift from civilian production to war matériel. Rationing was seen as the only way to allocate fairly what was left over from war needs. It was a joint effort of the Wartime Prices and Trade Board and the Wartime Industries Control Board. Initially, much was done by voluntary quotas. Only gradually did regulation limit consumption. Rationing of food and consumer goods affected every aspect of life on the home front and will be described in Chapter Six.

Controls remained in place even after shortages began to ease with the invasion of Europe in 1944. An increasingly restive citizenry was bombarded with an intensive campaign reminding them of the hyperinflation, boom and bust which followed World War I, and only after the defeat of

Japan were controls relaxed, and then only slowly, most lasting until the last half of 1946.

TRAVEL AND TOURISM

One casualty of war was travel, but it took a surprisingly long time before it was regulated out of existence. Gasoline shortages began to affect casual motoring by the summer of 1941, but rail travel, in spite of a special war tax of 10 percent on civilian tickets, was not discouraged until September 1942, when discount fares for holidays and long trips were eliminated and casual travellers were asked to limit trips to no more than 100 miles. The last gasp of pre-war tourism was a 2 June 1942 Canadian Pacific advertisement for the Banff Springs Hotel, offering "... a complete escape from the spectre of gas, oil and rubber."[40]

By November 1942, rail was the only way to go long distances, with the elimination of all bus travel over 50 miles. In May of 1942 the Mackenzie Bus Lines service from Glace Bay through Nova Scotia to Boston was suspended by the Transit Controller. It did not resume until August 1945, although it appears there were exceptions because a notice appeared the following May that heavy busses would operate again to Truro, to the Annapolis Valley and to the South Shore.[41]

Tourism remained important right up until Pearl Harbor blew it out of the water. As long as America was at peace, Canada at war held a grim fascination, and American curiosity and foreign exchange was welcomed. Tourism in 1940, for example, was just about as good as it had been the year before, even with stiffer American passport regulations. In Nova Scotia many tourists were, of course, from other parts of Canada. Nova Scotia, for better or for worse, had to stand in for the lure of America, after foreign exchange regulations on 1 May 1940 made it impossible to get foreign currency of any kind. Currency aside, Europe was out of the running, but civilians could and did travel back and forth to Britain, hazarding the wolf packs and, as long as they could convince the proper authorities that their reasons were compelling enough, which was the case for a young Rothschild who was seen off by his aunt, the Baroness in August 1942 on his way back to England and into the lion's den.[42]

The decline in tourism saw the demise of the Eastern Steamship Lines service between Yarmouth, Boston and New York, which reduced its service when patronage slipped owing to "clever propaganda spread by enemies of Canada."[43] The following summer, 1941, the service was suspended entirely when the American government, anticipating the inevitable, commandeered several of the ships of the E.S.L. fleet.

Another activity affected by a fear of German ocean raiders was off-shore sport fishing for tuna, very popular with Americans. Even so, tourism held up right through 1941. Nearly 3,000 American cars crossed into Cape Breton, and, in a spirit of *schadenfreude*, Halifax became a destination for thousands who watched in fascination from Point Peasant Park as convoys slipped out to sea and ships of the Royal Navy and Royal Canadian Navy sped in and out of the harbour on who knows what dangerous mission. That year the provincial government operated, as usual, its "Hotel Short Course" for some 200 at the Nova Scotian Hotel, offering lectures and demonstrations on wartime prices, blackout methods and techniques for meat cutting and broiling. Three window displays were sent to New York and over 50,000 copies of *Where To Stay In Nova Scotia*, as well as 39,000 road maps, were printed for distribution, for future as well as present use because of the rumours of a paper shortage. The market for this optimistic planning was not only Americans, but servicemen and women on leave and their visiting families, who might want to motor around the province. And so they did. For $15.00, in May 1940, Bobby and Jim Johnston, he an R.C.A.F. photographer posted to R.C.A.F. Dartmouth, rented a 1935 Chevrolet with no gas gauge and no speedometer and "did" Lunenburg.[44] However, all bets were off once America entered the war in 1942. Rationing and controls descended in force, and tourism dropped like a stone, despite a provision introduced in March 1942, the eve of gasoline rationing, that allowed American tourists to apply for a book of gas coupons good for 90 days.

The *Princess Helene* remained in service as an essential transportation link between Digby and Saint John, but the disappearance of the Yarmouth-based services prompted the closure of the provincial tourist booth there, and the Amherst booth closed early with the collapse of motor traffic; only 51 American cars made it as far as Cape Breton in 1942. Tourism officials were nothing if not optimistic, however, and thinking ahead, Mogull Film Studios of New York was commissioned to produce a Nova Scotia travel film to be shown in theatres for the war's duration and keep the dream alive. One of the first signs of a return to normalcy in 1945 was a call in July to "Enjoy Your Holiday in Nova Scotia this Summer. You May Travel 'Round The World But You'll Find No Better Place For A Holiday than Your Own Nova Scotia."[45]

CENSORSHIP AND GOSSIP

From the moment war was declared, censorship became a fact of life. It, too, fell under the aegis of the Dominion Government, initially as the Bureau of Public Information, then, as things got serious in 1942, in September as the Wartime Information Board with broader powers.

Everyone knew censorship existed. On the basis of keeping information out of the wrong hands, it was generally accepted. In the Canadian context it was imposed with a fairly light hand. Letters could be, and were, read, always if sent by a serviceman from a base or a ship. The media was expected to self censor, that is, within known guidelines write or broadcast what it chose, but check with an official Censor before disseminating any information which could be considered sensitive.

Some suspected other agendas. When Halifax author Clara Dennis wrote an American publisher only a year after the war began, to inquire what had become of her magazine Hobbies, she was tartly informed that, "You have very strict censorship in Canada and you are lucky to get any American magazines at all. They are putting an additional tax on the publishers now which they say, in this country, is deliberately aimed to keep American publications entirely out of Canada. This is only a starter. One of the magazines we publish has been excluded from Canada."[46]

On 29 October 1939, unaware of the new realities, Dalhousie law professor Allan Findlay sent his Danish fiancée a letter, which incorporated a sketch of Halifax Harbour. The Censor pounced and the professor was charged with having sent a treasonable letter. An uproar arose in the press and public despite the obvious fact that German intelligence until very recently had access to detailed charts of the harbour. In spite of representations at the highest level, Professor Findlay was found guilty when his case came to trial on 2 December, but the magistrate fined him only $1.00, plus $5.00 costs, on the grounds that while technically guilty the offense was inconsequential.[47] Professor Findlay finished out the academic year, but it was the end of his law-school career. He the joined the R.C.A.F. and at the end of the war became a successful corporation lawyer.[48]

Under wartime censorship, Halifax nominally lost its identity. It even disappeared from the postmark and for the purposes of the printed and broadcast word became simply "An East Coast Port," a euphemism whose meaning was transparent to everyone. The regional Censor of Publications was H.B. Jefferson, a well-known newspaperman and former editorial writer for the Halifax Daily Star, whose own uncensored observations are pithy and informative and supplemented by his probably illegal photographs taken from his office eyrie high in the Bedford Row Post Office. Unlike the rest of Canada, all correspondence from this "East Coast Port," civilian as well as military, was heavily censored, as Findlay and anyone else too chatty about what was going on around them soon found out.

Jefferson's job was not so much to ensure that no real news reached the public and hence the enemy, but that no useful or identifying details did. This job was not that difficult because press and radio, while forever pushing the envelope, were disposed to cooperate. Inattention rather than intent was the usual reason for a slip. The real issue was grounded in basic human nature, a need to gossip and rumour monger. Rumour was the favourite indoor sport of Halifax, where the war sat on the city's doorstep and ordinary citizens were daily witness to vital information, such as convoy departures or troop movements, that was impossible to conceal but illegal to discuss. To this end, Maritime Telephone and Telegraph Company presented its subscribers with a card to post by the telephone: "WARNING. It Is Forbidden to Mention Ships or Ship Movements, Aircraft, Troops, War Industries, or the Weather during Long Distance Telephone Conversations."[49] Rumours included the naval wife's worst nightmare when a well-meaning friend passed along that they had heard 'from someone on the inside that such and such ship had been sunk with all hands. Servicemen would say, only partly sarcastically, when they were heading out of barracks to talk to civilian friends: "We wanted to find out when we were due to sail." And the most common remark, which made military intelligence grind its collective teeth, was the casual , "Well, I suppose Joe is sailing with the troop movement on Wednesday," or "Did you see that big convoy go out this morning?"

Equally frustrating were the false tidbits circulating through the parlours and dance halls: the old favourite which told of the captured submarine crew being found with ticket stubs from a Halifax (or Boston, New York, Capetown, Southampton or Sydney) theatre in their pockets, a ubiquitous story the military hated for its inference of an undefended coastline. Every time the big guns off the harbour mouth at Fort McNab or Sandwich Battery practiced, rumours sprang up about a naval engagement off the coast with the truly nervous predicting imminent invasion. The fertile mind could do wonders with what was a common enough sight, a crippled tanker easing into port under an armed escort. With little difficulty this event was transformed into a grim traitor craft caught red-handed supplying fuel to a U-boat off shore. Some rumours were more humorous than dangerous. The regular flickering of a light from a harbourside apartment eventually roused the suspicions of the R.C.M.P. Upon investigation it turned out to be signal from a Halifax girl to her Dartmouth boyfriend that her father had gone out.[50]

Military security throughout the war complained that residents of "Eastern Canadian ports" were "... in many cases, a greater worry to the Allied cause than German soldiers ... Idle talkers at bridge parties, service-men on embarkation leave, ordinary people writing to friends and relatives, passengers on street cars, travellers on railway trains ... are helping Hitler by foolish talk." The recurring and only partly successful message was to keep your mouth shut and keep the information out of circulation entirely: "German submarines do not operate on the principle of luck, but on the basis of information. Where does their information come from? Very often from east coast ports."[51]

The campaign to quash rumour was a fight that the government never entirely won because it was a fight against human nature. Amid the dreary round of shortages and overcrowding, which was life in wartime Halifax, Haligonians had one advantage over more comfortable Canadians; gen-uinely exciting events, major comings and goings of famous people, famous ships, regiments of soldiers and real impact from war seen as shattered ships limping into port, or heard as distant offshore explosions followed by a rosy glow in the southern sky and a pillar of black smoke. It would have taken more resolution than even the most intense patriot could muster not to talk of the daily drama of World War II unfolding on Halifax's very doorstep, and focus instead on the weather, on the produce of the Victory Garden, on the travails of rationing or darning Johnny's socks.

With remarkable speed the residents of the "East Coast Port" saw their lives and their community transform from an easy-going if penurious existence on the periphery of the Dominion to a front line role. The city was the western gate of a military and merchant pipeline to a fierce war on the other side of the Atlantic. It was being stretched and squeezed to fill that role.

CHAPTER TWO:
The Military Presence

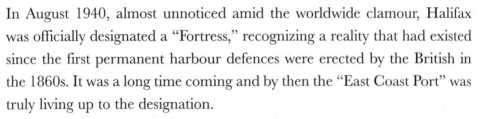

In August 1940, almost unnoticed amid the worldwide clamour, Halifax was officially designated a "Fortress," recognizing a reality that had existed since the first permanent harbour defences were erected by the British in the 1860s. It was a long time coming and by then the "East Coast Port" was truly living up to the designation.

Within days of war's outbreak, the army's 1st Division arrived in the unprepared city previous to a December departure overseas. Subsequently troop movements formed elsewhere, so, just this once, Halifax was more involved than it would be in the future with infantry deployment. The 1st Division was made up of many of Canada's best and bravest, who rushed to the colours for the finest of motives. The recruiting process was, however, more enthusiastic than selective, and many a recruit made it in who would not pass muster a year, even months, later. For many who had spent much of their youth on the dole, eating in soup kitchens and riding the rails, the prospect of a dollar a day, meals, a uniform and a warm bed was irresistible. They would worry about the implications later. It mattered little that many were ill-educated, run down and in poor physical and mental health; in this first go the army took them all. Colonel Edgar Mingo, Registrar for National Selective Service in Halifax later noted that men born between 1913 and 1918 had a high rate of medical rejection. His conclusion was that "they were in the age of adolescence during the great depression ... and did not enjoy the full nurishment [*sic*] or educational opportunity."[52]

For the first few years, Canada was able to maintain an all-volunteer army, unique among the allies. National Registration (officially the National Resources Mobilization Act) allowed men to be called into the army, although they could not be sent overseas against their will. This provision was not initially a problem as volunteers flocked to the colours for the first two years, even if motives were a mixture of patriotism, family pressure and need for a paying job. Cracks began to appear as losses mounted and in English Canada pressure grew for conscription. French-speaking Canadians, especially those in Quebec, were equivocal about fighting another overseas war, as they believed, on behalf of the British Empire. This made for a difficult political situation for the Mackenzie King administration whose power base owed much to the voters of that province. King called a plebiscite on the question, which, on 27 April 1942, authorized him to abandon a previous promise never to institute an overseas conscription policy, from which arose his characteristically ambiguous statement, "Conscription if necessary, but not necessarily conscription." The government was, however, able to maintain the volunteer aspect of overseas service until the autumn of 1944. Those who, despite great pressure and overt opprobrium, maintained their right to refuse overseas service, were generally known as "Zombies," a designation in no way intended to be a compliment. The community of Rockingham's resolve to have nothing to do with such a detachment stationed in a barracks at nearby Prince's Lodge was typical of the general attitude in English Canada.[53]

By November losses were mounting, and in Europe units were falling below strength. In the ensuing political crisis, the Hon. Colonel J.L. Ralston was replaced as Minister of National Defence by General A.G.L. McNaughton and some "Zombies" were sent overseas. In the end the number was very small and King, in his trademark way, prevaricated and delayed enough that the war was over before too much fallout could damage him politically.

One 16-year-old recruit remembered Halifax in the autumn of 1939, long before Zombies were an issue, as totally disorganized. He was billeted in the Garrick Theatre (today's Neptune), where he slept on the floor. He recalled:

> HMS *Repulse* was in the harbour with British sailors and
> Royal Marines who looked down on this motley collection
> of characters. Bootleggers on Water Street probably made
> the most money. In those days it was just bootleggers and
> whore houses down there.
>
> I don't think anybody could possibly be more relieved
> than the citizenry of Halifax to see the First Division sail
> out of that harbour ... An awful lot of them were sent
> back, some of them were medically unfit, some of them
> were psychopaths, some of them were alcoholics; they just
> piled them all on these boats, sent them over, and let the
> Brits sort them out.[54]

Later, raw recruits, who scarcely knew their left from their right foot,
were sent to Yarmouth for six weeks to find out if they were healthy enough
for what lay ahead. One 25-year-old from Greenfield, Queens County,
Colin Hunt, joined up as a forester and was sent to Lawlor's Island for basic
training, then on to Quebec for advanced training, before being sent overseas.[55] For the army, soldiers who passed basic training, or who had some
sort of World War I or militia experience, went to Debert near Truro, or
Aldershot near Kentville. These bases were tough places, where a combination of terrain and unsympathetic sergeant majors brought home the
concept that "war is hell," with Europe still an ocean away. Initially, for the
Royal Canadian Navy, HMC Dockyard was the training base; but later,
HMCS *Cornwallis* on the Annapolis Basin near Digby grew into a major
training establishment. Virtually all R.C.A.F. training was done out of
province, until the British Commonwealth Air Training Plan (B.C.A.T.P.)
took hold, and Stanley Airport just outside Maitland became the nearest
training base.

Once or twice Halifax saw tents on the Wanderers Grounds, but not the
sea of canvas which had filled the Commons with soldiers waiting for their
transports to Europe in World War I. Occasionally, regiments stationed
overlong in up-country venues sent a detachment or two for garrison duty

to keep soldiers active. The more fortunate officer class had access to passes to the big city. For most infantry or airmen, however, if it was daylight their only contact with Halifax was from the window of a crowded troop train as it rolled along the Basin, to the busy marshalling yards at the Ocean Terminals. If it was night, the trains were blacked out and they saw nothing until they were shunted onto the team tracks mere footsteps from the gangplank of their transport.

If he was fortunate, a soldier might find a place with hundreds or in the case of the big Cunard liners, thousands of his countrymen, along the rail as the busy tugs puffed and strained to haul his transport into the stream. Looking back, he might catch a glimpse of the city's wooden houses, Scotch dormers, coal smoke rising from a myriad of chimney pots, and over them all the looming Citadel. As the ship gathered steam, that scene faded and ahead appeared an assemblage of buoys marking the anti-submarine net, which stretched in a line across the harbour mouth between the long curving spit of Mauger's Beach, punctuated at its tip with an ancient Martello tower-cum lighthouse, and the steep forested cliff opposite crowned by the descendant of Prince Edward's 1795 York Redoubt. As his transport picked up speed, the departing soldier might not have noticed, because he was not supposed to notice, half concealed along the shores and hillsides on both sides of the harbour approaches, a series of bulky structures, gun batteries and searchlight emplacements.

From her home on McNab's Island, Marguerite Harding saw,

> ... the *Queen Mary* and the *Queen Elizabeth* side by side loading up the troops. It was an impressive sight. They would go along pretty slowly until they went past the gate boats and once they got past the gate boats you would see them start to open up.
>
> As I was watching them go out the harbour ... I could feel the urgency about these troop ships as they were heading out. And on a fine sunny day all those young, young boys on the top deck all looking out. It was really sad, you know. You couldn't help but wonder, well now, how many of them were going to come back.[56]

She was not alone in these thoughts; Clarissa Johnston wrote in her diary, "[I]t certainly was a sad sight, boatloads of airmen and soldiers all going to a real hell on earth."[57]

With each passing month between 1939 and early 1942, the number and complexity of the departing troop ships grew. In the heady early days of July 1940, the troop ships *Monarch of Bermuda*, *Duchess of York* and *Empress of Britain*, under escort by HMS *Revenge* and two destroyers, were serenaded by the cheers of the garrison of Fort Sandwich and the music of the 53rd Battery Band as they steamed past.[58]

Once the bow of the transport began to rise and fall with the North Atlantic swell, the soldiers were but birds of passage focused on the unknown future. When next the soldier came down that gangplank, all that was familiar, comfortable and safe was a world away.

PREPARATIONS

We have seen that the Canadian government, so as to emphasize its sovereignty, had waited a week to actually declare war on Germany, but in fact, during the night of 25 – 26 August, the sense of crisis had evolved to a point where the British Government had cabled the Canadian and other Dominion Governments to prepare for war, thus initiating the process of mobilization.[59] This was followed on 1 September by the full mobilization of the militia. The American lack of such foresight was to have serious repercussions at Pearl Harbor 15 months later.

THE ARMY PREPARES

Halifax rapidly developed a substantial and resident army garrison, mobilized early to provide manpower for the gun batteries and searchlight emplacements, which quickly rimmed the harbour approaches. Units included the Halifax Coast Brigade; Royal Canadian Artillery [R.C.A.]; the Ninth and Fifty First Heavy Batteries, R.C.A.; the First Anti-Aircraft Battery; the Fourth Light A.A. Battery (later replaced by the 14th A.A. Battery); and the First Field Company, Royal Canadian Engineers [R.C.E.]. Almost forgotten now was a group of specialists, the Tenth Searchlight Battery, a band of graduate engineers, skilled mechanics and electricians.

Local militia regiments, the Halifax Rifles, formed in 1860 as the Halifax Volunteer Battalion, and the Princess Louise Fusiliers, with roots back to 1749, were also mobilized. Supplementing these local boys were the Prince Edward Island Highlanders, originally sent to Dartmouth, where they were established on the grounds of the Hazelhurst Estate on Pleasant Street. Here in these first months, the "other ranks" lived in tents, the officers lived in the house and the extensive grounds were used for training. One of the first big weddings of the war years was the March 1940 double wedding of Lieutenants Lidstone and Holman to the Crichton sisters whose home was across the street from Hazelhurst.[60] They soon exchanged with the Halifax Rifles for whom a small headquarters was built on the grounds of Park Street School in April 1942, while the Highlanders set up quarters at the nearly moribund Halifax Citadel. From time to time they would be replaced as, for example, when the Kent Regiment from Hamilton, Ont. arrived in August 1941, so that the garrison troops could go to Sussex, N.B. for summer training.[61]

Many of the army's Home Defence and Coast Defence Battalions housed in the makeshift arrangements described above were eventually consolidated in what was known as Elkins Barracks (after Major General W.H.P. Elkins, General Officer Commanding, Atlantic Command). A vast establishment, it formed a component of A23 Coast and Anti-Aircraft Artillery Training Centre, inaugurated on 15 February 1941, just east of Eastern Passage. To many it was known just as A23 and the site is now home to Ocean View Manor, Ocean View School and a fire station.

For an able-bodied man, not wearing a uniform became difficult to justify, no matter how good the reason. Gordon McNeil, in a "designated" job in the Dockyard, was, for all intents and purposes, forbidden to enlist, but as the war intensified he found it difficult to walk along the street. Even though he was working flat out with almost no free time, "All my friends were in the service.... I said to the wife, I can't stick it out. I felt ashamed going along the street with all my friends in uniform .... I was walking the streets, [and] some of them said, 'Look at that fella, why isn't he in the service, everyone else is' — all the boys in the neighbourhood where I lived. So I went in...."[62]

Others were more equivocal on the subject of duty to King and Country. In an incautious letter intercepted by the Censor, one brother wrote to another in March 1942 from on board the S.S. *Waterton* at the Furness Withy pier in Halifax:

> If you have been hooked tell them you want the
> Mercantile Marine, for of the four services it is the best for
> you, I know you just as you know me, neither of us like
> being tied down or the discipline, so be smart the risk is
> high, for merchant sailors. But so is the dough (if you hit
> the right ship) you have more freedom and you travel. But
> don't get caught in the [Manning] pool, for then they can
> ship you where they please. If you are on the verge of
> being called up let me know and I will send you enough
> dough to get down here (I intend to pay you the rest when
> I get home). From here you can get lots of boats. Ours
> needs two firemen and two sailors, we are been [*sic*] fitted
> with a gun and machine guns, and degauzing [*sic*] cable.[63]

All the outlying forts had small, unlovely single-storey green tar-papered barracks. To accommodate the other elements of the expanding garrison, the Exhibition Grounds at Windsor and Almon Streets were leased and many more long, unlovely single-storey green-roofed wooden barracks, mess halls and offices were built. After 1941 the old Chebucto Airport dream vanished and was reincarnated as Chebucto Camp, a similar sea of temporary buildings, among which was housed No. 6 District Depot, organized in December 1939 to manage garrison personnel, recruiting services, such as the enlistment office on Cogswell Street, and personnel supervising the embarkation of troops overseas. Once women became a factor, two apartment blocks on South Street, the Alexandria and Hillside Hall, were purchased in 1943 to accommodate Canadian Women's Army Corps personnel.[64] And to keep them all clean, the City Market building was appropriated as a military laundry.[65]

Equipment needs were looked after by the Royal Canadian Ordnance Corps (R.C.O.C.), which supplied clothing and equipment of every kind.

The Royal Canadian Army Service Corps (R.C.A.S.C.) created the No. 1 Fortress Company in 1940 to supply food and transportation, including not only the more obvious trucks and cars, but also the duty boats *Alfreda* and *Burstall*, a water transport branch. These boats ran a twice-a-day harbour circuit: Halifax to Eastern Passage to Range Pier (Wreck Cove, McNab's Island) to Ives Point to Garrison Pier (McNab's) to York Redoubt to Halifax. This R.C.A.S.C. fleet was supplemented by about half a dozen private "bum boats," which served as water taxis. For a fee they took personnel to and from anchored ships and the flesh pots of downtown Halifax.[66]

The acquisition of land, which became known as Willow Park, on the east side of north Windsor Street (formerly the 1905/06 Intercolonial Railway roundhouse and servicing depot) provided a location, shared with the R.C.N. for an Engineering Yard to service the vast number of motor vehicles which provided transport for the Halifax Fortress.[67]

THE NAVY PREPARES

The rapidly growing fleet of the Royal Canadian Navy was based in the cramped environs of HMC Dockyard, whose headquarters was HMCS *Scotian*. Aside from Admiralty House, which housed the Officers' Mess, that was essentially it for the R.C.N. in 1939. Over the next six years the navy complement exploded from 12 ships to 270 ocean escort warships, and from 3,684 personnel to over 95,000 — 6,000 of whom were members of the Women's Royal Canadian Naval Service. It was the third largest navy in the world after the fleets of the United States and Britain. The property base expanded as well, when the Navy took over the Imperial Army's nineteenth-century Wellington Barracks and established HMCS Stadacona.

In 1939 the only permanent barracks in the Dockyard was the converted 1863 Royal Naval Hospital, since a Royal Canadian Navy Volunteer Reserve (R.C.N.V.R.) barracks built in 1933 to 1937 was soon converted for training purposes. There were a few other residences, including two sets of "Victualling Yard Residences," a set of double houses and, on Barrington Street above the Dockyard, a set of five permanent married quarters;[68] but these very soon became completely inadequate. The rapid expansion of personnel beginning in the first months of the war and barracks to house only a fraction of them became the root of many problems. For men returning from stressful and unpleasant sea duty, their home was the cramped and stuffy quarters aboard ship, where, even for officers, privacy was almost non-existent. Since there was so little shore accommodation, the only relief was to rent a hotel room or hope that some kind family would take them in for a few days.

Unwilling to build barracks for what was hoped to be a short war, the navy resorted to a Lodging and Compensation allowance, "Lodge & Comp," which set personnel free to find their own accommodation. This situation encouraged many personnel, shore based or sea duty, to bring wives and families to Halifax, since housing was effectively subsidized by the government. The shortage of rental accommodation of any kind meant that the cure was worse than the disease.

As well as being the home base for the Royal Navy's North Atlantic and West Indies Squadron housed in HMS *Seaborne* at the beginning of the war, and the rapidly expanding fleet of R.C.N. convoy escorts, HMC Dockyard also housed a multitude of other facilities which grew rapidly. This resulted in the demolition of many eighteenth-century buildings. The best of these buildings, the Capstan House, its two wings and the Sail Loft dating from 1759 to 1769 was destroyed in 1940. The only trace of its existence was the footprint of its more pedestrian successor, which maintained the same alignment and orientation.

THE AIR FORCE PREPARES

More out of the public eye was the equally rapid growth of R.C.A.F. Station Dartmouth located in Eastern Passage, which after 1948 became familiar to the public as HMCS Shearwater, shore base for the navy's carrier aircraft.

By the beginning of the war the R.C.A.F. station was well under construction. Even during the nadir of defence spending in the mid-1930s, the need for an air facility on the east coast was obvious. The grassed landing fields of the Chebucto Road airport could not be upgraded to meet the rapidly advancing capabilities of new aircraft. While that part of the city was still surrounded by open fields, it was evident that when the city expanded, it would be in that area. Further, the Chebucto Road airport was a municipal venture and city officials themselves had been contemplating the necessity and cost of a new airport, perhaps somewhere in the uplands to the west of the city, or else watch the burgeoning air age pass Halifax by. It was with relief that the city greeted the announcement in 1937 that a major R.C.A.F. base would be built in Eastern Passage, where the U.S. navy had established a seaplane base in the final days of World War I. The shelving beach and the sheltered waters were ideal for the big flying boats of the coastal patrol (first Stranraers, then Cansos), which rode easily at mooring buoys in the lee of McNab's Island, with ready access to the open waters of Halifax Harbour for takeoff and landing.

The 1937 proposals were, however, aimed at the next phase of aircraft development, focused on land-based facilities which could handle the needs of increasingly large and powerful aircraft. The new facilities were located across the road from the seaplane base and by the spring of 1938 clearing was completed. By September 1939 the mile-long runways were well underway. Pressure to complete them became intense and work was pushed seven days a week. New urgencies collided with old certainties when a freak hailstorm hit on the third Sunday after the war began. An asphalt crew paving one of the runways on that day quit en masse when faced with what seemed like the Lord's anger at this desecration of His day.[69]

Unlike HMC Dockyard, the expansion of R.C.A.F. Dartmouth was not restricted by an urban location. After initial stumbling, adequate barrack accommodations were provided for what amounted to a five-fold increase in personnel after 1939.

WOMEN BEGIN TO SERVE

Following generations of unquestioned civilian and military precedent, the response to the declaration of war was exclusively a male prerogative. That situation was about to change and it sowed seeds that altered western society forever. From the beginning of the war patriotic women urged the government to create women's branches of the armed forces. Resistance was strong. It was not enough to point out, although it usually was in pre-war Canada, that such innovations already existed in Britain. At every level of society, regardless of age or sex, the sense that "A woman's place was in the home" was entrenched. If the national emergency was so serious that it required the services of every able-bodied male, to make similar demands on women would gut the concept of family and deprive generations of children of the benefits of parental guidance and the moral foundation that only a mother could provide. Or so the argument went. The thought of unmarried girls working unchaperoned in society at large was too unsettling to contemplate. Still, women kept up the pressure and, finally, when manpower shortages in 1941 began to bite, the government reached an agreement to allow women to join the services.

In 1941 the intention was to release able-bodied men for active duty, radical enough for many. Even the most fervent advocates of women's involvement were not prepared to consider them in combat roles for a long time to come. Moreover, many well-intentioned people believed that a woman in a service uniform was by definition "fast." Despite the attitude of the more conservative elements of society, the women who served almost universally enjoyed the experience. They revelled in new freedoms, even in heavily circumscribed conditions. Fran Elliott, who was in the R.C.A.F., recalls hitchhiking around the province when on leave without a problem, something she never would have considered doing before the war.[70] The R.C.A.F. Women's Division barracks in Halifax housed 60 women in double-decker bunks, each supplied with two blankets, two sheets, a pillow and pillow case; the blankets, highly desirable items, had to be carefully guarded.[71] A cafeteria supplied three meals a day and there was a snack bar for evenings. Many women enlisted as much out of a sense of adventure as a sense of duty or loyalty. R.C.A.F. pay began at 90 cents a day and was raised to $1.05 in 1943; not much, but for a girl who might never have expected to have her own money, it was just fine.

One by one all three services came on board. The R.C.A.F. was the first in July 1941, with the Women's Auxiliary Air Force, later the Women's Division; then the Canadian Women's Army Corps (C.W.A.C.) arrived in August; and finally the Women's Royal Canadian Naval Service (W.R.C.N.S.). Initially, they were all full-time auxiliaries of the main force.[72] In March 1942 the C.W.A.C. was integrated into the regular army, shortly after the R.C.A.F. incorporated its Women's Division. In August the R.C.N. followed with the Women's Royal Canadian Naval Service, better known as the WRENS after its British sister service. WRENS first appeared in Halifax in March 1943, where some 100 eventually served. Generally, service women were employed in clerical duties, and Halifax WRENS were involved in merchant navy coordination, information processing and signals; they served also as motor mechanics, aircraft engine mechanics, radar and wireless technicians, as well as drivers, telegraphers, stewards and cooks.

In Halifax, the navy carried out its own recruiting for female personnel, but initially the air force and the army used the resources of the National Selective Service Office. From its lists, this office recommended candidates to air force and army recruiters, who in turn assessed them and, if qualified, recruited them. The R.C.A.F. grasped the concept quickly, worked with the Selective Service and within a short time took over its own recruiting for the Women's Division.

The army was a harder nut to crack. Despite direct instructions from headquarters, the local District Office wanted nothing to do with the concept and worked hard to frustrate it. An initial list of 38 carefully chosen candidates was supplied by Selective Service, but the army refused to set a reporting date. In the end both the time and place was set by National Defence Headquarters, but to no avail, because, in spite of the careful pre-screening, all the candidates were rejected by the District Office. To head off a public scandal by increasingly irritated candidates and their families, Ottawa took over the screening and all were accepted. The District Office remained recalcitrant until staff changes were made and they were forced to follow the lead of the other services and take over the recruiting process themselves.[73]

THE HARBOUR DEFENCES

Halifax was not well armed in September 1939, but the harbour defences were at least functioning. Their state reflected 1936 recommendations by Major B.D. Treatt, R.A., a British coastal defence expert. His five-year plan had been approved, but in 1939 it was behind schedule, not from lack of will but from the inability of Britain, the source of supply, to keep up with its own needs. Treatt's plan recommended upgrading of the defences based on the perceived threat of enemy submarines and cruisers with long-range 8-inch guns, operating far offshore and capable of deploying fast coastal motorboats for night raids. The result was the construction of "long range counter bombardment" batteries at advanced headlands – Devil's Battery, Fort McNab and Chebucto Head – armed with 6- or 9.2- inch guns, with a maximum range of 15 to 17 miles. Existing nineteenth-century batteries, supplemented by new installations at York Shore and Strawberry, served as "closedefence" and "anti-motor-torpedo-boat" batteries, more lightly armed with 6- inch, 4.7- inch and 12-pounder guns.[74]

On 26 August 1939, a call-out order was issued and the military sprang into action, a process solidified on 3 September when defence headquarters issued the order for Canadian ports to operate under wartime rules of engagement. Since the *Graf Spee* or the *Bismarck* was half-expected to appear in the harbour approaches, full alert of harbour defences was vital. The most respected naval theorists of the 1930s discounted submarines as having only a nuisance value and the Germans themselves were immensely proud of their fleet of "pocket battleships." In 1938 Canada's Chief of Naval Staff, Admiral Percy W. Nelles, echoed the prevailing wisdom when he wrote:

> If international law is complied with, submarine attack
> should not prove serious.
>
> If unrestricted warfare is again resorted to, the means of
> combatting Submarines are considered to have so advanced
> that by employing a system of convoy and utilizing Air
> Forces, losses of Submarines would be very heavy and
> might compel the enemy to give up this form of attack.[75]

On 28 October 1940, convoy HX84 (38 ships) left Halifax Harbour under the escort of the armed merchant cruiser *Jervis Bay*, an 18-year-old liner based in Halifax and refitted with eight World War I era 6-inch guns at the Saint John Shipyard. The ensuing action more or less followed the script as pre-war strategists envisioned. German intelligence, advised of the departure, in turn advised the battleship *Admiral Scheer*, which hunted down, found and attacked the convoy in late afternoon on 5 November. To give the convoy a chance to escape in the gathering dusk, Fogarty Fegan, captain of the *Jervis Bay*, steered his ship straight for the *Admiral Scheer* and its modern 11-inch guns, forcing an engagement which allowed 29 ships to slip away. The *Jervis Bay* had no chance and was sunk. Sixty-five of the crew were picked up by the Swedish *Stureholm,* which doubled back during the night. Subsequently, the crew of the *Stureholm* made it clear that they were not keen to wear the mantle of heroes, but the action provided the British cause with an immense propaganda victory that was exploited to the full.[76] Fegan received a posthumous Victoria Cross.

The entry of the United States into the war in late 1941 eliminated Hitler's anxiety about sinking "the wrong" ships, such as the *Athenia.* More importantly, the loss of the *Bismarck* on 27 May 1941, convinced Hitler that the submarine, of which he could have a whole fleet for the cost of one such battleship, was the route to follow. It was then that the threat switched from surface raiders to submarines. Ironically, the *Admiral Scheer* survived the war, more or less. Sidelined after 1942, it was bombed in Kiel by the R.A.F. on 9 April 1945, capsized and sank and is today part of the fill for a car park.

THE HARBOUR DEFENCES — THE FIRST MOVES

Halifax would have been ill-provided in September 1939 had the *Admiral Scheer* decided to test the defences. Old 4.7-inch travelling guns ("Long Toms") stored at R.A. Park were hauled out of retirement and the Ninth Heavy Battery's two World War I era 8-inch howitzers, kept at the Armouries for practice, were set up in a battery garrisoned by the Prince Edward Island Highlanders at Lawrencetown Beach.[77] This battery closed the back door on any German raiding party planning a sweep up Cole Harbour or Cow Bay Roads or the C.N.R.'s Musquodoboit railway line to destroy the refinery at Imperoyal or create havoc at R.C.A.F. Dartmouth. With these guns went their quarter-century old ammunition whose fuses were so corroded that they were as much a threat to the defenders as to the Germans.[78]

At this stage threats from the air were not so much from aircraft carriers, but from surface raiders capable of launching limited numbers of aircraft by catapult. This threat was covered by the Fourth Anti-Aircraft [A.A.] Battery, which in August wound up training in Picton, Ont. When the order came to mobilize, the now permanent soldiers put their 3-inch 20 cwt mobile A.A. guns on railway flat cars and headed to Halifax. Once there, the guns were set up at Burnside to protect the naval magazine, and at Eastern Passage to defend Imperoyal and R.C.A.F. Dartmouth.[79]

THE MILITARY PRESENCE

Army training was based on scenarios predicated on the landing of German forces and the capture of Halifax:

Information received enemy landing government wharf FRENCH VILLAGE HARBOR. Noise shipping off shore indicates three vessels. Size not determinable because fog. Two boats sixty men with machine guns now ashore ...

First thing we have to do is get scout cars out on the ST MARGARET'S BAY road and put in road blocks. They landed at least 10 minutes ago and have probably commandeered all the local cars they can get their hands on and are on the way to TANTALLON now....

We can expect the lights to go in a minute. They should be d—n near that power line by now.... we have to protect that AVON LINE pronto....

The lights cut out, but in a few seconds they are on again. "Well Bart Hays [N.S.L.& P.] was on the job. I bet we are on AVON power now. There's a record of when the German's reached UPPER TANTALLON, sir."

If I were Heine landing at FRENCH VILLAGE HARBOR my first troops would go all out to grab the roads as far forward as possible and then I would take a line along the crest of the highland that fronts along the Bay.... It would be a thin sketchy line but look at the country. A few F.D.L.'s would cover it tight. I'd try to grab HAMMONDS PLAINS or the ROAD JUNCTION here at 7076 [map reference] on the north road, FOURTEEN MILE HOUSE or, better still, SHELLDRAKE LAKE on the main highway, this ROAD JUNCTION at 6063 on the top of the hill near GATE LAKE and this ROAD JUNCTION at GLEN MARGARET. With those points protected by outposts and patrols on the ridge I'd figure I was pretty safe until I got my equipment ashore and was ready to move on HALIFAX.

"Look, sir, we can get a train of 'Flats' out from the

CNR and load some of Johnson's M.G.'s on it together with some of Gillis' crew and run it right out that road....

Hello. SAPO [5th Field Co., R.C.E.] I have a train for you to man at North Station yards right away. We are putting M.G.'s on her and some Bren's. Get a crew down to take over her operation. [Personnel] from [West Nova Scotia's, M.G.'s] will be along to fight her.[80]

While on the other side of the harbour:

24 September [1941] 0600 - General Alarm. Operational. All Ranks on hand at H. Q. Enemy in vicinity of Echo Lake, Upper Lawrencetown, Cole Harbour Road.

9th Heavy shoot 8" How.[itzer] Lawrencetown.

0745 - Enemy in vicinity of Echo Lake and Mineville.

0840 - Enemy in vicinity of Cole Harbour & Lawrencetown.

11:30 - Enemy attacked at Cole Harbour. Repulsed with heavy casualties.[81]

With remarkable speed Halifax became a heavily defended port, along with Sydney, Nova Scotia and Saint John, New Brunswick. The harbour batteries, including Fort McNab, York Redoubt, Connaught, Strawberry and Chebucto Head, were in relatively good shape, never having been abandoned, and they quickly upgraded and rearmed. Chebucto Head was totally rebuilt and Devil's Battery built from scratch. After 17 July 1940, Sunday drives to familiar harbour look-offs became another wartime casualty as army road patrols stopped all public access to the roads leading to the forts.

THE HARBOUR DEFENCES — THE BATTERIES

Since 1749, the design of Halifax's harbour batteries had been based on

British precedents. Major Treatt's report and World War II continued the tradition. All work was done from "outline plans" supplied by Britain to the Royal Canadian Engineers, who then adapted them to particular sites. In one respect the batteries were not as up-to-date as they could have been: unlike contemporaries elsewhere their guns were open to the sky and, thus, to enemy aircraft.[82] The defence of the batteries from hostile shore parties or from the sky was in the hands of strategically placed machine guns. The harbour defences were complete and fully functioning by 1941, with the exception of the most expensive site, Chebucto Head, emplacements for which had to be blasted out of solid granite, delaying the installation of its guns until the winter of 1941/42. The tedious job of constructing its complex of gun emplacements, magazines and shelters began in the winter of 1940, but, along with its partner on the opposite side of the harbour mouth overlooking Devil's Island, it was designed to be the strongest component of the port's defences and no effort was to be spared. Manned by the 54th Battery of the 1st (Halifax) Coast Regiment, its armament consisted of three 6-inch breech-loading guns.[83]

All batteries were built by private contractors, and although the final results were satisfactory, the army officer who supervised the entire process trusted only one firm not to over bill: T.C. Gorman. The Toronto firm of Angus Robertson made little or no money from Devil's Battery overlooking Devil's Island, and it was, in fact, the ruin of many a subcontractor. As a result, Devil's Battery was the last to be done on straight contract. It took its name from Devil's Island, exposed and isolated below the headland, home to a lighthouse establishment, a few families of fishermen, some sheep and a wireless station used for the transmission and receipt of newspaper despatches until it was taken over by the R.C.N. at the beginning of the war. The site was, however, a very good position from which to cover the eastern approaches, and paired with Chebucto Head on the western side could command the outer harbour to the distant horizon, a useful asset in pre-radar days. Now known as Hartlen Point, parts of which had long been military property, an extra 285 acres was purchased in 1940[84] and a community of houses was expropriated when the fortification project was initiated. This removed the inhabitants from danger in the event of action, and the houses were maintained for the duration of war so as to camouflage the existence of the battery.

As important as Devil's Battery was strategically, it was no surprise that contractors had difficulty. The problem was its complex system of hydraulically operated guns. To minimize the target and disguise its existence, the battery was buried below the surface. The lowest level contained the heating and air circulation, the second the plotting room, and the top, below the guns, the quarters, chart room, telephones, etc. All the components were connected by insulated sound-proofed tunnels converging on the command post, and the magazines were isolated from the rest of the complex. Like the other harbour batteries, Devil's Battery generated its own power, in a separate underground facility. Because of the demands of the gun's hydraulic system the complex was large; the diesel had a flywheel as tall as a two-storey house and took two starting engines to turn it over. It even had its own semi-underground cistern holding 150,000 gallons.[85]

Leaks in this subsurface environment were a nuisance, and the complexity of the hydraulic design caused problems. The guns were installed using cranes, one of which broke through a concrete apron which had been poured over frozen ground, sinking nine feet into thawed earth. The carefully crated and finely machined fittings were prefabricated in England to precise specifications, but could not be made to fit as they ought. Despite the misgivings of Major Callahan, the project manager, the R.C.E. in charge of the installation resorted to cutting and welding. When the time came to charge the system, fearing the worst, Callahan bought the cheapest hydraulic fluid he could find, some 1,500 gallons of the stuff. This cautious economy sort of paid off. When the guns were fired for the first time, before an audience of invited dignitaries, the welds failed and the interior of the battery was drenched in gallons of cheap rather than expensive hydraulic oil.[86] When finally completed it was manned by the 53rd Heavy Battery of the 1st (Halifax) Coast Regiment and its armament consisted of three 9.2-inch breech-loading Mark X guns.[87]

These two big new batteries were backed up by surviving components of the original British defences. Sandwich Battery, north of Chebucto, was built between 1900 and 1905 as Spion Kop. Its armament, taken out of action in 1943, was the original British: two 9.2-inch and two 6-inch breech-loaders. More or less opposite on McNab's Island was Fort McNab, originally constructed between 1888 and 1892 and furnished with two elderly 6-inch guns. More or less below it was Strawberry Battery, armed with two 12-pounders, which functioned throughout the war as the examining battery, providing artillery support for the anti-submarine net and its infrastructure that controlled the shipping entrance to the harbour. It was also geared to repel attacks by motor torpedo boats. Its twin on the other side of the harbour below York Redoubt, and at the other end of the anti-submarine net, was York Shore Battery, armed with two modern 6-pounder twin-barrelled duplex guns.

At the beginning of the war, other components of the original British defences, forts at Ives Point, Hugonin and Ogilvie, were operational; but in the first years of the war they were decommissioned and their armament moved.[88]

GARRISON DUTY

Duty in a coastal battery lacked the excitement of North Africa, Italy or Normandy. To keep the artillery men on their toes, daily "manning parades" went through the motions of bringing the guns into position, loading and firing them. These exercises were supplemented with actual target practice, so that city residents became familiar with the distant boom of the harbour artillery at almost any time of the day or night. On Victoria Day 1942, the Censor H.B. Jefferson reported that the firing from the harbour batteries was so regular and heavy that many feared it was not a practice. On the downtown streets the firing was loud and impressive enough to rattle windows. But, he said, there was no panic as the Air Raid Wardens had warned people to watch the street lights; as long as the lights remained on it was a sign that there was no danger.[89] This warning would pay dividends in July 1945.

Each battery incorporated not only guns, but also a Battery Observation Post, with its own Plotting Room equipped with a Depression Position Finder. These were supplemented by fortress observation posts at Spion Kop (Sandwich Battery, closed in 1940), Pennant and Whitehead (near Chebucto), and Flandrum Hill and Osborne Head (both at Cow Bay). Each was connected by telephone to York Redoubt, the location of the Fire

Command Post for the harbour defences, under the command and control of the Fire Commander, who, for much of the war was Major Victor de B. Oland. Its nineteenth-century rifled muzzle-loading cannon were still in place in 1939, and, thanks to the fact that it was not rearmed during World War II, they remain so. It was the nerve centre of the harbour defences and here the Fire Commander was the focus of a web of subterranean telephone and submarine cables bringing this officer range and bearing information for suspected targets from the various plotting rooms, supplemented by reconnaissance reports by aircraft and naval patrols. Every inch of the harbour approaches within range of a coastal battery had been charted in detail. When a target location determined by the Depression Position Finder was plotted on a chart, the resulting grid reference was sent to the plotting room of the Fire Command Post, where information was combined with corrections for wind, tide, temperature and speed of the target. The result was a range and bearing which was then sent to the gunners of a particular battery or batteries. Once a target was allocated to a particular battery by the Fire Commander, the battery commander was fully responsible for dealing with it and incorporating all new information.

The Fire Command Post at York Redoubt was an army responsibility. Along with the navy and the air force, it fed information to a heavily guarded enclave on Barrington and South Streets. The defence of the Atlantic coast was reorganized on 6 August 1940 as the Eastern Military Command, which covered virtually the entire eastern seaboard, including Labrador but excluding Newfoundland. Its first commander was Major General H.P. Elkins, a man of few words but apparently formidable presence. He was succeeded by Major General L.F. Page in December, 1943.[90] Command of the harbour batteries throughout the war rested with Colonel Charles Craig, much respected and well known, though not to his face, as "Shorty" in reference to his just over five feet stature.[91]

Mingo Sweeny, fresh to the army, was assigned a role in publicizing the new battery at Fort Sandwich early in the war. The test firing of the newly commissioned guns was to be broadcast live, and his task was to run up the stairs of the battery command post, a tar-paper shack high on stilts above the emplacements, and announce for the benefit of the broadcast audience and the crowd of guests invited for the event that "an enemy ship was in sight," that being the cue to initiate the ready-aim-fire procedure. So crowded with spectators was the command post, that Sweeny struggled to open the door. Finally inside, he made his announcement and the command was given to load and fire. The World War I era cordite in the cartridges would not fire, forcing the radio announcer to ad lib for awhile. When one of the guns did fire, unexpectedly, the explosion was so violent that the heavily laden command post teetered back and forth on its stilts, a test, certainly, of the guests' resolve to sacrifice all for King and Country, but a good reason to reassemble after the event in the officers' mess. Equally traumatized were the residents of Herring Cove where the shell landed harmlessly.[92]

From time to time there were other such incidents to enliven the routine of coastal artillery duty. On one occasion, one of the 6-inch guns at Fort McNab accidentally put a round into the bank above the York Shore searchlight batteries and gun emplacements. The officer commanding York Shore was so outraged that he had to be dissuaded from returning fire.[93] In April 1940 the M.V. *Avalon* approached the gate vessels with the wrong signals hoisted. The Examination Battery fired two rounds across the bow, and one in the air, which landed on the parade ground at York Redoubt.[94] On another occasion, the Roman Catholic priest from Herring Cove appeared at York Redoubt with a 3-inch shell, which had whizzed over the heads of a funeral party. Investigation revealed that an unfortunate gunner of the First Anti-Aircraft Battery at Eastern Passage was servicing his gun, accidentally hit the trigger and, as luck would have it, the gun was loaded and the safety catch was off. This mistake earned him 28 days at the Melville Island Military Prison.[95]

THE HARBOUR DEFENCES — ANTI-AIRCRAFT

Closer to home for the average citizen, though a forbidden topic of conversation, were the city's anti-aircraft defences. Perhaps the first ordnance to roll into town as a result of the invasion of Poland were the 3.7-inch 20 cwt A.A. guns that the Fourth A.A. Battery brought from Picton, Ont. These were set up at Eastern Passage to protect R.C.A.F. Dartmouth and Imperoyal, and at Burnside to protect the naval magazine. Installing this last battery was a baptism of fire, because the men had to build a road through the bush to the site before they could install the guns.[96]

A.A. guns were the closest the area came to actual combat involvement, so devastatingly familiar to inhabitants of British or European cities. But no hostile aircraft, with the possible exception of the *Hindenburg*, ever appeared in the skies over Halifax. Had they dared to do so, A.A. fire and, if at night, the accompanying searchlights, guided first by an acoustic sort of "radar" and by 1944 by a "Predictor," an early form of computer, would have burst forth. In 1941 there were four anti-aircraft batteries, at York Redoubt, Halifax peninsula, Navy Island Cove and Imperoyal. Once the network was complete,[97] it included seven heavy A.A. batteries and 23 light batteries, with associated Quonset hut accommodation. The original seven barrack establishments were later reduced to three. Fire could have burst forth from the roof of the Y.W.C.A. on Barrington Street (light), from the roof of the Nova Scotia Technical College on Spring Garden Road (light), from an emplacement on Tower Road at the corner of Atlantic Street facing the side of Tower Road School (light) and from Acadia Street below the City Prison. Batteries in Dartmouth clustered around the airport and oil refinery at Marion Heights (light), Morris and Russell Lakes (both heavy) and Indian Point on McNab's Island (light). The naval magazine and Bedford Basin convoy anchorage were defended by an original 1939 installation in Navy Island Cove, Rockhead in the north end of the city and Princes Lodge, all of them heavy batteries. The new guns were largely 3.7-inch or 40-mm Bofors and were supplemented by a mobile 3.7-inch hauled around on a truck.[98]

The students lucky enough to have classrooms on the south side of Tower Road School watched in fascination as the tall wooden A.A. platform was built at the corner of Atlantic Street; then, for the rest of the war, whenever the air-raid sirens went off, as they filed out of their own classroom, they looked back to watch the gunners rush up the stairs to man and train their weapons.[99]

THE HARBOUR DEFENCES — SEARCHLIGHTS

In September 1939 radar was almost a science-fiction concept . Although it was on the horizon within a year and played a critical role in the Battle of Britain, its development and, indeed, its very existence was highly secret. In spite of enormous technical advances by the end of the war, for the general public radar remained a vague concept, even though it became an increasingly significant resource for the Fire Commander at York Redoubt as the war progressed. For the coastal batteries, radar was a voodoo science, but searchlights were something you could get your teeth into.

Throughout the war, nighttime operations depended upon searchlights to locate targets for the guns as they had since the last years of the British garrison. The nearly half-century-old lights in seven locations were still operational in September 1939, and were under the jurisdiction of the Tenth Searchlight Battery, R.C.E., who operated out of the Engineers' Yard in downtown Halifax. A credit to their designers and builders, the lights still functioned well. It was said that the elderly kerosene-fuelled engines which powered the generators were so simple and dependable that once started up, which required a blowtorch, a boy scout could keep them running indefinitely.[100]

It was, however, 1939 and Boer War era searchlights left a lot to be desired in terms of power and range. Their coverage was limited to the waters off Point Pleasant. Military strategists now wanted to see as far as possible out to sea. A massive upgrade of searchlight capabilities was one of the priorities of the early days of the war and by late in the year new sites were located and work well under way under the immediate jurisdiction of the Fire Commander at York Redoubt. The new network of 17 searchlights was designed to light up the approaches and any potential targets on the surface of the sea or in the air above. Those at Strawberry Battery (the only one of the McNab's fortifications of Canadian origin) and McNab's were operational in September 1940; those at York Shore, below York Redoubt (numbers 5, 6, and 7), were the last to be brought into service in mid-April 1941.[101] This new network had two components. One focused on support for the harbour batteries in the outer harbour approaches, the examination area and the gate vessels at the submarine net; the other supported, although it was physically quite separate from, the various anti-aircraft batteries scattered around the harbour and Bedford Basin.

All of them were powered by their own diesel-electric plants, brand-new 50 horsepower Gardner diesel engines, costing between $50,000 to $60,000, and backed up by emergency standby compound-wound General

Electric generators. Although dependable and relatively quiet, these generators were fussier than the old kerosene engines, and required a crew of four to keep them running happily.

The searchlights had six-foot diameter reflectors, twice the size of their predecessors, and used the same, if more intense, carbon-arc illuminating principle. Of the harbour searchlights, the four on McNab's Island at Strawberry Battery below Fort McNab (numbers 10, 11, 12 and 13), and those at York Shore below York Redoubt (numbers 5, 6 and 7), had concentrated beams, like huge cigars, and little elevation, since they were intended to focus on the ship examination area just outside the submarine net. The others, on McNab's Island (numbers 14, 15, 16, and 17) Point Pleasant, (numbers 8 and 9), Sandwich Point (numbers 3 and 4) and Chebucto Head (numbers 1 and 2) had dispersed beams and greater elevation and flexibility in order to search for, locate and fix on moving targets at sea and in the air.

When the searchlights were on it was said that the entrance to Halifax Harbour was lit up like daylight and certainly the range of the two Chebucto Head lights stretched far out to sea. It was also said that you could read a newspaper 12 miles away in the light of one of the concentrated beams, but 30,000 feet was a more likely range.[102] The lights illuminating the examination area were always on at night but during World War I it was decided that it was a waste of money to keep the others going all the time, and that policy continued in World War II.

The Fire Commander could and did give the order at any time to "Expose All Lights," as part of a nighttime exercise or target practice. It took about 20 seconds for the generators to reach full power, and the Gardner diesels were always started before dusk so that they were warmed up for any emergency, be it a German raid or, more likely, a surprise practice. The searchlight crews and the gunners in the batteries kept their eyes peeled. During the evening of 19 July 1940, the crew of searchlight # 2 reported an unusual radiant glow to the Fire Command Post. Investigation revealed that it was the debris from Halifax's seagoing garbage scow, which on regular seaward runs challenged all lurking U-boats. Earlier that evening it had emptied its cargo at sea, but the debris clumped together, drifted inward on the tide, and when the unusually phosphorescent sea water broke over and eddied around it, glowed eerily in the warm summer darkness.[103]

Massive iron shutters over the front of the searchlight emplacements were normally kept closed, but despite their size and weight they moved very freely on wheels and could be opened wide with a finger. The searchlights were backed up by nighttime binoculars mounted on tripods. It was said that the combination of lights and binoculars made it possible for an observer to pick out a tin can floating in the harbour in the middle of the night. An acoustic device, a precursor to radar, focused in on an aircraft or ship engine to give the operator a bearing.

Each battery had a small barracks and attached kitchen for the men manning the lights and engines. Maintenance was constant, not only for the engines and generators, but for the lights themselves. The carbon rods, which provided the brilliant light, needed frequent replacement and the reflectors needed to be polished regularly with a buffing pad and jewelers's rouge, particularly at the top where the heat caused etching.

Of all the harbour searchlights, # 17 at the south end of McNab's Island was the most isolated. This circumstance was partly a feature of geography and partly because of it was at the end of the newly-built rifle range. Maintenance crews working at the emplacements made certain to stay inside the concrete buildings as long as stray bullets whizzed overhead. This isolated emplacement had another advantage. The small concrete barracks and kitchen was much cosier, especially in winter, than the main barracks on McNab's, which was just a vast tar-paper shack whose potbellied stoves barely coped with cold temperatures. Despite its isolation it was a popular spot and the maintenance crew asked for and was given permission to be stationed there permanently, until human nature got the better of them. One man, sensing a golden opportunity, set up a brewing operation in the ceiling above the stove. He made a batch, bottled and corked it and put it back up in the rafters to ripen. When the Orderly Officer paid one of his occasional visits, the corks started to blow and home brew foamed out of the ceiling, down the walls and across the floor. Thus, for the duration of the war, the searchlight maintenance crews had to travel back and forth, night or day, to service # 17s lights and generator.[104]

Entirely separate from the harbour battery searchlights were those associated with the anti-aircraft batteries. The A.A. searchlights had concentrated beams and, given their targets, virtually unlimited elevation. In 1941 there were seven sites in a ring around the harbour and Bedford Basin from Herring Cove (number 1) to Cole Harbour (number 7).[105]

THE HARBOUR DEFENCES — ANTI-SUBMARINE NET

Associated with the batteries and searchlights, the anti-submarine net was a critical component of the harbour defences. U-boats prowled up and down the coast, continually on the hunt for prey, which need not be a tanker or merchantship. In July 1942:

> Shells from the gun of a German U-boat for 45 minutes were hurled into a 30-ton fishing boat from Lockeport. With two of their number wounded eight of the crew tumbled with all speed into two dories and rowed away from their doomed ship.
>
> Three of the crew of 11 were not so fortunate in making escape from the craft, which was a target for other shells and machine gun fire. They were below deck when the first shells struck and by the time realization came as to what was happening they did not dare venture above.
>
> When finally they heard a lull in the steady round of firing they sped above and, launching a shattered and leaking dory, rowed away with all the haste they could with wounds proving a handicap.
>
> The three were transferred to one of the seaworthy dories with the others and a long row started to shore.
>
> But, before they left the scene of the attack, 100 miles off the coast, the surfaced submarine came within hailing distance. It was then, according to stories told by the survivors, that the commander, who spoke good English, told them, he was sorry to shell their ship, but that he was under orders and, having his duty to perform, had to obey.[106]

The net was installed by a private firm almost immediately when war was declared, so rapidly in fact that the contract for the job was not signed until 1940. It was a vast system of wire hoops reaching to the harbour floor, hung from buoys and armed with magnetic loops and ASDIC detectors. One end was anchored in Sleepy Cove below York Redoubt, more familiar as York Shore, and the other to the lighthouse peninsula reaching off Maugher's Beach on McNab's Island. The "back door" to the harbour, Eastern Passage, was scarcely navigable for anything but fishing boats but leaving nothing to chance, piles were sunk across the channel at intervals that ensured only fishing boats could pass through.

In order for ships to come and go, the net was in two sections. Towards its eastern end two "gate vessels," each permanently moored to a hinged end of the net, moved it inward or outward as required, to open or close the "gate" and let authorized ships through. The gate was located close enough to McNab's Island to be within range of the guns of Fort McNab and to provide enough draught for ships but not enough for a submerged submarine to slip in under the ship. It seems to have been effective, though navy men always suspected that submarines based themselves under the Sambro lightship, from which they could report the coming and goings of convoys to the German intelligence agency.

Just outside the gate was the "Examination Area" where entering ships were stopped under the guns of Fort McNab and York Shore Battery, and at night their associated searchlights. A vessel identified itself to a "boarding officer" who signalled Fort McNab by Aldis lamp (to maintain radio silence) giving tonnage, number of crew, nationality, cargo, etc. Fort McNab then telephoned the navy in Halifax, which cleared the ship and notified Fort McNab, which in turn signalled the gate vessels to let it through the gate. The gate vessels then winched their sections apart, allowing the gap in the net to open and the ship to enter.[107]

Initially, the net had weaknesses, which had to be remedied. For one thing, small boats could avoid the tedious wait by simply motoring over it. HMCS *Islander* made this intention clear when, reprimanded for going over the boom, it responded indignantly that it did it all the time.[108] In winter, frozen gear often left a line-up of ships waiting to get in or out as crews struggled to get ice-clogged winches operational, as happened on 16 February 1943.[109] The following day, net operators were further tested when

HMCS *Mulgrave* slipped in under cover of fog, unseen by Fort McNab, without bothering to report to the examination vessel.[110]

This work, however vital, tended towards the routine, enlivened only occasionally when an imposing battleship, conscious of its superiority, could barely be induced to play the game. While the men on examination battery gun duty did not toy with ships of that ilk, when smaller boats, such as the *Reo II* and the *Edith I*, tried to avoid playing the game in May 1940, they each got two shots across the bow for refusing to stop.[111] The watches were boring, particularly during the long hours between midnight and 8:00 a.m., and gunners itching for opportunity were known to fire warning shots across a bow on the slightest pretext, even the Halifax garbage scow. Perhaps once or twice it waited too long to properly identify itself on its return from a regular trip to sea, and got the message at close range.[112]

In this time of rationing, it was no surprise that the Royal Canadian Navy maintained its own lobster pots just outside the net. At York Shore Battery, the net had been set to an eight-foot depth for a short way offshore to allow fishing boats to come and go with a minimum of fuss, and this also allowed the garrison the opportunity to buy fresh lobster from the fisher-men. As time went on, the men began to lay their own traps, and the first order of the day was to haul them, supplementing army rations with boiled lobster for breakfast.[113]

The navy was not alone in supplementing standard issue rations. Opposite York Shore, on McNab's Island, garbage disposal had created a serious nuisance in the form of squads of rats who fed off the Army's largesse, not at all fazed by the fact that it had been buried. Rat shooting parties became a popular if not genteel recreation, even as a special garbage boat service was under contemplation to get the stuff off the island. In the autumn of 1941 some imaginative soul came up with a much more productive solution: to establish what became known as the McNab's Piggery. Edible refuse was fed to a herd of pigs which ended up supplement-ing the garrison diet with fresh pork and sausages in far more liberal quantities than was possible otherwise.[114]

The duty was occasionally tempered with danger. On 12 May 1940, one of the gate vessels, HMCS *Ypres*, a World War I era Admiralty steam trawler (Polson Iron Works, Toronto, 1917), was run down and sunk at her post by the battleship HMS *Revenge*, an honoured veteran of the Battle of Jutland, stationed in Halifax as a convoy escort. At around 8:30 p.m., *Revenge* was heading seaward through the gate when a loud crash was heard and the *Ypres* was pushed over by the bow of the *Revenge*. The next day all that could be seen of the *Ypres* was the top of its masts about 200 yards south of its normal position. The *Revenge*, in charge of a convoy of troop ships, could only proceed on to sea. No lives were lost, but the crews of the gate vessels got their own "revenge." For the next 18 months, before *Revenge* departed in October 1941 for convoy duty in the Indian Ocean, each time it returned to port, the crews of the gate vessels performed elaborate collision and "abandon ship" drills when it approached the examination area.[115]

HARBOUR DEFENCES — THE MINESWEEPERS

As soon as the gate vessels closed the net behind a departing convoy, an ocean of hostility lay before it. Shallow coastal waters, offshore Nova Scotia or Europe, were prime territory for mines. The British had not been hesitant to mine German-controlled ports, and both Germany and Britain laid mines along their own coasts to prevent unauthorized approaches or landings.

There was every reason to believe that Germany would try to harass convoys arriving or leaving Halifax, and each day, with monotonous regularity, a fleet of R.N. and R.C.N. minesweepers filed out of the harbour and launched their paravanes. Paravanes, rather like aquatic blimps, were towed on either side of the ship from the bow and were designed to pull away from the ship's side while maintaining a constant depth. They were intended to snag the tether which moored the buoyant mine to its anchor, and in sweeping it out to the paravane, cut the tether. When the mine popped to the surface, it would be despatched by gunfire with very satisfying results.

The daily monotony of it all was trying, but the very regularity must have convinced the ever-lurking U-boats that it was pointless to go to all the effort only to have their carefully sewn garden of destruction harvested first thing each morning. Minesweeping came to be seen as a non-hazardous duty, and the crews were often fairly young, teenagers picking up a bit of seasoning before going off to more gritty theatres. Only once, no doubt to the joy of the ships' companies involved, did the Germans make the effort.

In June 1943, U-119 laid a wide arc of 66 "moored magnetic" mines across the harbour mouth. Mines of this type exploded not only by direct contact but also by proximity to a ship. They were discovered almost immediately by alert lookouts on an R.C.N. escort, and the harbour minesweepers set about clearing a six-cable (1200 yard) channel to allow a waiting convoy to leave:

> All Canada can be proud of the cockleshell ships of her navy's minesweeping fleet who discharged their duty — to keep the sea lanes free — by sweeping a safe channel for ships within one day, who kept that channel clear, and who swept from the ocean floor all the deadly high explosive that Hun had sown to sink our convoys.
>
> [The men] now know the sickly emptiness of a man's stomach as the ship's hull rings like a gong from the sledge-hammer wallop of a mine touched off nearby ... [the crews] remember the tingling of bruised feet afterwards.
>
> [They] saw five mines geyser up one morning before breakfast [they] cleaned up messes of batter or whatever happened to be cooking when an exploding mine whacked the ships bottom [and] watched the blades on an electric fan crinkle up and rattle around from the force of the blow. [They] fixed boiler leaks and were jarred from their sleep in their bunks during their off watches.
>
> Their job is as tough as it was exciting and dangerous. The day begins at 4 a.m., and as the men prepare for sea the repair and maintenance crews who have been working all night go ashore. The day's orders come aboard and the sweepers cast off before daylight.
>
> They slip out through the mouth of Halifax harbour, gather speed and push past Neverfail buoy as the sun reddens behind a brilliant bank of cloud.
>
> At the "declared dangerous" area the ships slow to put the sweeps over. A crane lifts the float, which holds the sweep wire from falling to the bottom of the sea, and drops

it over the side. It looks like a domesticated but bad-humored shark, with its marker flag flopping on its upper side.

Next the multiplane otter goes overboard. It is like a piece of Venetian blind, frozen at a 45 degree angle, and its purpose is to exert a downward and outward pressure on the sweep wire.

Then the men go to the brakes on the huge drums, and play out cable after cable of hardened steel wire, serrated to cut the mooring of any anchored mine as it rasps along. As the ship gathers speed, the float marker moves far out to the side, indicating the channel we are now sweeping.

"It is just like plowing," a rating explains. "I was born and brought up on a farm. You sweep a field; you plow up, turn around and plow down, plow back again. The other ships are a couple of extra teams, and take their speed from you."[116]

Only one ship, a small freighter that strayed from the straight and narrow, was lost. A minesweeper that destroyed a mine was entitled to sport a white band on its funnel, and those who were awarded an "assist' got a blue band.[117] It was the last time the Germans attempted to close Halifax Harbour, though the adrenalin of frontline danger and excitement was still there because U-boats skulked, threatened and torpedoed off the harbour mouth. They took turns on six- to eight-week patrols, considerably aided by the development of the snorkel, which allowed them to operate submerged almost indefinitely. They continued to sink ships in the approaches; U-806 and U-1232 torpedoed five between December 1944 and January 1945. The last Canadian ship sunk in World War II was the Halifax based minesweeper HMCS *Esquimault*, torpedoed by U-190 in the approaches on 19 April 1945. So quickly did it sink that there was no chance to send a radio message. Forty-six of the 70 crew made it into the lifeboats, but by the time HMCS *Sarnia* chanced upon them hours later, the frigid weather ensured that only 26 survived.[118]

Ironically, U-190, which continued patrols to the bitter end, was commissioned into the R.C.N. following her surrender at Bay Bulls, Newfoundland. After a period based in Halifax for training purposes, the submarine was sunk in a theatrical display at the site of the *Esquimault*'s grave on Trafalgar Day, 21 October 1947.[119]

HARBOUR DEFENCES — ALARMS AND EXCURSIONS

Occasionally, Halifax's vast and complex assemblage of defences was tested. In the early days of the war, the port's defenders were particularly edgy. The arrival in port on 1 June 1940 from a collapsing France of the aircraft carrier *Bearn* and its escorts *Jean d'Arc* and *Emil Bertin* sparked off an alleged sighting of a submarine at 9:12 a.m. That evening at 6:00 p.m. the port was closed, double sentries were posted at the batteries and the searchlights were all exposed. When a small motor yacht, the *Dixianna*, came in, it was held in the examination area with orders to fire on it if it moved towards the boom. The alert lasted until 4 June and was almost immediately reinstated when on the morning of the fifth a submarine was reported off Chebucto Head. Bombs were dropped at the location of the sighting. There was another sighting 7 miles off the Sambro Lightship and then early in the afternoon the report of another from Stranraer 908. The harbour guns were fully manned, all passes were revoked and three minesweepers proceeded to sea at full speed. The next evening, bold as brass, the submarine appeared in the beam of #11 searchlight heading for the boom. Despite a full alert, it eluded destruction.[120] Much later in the war, on 24 December 1944, HMCS *Clayoquot* was torpedoed off the Sambro Lightship with the loss of eight men; in January 1945 two ships were sunk just east of the harbour and two more, the *British Freedom* and the *Martin Van Buren*, were torpedoed in the harbour entrance. Finally, weeks before war's end, the *Esquimault* was sunk.[121]

H. B. Jefferson recounted a real or imagined threat in early April 1942. On the morning of the ninth, the gate vessels reported that their equipment detected something passing through the channel between the two ships while the gate was open to let in merchant ships. Suspecting a submarine, a number of corvettes with ASDIC devices were immediately assigned to different parts of the harbour and Bedford Basin, to make a systematic check. A destroyer and several corvettes were sent to the gate to block escape. The search ended unsuccessfully about 3:00 p.m. that afternoon, but a large force of harbour craft remained on standby in case the submarine remained on the harbour bottom and surfaced at night for air and to charge batteries. Echoing Admiral Bonham-Carter's earlier speculations about sea-raiders, there was the possibility that a submarine could torpedo an explosives ship, with devastating consequences to the city, or torpedo one of the U.S. troop transports in the stream; or a ship lying at the Ocean Terminals, thus blocking a large part of the sea wall for months to come.[122]

In the wee small hours of Christmas morning 1943, a general alarm went out from Washington that an enemy air attack might be attempted on Christmas Day. The entire eastern seaboard was alerted, and in Halifax all military personnel were put on alert for nearly 24 hours. This alert was not as disruptive as it might seem because the unique frontline status of the city meant no special holiday leave for the garrison anyway. Radio bulletins kept the public advised of the danger, but gave few details, but they heard Mayor LaGuardia of New York City declare, "Today is a holiday, but the enemy respects no holiday. Remember in case of any emergency, act calm, avoid panic, obey orders."[123] Haligonians were reminded by their own mayor, O. R. Crowell, that they were still in the danger zone. At suppertime on Christmas Day an announcement was made that "protective measures" had been taken and around 10:00 p.m. the emergency was cancelled.

HARBOUR DEFENCES — KEEPING ALERT

The navy and the air force often returned to the Dockyard and Eastern Passage with hair-raising tales of corvettes or Cansos engaging the enemy directly; but for the harbour garrison it was a more difficult war. The above incidents were the exception but it was vital to keep focused; and when peaceful day followed peaceful day, that was hard. Harold Harding, on searchlight maintenance on McNab's Island, applied more than once for transfer to active service. He was told that he could not be replaced and, eventually, was bluntly told to stop asking.[124] Others on coastal battery duty found that a request for a transfer to an anti-tank regiment was often a successful way out. For some life wasn't so bad. Hunting and fishing could be good in the barrens behind York Redoubt or Chebucto Head, and the single-lane dirt road leading to Herring Cove was a dangerous place to meet a truck load of artillery men full of bonhomie, returning from leave to Fort Sandwich.[125]

In the early days of the war at least, the Fourth A.A. Battery, assigned to reopen the mothballed Connaught Battery, kept the cobwebs away by 10-mile route marches in full battle dress to the North West Arm — the first six at a run, the last four at a walk.[126] At Fort McNab, a Sports Committee was formed and organized a soccer team[127] and at Sandwich Battery in July 1940 a badminton court was completed west of the Officers' Mess, and volleyball games pitted the officers against the N.C.O.s and men.[128]

Entertainment also made its way out to these remote posts. Bill White and His (Coloured) Orchestra got a hearty reception in the Gunners' Mess at Sandwich Battery, and on 6 October 1940 the Halifax Concert Party group got an equally big welcome.[129]

That same month, Fort McNab was treated to a run of movies: *My Old Kentucky Home, Souls of the Sea, Magnificent Obsession* and *Breezing Home,* shown by volunteers from the Y.M.C.A., the Salvation Army and the Canadian Legion, who had trekked out by boat and over bad roads to deliver their cargos of escapism.[130]

DISCIPLINE

The military had its own mechanisms for enforcing discipline upon this great mass of humanity. Little was in place when the war began because in the tiny collection of professionals who constituted the services after World War I discipline was not a serious problem. It could usually be handled by a Sergeant, or a Warrant or Petty Officer. Strangely enough, the R.C.N. did not change its opinion on this matter until 1944, when a shore patrol with its own organization, rank, regulations and pay structures was established. Before that discipline was dealt with in the usual ad hoc manner. A Chief Petty Officer on a ship would be designated as Master-at-Arms (known as "Jaunty") or "Regulating Petty Officer," entitled to co-opt "volunteers" as required for Shore Patrol duty whether on ship or shore. Naval bases and property were in the custody first of the R.C.M.P. and later special constables of the Canadian Corps of Commissionaires.

The army and the R.C.A.F. were better organized. The former reconstituted its World War I Canadian Army Provost Corps in June 1940 and many were recruited or volunteered from the R.C.M.P. as Military Police (MPs); until, that is, the Commissioner of the Force, seeing his ranks decimated, forbade further transfers. Similarly, the R.C.A.F., in March 1940, established its Service Police (SPs) organization to maintain internal discipline and provide security for its bases.[131]

A belief that the expanded number of personnel in the Halifax Garrison were not, in their dress, discipline and courtesy, "reflecting to the credit of the Army," led to the re-establishment of the Garrison Military Police in January 1943,[132] a purely local agency which, after the World War I era Provost Corps was disbanded, garrison commanders had been authorized to establish if they felt it appropriate. In this case, it was felt that it was either not the duty of the Provost Corps to enforce the niceties of behaviour, or they were not interested in it.

The re-establishment of the military police probably reflects the dismay felt by some at the apparently lax behaviour of the "Zombies," those recruits who had opted out of overseas service, which, in Canada's all-volunteer army, they were entitled to do.

Each branch of the military had its own disciplinary infrastructure. The navy had ten cells in an old barracks in the Dockyard, the army inherited the old British military prison on Melville Island (now the Armdale Yacht Club) and a Detention Barracks on McNab's Island. For 85 cents a day, the City of Halifax was prepared to accommodate any service without discrimination in the granite cells of the City Prison in the north end.[133]

Career soldiers said that discipline in the garrison during the war was not what it had been in the pre-war army. Some recruits were always ungrateful, or could not take the routine and the discipline, or fell afoul of the liquor regulations. In the latter case, options depended upon your sentence. Seven days "confined to barracks" was served at the South Barracks, east of R.A. Park where you bunked in the Guard Room, were up at 6:00 a.m. to run around the Citadel for an hour fully kitted with great coat, pack, rifle, etc., a routine repeated in the evening within the confines of the South Barrack parade square, all the while under the malevolent eye of an ill-disposed N.C.O.

More serious offenses for a while meant Melville Island, a rough place run by the Royal Canadian Regiment. Absolutely no tobacco was allowed, a serious restriction in an era when smoking was deemed healthy and was ubiquitous. To ensure compliance, every article of clothing, even the seams, was searched. On Sunday a prisoner had two choices: reading or exercise. Reading meant the Bible and only the Bible; exercise meant two hours in full marching kit doing figure 8s.[134] But early in the war, Melville Island became an ammunition storage depot and the Detention Barracks were concentrated on McNab's Island, not only for the units stationed there, but for the garrison as a whole[135] and even the occasional German P.O.W. Among other things, prisoners held there built the Garrison Road, which joined the north and south ends of the island. For those who stepped out of line, the speciality of the guards was called the "hard bar," which required two offenders. Each offender took one end of a pole from which was suspended a 100 pound weight. They then had to run up a hill between two lines of guards armed with old bicycle inner tubes. Too slow (it was always too slow) and ...[136]

Minor offences were dealt with on site. When two gunners at Fort Sandwich appeared stark naked at "Working Party" parade, they were ordered to report for a week, at all times in full battledress. They explained in futile justification, that they had accepted a bet that they would not take off all their clothes, minutes before the parade. Their clothes promptly disappeared along with their mates, who responded to the bugle call. Since it was a greater sin not to report for parade than to appear naked, the two hapless victims had no choice but to show up.[137]

THE CONVOYS MID-WAR

The convoy system of escorting more or less defenceless merchant ships through hostile waters goes back to the Napoleonic period, and in one form or another much farther. The belief of late-nineteenth-century diplomats that war had been tamed and civilized by a series of international agreements did not long survive the beginning of World War I, and the convoy system was quickly reinvented.[138]

Although Halifax was a principal operational and assembly centre for the North Atlantic convoys for the entire period of the war, it was not the nerve centre. That was the preserve of the Tracking and Routing Section of the British Admiralty, thousands of miles away. The destination of

Halifax convoys was Britain, which, with the rapid collapse of continental opposition to the German advance, had become so isolated that if it was to survive and become the arsenal of democracy, it must be supplied from overseas. From day one Canada accepted this responsibility and Halifax became the epicentre of the country's effort, although with the entry into the war of the United States, ports such as Boston and New York began to take precedence.

Halifax's role was twofold. First, it was an operational base for the naval escort fleet, a responsibility shared uneasily with St. John's, Nfld. Priority shifted back and forth between the two cities. Although its harbour was small, St. John's had an intimate proximity to the killing fields of the cold grey North Atlantic, where the desperate struggle with Germany's U-boat wolf packs was played out as the Battle of the Atlantic. Halifax, with its vast harbour and links to the resources of the continental hinterland, had an existing, if antiquated, infrastructure. In the end Halifax prevailed with the accession in May 1943 of the R.C.N.'s Admiral Leonard W. Murray as Commander in Chief, Northwest Atlantic, and with it control of North Atlantic convoy support.

Second, Halifax's splendid harbour made it a natural place for the assembly and departure of merchant ships, which were the heart of the convoy because they were the only way to get the vast quantities of supplies, both guns and butter, across the ocean.

> "It can be no secret that Halifax has a vital role in convoy-
> ing merchant ships of Allied nations to beleaguered Britain
> and that the Royal Canadian Navy is playing a heroic part
> in this all-important task, having already safely escorted
> thousands of ships and millions of tons of cargo to their
> destinations in the Mother Country."[139]

Once war was declared all non-neutral ships immediately fell under the jurisdiction and control of the British Admiralty and they were more or less reduced to freight cars in a train, with the Tracking and Routing Section acting as dispatcher.

There were two choices to get ships across the Atlantic. If they could travel consistently at speeds greater than 15 knots they did so independently, under Admiralty control, because they could outrun any submarine. Foremost among this class were the great passenger liners which came and went from Halifax on their own schedules. The vast majority, however, went in convoys, which operated at two speeds; fast and slow. Until New York took over, Halifax was the base for the fast HX convoys (westbound they were OB and then, after July 1941, ON), which could maintain speeds of between 9 and 14.8 knots. Sydney, N.S., was the base for the slow SC group, which ran below 9 knots, but no less than 7.5 knots, and supposedly travelled in summer only.

The marshaling and organization of a convoy before it left Halifax was the responsibility of the Naval-Control-of-Shipping (N.C.S.) office, an arm of the R.C.N. On the one hand, it dealt with the Admiralty, naval authorities and intelligence services and, on the other hand, with ships' captains, organizing pre-sailing conferences, issuing code books, charts, special publications, sailing orders, etc. It did not, however, set the actual route. That task was the preserve of the Royal Navy's Trade Division, a responsibility shared with the U.S. Navy after America entered the war.

The command of the convoy rested with a Commodore, usually a retired Royal Navy flag officer, who might be assisted by a Vice and a Rear Commodore. It was the job of the Commodores to get their motley collection of ships and captains out of the harbour, form them up when at sea, keep them in order on the way across and disassemble them on the other side. The Commodore usually travelled at the head of the convoy and his Vice and Rear, if the size of the convoy warranted it, at the rear outer corners. The Commodore's ship was usually the largest and best appointed, not for prestige or comfort, but because it was best for visual and wireless communication.

Once the Commodore got his ships out of the harbour, he and they fell under the jurisdiction of the naval escort and its Senior Officer, Escort (S.O.E.) although usually he and the S.O.E. worked as a team. The escorts, which in Halifax came to mean the famous corvettes, fell under the local jurisdiction of the Captain (D) (i.e., destroyers), who had an administrative "flotilla" staff, ideally, specialists who supplied the needs and wants of escort groups as a whole, and individual ships and crews.

Initially, convoy escorts were under the jurisdiction of the Royal Navy and its Halifax representative, Admiral Bonham-Carter, within which the R.C.N. played an increasing role as its capabilities evolved. Until February 1942, Halifax-based escorts sailed only to a Mid-Ocean Meeting Point, where jurisdiction was transferred to a British-based escort. They refuelled in Iceland before returning to Halifax with or without a westbound convoy. Later they escorted convoys all the way across, where their base was Londonderry, Northern Ireland.

The captain and officers of a merchant ship, at least initially, found adapting to the convoy system demanding. In peacetime, once a ship dropped the pilot and left the confines of harbour, its officers and crew were on their own and the captain was monarch of all he surveyed. The engine telegraph, which had three speeds ahead or astern: slow, half or full — was placed in "full ahead" position and stayed there, perhaps for weeks on end, while the engine room crew kept the steam pressure up and moving parts lubricated. Now everything changed. In violation of a lifetime of training that had become instinct, a ship had to steam in a fixed position, in close and constant company with a myriad of others, for days and weeks at a time; to maintain its position in all weather in this mass of shipping the engineers had to be constantly vigilant so as to be ready to adjust the engine speed and under no conditions make smoke. Worse still, perhaps, the captain's authority was subordinated to that of the convoy commodore whose officers could and did harass him for any violations or variations. And over all hovered the very real prospect of attack and destruction at a moment's notice or less.[140]

As the Royal Navy came under increasing strain to maintain its command of the sea, it began to substitute Armed Merchant Cruisers for escort duty. In July 1941 it even recommended that Halifax be abandoned as an operational base and facilities consolidated at St. John's,[141] a proposal which did not fly as facilities there were minimal. Nevertheless, one of the results of the August 1941 Atlantic Charter meeting between Churchill and Roosevelt in Placentia, Nfld., was an agreement that the U.S. Navy would take over the Royal Navy convoy jurisdiction in the western Atlantic, an astonishing development when one recalls that the United States was still officially neutral. Accordingly, on 9 October 1941, Admiral Bonham-

Carter sailed for Britain on the *Cape Town Castle* to embark on an active wartime career which earned him a knighthood, leaving Mrs. Bonham-Carter to her Halifax friends for the rest of the war, and the convoys in the hands of the Americans.

After Pearl Harbor, American interest in this role diminished rapidly and shifted to the Pacific theatre. When the U-boat war moved into the Gulf of St. Lawrence in the summer of 1942, its most tragic victim was the 14 October sinking of the Newfoundland ferry *Caribou*, with a loss of 137 lives. Political pressure, coupled with the R.C.N.'s vastly increased capability, led to the withdrawal of the Americans and the appointment of Admiral Leonard W. Murray, based in Halifax, as Commander-in-Chief, North West Atlantic. Murray's crisp organizational skills, coupled with increasing Allied resources, including escort aircraft carriers and the advent of the R.C.A.F.'s long range Liberator patrols from Labrador, brought about a dramatic turnaround in the Battle of the Atlantic. Finally, the U-boats were forced on the defensive, suffered mounting losses and fell back into the role of dangerous nuisance for the remainder of the war.

Among the naval escorts, Halifax was not a popular base. "Slackers," as it was known, suffered in comparison with the warmth and responsiveness of St. John's, "Newfyjohn," where it seemed they could never do enough for you. Had the Royal Navy succeeded in eliminating Halifax as anything but a convoy assembly base, the R.C.N. crews would have been just as happy. Unfortunately for the crews, inadequate as Halifax's resources were, they were superior to those of St. John's. Therefore, for operational purposes, even ships based in St. John's had to go through Halifax for "additions and alterations" (A & As) or overhauls. Decisions made during this process were completely out of the hands of a ship's captain, and, what was more, he might, during such a layover, find himself stripped of the crew he had just worked up to a functioning unit, and forced to set out into the North Atlantic with a complement of green Prairie youths. The issue of training, which bedeviled the R.C.N. in the first half of the war, was yet another stick to beat Halifax with, and HMCS Sambro, the shoreside training or work-up establishment, was bitterly condemned for sending out crews which were "almost completely untrained."[142]

Stories of Halifax from the perspective of the naval escort service are legion. James B. Lamb spoke for many when he later recalled:

> When we came ashore to the soft civilian life of the shore-
> side navy, and were exposed to all its forgotten motivations
> of status and rank and petty privilege, we felt ourselves to
> be apart. We felt ourselves to be older, wiser, and tougher
> than these spoilt and silly people, preoccupied with illu-
> sions. They seemed unaware of the harsh realities of the
> uncaring universe that enfolded their little make-believe
> society; a universe whose awesome power and certainty
> could be glimpsed in the moon-lonely wastes of the winter
> ocean.
>
> To corvette crews, Halifax, or more precisely HMCS
> Stadacona, universally known as "Slackers," was the
> embodiment of the shoreside establishment; oh, how we
> hated to be sent to Halifax!
>
> Two pairs of Oerlikon guns, installed by the British
> aboard a corvette I was in to beef up our anti-aircraft
> defence, were taken away on return to Halifax because
> they were in excess of guns allotted to corvettes by author-
> ity. Nobody explained to us why the guns were more useful
> sitting in storage ashore than in action afloat.[143]

These unhappy deficiencies were only partly the fault of the shore-
based establishment, which had to cope with not only the astonishing
increase in the number of ships and crews required, but also the constant
need to retrofit ships with the many technological advances that war
brought in its wake. And then there was the stream of ships pummelled into
near incapacity, as much by incessant gales as by enemy action. Eventually,
the navy built its own facilities at small ports such as Shelburne to take the
pressure off Halifax; but for much of the war there was no real alternative
to Halifax or, with the long sail around, Saint John, N.B. Although most
corvettes were built in Great Lakes or St. Lawrence shipyards, once fitted
out for escort duties, they could not return for refits through the Saint
Lawrence locks for their draught was now too great. So Halifax it was.

THE ESTABLISHMENTS ADAPT — HMC DOCKYARD

Having come near to extinction more than once in the inter-war years, the naval Dockyard was almost intact at war's start, right back to a remarkable complement of eighteenth-century buildings. Although the navy's dramatic expansion was mostly in ships and men, its Halifax base also had to adapt. Change came after 1942 with repairs and extensions to the wharves, an ordnance depot, a temporary barracks and an administrative building:

> Many new buildings are going up and the whole place is an unbelievable clutter of pile drivers, steam shovels, concrete mixers, surveyors, parked cars, long rows of 4 and 6 inch guns, gun mounts, depth charges, paravenes [*sic*], minesweeping equipment, anchors and heaps of other equipment through which the road winds for miles. At the new jetty sixteen corvettes were berthed in groups of four. Farther south at the old jetties there were about 30 more corvettes, destroyers, minesweepers and a minelayer moored. Behind these jetties on the shore side there are a number of docks absolutely crammed with small craft. Behind the new jetty some sailors were taking instruction in handling whale boats. Mixxed [*sic*] into all this mess were groups of sailors running or marching along the roads to and from classes and hundreds of individuals [*sic*] officers and men travelling on foot in all directions. There did not seem to be as many private cars around but the taxi and truck traffic was as heavy as ever. As it was about 5 o'clock when we left, there were a large number of girls and women also moving about the Dockyard. These are people employed in various offices.
>
> So crowded has the Dockyard become that large numbers of corvettes are now being lined up on the Dartmouth shore or a short distance off it at mooring buoys and that side of the harbor threatens to become as crowded as Halifax.[144]

THE MILITARY PRESENCE

Additional land for the cramped facility, which was only some five hundred feet deep, was acquired from the army by their move to the old airport, and by leasing or purchasing from the National Harbours Board and the Canadian National Railways:

> The streets of Halifax are thronged with officers and ratings of the R.C.N., the harbour is lined with ships being readied for convoy, new buildings to accommodate the Navy's needs are going up on all sides, and the dockyard is a veritable beehive of activity as thousands of navy men are schooled for service on the seas.
>
> Proceeding to His Majesty's Canadian Dockyard, our party saw all phases of the technical training of the Navy, including the gunnery school, ordnance artificers' shop, machine shops, anti-aircraft school, and other departments of instruction. It is here that the officers and ratings receive their final training in gunnery, navigation, wireless telegraphy, signalling and able seamanship to fit them for their tasks. Stokers are taught their engineroom duties and there are schools for cooks, stewards and sickbay attendants. In one building the gunners were being trained on large naval guns. It was an unbelievable bedlam as the youngsters went through their paces, shouting and repeating orders and moving with speed and precision to their respective stations. Not all of these lads are Maritimers, in fact a great many are from the prairies and singularly enough they take to the water like ducks.[145]

In 1942 to accommodate its expanding requirements, the Dockyard took a lease of enough land and water lots from the National Harbours Board to build Jetty Zero at its south extremity, and in 1944 gave itself some manoeuvring room by acquiring additional land up to Pier 4.

Since 1924 the hillside above, on the other side of Barrington Street, had been a preserve of the army centred on Wellington Barracks, aside from Admiralty House, the Naval Officer's Mess. In 1941 the Navy took over Wellington Barracks and renamed it HMCS *Nelson*. From this grew what is today HMCS *Stadacona*, established in 1923 as a naval manning depot named after an armed yacht which had patrolled the waters of the port. It was based in the former Royal Naval Cadet College in the Dockyard, but grew dramatically with the onset of war. When Wellington Barracks was acquired, the training component of *Stadacona* was recommissioned as HMCS *Cornwallis*, and transferred into and subsumed the designation of HMCS *Nelson*. This change was always regarded as a temporary expedient, however, as it was recognized that Halifax could not accommodate a facility of its proposed size. Land was acquired at Deep Brook on the Annapolis Basin and during the first six months of 1943, Cornwallis' operations were transferred there. HMCS *Stadacona*, continued its operational role and annexed Admiralty House and its grounds to the south in 1943, built a naval hospital on the adjoining recreational field and, with the expropriations of 1942 and 1943, filled most of the rectangle between North, Young, Barrington and Gottingen Streets, its stomping grounds for the foreseeable future.[146]

By 1945, 40 or 50 buildings had replaced almost all the older buildings, and six modern jetties, four of them with cranes, transformed the yard to a cramped but more or less state-of-the-art ship-support facility.[147] Eventually a tardy solution to accommodation problem came with the 1944 takeover of the R.C.A.F. quarters at Windsor Park as barracks, renamed HMCS Peregrine.

THE ESTABLISHMENTS ADAPT — R.C.A.F. DARTMOUTH

For years the former American navy seaplane base at Baker's Point had been operated on a summer-only, shoestring "care and maintenance" basis by the equally shoestring R.C.A.F., but the serendipitous combination of burgeoning interest in airplanes and the desperate need for unemployment relief brought about a dramatic upgrade of its facilities beginning in 1934 and accelerated in 1938. As the war moved into high gear, the R.C.A.F. Dartmouth station became a separate community, larger than most Nova Scotia towns. Only war could account for the ease with which appeared hangars, machine shops, more unattractive barracks, a post office, docking facilities, not just for the flying boats but also for the small craft of the

R.C.A.F. Marine Section, and even lofts for a fleet of carrier pigeons. As the technology advanced, R.C.A.F. Dartmouth established satellite radar units both to detect threats and direct its own aircraft, at Preston, Osborne Head, Bell Lake and Port Dufferin. The first of these, at Preston, can claim to be the first radar station in North America.[148]

The first air patrol of the war was carried out on 10 September 1939, by Stranraer 908 and No. 5 Bomber Reconnaissance Squadron. Henceforth, a routine evolved whereby one or more aircraft took off from Eastern Passage at about 5:30 a.m. to provide cover for a departing convoy. The Stranraer, a biplane, had a maximum air time of nine-and-a-half hours. If weather permitted, because it was seaworthy, it could land in the waters off Sable Island and refuel. In the summer of 1941, the American Catalina, a Canso in Canadian service, began to replace the Stranraer. Although less seaworthy, it had a much greater range. The transition was complete by October and Cansos remained in service for the rest of the war.[149]

During the war, at one time or another, nine long-range Bomber Reconnaissance Squadrons were based in Dartmouth and flew Digby, Hudson and Liberator aircraft as well as the Stranraer and Canso.[150]

Once the initial reconnaissance was complete, coverage of the convoy might continue until maximum range was reached and taken over by Newfoundland-based aircraft, or it might continue as a general reconnaissance patrol. Patrols might not return to base until midnight. As the convoy system evolved, it became the practice, before the ships left harbour, for the aircraft to scour the waters outside the harbour. As the convoy left Chebucto Head and the Sambro lightship behind, a squadron of reconnaissance aircraft escorted by fighters radiated out in a fan shape from the lead ship in a "sector search," with each aircraft in a designated sector.[151]

Patrolling the harbour approaches was one of the Dartmouth station's most significant roles, but as headquarters of Eastern Air Command, it also carried out much broader functions of North Atlantic Patrol. In addition to accompanying convoys, its squadrons patrolled the Gulf of Saint Lawrence and Newfoundland and followed up fishermen's reports of suspicious activities with "special searches." A Canso might appear over an unidentified ship and give it a thorough inspection. In all but emergencies, radio silence was absolute and ship and aircraft communicated by the flashes of the Aldis Lamp in an elaborate code which changed with the time of day. If a response was not forthcoming or correct, a surface ship was located and directed to the suspect, which had been persuaded to heave to by threatening dives and bursts of machine gun fire. More prosaically, the squadrons also towed aerial targets over Halifax to give the shore and A.A. batteries something to practice on.[152]

The big flying boats, as well as smaller float planes, were maintained by the R.C.A.F. Marine Section, which also had its own fleet of boats and ships for rescue services and to supply remote radar sites as far north as Labrador. R.C.A.F. Dartmouth was also the home of a diving unit.

Supporting patrol and reconnaissance aircraft, R.C.A.F. Dartmouth was also, at one time or another, the base for six Fighter Squadrons. They flew the more or less obsolete Grumman Goblin, an open cockpit biplane, then the Curtiss Kittyhawk, two of which fought a brief action with a surfaced U-Boat 10 miles east of Halifax on 16 January 1942. Shortly afterwards the Kittyhawks were transferred to Alaska and for the rest of the war air cover for the East Coast Port was provided by Hawker Hurricanes.[153]

The Royal Naval Air Section also maintained a component at Eastern Passage. Originally blandly identified as Royal Naval Air Station Dartmouth, it was renamed HMS Seaborne, continuing the name of Admiral Bonham-Carter's temporary Dockyard headquarters. Their pay and administration unit, HMS Canada, was in Halifax in the King Edward Hotel. Also located in Halifax, for a time at least, was HMS Saker, in reality an umbrella establishment (then and now) covering Royal Navy personnel in North America with components in Washington, D.C., Brooklyn, N.Y., Maine, and probably other locations. In Halifax it was associated with the crews sent out to man the American lend-lease destroyers transferred to the Royal Navy.

Seaborne initially provided a home base for the Swordfish and Walrus aircraft assigned to the Royal Navy's 3rd Battle Squadron. When that presence withdrew, it shifted to assembling replacement Swordfish assigned to the "merchant aircraft carriers" (MACs). These carriers, conceived in 1940 but not put into operation until 1943, had been quickly converted from tankers or grain ships by adding not much more than a flight deck for three or four Swordfish. The grain ship MACs had a vestigial hangar, but the tanker version had none, so their Swordfish had to survive, more or less, as deck cargo in all weathers. Not surprisingly, Seaborne's establishment spent as much time repairing the resulting weather damage as that from active submarine surveillance. Until the American war machine produced more sophisticated escort carriers, these MACs were a very successful stopgap measure, protecting the convoys by providing constant air cover all the way across the North Atlantic.

The Swordfish was a remarkable aircraft. An open cockpit biplane of antique appearance, it was nevertheless so remarkably versatile that it served in a variety of theatres. Because they were so slow that the *Bismarck*'s state-of-the-art guns could not be geared down sufficiently to accurately train on them, Swordfish were responsible for disabling the battleship, leaving it a sitting duck for the pursuing ships of the Royal Navy. The Swordfish was so adept at fulfilling any assigned function that it was affectionately named "stringbags" for its ability to carry anything everywhere. The R.N.A.S. also maintained the Walrus, a single-engine flying boat. Like the Swordfish, it had a somewhat antique air, but nevertheless did sterling duty on anti-submarine patrols. For a time, one was based on the lake on Sable Island, from which forward location it carried out advanced patrols.[154] Seaborne also provided a land base and maintenance services for these and other Royal Naval Air Service aircraft attached to carriers or other ships while in port. Seaborne was finally disbanded in January 1946.[155]

R.C.A.F. expansion was not limited to the Dartmouth side of the harbour. Beginning in 1941, in its role as mentor for the British Commonwealth Air Training Plan (B.C.A.T.P.), the R.C.A.F. acquired land on the west side of the northern extremity of Windsor Street, the undeveloped remnants of the Willow Park Estate of the nineteenth-century agricultural pioneer John Young, "Agricola." At what became Windsor Park, an embarkation camp was built for newly trained graduates of the Plan. The large complex of long, wooden, green-roofed single-storey buildings housed barracks, mess halls and offices under the designation Y Depot. It handled as many as 2,500 men at a time: Australians, British, New Zealanders and Canadians. The success of the B.C.A.T.P. in training pilots, combined with Halifax's accommodation shortage, led to its phasing out in 1944 in favour of Lachine, Que. Y Depot was transferred to the R.C.N., which renamed it HMCS Peregrine, easing their housing shortage.

To adjust to its reduced needs, as the war drew to a close, the R.C.A.F. built an 85-man barrack block, combined mess and recreation centre on that part of the Gorsebrook property that faced on South Street at Wellington, and, a short distance away, behind All Saints Cathedral, it built Anderson Square, which housed an officer's mess.

INTERACTION WITH THE SERVICES

Even if gun batteries, airports and dockyards were off limits for most Haligonians the military presence was self-evident. Soldiers, sailors and airmen of many nationalities were everywhere. The Victory Loan Parade of 9 June 1941 brought together several thousand military personnel, many of them only passing through. As it marched along Barrington Street, Haligonians saw the Regina Rifles, Canadian Grenadier Guards, Princess Louise Fusiliers, Governor General's Foot Guards, a motorized battery of the Royal Canadian Artillery, units of the Royal Navy, Royal Canadian Navy, Royal Norwegian Navy, Royal Dutch Navy, Free French Navy, Royal Marines, Royal Air Force, Royal New Zealand Air Force, Fleet Air Arm and the Veterans Guard.[156] For most civilians, however, regular interaction meant watching the military bands which accompanied every occasion, great or small, military or civilian. Every regiment, unit or establishment had a band and there was no lack of opportunity to hear them. One sunny day, John Fisher told his listeners on CHNS's *Noontime Melodies* about one such encounter on Spring Garden Road. He found himself:

> ... actually marching to the tune of the military band
> which comes by here every morning on the way to chang-
> ing the guard. They play such sprightly pieces. The soldiers
> look very smart and the band master walks with such dig-
> nity. Several mornings ago I witnessed the same thing, but
> out in front of the bandmaster was another master. No, he
> didn't have the stripes — he wore no uniform and in fact
> the Army didn't recognize his rank at all. But we spectators

on the sidewalk did because this master put on such a grand show. You have often seen his equal. It was a little tiny boy about six or seven years old.... He had his stick; he swung it; he was in step and he was having the time of his life strutting down the street with real soldiers.[157]

CHAPTER THREE:

In Transit

Between 1939 and 1945, the communities on both sides of Halifax Harbour played host to an extraordinary number of visitors. Many of these visitors stayed to garrison its forts, man its ships and aircraft and operate the civil and military apparatus that burgeoned because of abundant war time spending and allowed the "East Coast Port" to function as "The Warden of the Honour of the North." For many others, however, the big harbour and its bustling communities were observed glimpses on the way to somewhere else.

The most obvious of these visitors were the vast numbers of men and women of the armed forces who surged into town, mounted the gangplanks of troop ships and disappeared across the grey North Atlantic. Most of them returned two, three or four years later on those same ships subdued, matured and damaged. But there were other, stranger cargoes; evacuees, internees, occupants of or exiles from Europe and German prisoners, some welcomed, some ignored, others unnoticed; but all of them made the port more of a frontline operation than any other Canadian city.

THE MILITARY EMBARK

For six years the railway sidings at the Ocean Terminals were as busy as any in North America, not only with freight, but also with the endless stream of passenger coaches, from the air-conditioned mainline cars to decrepit gas-lit wooden colonist cars rescued from certain doom by wartime emergency. There was no comfortable welcome in the vaulted waiting room of Union Station, just a siding on a pier, a cavernous freight shed, a gangplank leading to an unknown future and no chance for an illicit diversion in the fleshpots and speakeasies on Water, Hollis and Barrington Streets just a hop skip and jump away.

Getting thousands of men and women to this point was no small task because it had to be done under a blanket of security, if not actual secrecy. The average citizen's first glimpse of a troop movement might be the sight of a troop ship leaving the dock, its railing lined with hundreds of faces and waving arms. The security was in contrast to the World War I when troops bivouacked on the Commons, marched to their ships, bands playing, along Barrington Street lined with cheering crowds waving Union Jacks.

Part of the unseen and unnoticed wartime infrastructure, which crowded the city's apartments, trams and restaurants, was the staff of the army's "Embarkation Movement Control" (E.M.C.)[158] which handled nearly 150 troop convoys, including many individual trips by the huge liners notably, but not only, the *Queen Elizabeth* and the *Queen Mary*. Long before a troop ship announced its arrival to the radio operators at Camperdown, it was assigned a berth along the seawall or one of the piers by the Royal Canadian Army Service Corps officers, steamship and railway officials who made up the E.M.C.

Every large troop movement clogged the harbour and rail facilities to such an extent that it could take days to clear sidings of boxcars containing urgently required war *matériel* pushed aside by the troop trains. When the trains drew up before the piers, often at night or early morning for logistical and security reasons, the troops detrained and were drawn up for inspection. Only then were their commanding officers informed which men would be going on which ship, referred to only by a number unique to the particular movement. Part of the rationale for splitting up units was to avoid the worst case scenario of an entire regiment being wiped out by a single torpedo.

Although there were always exceptions, by and large large troop movements were either army or air force. The navy, by its very nature, absorbed the men into its frontline fighting force right on the Halifax waterfront. The R.C.A.F. could arrive from Prairie airfield, while the Army could arrive on the trains of the Dominion Atlantic Railway from as close as Kentville, where the training base at Aldershot had whipped recruits into shape and instilled in them the techniques of advanced infantry warfare.[159]

Initially, unlike the army, the R.C.A.F. had a manning depot at Windsor Park; but toward the end of the war it was moved to Lachine, Québec, from where Keith Craig, a navigator, shipped out. He came down by train straight to the Pier 21 siding and right onto the *Empress of Scotland* only a few hundred feet away.[160] With large movements involving one of the Queens, or a convoy movement of a number of smaller ships, trains ran every hour for days, an amazing logistical accomplishment to later generations of railway men, and the planning all had to be done under conditions of absolute secrecy. Railway employees dealing with troop movements answered the telephone with only "hello," with strict orders not to give out information about the movement. Only the railway's private dispatcher telephone network was used, never the public system.[161]

As raw new recruits, still awaiting their assignment to basic training, loaded mail and other baggage, each unit of soldiers was led onto their ship by an R.C.A.S.C. officer. Each soldier received a card identifying his berth and cabin. He could bring anything with him that he could carry, in addition to his regular gear, a load which effectively limited him to extra cigarettes. Another group, Pay Corps officers, verified and processed pay documents for each man, ensuring, for example, that deductions for dependents at home were in order. Medical officers kept an eye open and at the slightest hint of contagious disease a soldier, or a whole group at risk of infection, would be removed and sent back to wait it out until the next draft. If one man delayed his comrades, he found himself one very unpopular soldier.

Once on board ship the men were turned over to shipboard staff. Now there was no turning back, something gangway sentries were to make sure of, a necessary precaution as it could take as long as a week to load one of the big Queens. Special Service Officers organized singsongs, concerts, movies and entertainment for those off duty. Duty, even on a troop ship, was inescapable. Drills, physical training and even invented work was intended to ensure military discipline remained tight. As an officer, R.C.A.F. navigator Keith Craig had it a little easier. Once at sea he had two[162] half-hour shifts a day on submarine lookout and the rest of his time was free, most of which he spent looking after buddies who were consumed with seasickness.

Sometimes soldiers protested and rebelled. H. B. Jefferson reported that on 9 April 1942, some soldiers walked off the transport *Banfora*, citing a number of grievances. Rumours claimed it was as many as 1,900, but a later estimate put it at 300. They marched into the city, the guards making no effort to stop them. During the night some of them broke into the Hollis Street liquor store and peddled $5 hootch for $2 along the street. They were eventually picked up and brought back to the *Banfora*. Instead of going up the ladder, where the NCOs were waiting to take their names, they swarmed up the ship's side and disappeared into the crowd of soldiers on deck and escaped penalties, an outcome which saved everyone a mass of embarrassing courts martial.[163]

Some troops, troops movements and troop ships were even more transient. On 8 November 1941, eight ocean liners arrived from Britain loaded with British troops headed for Singapore. During their brief stay they transshipped to six American Army Transports, four of them former passenger liners, and left two days later, arriving a few months later just in time to surrender to the Japanese.[164]

Also at dockside was a group with a somewhat lighter duty: the 30-piece depot marching band of the army's Military District 6. As well as participating in bond drives, parades and concerts in town, from time to time the band saw off troop ships and later on, welcomed them home. They also had a more crucial role. As the war progressed, returning troop ships brought home the healthy and the wounded. The latter who were ambulatory milled around the shed, and while they waited to get on their hospital train, enjoyed the coffee and doughnuts at the Salvation Army canteen. For those more seriously wounded, the band played a half hour or so then put down its instruments and became highly trained stretcher bearers. If soldiers returned on a hospital ship, it was an easier job to get them off as the ships had been modified to accommodate stretchers or gurneys and their associated IV equipment. Frequently, however, wounded soldiers returned on a regular troop ship with awkward corridors, doorways and stairwells that reflected a more peaceful era.

Getting badly wounded and bed-ridden men off without making a bad situation worse was a job for which the bandsmen received special training in an obstacle course constructed at the Cogswell Street barracks.[165] Volunteers with simulated serious wounds described on an attached tag were located around Citadel Hill. The bandsmen/bearers had to find them, get them on a stretcher and bring them back to a waiting ambulance over a series of walls and hurdles, then report to the Armouries for an inquisition on their performance. They were also tested on site at Pier 21 and had to demonstrate an ability to carry a stretcher at shoulder height, keep the IV bottles steady and lower it over a ship's side using attached straps. Four men comprised a stretcher team, the tallest at the front. Victor Gray recalls that some of the wounded men were in rough shape because the last doctor they saw in England had "glued" them together sufficiently to get them aboard a ship, where they received no further treatment other than the care of a nurse for the week it took to get to Halifax. On the other hand, one of the properly equipped hospital ships might actually take longer on the voyage since, if weather permitted, their immunity from attack allowed them to heave to for an urgent operation. For the most part, the stretcher bearers would transfer their charges to a proper hospital train, but from time to time scarcity of equipment meant the wounded were sometimes strapped in and tipped sideways through the narrow corridors of regular passenger and sleeping cars, which like the troop ships were never built with this sort of purpose in mind.

By May 1943 there was a specifically Canadian hospital ship, the *Lady Nelson*, a former C.N. Steamship in West Indies service, which made its first trip to Halifax that month. The ship had been torpedoed and sunk in St. Lucia in 1942, but the water was shallow so that it was raised and converted for this new service. Like other hospital ships it was highly visible, painted white, ornamented with red crosses and a green band around the hull and brilliantly floodlit at sea. Officially, it was called Canadian Army Ship # 46, a bureaucratic handle that did not catch on. After the D-Day landings, the *Lady Nelson* was joined by the addition of the SS *Letitia*, sister ship of the *Athenia*, sunk the first day of the war.[166]

On 14 February 1944, the hospital ship *El Nil* arrived and the following evening demonstrated its invulnerability when it switched on its lights:

> ... and appeared like a floating fairyland in a harbor that for 4 years has seen nothing but meager riding lights and an occasional search light display. Around her [*sic*] hull at deck level she had a belt of green lights and the red crossed [*sic*] on her stack and decks blazed in red Neon lights. In addition she had many white lights, for identification by aircraft she had a number of Neon light Red Crosses lying flat on deck, one very large one ahead of the main mast and another behind the main mast.[167]

INNOCENTS TRAVEL ABROAD

Before the flow of military personnel reversed itself, starting with a trickle in 1944 and becoming a flood in 1945 and 1946, there were little-noticed westward flows of people from the earliest days of the war. One which did register in the public mind and imagination was the short-lived transfer of British children from the maelstrom of the Blitz to the bucolic safety of Canadian towns and cities. Known as the "Guest Children," this rescue was a hugely popular concept with Canadians, who saw themselves as protecting British children from cities reeling from the horrors of aerial bombing and possible German invasion. Governments were less enthusiastic. Churchill took a dim view of the whole process, echoing a cautious reprimand made amidst the euphoria over the successful evacuations of Narvik: "Wars are not won by evacuations." When asked if he would send a message to the Canadian Prime Minister by the hand of one of the children, he said, "I do not propose to send a message by the senior child to Mr. Mackenzie King, or by the junior child either. If I send any message by anyone, it would be that I entirely deprecate any stampede from this country at the present time."[168]

Britain and Canada began to focus on the evacuation of children as early as 1938. As soon as war was declared, 100,000 Canadians indicated to the National Council of Women that they were ready to offer homes to British evacuees. Canadian authorities were cool to the idea because of the potential pressure to expand the concept of "evacuee" from British children to continental Europeans in Britain, who although they were refugees from Nazi tyranny were nevertheless considered foreigners and a generally undesirable commodity.

Despite the declared intention of the Royal family to stay put in London, large numbers of well-to-do Britons, including entire schools, took to the boats, where if you were not bumped by individuals with a higher priority, passage could still be bought on liners by anyone who had the fare. This process looked elitist and bad, and under mounting pressure the British Government, with Canadian concurrence, initiated a state-sponsored Children's Overseas Reception Board (C.O.R.B.) at the end of June 1940.[169]

Within weeks 211,000 children were registered. So enthusiastic was the response in Canada that Hon. T.A. Crerar, the minister in charge of immigration was under heavy pressure to say something on the matter. He chose to say exactly the wrong thing to a waiting world, the date the first group of children would be sailing, forcing a horrified Admiralty to cancel the voyage immediately.

Chastened, Mr. Crerar kept the veil of secrecy intact in July 1940, when the first ship finally sailed. Despite the numbers registered, only small groups of children, chosen from cities being bombed or in the flight path of bombers, came on each ship. Still unenthusiastic, the British government was much more interested in getting prisoners of war and enemy aliens out of the country than its children. Despite the real and perceived danger, when it came to actually sending their children away, perhaps never to be seen again, many British parents got cold feet. Those who came were generally between eight and fourteen, occasionally younger if they were with an older brother or sister, but rarely older, as many teenagers felt keenly that they were deserting their country at a critical moment. Peter Rison, a 14-year-old who stayed with the Hare family on Willow Street, was so determined to return home after he arrived that in January 1942 he scoured the waterfront until he found a merchant ship that would take him as a cabin boy. When he was found by the police after a day's hue and cry, he adamantly refused to leave the ship and only with great difficulty was persuaded to return to Willow Street.[170]

For the younger ones, not yet motivated by teenage angst and patriotic yearnings, the evacuation was a great adventure. Only one suitcase was allowed and Marks and Spencer's saw to it that every child who needed help was properly outfitted. Most left from Liverpool or Glasgow, organized in parties of 15 with an escort. Most of the liners that served as their transports had not yet been gutted to provide mass accommodations for troops, and still reflected their pre-war elegance. With the portholes closed, the insides blazed with light that most had not seen since the previous September. Meals were fine unrationed affairs with second helpings, formally served by indulgent uniformed stewards who enjoyed spoiling them. None of which mattered for many once the ships rose to the first swells of the North Atlantic.

On 19 August 1940, HMS *Revenge* escorted into Halifax Harbour, the *Duchess of York*, *Georgic*, *Empress of Australia*, *Antonia* and *Oronsay* with some 750 sponsored children on board and almost as many more coming out to stay with relatives and family friends.[171] Spectators waved, the children on board lined the rails and sang popular songs such as "Roll Out the Barrel" and "There'll Always Be An England." Almost all of them looked for Mounties, hoping and expecting to see them as soon as they landed. Eighty-six were destined to stay in Nova Scotia and went to the School for the Blind, and later Truro. They were matched with a family by the provincial Department of Child Welfare, which wanted at least five applications for each child to ensure a good match. Christopher Nolan, who caught the public fancy by coming ashore in full highland regalia, lived with the Vickery family on Chestnut Street. Most went straight onto trains that deposited them in communities across the country. The children were fascinated by the size of the trains, the black porters, the sleeping cars, easy use of automobiles, telephones everywhere, plenty of butter, mosquitoes and window screens. Canadians were entranced with the whole concept and as news spread that a train of evacuee children was en route, crowds massed at stations to meet them, handing out candies, apples and bananas, making such a fuss that authorities worried that the attention would turn impressionable young heads. Twenty-five children who arrived in Saskatoon were met by a crowd of 3,000.

The euphoria would be shortlived. On 30 August 1940, the *Volendam*, with 321 government-sponsored children on board, was torpedoed. All but one of the children got off in the lifeboats, and that child was found wandering around the still floating hulk a day or so later and taken off protesting. They all made it back to Glasgow, keen to re-embark as soon as possible; but they turned out to be the lucky ones. Two weeks later, on 16 September, the *City of Benares* was torpedoed with a tragic outcome: 83 of the 90 children on board died. Initially, it was thought that all but one had been lost, but eight days later a patrol plane sighted a lifeboat and among those clinging to life were six boys who had been kept alive by the heroic efforts of two escorts. Thirty-one more sponsored children arrived in Halifax on 3 October, of whom 29 stayed in the province,[172] but this group was the last. The *City of Benares* tragedy effectively ended the programme. Officials stated at the time that it was being suspended only for the winter, but it never resumed, even though there were still 14,000 children on the C.O.R.B. list waiting to go. Both governments were glad for the excuse, whatever their motives.

Child evacuees began to dribble back to England as early as 1943, when the Royal Navy sponsored the return of eight 16-year-old boys willing to become cadets. In May 1944 a chartered ship took back girls under 17 who volunteered. Those from areas deemed free from air raids returned after November 1944. All but 205 of the C.O.R.B. children had returned by February 1945. They returned to Britain with mixed emotions, having spent formative years amid the relative peace and plenty of Canada, and in homes that were by and large supportive and well chosen. Returning to a family of near strangers to live in straitened circumstances in post-war Britain could be hard. It was easier for boys, who were expected to be independent. Girls who had experienced a relatively free-and-easy Canadian lifestyle were dismayed to find that their equally dismayed parents expected them to revert to a demure pre-war behaviour, while they stayed at home to await marriage. Canadian accents and makeup caused consternation. Family and friends were surprised by the size — huge they were called — of the returning teenagers. The returnees were chastened to find that Blitz or not, their contemporaries who had stayed home were two years ahead of them in schoolwork and taunted them, as many had feared, as being "draft evaders," who had skipped out during Britain's hour of need.

RELUCTANT VISITORS

It might be assumed that the troop ships, which left port loaded to the gunwales with military personnel, would, aside from the wounded, be largely empty on their return. Far from it, there was a constant stream of military and civilian officials coming and going. As soon as the "Phoney War" turned deadly serious, Britain persuaded the Canadian government to relieve it of enemies within its borders, that is, not only the resident enemy aliens who had been interned at the outbreak of war, but also a large number of German prisoners of war, many of them Luftwaffe pilots shot down before and during the Battle of Britain.

For most of these individuals, Halifax was a barely observed blip on a long voyage. Internees were a mixture of genuine Nazis and anti-Nazi refugees perhaps long-resident in Britain who, caught in a bureaucratic catch-22, were still legally German citizens and therefore enemy aliens. Despite mountains of evidence to the contrary and a general admission that it was so, these people were technically considered hostile.

Prisoners of war were a clearly defined commodity. Most of those sent to Canada came to Halifax only to head, immediately, far inland. The only prison camp in the Maritimes, Camp 70, was near Fredericton, N.B. Most camps were in isolated bush far enough from civilization to give even the most ambitious escapee pause, even if he was able to foil guards and barbed wire. Most camps were set up when America was still neutral, and therefore tended to be far from a border, which, until December 1941, promised freedom and a route home. After that, escape was useful only for its entertainment value as Mexico, the only possible destination, was an impossible dream.

Only one P.O.W., Luftwaffe pilot Franz von Werra, appears to have made it home once he arrived. He landed in Halifax at Pier 21 on 22 January 1941, along with about a thousand others, on the *Duchess of York*, the first group to come through. Likely he was surprised and probably relieved to have survived the crossing, so firmly had he been led to believe that U-boats held the North Atlantic and all allied shipping in such a crushing grip that a transatlantic voyage was almost a sentence of death. Two 15-car trains awaited this group to transport them inland to a camp on the north shore of Lake Superior.

The boat had been docked for an hour or more before troops appeared and lined up around the special train and formed an avenue between the train and the shed, a distance of about 75 yards. The unloading of the prisoners began about 4 o'clock instead of two, as had been planned. They passed between two lines of soldiers about 10 or 15 feet apart within easy bayonet reach of each other. Each squad of prisoners was preceded by a close rank of three or four soldiers and followed by another close rank. They marched in twos and threes carrying their blue kit bags, some slung over their shoulders much like embarking Canadian troops.[173]

Von Werra, whose ingenious and frequent attempts to escape in Britain had made him a nuisance, must have had a good idea of Canadian geography. He bided his time until the Canadian Pacific train was just outside Smith's Falls, Ont., as close as he was likely to get to America. Along with seven others who were soon recaptured, he escaped through a window. Armed with little more than a good command of English, much charm and an abiding confidence in himself and the fatherland, he walked and hitch-hiked to the frozen St. Lawrence River. Despite open water in the middle, he made it across and gave himself up to the police in Ogdensburg, New York, at 10:15 a.m. on 24 January. German authorities foiled Canadian attempts at extradition by smuggling him to South America, from where he returned to Germany to a hero's welcome and an Iron Cross from Adolf Hitler. Sadly, his was not a storybook ending. Von Werra disappeared in October of that same year while on a routine fighter patrol over the coast of the Netherlands.

Von Werra was not the only prisoner in this group who escaped. The others were not so successful. Two prisoners escaped at Moncton but were soon picked up because their clothes were so obviously unsuitable for a New Brunswick winter they attracted immediate attention. More exciting for Halifax was the successful escape of two Luftwaffe pilots, Helmuth Bruckmann and Peter Schering, who had whiled away their idle hours at sea plotting escape. While on board, Bruckmann stole civilian clothes and some I.D. from the cabin of the ship's Master-at-Arms. The fact that this official did not notice or did not care enough to raise an alarm is indicative of the lax security that seems to have prevailed. Schering went to more trouble, stealing enough tarpaulin to make a pair of overalls. He also stockpiled hand-drawn maps, a can of beans, three pieces of steel wire, some nut bars, three onions, a piece of soap and a needle and thread. While he seems to have spoken some English, he had written out two key phrases: "I am a British Subject" and "I am going to see my aunt in the United States." Both of them got off the ship undetected, Bruckmann by presenting his stolen I.D., Schering, in his tarpaulin trousers, by mingling with the amazingly incurious stevedores as they went off duty.

They may or may not have acted independently, but they went their separate ways once they made it ashore. Bruckmann had the freedom of the city for only a few hours before he was captured in the early morning of 23 January at the Rex Café on Sackville Street. He had rented a room but had only a ten shilling note to pay for it, which the proprietor refused to accept. An R.C.M.P. special constable staying there heard the argument, got suspicious, and the jig was up for Bruckmann.[174]

Schering was relatively more successful, spending the day at liberty, working his way across the peninsula towards the Fairview underpass, one of only two road exits from the city and within sight of the railway marshalling yards, probably his goal. By the next afternoon Schering was at the Robie Street reservoir. From here he could see the underpass, where by now the Mounties had established a road block. Two small children, Marguerite Little and Charles Malloy, were playing in the snow and found his presence odd enough that they ran to Marguerite's nearby home on Prescott Street to tell their mothers, who were having a cup of tea. Since the city was abuzz with the news of escaped Nazis, the police were called. The "radio car" was alerted and "across the north-end of the city and down Kempt Road the patrolmen sped."[175] Constables Montague and Feener caught sight of a figure with baggy trousers and smoking a pipe, stopped him and, despite his protestations that he was a British subject, knew they had their man when they saw his Luftwaffe tunic under his coat.

Because of the leaky condition of this particular shipment, the whole system of transporting German P.O.W.s was thoroughly overhauled. Similar escapades never happened again.

The actual transfer from ship to train was slowed down, the better to account for each prisoner. On the trains there would be three guards in each car, one at either end and one to patrol the aisle, though they were armed only with a leather billy club and a whistle to call the men with guns. Washrooms had no doors, only one man could be out of his seat at any time, windows could be opened only four inches and at night each man's face had to be visible at all times.[176]

A year later, on 1 January 1942, another 700 prisoners arrived on the *Moreton Bay*, and were taken away on two trains. This group included a number of Luftwaffe pilots who wore R.A.F. uniforms with German insignia in place of British, because their own had not survived their travails. Also among the contingent were the 116 survivors of the KM *Bismarck* sunk on 27 May 1941. Another 1,000 came on 6 April on the *Rangitki*, sweet revenge for it had been shot up by the *Admiral Scheer* during the attack on the *Jervis Bay* and Convoy HX84 in November 1940. Among these prisoners was the famous U-boat captain Otto Kretschmer, whose record of successful sinkings was never beaten. Thanks to his capture and incarceration in Canada, he lived until 1999 to tell his tale, employed by N.A.T.O. and lionized by friend and foe alike.[177] Authorities were so nervous about this group they had painted circles on the prisoners' backs and on the back and front of the knees of their trousers.

Prisoners were, generally, well treated, so much so that when von Werra got back to Germany he made an issue of it and may have helped improve conditions for British P.O.W.s in German camps. One Canadian soldier on duty at Pier 21 was confined to barracks for 21 days when he kicked a German who spat on him.[178] Once they boarded their train prisoners were given a paper bag with meat sandwiches, apples, bananas, etc., which they hoarded, assuming it would have to last for the rest of their trip. To their astonishment, as much for the waste as the generosity, after a while it was taken away, thrown out and replaced with more for the next meal.

For many prisoners, the return home in 1945 was a bittersweet experience. For those who remained convinced Nazis, returning to a ruined defeated fatherland was traumatic. For the less dogmatic, who had begun to enjoy the relative plenty in Canada and the often relaxed and pleasant relationships they formed during work assignments on farms and in communities, repatriation meant only privation, misery and a burning desire to return to Canada.

ITALIANS

In April 1943 the Canadian National Railways established a large railway labour camp at the south end of Atlantic Street to accommodate hundreds (H.B. Jefferson says seven or eight hundred) Italian internees and prisoners of war.[179] By the end of that summer, the formerly quiet street was busy with the activities of its new residents, who by then, with the sudden transformation of Italy into an ally, were quite free to come and go.[180] This camp was not established without some angst. It probably began when the C.N.R., strapped for labour on the docks and marshalling yards, initially set up 117 workers in "boarding cars," that is to say bunk houses on railway trucks, which it parked on a siding in the railway cut under the Young Avenue bridge. They were brought up short at the beginning of April by Dr. Arthur Pettipas, the city's Health Superintendent, who condemned the unsanitary conditions which resulted.[181] The C.N.R. then began construction of seven bunkhouses on vacant land which it owned on the edge of the cut in the vicinity of Atlantic Street and McLean Street. This action did not go unnoticed by the local residents, who took great exception to a development they felt would have a serious effect on their real-estate values, especially if, as they feared, it became a slum after the war. These views were expressed in no uncertain terms by, among others, Lieutenant Colonel S.C. Oland and J.W. Payzant, at a public meeting held on 24 April.[182] Protests were to no avail, however, because the War Measures Act trumped the local concerns, despite the support of the mayor, who claimed the city had no more notice or information on the matter than the residents, and despite a telegram sent to cabinet ministers C.D. Howe, J.E. Michaud and Humphrey Mitchell.

TRAUMATIZED VISITORS

Throughout the war, but particularly in the U-boat glory days of 1941 and 1942, the city's hostels provided emergency shelter to a multitude of survivors, whose prelude to arrival was a nasty interlude in a lifeboat ranging from hours to days. They were often soaked and suffering from the shock and horror of watching their ship founder and seeing many of their companions die either instantly or slowly. Sometimes it was only a matter of sheer luck that a passing R.C.A.F. Catalina located them, or one of HM ships or a fellow merchantman picked them up.

H.B. Jefferson was there to report it all. In the first few months of 1942 he chronicled some of the carnage:

23 January — *Belle Isle* Br. liner comes in and docks at Pier B40. She brings in 42 survivors of the *Thirlby*, Br. freighter. She was torpedoed at 1:30 a.m. Jan. 23 ten miles south of Seal Island, 17 miles west of Cape Sable Island, and the ship sank at 6:30 a.m. They were picked up at 8:30 a.m. by the *Belle Isle*. Both ships were on their way from New York to Halifax.

24 January — Five survivors from the Tanker, *Inneroy*, Norse, torpedoed Thursday afternoon (Jan. 2) at 4:45 p.m. and picked up Friday morning, Jan 23, were brought into Halifax by a Br. Tanker Saturday Morning (Jan, 24). They were torpedoed 177 miles off Halifax 44:30 n 61:36 w.

27 January — 4:20. Learn that 24 survivors of a Canadian tanker had been brought into hospital. They were mostly Norwegians and were in the boats 9 days. Two days after being sighted by an R.C.A.F. plane they were picked up by an RCN destroyer and brought here today. The Destroyer was the I-65 *St. Croix*. This ship turned out to be not a Canadian tanker but a Norwegian tanker under charter to Imperial Oil. They were torpedoed at 10:30 at night on Saturday, Jan. 17. The ship did not sink and about 2 hours later they fired 2 more torpedoes into them and then she sank. There are 14 Norwegians and one Englishman missing. The Captain died just as they were entering the harbour.

30 January — At 10:40 AM T. called and told me that he expected 120 more survivors to reach the Navy League House in about an hour. At 12:17 Ed Ingraham called to say that the 120 had arrived and he sent a bulletin to the Star. In the evening the Canadian Press called in considerable trouble because they had sent out a story saying that there were 29 at the hostel and 54 more in port. This

turned out to be incorrect. There were 29 at the hostel who had been brought in by a Greek steamer. They are survivors of a Norwegian tanker, the name of which I do not yet know. Five of their comrades were lost. The remainder of the 120 will be in on one or more other vessels within the next 24 hours. Reg. W. who interviewed the survivors said that the ship was the tanker *N.B. Leiesten,* Norse tanker, on a voyage from Manchester to New York. At 9 a.m. Friday, January 23 they were torpedoed 400 miles off Newfoundland.

Jan. 30/42 — This is the finish of *N.B. Leiesten* torpedoing in last note on Jan. 30. The first torpedo struck them at 9 a.m., Jan. 23/42, in the bow, the second at 9:15 wrecked the engine room. As she did not sink fast enough to suit the Germans, the sub surfaced and began shelling them with a gun. 6 men were killed. The rest got away in 2 boats and after 32 hours afloat were picked up by a Greek freighter *Athos Georgios.* (Other survivors said the tanker used her guns and fought with the U-boat as long as she was manageable.) Reg says the sub came within 50 yards and her skipper waved his hand at them before giving the order to submerge.

February 24 — Learn tonight that Tanker torpedoed and Burning Off Ketch Harbour Feb 2 Is *Kars.* Their story was that in broad daylight Sunday (Feb. 22) afternoon off Ketch harbor at the mouth of Halifax Harbor this tanker was torpedoed. A hole was made in one of the tanks igniting the gasoline which ran out and spread a burning field all around the ship and also set fire to the vessel from stem to stern. Some of the men trapped on board and had no chance to get away. Others managed to launch 2 lifeboats but in the excitement upset one of them among the burning oil which covered the water and the men in them were all killed either through drowning to escape the gas or inhaling flames. The men became panicky and jumped overboard to get away from the flames. Black and 2 companions, the Norwegian fireman previously mentioned and a friend named McNeil succeeded in getting to the edge of the field, jumped overboard and swam.

They would swim until the burning oil overtook them, then dive and swim under water for a distance and come up for a breath of air until overtaken again by the slowly spreading oil. Finally they got outside the fire circle and saw a steel lifeboat which had drifted away from the ship. They swam to it but it was still hot from contact with the ship and they burned their hands badly in clinging to it. Black lost consciousness and did not know what happened to him until he came to on board a Canadian corvette which reached the scene about half an hour after the alarm was given. The Norwegian fireman had also been picked up but was already dead. McNeil had disappeared. Black was told by the coxwain of the boat that both had let go of the lifeboat and were sinking when hauled in just in time. I now hear that a second seaman named McLean also survived the wreck but this is not official. A Ketch harbor man told me tonight that the torpedoing and fire took place off their cove and was seen by hundreds of people until darkness shut down. This must have been the glow that we saw in the sky on Sunday night. Learn tonight from the Dy that this tanker is the *Kars* and that she is being towed in, the fire having burned itself out. C says there is another tanker over back of the *Egda* with two holes in it. He added something to the effect that this was now at Imperoyal having its cargo discharged. That sounds like the *Corilla* but there was another one just south of the *Egda* this afternoon pumping a lot of water over the stern like the *Egda* was doing yesterday.

Learn Tonight that *Edga* Was Torpedoed Feb. 21, 400 Miles Off Halifax. According to ED who was aboard this afternoon the *Edga* was torpedoed last Saturday morning

(Feb. 21) 400 miles off Halifax and 260 from Cape Race. Only 1 man was injured. He had his arm bruised but the captain and others on bridge got quite a bouncing. The torpedo exploded under them.

11 March — *Tyr* Norse Freighter Torpedoed Mch 9/42 Eighty Miles From Halifax. This occurred on Monday afternoon. A submarine broke water and circled the sinking ship which went down in 10 minutes and later came up to the lifeboats where the U-boat captain had a conversation with the ship's captain, the nature of which the crew could not make out. The boats stayed together until midnight and then became separated.

19 March — First Mate Fred Shaw, Captain D. N. Nolan and the 2nd Engineer arrived home on a Norske freighter last night [March 18] and reported that their small steamer *Lennox* was torpedoed off Demarara [*sic*] on Feb. 23 about the middle of the afternoon. When they were in the boats the submarine captain came up, asked them it they had lots of food and water, offered to supply any provisions they needed, and set a course for them to Demarara [*sic*]. As they had no wireless on the ship they could not call for help. But a molasses tanker, torpedoed the day before, had sent out an SOS, and a ship that came out from Georgetown looking for them, picked up the *Lennox* people instead.

11 April — T. Says that the ship whose survivors arrived yesterday on the *Franche Comte* was the *Nemanja*, a Yugoslav freighter that was here about a year ago. The crew say they were torpedoed only three-quarters of a mile off Bear Cove, at the entrance to Halifax Harbor. A high wind was blowing at the time and instead of making shore at once they were two days and a night in the boats before being picked up.

One of the grimmest visitations was by the former United States Lines New York to San Francisco passenger ship *Manhattan*. Taken over as a troop transport by the U.S. Navy in July 1941, it was renamed the USS *Wakefield*. Evacuating civilians from Singapore in January 1942, it was strafed and bombed by Japanese aircraft but survived the event. As part of an August 1942 troop convoy from the United States to Britain, it called in briefly at Halifax. Returning home, it caught fire off the Nova Scotia coast on 3 September and was completely gutted, forcing a complete evacuation of passengers and crew. The gutted hulk was towed to Halifax by the *Foundation Franklin* where Carl Fader, a boy living on McNab's Island, watched as it was first brought alongside the island's Garrison Pier. There the bodies of those who had died in the conflagration were removed. Fader remembers the bodies "stacked like cordwood on the wharf," later to be buried at sea. The ship was later taken across the harbour and made fit to be towed to the United States. It was rebuilt and continued to serve as a troop transport until 1947.[183]

DIPHTHERIA

Another unwilling, although more welcome, group of visitors was the Norwegian whaling fleet, three factory trawlers, stranded in the Antarctic in the summer of 1940 when their homeland fell under German occupation. The Norwegian government-in-exile diverted them to Halifax and at the end of August they were ordered to Lunenburg, where they became the nucleus of a Norwegian exile community and base for the Royal Norwegian Navy.[184]

Some of the Norwegians brought with them an unwelcome fellow traveller that left its mark in Halifax. In September 1940 a Norwegian tanker steamed into the harbour and anchored in the Basin next to a Norwegian whaler. The crews of the two ships went ashore. Within 24 hours some of the crew developed symptoms of the diphtheria they had been carrying. Diphtheria, like tuberculosis and typhus, was a disease of poverty, poor sanitation and overcrowding. Caused by bacteria infecting the tissues of the throat and nose, it was one of the most common killers of children. Treatable in the early stages, if neglected the bacteria produces a virulent toxin which damages the muscles of the heart and, ultimately, kills. Although inoculation existed and was practiced, it was a strictly voluntary process and in the initial stages of public acceptance.

The situation was worse in Halifax than anywhere else in the Dominion, because the chairman of the Halifax Board of Health from 1925 to 1939 had been Dr. William Duff Forrest (son of John Forrest, the former President of Dalhousie University), a firm, vocal and effective opponent of immunizations against disease and other innovations such as TB testing and the pasteurization of milk, in spite of ready acceptance in the rest of the province. During his tenure Halifax earned the unenviable reputation of "diphtheria capital of Canada."[185]

As diphtheria spreads easily from routine human contact, it ran like wildfire through the crowded streets, speakeasies, restaurants and bordellos of the waterfront area. By year's end there were 291 civilian cases. In 1941 there were 622 cases. Through September 1942 there were another 475 cases. By that date there had been 33 deaths, all but two of them under 20.[186] At the height of the epidemic over the winter of 1940–1941, the city leased the clubhouse of the Gorsebrook Golf Club to serve as an overflow infectious disease hospital until 21 July.[187] The worst area of the city was between Gerrish and Almon Streets.[188] Between March and May 1941, virtually all of the armed forces were inoculated. Although a massive campaign of free inoculation was rapidly instituted, particularly for school children (at least 10,000 children went through the required three doses), it was not enough. The procedure was actually quite complicated, involving a "Shick Test," then a series of precisely timed visits to the doctor, followed by another test to ensure the patient was now immune.[189] Many parents of very young children, suspicious of the whole process of vaccination, which induced a mild form of the disease to build up resistance, refused to participate.

It took until 1944 before officials considered the epidemic vanquished. In 1945 with the prospect of the return of troops from war-ravaged Europe, the now-alert public health authorities initiated a massive publicity campaign to encourage the civilian population of the Halifax area to have themselves and their children tested or inoculated. On 15 May the provincial Department of Public Health issued a Diphtheria Warning, advising that central and northern Europe were in the middle of an epidemic, "brought to many of the countries now heavily infected by the invading Germans." Parents were urged to have their children immunized if not done already, or have reinforcing doses given to those already immunized, either by their doctor or at free clinics:

> Soon large numbers of men, many of whom may be the
> carriers of foreign strains of diphtheria bacilli, will be
> returning to Nova Scotia and Canada from the European
> Countries. We all know what happened in our Province
> in 1940 when the 'Gravis Strain' of this disease was
> introduced. It spread rapidly among those who were
> not completely immunized causing grief, suffering and
> death.[190]

The warnings worked and the return of the troops only brought happiness. If there was a monument to the epidemic, it was the new Victoria General Hospital, its cornerstone laid 5 September 1945.

THE GOLD RUSH

The mind boggles at the job of keeping thousands of young, bored men in the prime of life under tight control from training camp to railway car to troop ship to battle front, or overseeing hundreds of energetic and curious children, or guarding hundreds of resentful and arrogant prisoners. While this activity was unannounced, everyone was well aware that it was going on. From time to time there were other less obvious, if enormously significant movements, through the harbour city.

On 16 October 1939, HM ships *Resolution, Caradoc, Repulse, Enterprise* and *Emerald* slipped into Halifax Harbour, a movement that raised no eyebrows because such comings and goings six weeks into the war were already routine. Their movement, however, was triggered the moment the Luftwaffe and the Wehrmacht stormed into Poland. Stored in the central banks of Britain and Europe were vast quantities of gold bullion, which during the years of the gold standard, represented the nations' currency and stood security for a nation's financial credibility.

The deteriorating political situation in Europe led central bank officials to think the unthinkable — if Germany continued in its aggressive ways and got its hands on any or all of this treasure, it would finance an almost unlimited expansion. Moreover, the quantities of treasure stored up over half a millenium represented security for foreign military purchases, particularly in the United States. The solution was to find a safe haven. For Britain it was the vaults of the Bank of Canada on Wellington Street in far-off Ottawa. For France it was the Federal Reserve Bank, New York City. So it was on that October morning in 1939 that five ships of HM fleet steamed into the harbour carrying between them 741 boxes of gold bullion with a combined 1939 value of $44,300,000.

In the case of Britain and France, this movement was not a last-minute decision, but involved complex planning under a blanket of absolute secrecy.* Other less far-sighted countries were not so fortunate, but Norway was able to take ad hoc measures which saw some of her national treasure dock in Halifax.

The fall of Czechoslovakia in 1939 raised international tensions to the point where British officials seriously proposed that the naval vessels escorting the King and Queen across the Atlantic on their spring visit to Canada and the United States be used to initiate gold shipments. The Governor of the Bank of France had so little faith in the 1938 Munich Accord that he had already sent 300 tons of gold to the United States and began the dispersal of the rest of the nation's bullion to 51 depots in those départements with easy access to Atlantic and Mediterranean naval ports.[191]

In Britain's case, hand in hand with the bullion transfer was a paper hoard of the sequestered foreign stocks and bonds of the British investor. Without the consent of their owners officials confiscated these private holdings and shipped them off across the Atlantic all unknown, where they were deposited in the basement of the Sun Life Building in Montreal in the custody and management of the United Kingdom Security Deposit Agency.

This sweeping Bolshevik-style confiscation was necessary to pay for war matériel purchased in the United States in the first days of the war. Before Lend-Lease came into effect in March 1941, the neutral United States was prepared to be the arsenal of democracy, for a price and in American dollars up front please. Fortunately for the investors, Lend-Lease arranged other means of payment and most of their stocks remained intact.

Although general knowledge had leaked out that British and European gold was on the move, Haligonians had little inkling of the vast gold and

---

* see Alfred Draper, *Operation Fish*, Don Mills, Ontario: General Publishing Company, 1979

paper hoard that flowed through their rather shabby little city. Nor did they have any idea of the continuing drama when the treasure arrived here, as it was still a thousand miles from its final resting place. That every penny's worth made it through the gauntlet of North Atlantic wolf packs was no reason to relax the vigilance that had got it this far.

The procedure for unloading in Halifax was tightly scripted. When HMS *Revenge* arrived at Pier 6 with the *Monarch of Bermuda*, the *Batory* and HMS *Bonaventure* on 13 July 1940 with their cargoes of gold and securities, C.N.R. Express cars were already lined up along with a squad of C.N. Express armed guards, dressed in civilian clothes to avoid attracting attention. At 8:00 a.m. *Revenge* was alongside, but there was no opportunity for the crew to go ashore as the ship was sealed until the cargo was transferred. The ships had to be unloaded in daylight to avoid the necessity of floodlights that would inevitably attract attention. The boxes were winched out of the hold a dozen at a time, counted, then, initially, winched ashore. This procedure was found to be too slow. With four other ships in the lineup and a clear track awaiting the line of Express cars there was no time for delay. A solution was found in large pieces of sheet metal left over from an old sign, bent into U-shapes and fitted onto the gangway between the handrails, making a chute down which the boxes were slid onto the dock, then loaded on to hand carts, weighed and transferred to the C.N. Express cars. To an observer, a fully loaded car appeared virtually empty, because the weight of gold meant only one layer of boxes was laid on the floor, and even then there was occasional trouble with springs breaking. Car 8684, for example, from the 13 July landing had a capacity of 55,000 pounds and on this occasion was loaded with 380 boxes with a total weight of 49,000 pounds spread evenly over the floor.[192] The weight caused other problems as well. C.N. officials were reluctant to have gold shipments use piers 22 and 23 because the rail curves were so tight there was a chance the cars could jump the rails. If those piers had to be used, trucks transferred the golden cargo to waiting Express cars. Not surprisingly, truck movements were carefully regulated:

> Each truck must have two armed guards, one to ride in
> the cab with the motorman and the other to ride in the
> body of the truck. The truck gates must be locked. The
> motorman must not under any circumstance leave the cab.

It will also be necessary for you to arrange for an armed
car with C. N. R. Police, to ride immediately in front of
our motor truck or trucks, and another armed car to follow
immediately behind our motor truck or last truck, if more
than one, and our trucks are to be kept together, one
immediately following the other, leaving no gap in between
where other vehicles might cut in.[193]

Security was equally intense on the trains which took the gold to
Montreal and Ottawa. The railway employees who guarded the
$89,400,000 of gold bullion off loaded from HMS *Furious* on 22 June 1940
were armed with 26 revolvers and ten riot guns.[194] The many personnel this
level of security demanded had to be accommodated. The "fish trains" as
they were usually called could have as many as 50 railway and express
guards on board, who worked four-hour shifts, including two men locked
inside each express car allowed out only at the end of their shift. When they
came off duty, they were searched by guards posted outside in the vestibule
of each car. Because there were more men than berths, these were never
made up because there was always someone in them. A memo of 24
October 1939, noted "... a special train consisting of several baggage cars,
one non-air conditioned sleeper and one dining car reduced to 18 chair
capacity left Montreal October 13 for Halifax, returning from Halifax
October 16 to Montreal and Ottawa, and returned from Ottawa to
Montreal midnight on October 18 and 19, for accommodation of Express
Department officials."[195] Senior staff were expected to escort each shipment: "I was astonished to learn", wrote the C.N.R.'s Vice President and
General Manager on 26 March 1940, "that the important fish train, consisting of fourteen cars, operated over your Division recently without either
the Assistant Superintendent or Master Mechanic accompanying it."[196]

In the beginning, references to the shipments in official exchanges were
direct about the contents of the Express cars, but by early December 1939,
it became apparent that "... rather than using the wording 'gold bullion',
that 'Special Shipment' would be better."[197] This suggestion was so obvious
that within days instructions were issued declaring the need for "utmost
secrecy ... in the movement of this traffic, whenever there is any need to
refer to the movements in correspondence, debits or audit advices or

communications of any kind, the term 'Special Shipment' should be used for descriptive purposes."[198]

"Fish train" was one of the euphemisms for the shipments from their early days and had its origins in similar, if smaller scale, movements during World War I. It was a logical way of referring to the movements because employees and the public were accustomed to high-priority transport of special fast trains of fresh or frozen fish destined for the Montreal and Toronto markets. In coded messages or regular correspondence, the cargoes of the arriving bullion ships might also be referred to as shipments of "peanuts" packed in boxes, or "rivers," while the Royal Navy referred to their unique cargo as "margarine."

It was almost impossible, however, given the attention these trains received, for them to pass entirely unnoticed. The very fact that the buffet restaurant car Val Brilliant was regularly assigned to a "fish train" quickly led railway employees to associate it with one of these "special shipments." The wartime scarcity of equipment made it impossible to supply a different car for every trip and the only solution was to remove the name of the car "… as no doubt the name Val Brilliant suggests movements that perhaps would not otherwise be thought of."[199]

The quantities of British gold that passed through the port were immense and the shipments, some 50 in all between 16 October 1939 and 10 March 1941, were regular in the first few months of the war, amounting to an overall total of $ 2,554,000,000 in bullion, and about five billion in negotiable securities.[200] The shipments were independent of the convoy system, counting upon the speed and manoeuvrability of HM ships or passenger liners. The only hitches were minor ones. On one occasion, a bag of gold sovereigns burst and quarts of them fell in a golden shower down into the hold. After the scramble to retrieve them, they were weighed and every ounce accounted for. On a more trying occasion, a concerned Sydney Perkins of the Bank of Canada could not account for three boxes of bullion. With the dockside express train anxious to depart on schedule, the ship was searched high and low, stem to stern but no luck. Puzzling over the loss in the wardroom with the captain, the steward interrupted to say that he might have the solution. Under the bar, beneath several cases of Scotch, were the boxes, where they had been stowed hastily in the rush to leave the

Clyde in advance of an air raid.[201]

Tenser drama and near misses befell the Europeans, who, however suspicious they were of Hitler's motives, had not expected his sudden arrival in the spring of 1940. Some countries, such as Norway, had little opportunity to clear out their bank vaults. On 8 and 10 July 1940, three small Norwegian ships, almost too small to cross the Atlantic, steamed into the harbour. Among them, the *San Andres*, the *Bra-Kar* and the *Norma*, they brought 439 boxes of gold coins worth nearly $17,000,000, destined, like the British gold, for the vaults of the Bank of Canada in Ottawa.[202] The drama lay in the fact of their escape from under the noses of the occupying Germans. It is said that gold was smuggled to a coastal rendezvous on sleighs pulled by Norwegian children, all golden-haired innocence, the one pulling and the other seated on a blanket hiding their priceless cargo, and scampering past indulgent German patrols. Posing as coastal freighters or fishing boats, the freighters successfully evaded Nazi coastal patrols. Had they been stopped, they might have hoped to save their cargo by hiding it in plain sight. On the *San Andres*, "The boxes were in a raft on top deck, with empty oil barrels constituting the raft. There were three rafts in all." On the *Bra-Kar* and the *Norma*, "Shipment was packed in water barrels — three boxes to a barrel — barrels loaded on top deck." The real reason for this arrangement, however, was more pragmatic if equally dramatic. Had the ships been torpedoed, the crew were to cut the rafts and barrels loose in the hope and expectation that, if the ship sank, the cargo would float away ignored by the attackers, to be picked up later by search parties. And so it was in the case of one Norwegian ship that was sunk.

Even greater drama befell the French. The first wartime shipment of what they, like the British, called "margarine" arrived in Halifax from a still confident France on 2 December 1939, on board the *Lorraine* and *Jeanne de Vienne*. Valued at $123,258,751, its transfer was intended more to reassure America's financiers than from fear of Germany. It was followed immediately by the *Dunkerque* with a shipment · of almost equal value. And pragmatic to the core, the Bank of France officials argued fiercely with the C.N.R. over the freight charges to ship it to New York and the vaults of the Federal Reserve Bank. The New York destination may have reflected a lingering Gallic suspicion of consigning their treasure to a British Dominion, but there was probably no room for it in Ottawa. That being the case, why not go straight to New York and save all the trans-shipment trouble? Neutrality laws forbade a belligerent warship from remaining in port long enough, in this case, for the gold to be unloaded, so Halifax it was.

The last of the easy-going shipments from France, over $180,000,000 worth, arrived in Halifax on board two cruisers on 23 March 1940. Then suddenly, the Phoney War was over and survival became a deadly serious business. To their great surprise, the French found their vaunted defences crumbling before a German army that flowed across the border and across their countryside like a river in spring flood. Of the three French ports with gold depots, Toulon on the Mediterranean was initially fairly safe, but after the fall of Dunkirk, Brest on the Breton peninsula and Le Verdon on the Bay of Biscay fell into chaos before daily advances of the enemy. Getting the gold to dockside was the stuff of an espionage novel. France's sole air-craft carrier, *Bearn*, arrived in Halifax on 1 June 1940, with nearly $240,000,000 worth of bullion. On the 2nd, the *Jeanne d'Arc* and *Emile Bertin*, with just over $260,000,000 worth arrived, and, finally, on 9 June, the liner *Pasteur* with over $250,000,000.00 worth of bullion arrived. Chillingly, as the *Bearne* and *Emile Bertin* slid out of Brest, a German radio broadcast wished "... bon voyage to the two French cruisers which leave France tonight carrying the Bank of France gold to the United States."[203]

France's Third Republic was now on the verge of collapse and allegiances were becoming fluid. Although hints of the flight of Europe's gold had appeared in the press, Haligonians were oblivious to the high-stakes drama being played out under their noses. With the arrival of the *Pasteur* they got an inkling of the cracks appearing in the façade of their erstwhile ally. What was the third-largest liner in the French merchant marine to do now? If it returned to France it was clear that it would soon be flying the swastika or a variation of it, something the Royal Navy, which controlled Halifax, would never allow. Rumours flew that on 4 July the *Pasteur*'s crew tried to scuttle her at her berth at the Ocean Terminals, only to be thwarted by a Royal Navy boarding party, which closed the sea cocks before it could settle. True or not, the Admiralty took it over and by mid-August 1940, the officers and some of the crew were on their way home via neutral Portugal, while some stayed behind to serve in the Canadian merchant marine.[204]

To this degree, Haligonians participated more than the rest of Canada in the agony of France's collapse. The personal agony of Frenchmen also played out in the person of M. Jean Poissonier, Deputy Governor of the Bank of France, who accompanied the *Pasteur*'s gold shipment. His world collapsing around him, he then accompanied the eleven Express cars to Ottawa, the one French shipment not consigned to New York, from where on 15 June he wrote to the C.N.R. Express Superintendent, F.M. Smith, "Since I am here I have sent 4 cables to France to get news from my wife and daughter. I have no answer and am very anxious about their fate. They too are certainly anxious to receive Something of me. I will try another way. I herein enclose a letter and I kindly ask you to give it to an english [*sic*] or french [*sic*] officer of an english or french ship leaving for France, for Bordeaux if possible."[205] There was no happy outcome, however, because France sued for peace just days later, quashing M. Poissonier's sanguine expectations that despite all the bad news, "... the war will continue and our strong and splendid soldier General Weygand will find the right way to drive back and beat our enemies."[206] In the end all Smith could do for Poissonier was ask an Ottawa colleague to take him under his wing.

Still more high drama began to unfold on 7 June when the *Emile Bertin*, one of the fastest ships in the world, left Halifax for a high-speed return to Brest to clean out the remaining gold. On 18 June, after a remarkable passage, it arrived back in Halifax with some 245 tons of bullion, mere hours before the French government signed an armistice with the Germans. A tense game of cat and mouse, invisible to all but the participants, now began as Captain Robert Battet of the *Emile Bertin*, Admiral Stuart Bonham-Carter and Canadian officials jockeyed for position. HRH Princess Alice, who with her husband the Earl of Athlone, arrived in port during these tense hours to take up the role of Governor General, later recalled press reports telling of a dramatic dawn escape as the French cruiser, guns manned, fled the harbour pursued by the Royal Navy. This tale was an unlikely fiction given the harbour defences, but the real story as related by the C.N.R.'s Mr. Smith was dramatic enough.[207]

French cruiser *Emile Bertin* left Brest 12 June and arrived Halifax June 18 at 1200 noon, standard time, with 3986 bags and 796 boxes. Mr. Edoard de Katow, Attache Bank of France in charge. The Captain of the ship had sealed orders to open on arrival at Halifax which called for his communicating with the French Admiralty at Paris before unloading his cargo. He rec'd advice Wednesday from his Admiralty to go to sea and not unload the cargo.

Notice was served Wed. aft. at around 5 PM on the Captain by Commodore Reid of the British Admiralty, forbidding him to leave port: further notice was served by the Collector of Customs, Mr. Collins, and Mr. Staden of the Bank of Canada served a notice in letter form demanding the cargo.

On telephone instructions from Mr. G.E. Bellerose, we were instructed by the Governor of the Bank of Canada, Mr. Graham Towers, to be ready at a moment's notice to handle the cargo from the ship.

On Friday, June 21 around noon, was advised by Mr. de Katow that the ship and cargo had been released and they were putting to sea for an unknown destination. The ship left Pier No. 40 at 5 PM std. time June 21 for sea without unloading.

During these tense three days, Captain Battet, like so many of his fellow French officers, had to give serious consideration to where his loyalties lay. His superiors told him one thing, but here in Halifax he was surrounded by the baleful gaze of recent allies, who now regarded his superiors, their motives and perhaps him with dark suspicion. Fortunately, reason prevailed. The Royal Navy could not sanction the return of the *Emile Bertin* to France, which was being occupied by the Germans. A compromise was worked out in those three days that allowed the *Emile Bertin* to sail to the relative neutrality of France's West Indian colony of Martinique. Not only were vaults of the Bank of France located there, but it was within range of the Royal Navy's West Indian squadron; and perhaps of greater significance, it was under the wary eye of America, sensitive about Martinique's proximity to their Panama Canal. America had already demonstrated that its concept of neutrality was a fluid one. Regardless of what happened in France, nothing would happen in Martinique that the Americans disapproved of. There the *Emil Bertin*'s gold slumbered until 1946, when in the *Halifax Herald* of 20 March, there appeared a brief notice that 235 tons of French gold had been returned to France from Martinique, a notice on which Mr. Smith had pencilled, "What a night — long, long ago."[208]

The French drama in Halifax Harbour did not stop here. The French aircraft carrier *Bearn*, which had arrived with its golden cargo on 1 June, had a double mission. The United States had agreed to supply France with a small fleet of fighter aircraft for its air force. None of these, most of them open-cockpit biplanes, were cutting edge, and they numbered, depending on the source, between 65 and 100. An American magazine described them as Curtiss SBC-4 dive bombers, Curtiss "Hawk" fighters, Brewster 339 fighters and Stimson trainers.[209]

Having divested itself of its cargo of gold, the *Bearn* was now commissioned to pick up the American planes, which were waiting in Halifax, and return to France in what had began to look like a last-ditch effort to beat back the Luftwaffe.

As with the fleet of 50 destroyers delivered to Halifax by the Americans a few months later, the conventions of neutrality, however much in tatters, allowed the Americans to deliver the planes only to a point of exchange. It was then up to the French to get them off the dock and onto the flight deck. To assist them in this task and to train the French pilots and mechanics in their operation and maintenance, the R.C.A.F. lent a detachment of men under Squadron Leader Adelard Raymond, a Montreal native stationed in Saint John, N.B. Once loaded, Raymond and a hand-picked squad were to accompany the aircraft to France. It must have seemed ominous that on one of his last official acts before leaving port, Admiral Pierre Rouger, commander of the *Bearn*, paid a courtesy call upon Princess Juliana of the Netherlands, heir to the Dutch throne, who had just disembarked in Halifax en route to wartime exile in Ottawa.

For the French sailors the next 16 days must have been depressing and confusing as each day's wireless news broadcast fresh evidence of their country's collapse. Their intended destination had been the naval port of Brest, but with the fall of Dunkirk they were diverted to Bordeaux. The day before arriving there, Bordeaux was seized by the Germans, so Casa Blanca, Morocco, became their destination. By this time loyalties in the French navy had become so equivocal that some of the crew were preparing for a fight, but for and with whom? Perhaps to avoid that outcome, and since delivery of the aircraft had suddenly become pointless, the *Bearn* set course for Martinique, where it arrived on 26 June, two days after the government of Marshall Petain signed an armistice with Germany. The signing of this armistice instituted an order to all of the Halifax Harbour batteries that effective 15 July all French warships approaching Halifax were to be treated as "neutral war vessels."[210]

Meanwhile, Squadron Leader Raymond and his men watched their status shift from honoured ally to potential belligerent. Fortunately, the French navy maintained a gentlemanly attitude during it all and there was never any suggestion that the Canadians would be interned, either on the ship or after their arrival in Martinique. Whether this would have been continued had they still been at sea on 3 July was a moot point. That day the Royal Navy bombarded a French fleet in Oran, North Africa when it refused to declare its intentions, and 1,300 French sailors died in the attack.

In Martinique, the *Bearn*, in company with the *Emile Bertin*, initially prepared to resist an attack on the island by the Royal Navy. The planned attack withered away with American assurances that despite the island government's Vichy sympathies, it and everything in and on it was effectively interned. The ships mouldered away at anchor until Vichy France was occupied by the Germans after the Allies landed in French North Africa in November 1942, and they associated themselves with the Free French forces for the duration of the war.

Once on Martinique, Raymond made himself useful as a liaison between the French and the British in the touchy days before the American-imposed armistice. He and his men finally embarked on a Royal Navy blockade ship, which was allowed to enter Fort de France to pick them up. After many vicissitudes Raymond arrived back in Canada. He had changed ships 14 times. Clearly a resourceful man, Raymond ended up an Air Vice-Marshall, a Commander of the Order of the British Empire, a Chevalier of the Legion of Honour, and holder of the Croix de Guerre (avec Palm).[211]

The drama now over, the remainder of the gold transfers, now all from

Britain, proceeded in an orderly fashion until the last, on 10 March 1941, when Express cars set off with six boxes of bonds and securities worth $550,000 and 157 boxes of gold worth $9,834,000, a mere pittance compared to some of the predecessor shipments. No doubt all those involved were much relieved that it was over, not only because of the intense security, but also because, despite a flawless performance, they could breathe no word of it even to their nearest and dearest until war's end when it was yesterday's news.

THE GREAT AND THE NEAR GREAT

A number of what later generations would call celebrities passed through the port in these tumultuous years, people who in another time would never have come near the place. First among them was Winston Churchill who, along with his wife Clementine and their daughter, boarded the *Queen Mary* in Glasgow and arrived in September 1944 en route to the second Quebec Conference with President Roosevelt and Mackenzie King. It was supposed to be very hush-hush and a train was waiting dockside to whisk them away. Years of preaching the virtues of sealed lips cut no ice with many Haligonians, and a crowd of some 200 or more gathered around the train. Not one to miss an opportunity, Churchill stood on the observation platform of his car for 20 minutes waving and talking to the crowd. The great man led them in the singing of "The Maple Leaf Forever" and "O Canada," and, he said, needed only a band to launch into "Rule Britannia." When the train pulled out he flashed his famous V signal and as the car rolled out of sight called out "God Bless You" to the crowd.[212]

It was not Churchill's first visit. Just a year before he had arrived in port on 9 August with a high-profile delegation en route to the first Quebec Conference. There was much more security and less public contact with so many important personnel floating about, but he endeared himself to locals by commenting, "Now we know that Halifax is not just a shed on the wharf as we had known it to be before."[213]

The presence of the Royal Norwegian Navy in nearby Lunenburg brought to the city from time to time, not the elderly King Haakon, who remained in London, but Crown Prince Olav and his consort Princess Martha. On a January 1942 visit they kept a punishing schedule, leaving

Lunenburg in the morning and arriving in Halifax about noon to spend the afternoon visiting every Norwegian ship in the harbour. They dined at Government House in the evening and the following day paid rounds of official calls, visited the Allied Merchant Seamen's Club and in the evening entertained the personnel of all the Norwegian ships at dinner. HRH was an Olympic gold medalist, and a good thing too, his fitness stood him in good stead.[214]

Canada's Governor General, Alexander, Earl of Athlone, was ironically by birth Prince Alexander of Teck, son of the Duke of Teck in the Kingdom of Wurttemburg. Along with many members of the Royal family, his German titles were "sanitized" in 1917 when he became Earl of Athlone. As brother of Queen Mary, however, his entire career had been as an officer in the British military, where he served with distinction in South Africa. With his wife, Princess Alice, he was indefatigable in touring the country to encourage the Canadian war effort. They arrived in a downpour on 20 June 1940, at Pier 20, almost secretly, after an eight-day voyage, sharing their ship with hundreds of refugees, many from Czechoslovakia, on their way to the United States. No time was spent in the city on this trip and they embarked immediately on their special train for Ottawa. They had not come alone. With them was their bull terrier, Bronk, who watched from the rear platform as the docks receded in the soggy gloom.

Bronk was not the only distinguished canine visitor to come through the port in these busy years. Many survivors of torpedoed ships paused in Halifax as they recuperated from their ordeal. One of them was a purebred springer spaniel of the merchant navy with the name of "Homer the Outlaw." In February 1942 he was relaxing at the Malone household on Quinpool Road before continuing on to Montreal where, notwithstanding rationing and other scarcities facing ordinary citizens, T-bone steak was on his menu. He had survived two torpedoings, and after one he had spent two days in a lifeboat. When the torpedo struck he was in the middle of dinner and when rescued dripping from the water was still grimly holding onto his bone.[215]

Ten days before the arrival of the Athlones on 11 June, two warships of the Royal Netherlands Navy slipped into port, one of which carried Crown Princess Juliana of the Netherlands, two-and-a-half-year-old Princess

Beatrix, and nine-month-old Princess Irene. The second warship carried refugees from the German invasion of the province of Zeeland.[216] Although her special train was waiting at dockside, it did not leave until the morning of the 12th, when it took her and her family to the C.P.R. resort hotel at Montebello, Que., to await the arrival of the Athlones, with whom they stayed until they could find a house. The Crown Princess was on the Gestapo hit list and since she was heir to the throne it was deemed politic to get her and her children to safety, while Queen Wilhelmina stayed in London with her government-in-exile. Juliana's husband, Prince Bernhardt, spent the war years in active service. Their arrival was no secret. Bobbie Johnston noted in her diary that there were lots of Dutch sailors on the streets, "... having come over here on a Dutch destroyer, bringing their Princess Juliana, to the peace and quiet of Canada. She is to stay at the Seigniory [sic] Club, nice choice on her part, as that is where we spent our honeymoon."[217] Then she added thoughtfully, "The Dutch sailors were innocent looking lads, too bad they aren't left alone with their dikes and tulips."

Just over a year later, on 21 August, Princess Juliana was back in Halifax, this time to open a hostel on Bishop Street for the Dutch navy and merchant service, coming not from Ottawa, where she was living, but from the C.N.R. resort hotel, Pictou Lodge, where she was spending part of the summer with the two princesses.[218] The Dutch presence was strong in the war years, strong enough that on Queen Wilhelmina's birthday, 31 August, all of the naval ships who could muster one flew a Dutch flag from their mastheads.[219]

Other greats and near greats included the film actress Anna Neagle, who arrived on 16 April 1942.[220] She had just starred in *There Too Go I*, a film on the wartime work of the Canadian Red Cross, and was about to embark on a national tour supporting the agency's National Appeal for $9 million. Noted earlier was the young Rothschild, prepared to step back into, or very close to, the lion's den in August 1942 when he was seen off at the Ocean Terminals by his aunt.[221]

HRH the Duke of Kent, who traded his pre-war playboy role for that of Air Marshal of the R.A.F., while visiting British Commonwealth Air Training Plan facilities across the country, toured Halifax in September

1941. Among other events, on the 4th he visited Sandwich Battery, where he inspected the garrison and watched the guns aimed and fired.[222] His Royal Highness, whose 1941 visit made him the first member of the Royal family to fly the Atlantic, was killed on 25 August 1942, when his Sunderland flying boat, en route to Iceland, crashed in the north of Scotland.

And so it went, back and forth, ships and trains coming and going as fast as the facilities could handle them, with thousands of passengers, a river of humanity that Halifax had not seen before and would not see again. For the six years of the war, the port facilities handled a constant flow of humanity in both directions. Although the numbers were greater than had ever been contemplated in their design, nevertheless its years as one of Canada's principal points of entry for immigrants gave it a base of both facilities and expertise from which to operate. All that was necessary to make it all work smoothly were long hours, erratic schedules and hard work.

CHAPTER FOUR:

A Hard - Working City

As the 1930s drew to a close Halifax, like so many communities elsewhere, was struggling to its feet after a decade of economic depression. The city had never recovered from the economic consequences of the departure of the British garrison in 1905–1906 and the slow decline in maritime trade. The boom brought by World War I was cruelly crushed by post-war inflation and the depression of 1920–1921. Because the city was primarily a service centre for the military and the provincial economy, and post-Confederation attempts to create an industrial infrastructure had come to little, it did not have the base to participate in what the rest of the continent recalled as the "Roaring Twenties."

When war clouds formed and the storm broke, and six years later when victory was declared, there was little difference in the industrial capacity of the Halifax/Dartmouth region. Indeed, one could say that it was slightly less, for the Acadia Sugar Refinery located in Woodside, deprived of a steady supply of raw material and battered by rationing, shut down in 1942 and never reopened. Despite the tremendous demands on the industrial capacity of Canada, Halifax and Dartmouth received no new infrastructure for a fresh start once the world had been made safe for democracy. To meet the demands placed on it, the area's existing industrial capacity simply ramped up and, then, when that demand evaporated in 1945, slumped back down. As Jay White has pointed out, glamorous new industries such as aircraft manufacture, which brought the best jobs and cost-plus contracts, went largely to Central Canada. The East Coast Port boomed, but the boom was in hotels, restaurants, cafes, hostels, laundries, cinemas, dance halls and retail stores.[223] However, although these did not generate high-paying jobs, there were lots of them where there had been none before.

There was one exception to this — the Clark Ruse aircraft plant on the shore below the R.C.A.F. Dartmouth air station. Even though maintenance rather than manufacture was the order of the day there, it employed hundreds of workers, enough that the Department of National Defence built houses to accommodate them.[224] This plant was more or less the only purposely established brand-new wartime industry in the Halifax/Dartmouth area and was intended to support the aircraft stationed at R.C.A.F. Dartmouth. The founders were a Montreal-based group of aviation pioneers and bush pilots with connections to Noorduyne Aircraft, manufacturers of the sturdy Norseman beloved of bush pilots and used by the R.C.A.F. for training and light cargo.[225]

Clarke Ruse was typical of the new wartime industries which sprang up across North America in that it did not hesitate to employ women in non-traditional occupations. Clara MacCormack was trained by a woman who came from Montreal to show them how to rivet pieces and panels on planes. "It was exciting," MacCormack remembered. "You used electric guns and drills and you got used to it. I was 17." The closing of the plant in the autumn of 1944 was but one signal that the war was coming to an end. Before the decade was out, however, Clark Ruse was succeeded in the same facilities by Fairey Aviation.

The government of Canada's focus for new investment was Central Canada, with the implication of a post-war shift to a continental rather than an Atlantic Triangle economy. Because the federal government's wartime control of the economy and investment was total, the post-war industrial map of Halifax and Dartmouth changed little from the pre-war version.

Strong arguments have been put forward[226] that the architect of this policy of centralization was the powerful and effective Minister of Munitions and Supply, Clarence Decatur Howe, who, despite or because of years of residence in Halifax (1908 to 1913) as a Professor of Engineering at Dalhousie, resisted attempts to make the city the focus of more government investment than was absolutely necessary to maintain basic support to the R.C.N., the R.C.A.F. and the convoy system. Even in the face of the huge expansion of the R.C.N., for example, Howe preferred to focus investment on the shipyards of the Great Lakes and the St. Lawrence, this despite severe constraints of St. Lawrence locks and winter freeze-ups, the urging of the British Admiralty and the representations of Hon. Angus L. Macdonald, a Nova Scotian and Minister of Defence for the Naval Service. Anticipation of the St. Lawrence freeze-up led to traffic jams in Halifax, as new or repaired corvettes, minesweepers and other craft flooded into port from central Canada, as many as 150 in December 1943, filling every pier and jetty, with the overflow anchored out in the stream.[227]

This said, the industrial complex at Halifax, such as it was, did not drowse away the war years. Busy it was. In fact the word "busy" scarcely applies; "frenetic" is more appropriate.

2 000 Killed 9000 mortally injured

THE HALIFAX SHIPYARDS

Of what was considered "heavy industry," the type that darkened skies with smoke and deafened the ear with its clamour, the Halifax Shipyards truly qualified. Although ready, willing and able, the yard had never attracted much shipbuilding business; but it had survived the lean 1930s rather well by focusing on the repair business. Supporting or supplementing the ship-yards was a selection of specialized and purely local repair firms, foundries and machine shops, often modest operations, that found themselves under heavy pressure when the war began.

The Halifax Shipyards was in fact two establishments. The one on the Halifax shore at the Narrows contained the graving or dry dock, built in 1889 to support a mixture of commercial and military needs. The old Halifax Graving Dock Company, managed by Samuel Brookfield, was dev-astated by the 1917 Halifax Explosion and expropriated by the Canadian government in 1918. It was then absorbed first by the British Empire Steel Corporation (Besco), then its successor the Dominion Steel Corporation (Dosco). Under the Besco administration, considerable investment was made to fit the yard for shipbuilding. Even though some hulls were built, this venture had limited success.

Although the shipyard failed to emerge as a major builder, during the 1920s and 1930s, under the careful oversight of its General Manager Robert John Roddick Nelson, it established a solid reputation for quality repair work that kept it afloat and profitable while contemporaries struggled. Nelson, who took charge in 1924, along with his colleague, John Paterson, Superintendent of the Dartmouth Marine slips, saw the yard through the maelstrom of World War II and out the other side.

Nelson was not, however, master of all he surveyed. In November 1940, the Director General of Shipbuilding was appointed Controller of Ship Construction and Repairs and the following spring the duties were separated with a separate Controller of Ship Repairs. In liaison with the British Ministry of Shipping, along with shipyards and ship owners, the Director established priorities, the foremost of which were naval vessels and merchant vessels engaged in essential war work.[228] It was not long before it would be difficult to find a ship that would not fit in either one of those categories.

Most new work went to yards in Quebec and Ontario even though the British Admiralty, confused by the illogicality of building and repairing naval ships in so far from the Atlantic battlefront (1,500 miles each way), urged Howe to expand Halifax's capabilities. They could not budge him nor, on appeal, Prime Minister King.[229] The official reason was that Halifax was busy enough with critical ship repair business, which was certainly true. To have encouraged shipbuilding would have meant expansion of the plant, probably in the vicinity of Tuft's Cove. Although never so baldly stated, that was never going to happen. The Halifax Shipyards footprint in August 1945 was pretty much what it had been in September 1939.

After heavy pressure from Angus L. Macdonald and amid much patriotic rhetoric, two tribal class destroyers were laid down in the shipyard, *MicMac* and *Nootka*. As far as Ottawa was concerned, far from representing a breakthrough, these two ships the (first was begun in September 1942) were backups to keep the workforce busy during periods when repair work slacked off. Neither ship was finished until after the war. Within a year of their start, the contracts for six new corvettes went to British yards.[230] Thus, they had about them the aura of a "sop" to keep the locals happy, which was no reflection upon their subsequent honourable careers as HMC ships.

Refits and repairs it was to be for the Halifax Shipyards. Initially, efforts focused on making warriors out of an unlikely fleet of peacetime passenger steamers, many of whose careers had been spent on calm, warm, sunlit seas, the music of the afternoon tea dance trailing aft from the Verandah Lounge and dissipating over the sparkling wake. The immediate institution of the convoy system required armed escorts to protect it from attack, but there were no suitable escorts in the Canadian navy and few in the British. The now largely redundant passenger ships were requisitioned to fill the role of Armed Merchant Cruisers (AMCs). Shipyards, including Halifax, filled first wartime contracts by welding, bolting and screwing big guns, small guns, 12 pounders, Oerlikons and Bofors guns, Hoskins, Browning and Marmon machine guns, whatever could be scraped up in armouries and ordnance yards around the country, to the decks of ships large and small. Usually, the size of the ship was out of all proportion to the makeshift armament installed. And not only guns. To combat the threat from below, brackets were welded on from which to hang nets to keep off torpedoes and mines. To cope with the threat from above, rocket launchers were installed. As an enemy flew in low over the water, a rocket trailing 500 feet of piano wire could be launched in the hope that it would shear off a wing or tangle a propellor and bring the plane down.[231] As makeshift as these arrangement often were, many of these ships and their crews acquitted themselves magnificently in situations scarcely contemplated by their builders and designers, the Halifax-based *Jervis Bay* being but one of many such.

As the war evolved, AMCs were replaced, as intended, by corvettes and destroyers of the regular navies; but the process of adding armament to civilian ships continued with the Defence Equipped Merchant Ships (DEMS) programme, where selected freighters were outfitted with light armament. The shipyard's role shifted as the war evolved to scheduled refits for the navy, which invariably came to mean the installation of the new and upgraded equipment that soon reduced the effectiveness of the U-boat wolf packs. This activity was incidental to the incessant and unscheduled demand for emergency repairs to a corvette or merchantman staggering in past Maugher's Beach. When a ship survived to limp or be towed into port the damage could be spectacular. On 24 July 1942, the SS *Kronprinzin*, a

Norwegian ship, struggled into harbour. Torpedoed off Yarmouth, it had beached at Lower East Pubnico to remove part of its cargo, then was towed to Halifax with a huge hole in the bow and a virtually collapsed stern.[232]

In early March that same year, there were at one time four torpedoed tankers in harbour awaiting some kind of repairs: The *Kars*, torpedoed off Ketch Harbour and temporarily beached on Ives Point where the high octane cargo lit up the night sky for days; the *Egda*, which had arrived with a perfectly round hole right under the bridge; the *Diloma*, whose deck bulged up from the torpedo strike that had torn a gaping hole in the hull and left a large flap of steel bent back toward the stern, and the *Corilla*.[233] To Thomas Raddall, many of these torpedoed ships resembled nothing so much as burst paper bags.[234] Sometimes these half-submerged tankers were kept afloat by stuffing their holds with empty oil barrels.[235]

The Atlantic was also a formidable enemy. In March 1944 a convoy en route to Russia from New York encountered gales of such ferocity and was in such parlous condition it sought shelter in Halifax. With reports that a U-boat pack was waiting for them the 28 ships required urgent repairs before they dared face them. In addition to the damage that mountainous seas had done to superstructures and decks, tanks and trucks had dislodged in the holds, compounding from within the damage by the sea without. Parts were ordered, but it was urgent that the convoy get on its way. The shipyard workers scoured every ship then in harbour, lists in hand, stripped them of the parts needed for the Russian convoy, repaired the damaged ships, which then departed with desperately needed supplies for an eventually ungrateful Stalin. When the new parts finally arrived, they were then installed on the plundered ships.[236]

Not all repair jobs arose from life-and-death struggles with a relentless enemy. In August 1943 the *Queen Mary* brought Winston Churchill across the Atlantic to the Quebec Conference with President Roosevelt. The garbage scow assigned to service the great liner most embarrassingly sank right at the stern. The ship could not budge without damage to the propellers or hull. Heavy equipment was brought in to lift the scow so that it could be taken away for repairs.[237]

In February 1942 a freighter loaded with foodstuffs en route to Britain docked at the Ocean Terminals caught fire. The freighter, whose name was felt by the censor to be unnecessary information, listed over and sank, rendering the pier useless, a result similar to the interned French liner *Normandie*, which caught fire while under refit in New York, tipped over and sank under the weight of the water poured into it by the fireboats. For five months, in the Halifax case, Foundation Maritime struggled to pump it out and right it, during which process one man died when, cutting into the hull, he was overcome by the fumes of the rotting cargo. Another two months was required to make it fit to sail the short distance to the Halifax Shipyards. Finally, by year's end, it was seaworthy again.[238]

Equally undramatic were the many repairs from collisions, almost inevitable before there was radar in tightly packed convoys or crowded harbours, when ships simply ran out of room and into each other.

Between 1939 and 1945, over 7,145 ships passed through the Halifax Shipyards, fairly evenly divided between Halifax and Dartmouth, generating for the company a profit of some $20,000,000. Jobs under 3,000 tons were carried out in Dartmouth. Because this tonnage included classes such as corvettes, frigates and destroyers, and almost all wooden vessels, it amounted to about half of the Shipyard's work. To handle the load, one of the existing marine railways was upgraded from 800 to 1,800 tons capacity and two of 3,000 tons capacity were added, bringing the total to five. A new machine shop was built, which included space for administrative offices and a drafting room. The Dartmouth yard was so productive that it was awarded a collective O.B.E. by King George VI.

The larger repair jobs were handled at the Halifax yard. Two 615 foot building berths were overhauled for the construction of the *MicMac* and *Nootka* and to handle the repair work. The existing plant was upgraded to cope with the unrelenting demand for faster turnover. A floating dock of 25,000 ton capacity was built and complemented the 1889 graving dock. What was for a time the world's largest "kettle" for galvanizing metal was added, along with the floating Halcrane "Lord Kitchener" capable of lifting 75 tons, which could move about the harbour as required. Additionally, the machine shop, boiler shop, pipe shop, blacksmith shop, coppersmith shop, electrical shop, mould loft and rigging loft were upgraded. A 6,500-cubic-feet-per-minute compressor supplied air-operated tools in every corner of the yard. Welding, which had been a small component of every pre-war shipyard, rapidly proved itself to be not only strong and reliable, but also much cheaper than the traditional riveting. By 1945 it had become the norm in new or repair work.

During the years of most intense activity there was no time to putter away leisurely at a wounded ship, at rest in drydock until it was all tidied up and ready to go back to sea. Careful scheduling was an impossibility as the yard had to cope with last-minute emergency repairs, sudden priorities for the installation of newly approved equipment, security alerts, bad weather, constant secrecy over arrivals and departures and a myriad of other factors. Delays compounded so that by late 1942 there were bitter complaints that the three-month period now required for the routine refit of an R.C.N. convoy escort was far too long, causing hardship for the backed-up ships and crews forced to stay on sea duty long past their due date and in a badly run down condition.[239] With the entry of the United States into the war, pressure eased somewhat. American shipyards were now open to the Allies and damaged ships were towed to Boston or New York and repairs carried out there. Combined with increasing control of North Atlantic waters, by the beginning of 1944 there was capacity in Halifax for 12 minesweepers to be under refit at once, readying them for the coming invasion of Europe.[240]

The worst-damaged ships were drydocked or hauled out on the marine railway, and as soon as the hull was sound, refloated and towed to a vacant mooring or pier where the necessary work was completed. Thus, work parties were not confined to the property of the Shipyards, but were constantly on the move around the harbour or out in the basin. One of these repair runs had a tragic outcome when 19 skilled workers on their way to a ship moored in the Bedford Basin died when their shipyard tug *Erg* was run down by the freighter *Norg* and sunk on 6 July 1943.[241] The Halcrane "Lord Kitchener" was as mobile as the working parties and was towed around the harbour as required. Its crane, its working parties and a plethora of equipment might well labour side by side with gangs of stevedores, both racing against time as zero hour for the departure of a convoy loomed ever closer.

Donald Purchase, just into his teens, was recruited by his father's firm and once found competent was told to be the gofer for one of the machinists.[242] His most nerve-wracking job on these mobile work parties was getting the tools from the tender up the side of the ship on a rope ladder dangling against the steel hull and onto the deck. Dropping any of these expensive tools into the cold depths of Bedford Basin was unthinkable, and he never did, but he still remembers the stress.

Purchase and his father, Walter Purchase, worked for the firm of William Collings & Sons, on Barrington Street. Collings was one of a handful of firms that carried out smaller repairs in conjunction with, or in addition to, the shipyard. These companies included, at one time or another, T. Hogan & Co., Lower Water Street; W. & A. Moir, Ltd., Barrington Street; Purdy Bros., Upper Water Street; Fleming Bros., Barrington Street; Thomas P. Way, Robie Street; Wm. Kennedy & Sons, Barrington Street; Dartmouth Iron Foundry, Maple Street; Austen Bros., Hollis Street; Burns & Kelleher, Grafton Street; Hillis & Sons, Kempt Road, and some half dozen others in various trades.[243]

To handle the load, always under pressure for one urgent reason or another, for merchant ship or convoy escort, the Halifax Shipyards was soon working 24 hours a day and the workforce expanded sevenfold.[244] The subject of the shipyard workforce was a delicate one on two fronts. The first of these, the introduction of women into the workforce of what had been generally accepted as a male environment, went surprisingly smoothly, within very limited parameters. The second, relationships between labour and management, proved to be a more tricky problem, never really resolved before war's end.

Officially, once the war began, capital and labour were as one, marching hand-in-hand together to achieve the ultimate victory over fascism. In practice, and not only at the shipyard, sometimes this fusion worked and sometimes it didn't, as years of ingrained attitudes were not easily swept away.

On the plus side, as soon as the war began, Shipyard management realized that it needed more workers. In concert with the provincial government and the Nova Scotia Technical College, under the aegis of the "National Youth Training Plan," it instituted courses in machine-tool operation, machine fitting, sheet-metal working and welding, all of which were created from the ground up since the province had no vocational training in the school system.[245] The urgency of this need was evident as early as July

1940 when it became clear that the nation's pool of surplus "man" power, would soon be exhausted, and bringing women into the workforce would have to be seriously considered.

Hand-in-hand with this issue arose the competition for the pool of new talent that was coming into the shipyard — the same pool of young, trained men the army so desperately wanted and needed, which was identified by the National Selective Service Act.[246] Men in vital occupations could be and were deferred, but these deferrals were intended only as temporary, for six months at a time, and the recurring process of renewal led to uncertainty for the yard and bad morale for the men. Interestingly enough, it was the navy, in one respect a competitor for the same pool of recruits, that recognized the vital importance to itself of a stable, skilled workforce to keep its ships at sea. By June 1943 the navy won the acceptance of regulations that allowed for more-or-less permanent deferrals of these essential workers.[247] Moreover, to keep them happy in the harsh world of the Halifax housing shortage, one of the first efforts of the Dominion government's housing authority was the construction of accommodation for single workers, complete with dining facilities, on vacant Crown lands at Mulgrave Park, to be followed by colonies of "pre-fabs" for married workers.

By then, the government had accepted the necessity of bringing women into the workforce not only in the armed forces but also in "non-traditional" occupations. Most of these women went into aircraft production, located in Upper Canada, although Clark Ruse in Eastern Passage was a local exception, and it was relatively easy to do since the industry itself was so new there were few vested interests to surmount on either side of the capital/labour divide.

Five women, in a joint Shipyards/Department of Education venture, were trained as welders in 1943 and joined the Halifax workforce in June of that year. They were well accepted perhaps because their conditions of work were restricted and they could never qualify as "journeymen." Their hours of overtime were limited and certain jobs, such as overhead work, were off-limits because they were not considered good for a woman's health. Everyone, women included, understood that their involvement was a temporary measure, an emergency reserve that would disappear when the emergency did. It must be noted, these five women were not the vanguard of an army of Halifax "Rosie the riveters" — they were all that were ever hired.

This restricted involvement might not seem like a big deal, but in some ways it was a huge advance. Helen Pilicoski later recalled that they "encountered no prejudice at all — no resentment from the men; in fact they were helpful."[248] Limited it may seem, but for the women, it was a wonderful opportunity. They could earn upwards of $2,000 a year compared to an average of $376 for their contemporaries.[249] Even though the moment the war was over they were off the payroll, making hay while the sun shone seemed quite acceptable. Some, more than others, recognized the signs of change. Radio host John Fisher mused publicly that although the idea of women in the workforce was a new thing in these parts, it was just possible that in the future there might be women conductors, truck drivers, delivery boys and elevator girls. He added coyly, "Well the women always told us what to do before and now they actually do it themselves."[250]

Joan Murray, hired at Clark Ruse for the summer of 1943, has equally fond memories of being a pioneer in a man's world. She took in her stride the perhaps inevitable side effects of such a new role. "One of the hazards of working at Clark Ruse for *any* female was having to walk through the huge hangar and keep cool, turning a deaf ear to whistles and comments from the mechanics. If she survived that experience, there was a further test to pass. Between the main office and the hangar, at second floor level was a long covered walkway. To walk the length of this, facing a couple of high spirited young men coming the other way was another unnerving experience."[251]

Less sunny were the labour squabbles that bedeviled the Halifax Shipyards, something it had in common with many wartime industries. In almost all cases the root cause was the "hands together" wartime rhetoric, which operated under the premise that there would be no labour actions, and no dubious management practices before fascism was driven from the earth, which clashed with the daily realities of incessant emergencies, never-ending deadlines, inflation and ingrained attitudes. In the case of the shipyard, the unwillingness of management to accept the provisions of the province's 1937 Trade Union Act, which authorized the "check-off" of union dues from workers' pay cheques, led to a month-long walkout by union members in August 1944. The problem faced by the union (Local # 1 of the Union of Marine and Shipbuilding Workers of Canada) was ironic. The workers were willing enough to go out on strike when push came to shove, but the Local was almost bankrupt because, as long as payment of dues was voluntary, the men could not be induced to pay them. Equally ironic was the position of the Local's business agent and one of the stewards, both hard-line communists, who followed the Communist Party line that "strikes, slowdowns, and absenteeism were ... the weapons of fascism." Although they fell in line once the pickets went up, they opposed the strike from the beginning.[252]

In 1942, at the height of the Battle of the Atlantic, such an action would have led to a swift takeover by government, but by now everyone except the Nazi hierarchy recognized that the war's end was only a matter of time. Increasing control of the North Atlantic meant less repair and refit business, and the destroyers on the stocks were not a priority. The strike ended on an equivocal note. In February 1945 the Nova Scotia Supreme Court handed down a decision confirming the validity of the automatic check-off of dues, seemingly a union victory. But an unintended consequence was the departure of a number of skilled workers, who had taken advantage of their temporary unemployment to apply successfully to the War Labour Board for permission to move to other jobs, good judgement on their part. The war's end meant the end of the gravy train, and the shipyard faced a more familiar kind of pressure, the relentless hunt for new work.

NOVA SCOTIA LIGHT AND POWER

Somewhat to its initial surprise, Nova Scotia Light and Power found itself recruited into a specialized group of marine workers. Early in the war, the Germans developed a magnetic mine which was set off by the natural magnetic field of an iron or steel ship. Initially, this mine caused great havoc until British scientists developed the process of "degaussing." Degaussing involved running a heavy electrical cable around the perimeter of a ship and when energized, it neutralized the ship's magnetic field. The process evolved during the war as German scientists sought to outmanoeuvre the British scientists, a battle of wits in which Dalhousie professors of physics played an important role.

Degaussing was so effective that it was soon a necessity. Until it became universal, every ship not so fitted that entered Halifax Harbour was a candidate. Nova Scotia Light and Power was asked to coordinate the effort. After finding that there was no spare capacity anywhere to coordinate, in April 1940 it set up its own "Marine Department," drawing on its own staff. As with everything to do with wartime shipping, the Marine Department worked under immense pressure, beginning with the massive job of installing cables on the battleship HMS *Ramilies* and the cruiser HMS *Emerald* (both soon to pursue the *Bismarck* to its doom). Priority was also given to the Armed Merchant Cruisers doing duty as convoy escorts, then to the merchant ships themselves. On a large ship, such as the liner *Pasteur*, this refit involved the installation of more than 30 miles of electrical cable plus the appropriate circuitry. The work never let up. On one occasion the *Lady Rodney* arrived in port and was deemed the highest priority. Not a spare electrician could be found in Halifax, given that every job had the same priority. Desperate, the Marine Department called the Nova Scotia Technical College. The Principal, Dr. F.H. Sexton, said that he had students he considered qualified. To a man they volunteered, classes were cancelled for two days and the budding electrical engineers laboured for two days under the supervision of the Marine Department, then stepped back to watch the *Lady Rodney*, fully degaussed, sail on time.[253]

In an imaginative gesture, Nova Scotia Light and Power presented to every ship it degaussed with a framed quotation from Homer: "This magic circle round thy bosom bind, Live on — and cast thy terrors to the wind."

The Marine Department's mandate expanded to the installation of the still top-secret radar on R.C.N. ships, installation and maintenance of alarm and telephone systems, generators and gyrocompasses, a multitude of general electrical work on a multitude of ships and even the repair of elevator motors on aircraft carriers.[254] Ingenuity was a must. On one occasion the Armed Merchant Cruiser *Rampura* staggered into port sheathed in ice and in need of serious repairs that involved shutting down the boilers and generators. The 600 people on board could not be left on a dead ship in winter, but her 220-volt DC system could not be connected to the regular 120-volt AC power grid. Of course, it was an urgent situation because the convoy could not depart without her. To allow the boilers to be shut down, one of the 550-volt DC generators of the tram system was conscripted from its regular duty, its voltage stepped down, cables strung from the Water Street plant, up and over the roof of the Harbours Board offices, down the hatches of the *Rampura* at the Ocean Terminals and up to the main switchboard. The trams may have gasped for current for a while, but life on the ship carried on and, repairs completed, the *Rampura* and its convoy sailed on time.[255]

IMPERIAL OIL

Equally vital, both locally and nationally, was the operation of the Imperial Oil Refinery at Eastern Passage, in an enclave known as "Imperoyal," where employees lived in company-supplied houses, children attended a company-funded school, and families relaxed in company recreational facilities. The Maritimes had depended upon its products for over 20 years, but in September 1939 first priority shifted to the ships of the R.C.N. and the R.N., the aircraft of the R.C.A.F. and the merchant ships which made up the Britain-bound convoys.

Although Imperial Oil traced its roots in the Halifax area back to the 1880s, the Eastern Passage refinery and Imperoyal dated from 1918. It was a product of World War I and the urgent need to supply Britain with refined products from North American and South American crude, without going through the extra 3,000 mile voyage to and from Montreal refineries. The refinery's vital importance was obvious. One of the first responses after the declaration of war was to take steps to protect it and the R.C.A.F. station from the threat of German raiders landing at Lawrencetown Beach, and by war's end both facilities were ringed by anti-aircraft installations.

The largest tonnage coming in and out of Halifax Harbour during the war was crude oil and petroleum products in from the Caribbean and out to Britain. During the final three years of the war petroleum crude and fuel made up half the total tonnage. The first, nasty years saw Imperoyal, the navy and at the bottom of the supply chain, the civilians holding useless gas-ration coupons, staggering from the lack of crude owing to the effective operations of Nazi submarines. Moreover, the desperate need to get petroleum to Britain meant that as the Battle of the Atlantic raged, for every tanker lost to a torpedo, another was sent from the coastal fleet to replace

it. Even though shipyards geared up rapidly and the United States eventually began to contribute, at this early stage there was no way to replace
those lost. Railway tank cars could not take up the slack. The steel was just
not there to build more. Even had it been possible, increasingly overloaded
railways did not have the capacity to haul them.

In February 1942, 23 tankers heading up the Eastern Seaboard were
sunk. Seven tankers owned or chartered by Imperial Oil were lost, including the *Montrolite* en route to Eastern Passage from Venezuela with the loss
of 28 of her 48 man crew.[256] One of Imperial's Norwegian-registered char-
ters took two torpedoes at 10:30 p.m., 17 January 1942. It was still afloat
after two hours, so the frustrated U-boat fired two more which finished it
off. By some miracle the survivors were sighted by an R.C.A.F. patrol and
24 were brought into Halifax by HMCS *St. Croix* after spending nine days
in lifeboats.[257] It was no surprise when, on 12 May, the Imperial Oil tanks
ran dry and the refinery shut down until a new supply of crude had run the
gauntlet.[258] In order to prevent such events happening again, by war's end,
the storage capacity at Imperoyal was four times larger than at Montreal.[259]

In the desperate early days of the war, the refinery's production, which
had been 3,960,000 barrels a year, was ramped up to a 24-hour-a-day operation, and by 1945 it was putting out 6,850,000 barrels a year. Additionally,
from the tank farms on the hillside above the plant, bunker oil was supplied
in vast quantities, some 25 million barrels, to 10,500 ships — everything
from the *Queen Elizabeth* to corvettes and fairmiles and, of course, huge convoys of freighters. In the early days of the war, the *Iocoma* was transferred
from Montreal to Halifax to handle the job of bunkering these ships. It
never stopped, a mammoth, endless task, back and forth from Eastern
Passage to the Bedford Basin or the Ocean Terminals, trip after trip after
trip, in the days before a convoy set sail. It took seven or eight hours, and
three trips, to bunker the *Queen Mary* with 5,000 tons of fuel.

Supply could well have been a problem in September 1939, for much of
it came from presumably neutral American tankers, which strictly, speaking,
should not have engaged in supplying Britain and Canada with war
matériel. This detail was, however, taken care of by a top-secret agreement
known as "Operation Shuttle," which saw American tankers hauling oil
from the Caribbean to Eastern Passage. It was delivered to five 80,000

barrel tanks, rented to the British Petroleum Board. Whatever they suspected, officially the tanker captains did not know that. This subterfuge became unnecessary after December 1941, but to improve the flow from "the Shuttle" the British government built seven more storage tanks of 100,000 capacity each, along with two docks and associated pump houses and lines. This expansion required the demolition of the 1860s Fort Clarence, site of a gun battery since the establishment of Halifax and Dartmouth and acquired by Imperial in 1927.[260] By the time it was all over, "the Shuttle" had transported over 33 million barrels of oil and oil products through the Imperoyal facilities.

The Germans, who must surely have been aware of this activity and many other flagrant violations of the laws of neutrality, had their revenge in 1942 in the havoc they wrought among the American east coast tanker fleet, which the American authorities unwisely left unprotected and exposed to the wolf packs for months. The Germans had other, more subtle tactics as well. On a number of occasions, the R.C.M.P. called in Imperial Oil technicians who confirmed their suspicions of sabotage by identifying soap and sugar in the fuel and lubricants of ships' engines.

Refueling ships was not the only concern of the refinery. Since 1928 it had been producing aviation fuel, not only for the tiny R.C.A.F. operation located a stone's throw away, but also occasionally for such notables as Charles Lindbergh and Amelia Earhart, and, more regularly, from 1938 on, for the big Pan American Clipper flying boats on their transatlantic leap between Newfoundland and Foynes, Ireland. In addition to fuel supplied to the army and navy, millions of litres of aircraft fuel and lubricants were sent around the Atlantic Provinces from Imperoyal aboard tankers, such as the *Icolite*. Fully loaded the tanker carried 21,000 barrels of petroleum products and during these years the crew of 26 had an average age of 25, the oldest, 33, the youngest, 16.[261]

OTHER INDUSTRIAL CAPACITY — MOIRS

Probably the only local industry that had a prominent national and international profile was Moirs Chocolates, whose large factory, under the right conditions of wind and weather, enveloped the neighbouring Grand Parade, City Hall and St. Paul's Church in a fragrant embrace. Marginal to the war effort in an industrial sense, it nevertheless maintained an important role in the harder-to-define realm of public morale.

Moirs Limited was a major employer, with 900 workers, a large proportion of them women in the downtown plant, but a higher proportion of men in its Bedford operation. The latter facility was a substantial and self-sufficient operation, generating its own electrical power from Paper Mill and Kearney Lakes, and cutting its own wood from its hinterland of lakes and forests behind the town. Here the chocolate was made, refined, blended and stored until needed downtown, and here a sawmill and shook mill made shooks and wooden boxes for its own purposes, as well as general sale. Wartime brought with it serious shortages and, eventually, quotas of most of its raw materials. The problem was not so much from enemy control of the sources. It was, for example, able to replace cocoa butter formerly supplied by Holland and Germany, and walnuts supplied from France.[262] The problems came from losses of supply ships to U-boat attack, and the diversion of shipping to more essential purposes, problems all domestic industries faced.

During the war candy, and chocolate in particular, was seen as a luxury, and restrictions on raw materials made it hard to get. By December 1942 sugar supply was reduced to 70 percent of the previous year and both cocoa and honey were in short supply, and much of that was being devoted to the manufacture of Christmas cakes. Moirs did not suffer, however, because there were no restrictions on the manufacture of chocolate bars destined for the military, and production of these was enormous.[263] By 1943 even going directly to Moirs Halifax store did not guarantee success. A shopper wanting to stock up for Christmas might find only empty showcases with none of the company's famous "Pot of Gold" line and no fancy seasonal boxes. Twice a day, if the patient consumer was there at the right time, a few one-pound boxes were brought down to the retail store. When those were gone, that was it until the next day.[264] Dorothy Brackett, who moved from Sydney in the spring of 1940, worked on the chocolate line during the war. Moirs was a good place to work and employees got along well with each other. She remembers that one Christmas one of the floor supervisors, who kept things moving in the different departments, met her as she was leaving the plant to head back to Sydney for Christmas and, very much under cover, gave her a whole box of "Bonbons" to take home to her family as a treat.[265] Among those one might think most affected, the young, scarcity even of chocolate was just one of those things to accept. Donald Purchase recalls that he could get one chocolate bar a week, and he never felt hard done by.

OTHER INDUSTRIAL CAPACITY — BRANDRAM-HENDERSON

The national paint company Brandram-Henderson Limited operated its Halifax Paint Factory on the cotton factory siding at Kempt Road and Young Street. It supplied only the Maritimes and looked after the rest of Canada from other factories in Montreal and Vancouver.[266] Having a paint factory did Halifax little good during the war because none of the paint stayed. Paint was a restricted commodity in the civilian world, a fact painfully evident and often commented upon by transients when they passed through the increasingly shabby and depressed-looking wooden buildings of the city.

OTHER INDUSTRIAL CAPACITY — CLAYTON'S AND MURPHY'S

From its vast assemblage of buildings at nearby Barrington and Jacob Streets, Clayton & Sons clothing factory began to hum under the capable if somewhat reluctant direction of Louise Clayton. Capital provided by a Montreal investor enabled the company to take on military clothing contracts with new or refurbished machinery.[267] Miss Clayton wisely focused much of her effort on the family's extensive real-estate holdings, and while the clothing firm survived the war by only ten years, entering into bankruptcy in 1955, she had cleared off years of accumulated mortgages on other properties in time to take advantage of the post-war expansion in to the suburbs.[268]

J. & M. Murphy Ltd., long famous for their work clothes — "Murphy-Made" and "Strong As An Elephant"— manufactured by its subsidiary, Murphy's Limited, expanded operations in 1940, just before growing restrictions made such a move impossible. It purchased and remodelled the Taylor Shoe building at Brunswick and Duke, installing new and up-to-date machinery, putting it in a good position to cope with the burgeoning demand. Joseph Murphy echoed the sentiments of many private-sector employers who suddenly found themselves facing the wage competition of the expanding government sector. He complained to an unsympathetic Angus L. Macdonald that he had to compete with HMC Dockyard, which was paying seamstresses $22 per week against his $12 to $15.[269]

OTHER INDUSTRIAL CAPACITY — DARTMOUTH ROPEWORKS

And as the Royal Canadian Navy ballooned, over in Dartmouth the "rope works" found itself turning out as much cordage as it could handle. Established in 1868 as the Dartmouth Ropeworks during the heyday of Nova Scotia's sailing fleet, it was taken over in 1938 by the Plymouth Cordage Company of Plymouth, Mass. At war's beginning the traditional manual method of making rope by twisting the fibres in the echoing length of a ropewalk was still in place, along with the traditional natural raw materials, mostly manila hemp. Both were replaced after war's end by mechanization and artificial fibres, but in 1939 and 1940 it was a crisis when the Japanese seizure of the Philippines cut off the supply of manila. Just as the R.C.N. was beginning its major expansion, and the merchant navies of the world began to crowd into the harbour, the company had to cope with severe government conservation measures until alternatives, abaca from Central America and hemp from the United States, could be brought online.[270]

OTHER INDUSTRIAL CAPACITY — CANADIAN NATIONAL RAILWAY

Industrial in theory but not in practice were the maintenance facilities of the Canadian National Railways on Windsor Street. The eastern terminus of the company's Canadian system, the facilities were capable of modest repairs to locomotives and cars, but the Moncton shops, established by the Intercolonial Railway 60 years before, undertook all major repairs.

CONCLUSION

Although the population of Halifax jumped dramatically during the war, the influx of workers was in the military and service sectors, not the industrial. Few new industries came to town and most of those that did were temporary branches of firms headquartered elsewhere, such as Anglin-Norcross, Canadian Allis Chalmers, or the Montreal engineering firm of Porters. By and large, existing firms simply expanded to fit the new realities.

In 1939 Halifax had 87 "industrial establishments," employing 10,000 workers. Dartmouth had 11, employing 1,120. By 1942 the number of employees had grown to 12,000 in Halifax and 1,400 in Dartmouth. By the following year, with only one more industrial establishment listed in the city directory, employment figures reached their wartime peak of 15,000 in Halifax and 1,500 in Dartmouth.[271]

Although the relief at the end of restrictions and shortages was palpable when peace came in August 1945, women workers soon found themselves back in the kitchen or the nursery or earning women's wages in retail. Men still in industry, or returning soldiers, saw the plentiful wartime overtime evaporate, and contracts for new work suddenly resumed the old familiar pattern of distant prospects and pre-election goodies. Halifax's mini-industrial boom was over as quickly as it began.

CHAPTER FIVE:

Day by Day

Halifax was a crowded place during the war and, in many ways, life returned to the basics of previous generations. For children, the focus outside home was school, as it always was, but with war-related extracurricular activities. For civilian adults, outside of work, the horizons of their social life resembled that of their grandparents. The automobile, a growing influence despite the Depression, disappeared and it was back to walking or the tram. Rationing made entertainment difficult and restaurants were crowded. Professional entertainment was limited to the radio or the movies. War-related activities, inspired by duty and patriotism, took up much of the slack. For women, this activity meant making inroads in the working world. With marriage, women were expected to dedicate their time to housekeeping and children, but with forays into volunteer work and the labour force, an increasing number began to defy convention and bring home a salary of their own. For men, the Air Raid Patrol, the street-level component of Civil Defence, provided an absorbing focus. For the armed forces stationed in Halifax there was little for the young men in the prime of life to do when on leave. Halifax tried its best, out of all proportion to its size; but not until the end of the war was in sight did military authorities awaken to the maxim, " The Devil makes work for idle hands," and begin to organize athletic and social activities that provided an alternative to the street.

CIVILIAN LIFE — YOUTH

For the city's youth, wartime life was exciting in a way it has not been since. The routine of regular school work was supplemented by activities under the heading of current events. Updates on the progress of the war and lessons in the geography of Europe and the Pacific enlivened classes. Children were encouraged to bring clippings and keep scrapbooks. Those with fathers at sea or the front took a deep interest in these subjects.

Although the likelihood of a Stuka dive-bombing the city, or a Messerschmitt ME battling it out overhead with a Hurricane or Spitfire, became remote as the war progressed, had one appeared, a crescendo of piping voices from schoolyards would have provided more advance warning and identification than any new-fangled radar set because aircraft recognition was a skill that school children of every age learned, just in case.

Boys were mandated to belong to a cadet corps of one of the services, organized in virtually every school. For Donald Purchase, in 1939 an elementary pupil at Richmond School, this meant the thrill of army cadets and rifle practice. When he arrived at Queen Elizabeth High School (Q.E.H.) and joined the air cadets, it meant the excitement of visits to the R.C.A.F. station at Dartmouth, where they were taken on a flight in a Digby bomber on at least one occasion.

Cadets quickly became a regular and required subject on the school curriculum for older boys, and at Q.E.H., all three services were represented. Army Cadets were a detachment of the 35th High School Cadet Battalion, Royal Canadian Artillery, one squad at Q.E.H. the other at Saint Patrick's High School. Friday afternoon at the Armouries was the regular drill period and during the winter they were given additional training in small arms, physical education and marksmanship. Special Wednesday afternoon lectures provided the fundamentals of basic training, map reading and internal combustion engines. Sea cadets were members of the Drake Division of the Nelson Sea Cadet Corps. They drilled at Stadacona Friday evenings, while Saturday mornings at the Navy gymnasium were given to physical education and special classes in subjects such as the Naval Code of Signals, operation of a 4-inch gun and seamanship. During the summer they operated the North West Arm Patrol out of the Waegwoltic Clubs whose resident manager, George V. Guy, happened also to be their commander.[272] At Q.E.H., air cadets were members of # 250 Squadron Air Cadets. At Dartmouth High School, 110 boys joined the # 18 Dartmouth Squadron, their School Board paying half the cost of their uniforms. In Halifax the Air Cadets also met on Wednesday and Friday afternoons with drill and physical education. Their turn at the Armouries rifle range was on Wednesday afternoons. Friday-afternoon lectures focused on navigation, service familiarization, progress of the war and aircraft recognition. The Dartmouth boys had a similar schedule, plus their own rifle range in the basement of Findlay School.[273]

Don Munro, a Grade 12 student, wrote in 1945, "... the average cadet ... realizes that the war against the Axis powers is far from won and hopes that the training he will receive in the cadets, ... may give him a suitable background when he takes up arms against the enemy. Already this year a number of our cadets have enlisted and found their cadet training of great benefit to them."[274]

For those really keen the opportunity was there after January 1943, when 17-year-olds, with parental permission, could join the regular army, but not active service for another year. Once he hit 18, a young man was promised grants to continue his education, extended the next year to cover university.[275] By that autumn, the R.C.A.F. was offering to take any physically and mentally fit 17-year-old, irrespective of his education, and turn him into an airman.[276]

Cadets for girls was still far in the future, so while the boys were off on drill, the girls spent their time at the Red Cross or other volunteer projects. Most schools had Red Cross auxiliaries, and the groups adopted specific goals to raise money for the organization.

Reflecting the population explosion, schools were crowded in the lower grades. Some classrooms were enlarged by taking out the cloakroom wall. Fifty pupils to a room was common, an often unnerving experience for children transferring from small country schools.[277] Joyce Ripley went to a three-room elementary school in Rockingham on the city outskirts with no indoor plumbing, only an outhouse. There were ten grades, Primary to Nine, with five grades in each room. One teacher was Protestant, the other Roman Catholic. For 10 to 15 minutes each morning, the students would shift to the room with the teacher of the correct denomination, regardless of age or grade, for daily religious exercises. Then they would go back into their grades and the day's learning would begin.[278]

The amalgamation of the two Halifax Protestant high schools, Bloomfield and the Halifax Academy by 1942, left Q.E.H. and Saint Patrick's as the only available high schools on the west side of the harbour, with Dartmouth High School newly relocated to the Greenvale building, on the east side. Suburban students were expected to commute or board. When Joyce Ripley graduated from Rockingham elementary school, she and other students took Pender's Bus to Q.E.H. It was a 20 minute trip and they were dropped off at the Willow Tree intersection en route to its terminus on Doyle Street. A weekly pass was $1.25 and the driver punched it for each trip. Sometimes he forgot and that meant a free ride some other time.[279] Many male teachers of military age, and later some of the women, joined up, which led to the recall of many former teachers from retirement. Despite the scarcity of teachers, however, the Halifax School Board stuck to its guns; once married a woman could not teach unless she became a widow. Still, change was in the air. When one of its teachers married during the Christmas holidays in 1941, her offer to finish out the term was gratefully accepted by the Dartmouth Board. Only a couple of years before the Board would have expected her letter of resignation as soon as the wedding register was signed.[280]

In an era when many considered going beyond Grade 6 was icing on the educational cake, during the Depression many youths remained in school because there was not much else to do. But as soon as opportunities in the military or the working world began to open up, youths, especially boys, disappeared into the armed forces or labour force. In contrast to the elementary grades, in high school the situation only got worse as the war progressed. When faced with the choice of classroom study or adventure and excitement in military service, for many a boy it was no choice at all. Many too young to join up were also lured away to mediocre (and illegal) jobs at a dollar a week such as bicycle delivery boys. In Dartmouth, a School Board census in 1940 discovered that although the town's population had jumped, the school population, particularly the high school, had dropped.[281]

Enthusiastic teachers might insist that pupils come in at 8:30 rather than

9:00 a.m. and use the extra time to sell war savings stamps, whose sales charts might feature a "Sink the German submarine" poster, which could be accomplished by selling enough stamps to fill in all the stars. Classes competed to collect the most and largest lumpy balls of string and shiny balls of foil from gum and cigarette packages. War also meant "air raid drills," an exciting innovation which meant occasional breaks from routine, as students were trained to exit their classrooms in a calm and orderly fashion and head to a shelter area. In Dartmouth, the School Board Commissioners toured all the schools in November 1939 and selected the safest room in each as the official shelter.[282]

Volunteer work was encouraged and youthful obsessions were redirected from cowboys and Indians to wartime exploits. The school focus on aircraft recognition was translated into building model Spitfires, Mosquitos, Lancasters, B 17s and B 25s. Ten- and eleven-year-olds discussed and argued aircraft gunnery, ranges of bombers and fuel consumption, Thompson sub-machine guns, bazookas, tanks and regimental crests.[283]

The war was taken very seriously by the young because everyone knew someone overseas. A knock on the classroom door could mean that a father had been lost at sea or over Germany. Margaret Louise Potter, a grade 10 student at Q.E.H. wrote "War Poem of 1944":

> Five years of battle; soon we see the close ...
> Prayers still to sigh as thoughts go back to those ...
> The 'Ottawa", the 'Valleyfield', and more,
> They died a gallant death in this ... our war
>
> ....
>
> Look to the hills and find your comfort there,
> Look to the sky, and greater works prepare,
> Call to the world in not unhappy pride,
> There is your light; In vain they have not died.[284]

In 1943 Bruce Knight, a Halifax businessman, offered the Knight Trophy for an annual hockey competition between Kings County Academy (K.C.A.) in Kentville and Queen Elizabeth High. Both the game and the train trip to each others' communities quickly became the event of the year for the two schools. On Friday, 23 February 1944, 250 Q.E.H. students boarded five reserved cars on a Dominion Atlantic train at 3:40 p.m. and for the next three-and-a-half hours sang songs, played cards and snacked on apples and candy provided by the Home and School Association, while the daring few smoked forbidden cigars in the vestibule. Arriving in Kentville at 7:20 p.m. was just the beginning. The horde of students invaded every food joint on the way to the arena where K.C.A. beat Q.E.H. and clinched the series for that year. There was still the big dance and the return train trip, to be met by parents in the early morning, the regret of their loss on the ice tempered by the thrill of "unessential" travel.[285]

The jitterbug and jive were the parentally disapproved of dances of the day. Joe Levison, a Grade 11 student new to the technique, reluctantly found himself at a school dance infested by "jitter beetles," where, he says, some Amazon grabbed him and he was "flipped from the floor and flung around through the ozone ... in breath-taking style. From time to time collision appeared in the offing as I flew in between, under and over couples indulging in the same sport, and with hands over my eyes and wind whistling in my ears, gray hairs in profusion sprouted in my scalp."[286]

High-school students of the day were considered young adults, most of whom, on leaving Grade 12, if they had not done so already, embarked on an adult working career, very probably with the armed forces. It was another decade before Marlon Brando defined the "generation gap" and "youth" became a culture of its own. Therefore it did not set off any alarm bells when a group of them got together, rented space on Isleville Street, and organized a dance hall of their own, "The Caper Club" (i.e., capering about).

For the still relatively few who went to university, life went on, but not quite the same as before. Roman Catholic students were divided by sex, with girls going to Mount Saint Vincent College under the jurisdiction of the Sisters of Charity and a safe distance from the temptations of the city, overlooking Bedford Basin in Rockingham. Some 300 men went to Saint Mary's College on Windsor Street at Quinpool, which was in a state of flux. Until 1940 it was run by the Christian Brothers of Ireland, who were well-liked by the students; but relations with Archbishop John T. McNally were cool, he being of the opinion that the cost was too much for the meagre scholarly results. Accordingly, the Brothers were replaced by the Jesuits of Upper Canada and land was purchased at Gorsebrook for a new campus, for which planning, but no development, continued during the war.[287]

The campus of Dalhousie University, which incorporated the Anglican University of King's College, was heavily compromised by the war. The entire campus of King's was sequestered by the R.C.N., its students and faculty exiled to pass their days in forced ecumenism with the United Church at its theological college, Pine Hill, on the North West Arm. The navy took over King's lock, stock and chapel to serve out the War as HMCS Kings, an officer's training school. The Red Cross announced in December 1940 that in the event of an emergency, it would requisition Shirreff Hall, the women's residence. In the summer of 1942 the Canadian Women's Army Corps indeed took it over, but returned it in time for the autumn term, cleaner, it was said, than it had ever been. The Dalhousie gymnasium, one of the few in town, was heavily used by the armed forces, 24 hours a week by HMCS Kings alone. The medical and dental schools, in the early days of the war, were major resources for military doctors until their own corps was built up. The Public Heath Clinic, funded by the Rockefeller Foundation and by Dalhousie as a component of its medical school, was essentially the city's out-patient department, and it struggled to cope with the VD load from the navy, the merchant marine and their civilian partners.

University staff were prime targets for secondment. Two members of the Physics department were seconded for degaussing work and never reappeared for the duration. By 1944–1945, 19 faculty members had been seconded for government work of one kind or another, which created a national problem of such dimensions that the presidents of McGill and Queen's suggested that faculties of law, humanities and social sciences be shut down entirely.

This recruitment had an effect on enrollment, which dropped by 25.5 percent by autumn 1942, with a concomitant drop of $50,000 in student fees, no small item in the budget of any institution. Male university students received a deferment of military service as long as they were enrolled, but from the fall term in 1940 until January 1945, all physically fit males were required to put in 110 hours of training in a campus military unit, plus spend two weeks at training camp.[288] By the fall 1942 term failure at the

Christmas exams brought with it automatic eligibility for military service, although the university retained the right to have final say on academic standing. Dalhousie came out the other end of the war with 650 students. With the beginning of first semester in September 1945, that enrollment doubled with the arrival of the first of the government-funded servicemen.

In the Roman Catholic colleges, men and women were literally miles apart, and even at Dalhousie interaction between men and women was regulated. Although they took classes together, study in the Macdonald Library was carefully controlled, with men on the east end of the main hall and girls on the west end and never the twain met if the librarians on duty had anything to do with it. Social life survived the separation, however, and there were dances and good times. Shirreff Hall was the focus of much social activity and, war or not, formal dresses and tuxedos were still the norm at dances. Callow university males suffered in comparison to servicemen, whose uniforms, better manners and broader experience made them more interesting. The year 1941 saw Dalhousie's first "sweater queen," Susan Morse, who, with other girls managed to look good in spite of the disappearance of silk stockings, then nylons, and were left with the only available replacement, lisle. One Shirreff Hall girl moaned, "The same thing happens to girls who wear lisle stockings as it does to girls who wear black woolen stockings — Nothing!"

University education was a much more intimate experience than it became later. J.R. Malloy remembers the civil and charming presence of the President, Carleton Stanley, and in that vanished era freshmen students would often be invited by Mrs. Stanley for tea.[289]

CIVILIAN LIFE — ADULTS

Adults had a good time, too, despite shortages and overcrowding. Since everyone was in the same boat, most people were prepared to make the best of it.

Commercial entertainment focused on movies. Halifax had nine theatres, seating 7,400. Dartmouth had two theatres, with 1,380 seats.[290] At the top of the heap was the Capitol on Barrington at the foot of Spring Garden Road, a movie palace of the first rank, whose patrons began to enjoy its mediaeval splendour on 31 October 1930 when it featured George Arliss in

Old English.[291] It might have seemed an appalling time to open a lavish movie palace, but the Capitol was selling dreams, not reality, and the Great Depression presented no threat. It and the city's other movie theatres went flat out during the war years, and although there was rarely an empty seat, they complained bitterly when the government slapped a ten-cent entertainment tax on every ticket. In their high school years, Donald Purchase and his friends got jobs as ushers at the Capitol. They had a neat uniform with a pill box hat, a red jacket and blue pants, and worked every few days. The theatre was always full and there was always a lineup, which ran along the front of the building and down Blowers Street. Movie-goers did not make a point of arriving on time for the beginning of the show, but came and went on their own schedule. Accordingly, Purchase and his fellow ushers constantly patrolled the theatre looking for empty seats and when they found one or two or three, went to the line, called out the number of seats and the location and asked if anyone wanted them. If there were only two separated seats, a husband and wife often took them; but, he said, a couple on a date always wanted to sit together.

Most theatres had a daily matinee, as well as evening shows. Given the lack of alternatives, it was a popular way to relax, and not just singles or couples, but whole groups of friends got together for a night at the movies, the way later generations congregate at the pub. The films changed like clockwork twice a week, but never on Sunday, with the first run shows going to the Capitol and the Orpheus (later the Paramount) on Barrington, or the Casino on Gottingen Street, with the Gaiety and the Empire further down the pecking order picking up the re-runs and the B grade double bills. Most of the movies featured worlds far away from the reality of Halifax, but at least once the city took pride of place, shared with the movie star Randolph Scott. *K225*, released in October 1943, was the story of a corvette based in Halifax, and residents were thrilled to recognize the Dockyard, HMCS Kings and Bedford Basin.[292]

Radio, in Halifax, meant CBA, the national network of the Canadian Broadcasting Corporation, and the local CHNS, (broadcasting from old Saint Andrews Church on Tobin Street newly remodelled as up-to-date studios), plus the BBC's "London Calling." Clear enough, for a powerful radio set, to supply daily newspaper programme listings, were WEAF (NBC network, New York), WJZ (Blue network, Newark), WABC (Columbia network, New York), WOR, (Mutual network, New York), plus a multitude of other American stations, drifting down from the ionosphere on to the long-wave band as night descended.

Radio, less than two decades old and still an amazing technological novelty, brought war news right into people's homes, rain or shine, winter or summer. One of the most popular programmes featured interviews with servicemen overseas, and families listened faithfully, hoping against hope to hear a husband, father or son say hello from Britain or Europe and thereby assure them that, yes, he was still alive. For a wife living in some seedy room, with a husband away at sea, radio was a godsend.[293]

This liberating aspect did not pass unnoticed. John Fisher saw radio, and no doubt himself, as a great emancipator, particularly of the hitherto isolated housewife:

> Radio in my opinion is quietly and slowly revolutionizing
> society... it has done more than the car and the electric
> light — for radio has offered an escape to the average
> woman — What is the implication of all this? It means that
> the vision of women is being widened every day — every
> year — in time what will that mean? Over the years ...
> women are bound to take a greater interest in fields associ-
> ated with men — with television around the corner — with
> static-less radio [FM] already a fact — we are just begin-
> ning to see one of the greatest changes in our way of
> living.[294]

Within a year of that 1941 prophecy, W.C. Borrett, Managing Director of CHNS advised his accountant that because so many men had been lost to the services, "It will be necessary for the trained female members of our staff to replace men in certain phases of the senior work of the Station." Nancy Forrest and a Miss Carter were promoted to the announcing staff, thus introducing the radio audience to the female voice in an official and authoritative role.[295]

Radio, like the movies, tended to put a positive spin on wartime issues when dealt with in the daytime soap operas or evening variety shows. The American comedy standbys, "Jack Benny show," "Charlie McCarthy" and

"Fibber McGee and Molly," were hugely popular, but there were a number of Canadian-made dramas which also caught the public imagination. Casual conversations often revolved around the trials and tribulations of the crew of an R.C.A.F. Lancaster bomber in "L for Lankie," as they fought their way through the skies over Germany on missions to bomb the factories of the Rhineland.[296]

CHNS, on the air for 16 hours a day, produced three hours a day of local programming, including not only long-standing radio auctions for various charities, but also, now that the war was on, the regular weekly army show "On Parade," the air force show "Wings Over Canada" and the navy show "Hearts of Oak," all featuring a variety of the talent that had found a temporary home here, as well as their establishment bands. The talent that could not make it into the studio was recorded for broadcast by a "Special Events and Remote Control" truck, which visited outlying camps and sites. Other wartime shows on CHNS included special Victory Loan features during campaigns, a Norwegian Hour and a weekly broadcast by the Hugh Mills Concert Party Division. Programmes carried over from more peaceful days were weekly interpretation of the news by Dr. H.L. Stewart of Dalhousie University, a Children's Quiz sponsored by Farmers Dairy, a weekly drama CHNS Playhouse, historical "Tales Told Under The Old Town Clock" and the always popular Dick Fry on the Hammond organ.[297]

War news, intoned in Lorne Greene's bass voice on the CBC's nightly news, or direct from London by Matthew Halton, or, for the late night listeners by Edward R. Murrow from New York, was a staple for all ages. So too were warnings against saboteurs, fifth columnists and spies, against whose activities constant vigilance was urged. There was also music. For the first time a listener could hear live music without leaving home just by flicking a switch and twisting a dial. Every few weeks the radio featured new catchy American hit tunes and the big band sound was everywhere, with Glen Miller or Harry James orchestras from America, or perhaps Mart Kenney and the Western Gentlemen from Canada. Some music was escapist: "That Old Black Magic" and "Chattanooga Choo-Choo." But some of it, with a sentimental bent, was war related: "There'll Be Blue Birds Over the White Cliffs of Dover" and "When Johnny Comes

Marching Home."[298]

Some of the big bands (Tommy Dorsey, Lionel Hampton and Mart Kenney) actually came to Halifax. Usually the Forum (the Navy League Forum for the duration) was their venue. Mart Kenney appeared in April 1943, along with singers Art Hallman and Judy Richardson, who were backed up by a quartet and could have been seen and heard for 55 cents, or $1.50 if you wanted one of the 1,200 dancing tickets.[299] It was the same old story for any such event, more lineups, a mile long and four deep.[300] Less crowded were the Sunday afternoon concerts at the Public Gardens featuring one of the many military bands attached to the army, navy or air force.

Regular dances took place at the Nova Scotian Hotel for the gentry. For the hoi polloi dancehalls, which had not existed before the war, began to appear: the Silver Slipper on Barrington just south of Cornwallis Street in 1941, the Roseland Dance Hall on Cogswell just west of Gottingen in 1942, and in Dartmouth, 1943 saw the appearance of the Cinderella Dance Hall on Commercial Street near the Dartmouth Slips. While Marjorie Whitelaw recalled them fondly, some evenings of dancing and laughter were bittersweet, mixed with thoughts of partners who never returned from an Atlantic crossing.[301] And truth to tell, though the bands at these dances were lively, they could be uneven. Orchestrations of popular tunes were impossible to get, and band members, a mixture of civilian and military, came and went constantly as duty called.[302]

The peculiar Halifax liquor problem was the uninvited guest at every one of these dances. There was no way it was not going to be on hand even though the law forbade it. It seemed to be the woman's role to slip a bottle into her purse which, once opened of course, had to be consumed. Sometimes it meant a roaring good time, sometimes it meant a brawl. Simply because a dance was held at the Nova Scotian, frequented by officers and their dates, was no guarantee of genteel behaviour. During the summer of 1942 the supper dances at the Nova Scotian were suspended, ostensibly because of the hot weather and scarcity of help, but really, it was said, because they were getting too rowdy. Supper dances were reintroduced in early September, though management had cut out the supper. The reinstated dances were inaugurated by a fight between army officers in civilian clothes and a woman was carried out with two black eyes.[303] Helen

Creighton felt that it hardly seemed worthwhile for a girl to fuss over her appearance because once the fights started, nobody cared what she looked like.[304]

Given that the supply of local young men had been diminished, the availability of "come from away" replacements in snappy uniforms was a heaven-sent opportunity for the local girls. It was important, however, not to seem too eager. Margaret Chase recalled that in order not to encourage loose living, organizers of dances and parties made it easiest for "engaged" couples to get in. So Margaret and her friends became "engaged" almost every week so as to enjoy to the full the wartime social round.[305] Highly desirable in this situation of scarce resources were invitations to dances at Admiralty House to meet midshipmen or other eligible young officers of visiting ships.

Halifax had no local professional theatre, but stage shows came through town on occasion, some of them the professional variety put on by the army or navy as morale boosters and recruiting devices. Hugely popular were the occasional visits of stars such as Gracie Fields, who wowed audiences at the end of September 1940, and the equally professional New York based "Marcus Show," featuring good music, stand up comics and lots of pretty girls with long lovely legs.

Most of the time, ordinary Haligonians depended on the home-grown variety, especially if they did not have entrée to one of the Concert Party shows. One such local production was hosted on an outdoor stage at the Dingle by the boys of St. Patrick's Home on Mumford Road. Music, singing, dancing, tumbling, acrobatics and step dancing were enjoyed from a blanket spread out on the grass, or from the water by those with boats or canoes.[306]

More serious war-related distractions for the home-front citizenry was the organizing of the population for civil defence, wartime fund-raising and salvage campaigns. In spite of the grim rationale for these activities, they involved more social interaction that kept adults and children busy and replaced peacetime diversions such as drives in the country and summers at the cottage.

CIVIL DEFENCE

In November 1940 the population was warned:

> ... that there is a possibility that the enemy may some day
> endeavor to cripple Canada's war effort in an attack on the
> port of Halifax. It might be by sabotage, bombing from the
> air, shelling from naval vessels, or even an attempt to land
> troops. Should an emergency arise, every man and woman
> of the civilian population will have their part to play. You
> will remember how Hitler's invasion of Poland, France and
> Belgium was greatly helped by the fact that the population
> was taken by surprise — they did not know what to do in
> an emergency. As a result they crowded the streets and
> roads with traffic and prevented the armed forces who
> might have accomplished something, from doing their
> task.[307]

It was certainly not going to happen here. From the beginning of the war the citizenry was mobilized to deal with the effects of enemy attack and civil emergency. The Civil Defence Directorate for Halifax was under the direction of the mayor, who was in turn responsible to the Provincial Minister of Health, Dr. F.R. Davis, and linked directly with the army's Fortress Commander and the Anti-Aircraft Operations Room. The Directorate was responsible for the civilian population during any military action, including an evacuation of the city.

It comprised about 4,500 men and 1,500 women, incorporating wardens, fire-watchers, auxiliary police and firemen, doctors, nurses, first aid workers, reserve squads, decontamination squads, demolition and clearance crews, as well as groups dealing with telephone cable and radio communications, gas, electric and public utilities (workers, drivers, messengers), and in an emergency, the entire Red Cross organization.[308] There was even a brand new ambulance presented to the Saint John Ambulance Brigade by the American Consul in February 1942 and donated by the British American Ambulance Corps of New York City.[309]

The most visible component of Civil Defence were the Air Raid Patrol

(A.R.P.) wardens, who were neighbourhood based. Every male householder was encouraged to join the local patrol, which was based in a "hut" in a centrally located spot. The huts stored firefighting equipment, which initially might be no more than stirrup pumps and buckets, but by the end of the war could include gasoline-powered pumps and proper hoses. Dartmouth was small enough that the A.R.P. from the beginning, in October 1939, held its Monday night meetings in the assembly hall of Dartmouth High School and stored its emergency fire equipment at Victoria School.[310] At the end of the war, this equipment was returned to the War Assets Disposal Corporation, though many smaller communities were allowed to keep what for them was the first proper fire fighting equipment they ever had. In every part of the "East Coast Port," the neighbourhood A.R.P. hut provided a social focus for men in the same way as volunteer work in huts and canteens engaged women.

A.R.P. wardens patrolled the streets during a black out, shooed the curious back into their homes, and looked for chinks of light that might guide a Stuka bomber into a screaming dive over Almon Street or Connaught Avenue, if not the Dockyard or Imperoyal. They were also tasked to see that every household in these neighbourhoods of wooden houses had at least a bucket of sand ready and waiting to douse incendiary bombs, or even better, their own stirrup pump. Failure to have this basic equipment could leave the householder open to a fine of $100 or three months in jail.[311]

A.R.P. wardens were discouraged from using the telephone during an air raid and used either a messenger, usually a boy on a bicycle, or, for basic communication, a whistle code. One long blast called a policeman, a long and a short called another warden, a long and two shorts called a messenger, and a long and three shorts called a fire watcher. Two short blasts meant that a passing car must stop, three blasts and it could carry on.[312]

Eleven-year-old Robert MacNeil, consumed with envy at the sight of an A.R.P. messenger friend's casually flaunted steel helmet, lived to move up from Cubs to the Boy Scouts. That object attained just before his twelfth birthday, he was now eligible to join the Halifax Civilian Emergency Corps (H.C.E.C), which he promptly did. On two evenings a week he trained in the Saint John's Ambulance First Aid course and, on passing, he became a first aid messenger. Finally, he was issued his heart's desire, a steel helmet, along with a gas mask and a white H.C.E.C. armband. Immensely proud of his new responsibility, he would, if necessary get up at night and get dressed, when the air-raid siren at Inglis and South Park Streets went off, and pedal off alone on his bike into the unlit dark to his mustering station at Pine Hill Divinity Hall.[313] Youngsters like Robert took their A.R.P. responsibilities seriously. Called in to duty at the huge Piercy's fire on 9 September 1944, the youths of A.R.P. Platoon #9 were credited with saving the adjoining premises of John T. Bottomley Woodworking Company by forming a bucket brigade that kept the building roof from catching fire. A grateful Mr. Bottomley threw them a Christmas party that December with all the trimmings wartime restrictions allowed.[314]

Blackout regulations were first issued in February 1942, although the first application occurred the evening of 19 September 1939, and they were thereafter compulsory.[315] Unlike in Britain, blackout was not a permanent feature of every night in every town, and was only fully implemented when the sirens sounded for a practice. Nevertheless, all outdoor electric signs were forbidden between sunset and sunrise, and all light sources, exclusive of motor cars, were to be invisible from the sky. Street lights, for example, were shaded so that their light focused downward. Occupied buildings, whether homes or offices, could have lights on as normal outside of air-raid practice, but unoccupied buildings, with no one around to turn the lights off if necessary, could not without written permission. During an air-raid practice, casual use of the telephone was discouraged to keep the lines open for emergency use.[316]

It was not necessary to black out every window in the house, a major job since it involved fitting special black-out material, heavy blankets or sheets of Beaverboard into the window opening to keep light in and flying glass and debris out. All that was necessary was to designate one room as a "refuge" or "blackout" room, ideally the kitchen since it had food, heat, water and an exit. People were urged to resist the impulse to turn out the lights and watch the action, whether real or simulated, as they would not only be better protected, but sitting in the dark for long periods once the "fun" wore off was bad for morale.[317] After the initial enthusiasm, or genuine expectation, of an attack evaporated, few people went to that sort of trouble. The regular air-raid and blackout practices themselves were short, never much longer than half-an-hour, and the novelty of putting all that stuff up just to take it right down again wore off very quickly. Compared to Britain, regulations were lax. Compared to the rest of Canada, they were stringent, and sometimes it was hard to motivate people. Office workers went home and left lights on in downtown buildings. H.B. Jefferson commented sourly that the practice of 16 July 1942, was the worst for months: "There were at least 25 big lights visible from the [post office] Tower including Leed's Store, Roy Building, Halifax Hotel, National Fish, Maritime Towing and many others." Nevertheless, the papers "printed the usual fatuous official statements that the blackout was very efficient."[318] It would seem that the rest of Canada took this less seriously than the East Coast Port, for Halifax's mayor had to remind the organizers of a planned coast-to-coast Victory Loan campaign chain of beacon fires that Halifax and area could not participate because of the blackout regulations.[319]

In order to keep everyone sharp, to train A.R.P. wardens and the general population, simulated attacks and disasters were from time to time added to regular blackout practices. Sometimes it was a real showstopper. On the evening of 21 June 1943, as part of A.R.P. Week, formations of fighters, bombers and flying boats roared over the city in a simulated attack and defence, with dogfights and aerial pursuits filling the sky thrilling the watchers below, who had seen exactly the same thing in newsreels of the Battle of Britain. As dusk fell, the searchlights came on and their pencil beams probed the sky until they had pinned an enemy in the glow of their shaft. Just after 10 p.m., the entire city was blacked out and magnesium flares were dropped, explosions simulated bombs and fires were started around the streets which the A.R.P. wardens then put out.[320] Technically, everyone should have been huddled in their blacked-out kitchens, but there was no chance of that.

In January 1942 the Roy Building was "bombed." Traffic was halted on Barrington Street and two trucks, loaned with their drivers by Cousins Laundry and Dry-cleaning, rushed up to the front and unloaded Auxiliary Police, who sealed the entrances. The injured were brought down from the second and third floors and whisked away to a clinic. The emergency over, the volunteers formed up and marched to the Police Station to dissect their performance.[321]

In May of that same year, during a blackout drill, the Red Cross mobilized according to their emergency plan, sending nearly 700 workers to 70 hospitals, relief stations and depots around the city, all of which had been designated as assembly points by the Red Cross Civilian Emergency Organization.[322]

In the event of an actual air raid, residents of the "East Coast Port" were pretty much on their own in terms of shelters. Indeed, there were only two, finished in July 1942 by Foundation Maritime and both at the entrance to their wharf on Water Street. Because the high water table at that location guaranteed inundation of any underground structure by a spring tide, they were above ground, but the Foundation said proudly that they were so strongly built as to be proof against anything the Luftwaffe could throw at them.[323] For everyone else the kitchen had to do.

It was an indication of coming victory when the Department of Health issued revised blackout regulations in December 1944. Although it was still forbidden to have lights on in unattended buildings after dark, other lights, indoor and outdoor, could now stay on, so long as someone was around who could turn them off in the event of an emergency.[324]

By then it seemed that it was time to relax, put away the helmets and stirrup pumps and say goodbye to the A.R.P. hut on the corner. With the collapse of Germany in May, and Japan clearly on the ropes, such precautions could surely be put to bed. But no, not just yet.

FUNDRAISING AND SALVAGE

The "East Coast Port," like the rest of the country, was awash in Victory Loan parades, War Savings Stamp campaigns and salvage drives.

The Government of Canada, through an intensive publicity campaign, was remarkably successful in persuading Canadians to invest the "excess profits" of their personal wartime prosperity in the prospect of "jam tomorrow," not "jam today." Since this "voluntary" saving represented 48 percent of the government's annual income, success was vital to the war effort.[325] What with taxation, Canadians financed a significant portion of the country's part in World War II from their own resources, so that in 1945 Canada owed scarcely a nickel to foreign bondholders.

It helped that between rationing and outright unavailability, many big-ticket items were off the market entirely, but Canadians in their millions bought into the idea that saving now would build up a nest egg to give a couple a head start when Johnny came marching home. Surprisingly enough, that is just about what happened.

The first "War Loan" (soon to become "Victory Loan") campaign was launched in January 1940, with the final one in April 1945. They were in effect Government of Canada savings bonds which could be purchased outright, but more often through payroll deduction plans at work or at the bank. Like any government bond, once bought, it could be redeemed for cash, but naturally, there was heavy pressure to hold on to them until they matured. The 4th Victory Loan, for example, came in two groups: the long term, maturing 1 May 1957, paid interest at 3 percent and came in denominations of $50, $100, $500, $1000, $5,000, and $25,000; the short term, maturing 1 November 1946, paid interest at 1 3/4 percent and came in much larger denominations of $1,000, $5,000, $25,000 and $100,000.[326] A Victory Bond could be purchased at any time, but the launch of each new issue was heralded by a massive publicity campaign.

Huge parades of all available armed forces in Halifax were a feature of each Victory Loan campaign. Bonds might be given away over the radio in a promotion scheme that, for example, saw a householder picked at random from the telephone book. While the city listened with bated breath, somewhere a telephone rang, and the excited householder was asked a question about the war. If the answer was right, they were the winners of a bond in the days when a hundred dollars was a lot of money.[327] On one occasion, tragedy followed the two winners of a Victory Bond Campaign at the Clark Ruse aircraft plant in Eastern Passage. Their prize was a flight over the harbour in a Hudson Bomber. On 3 December 1942, they took off from the R.C.A.F. Station. Circling Point Pleasant Park the plane was overtaken by a sudden snow squall, the pilot lost his orientation and plunged into the water just off the breakwater south of the Ocean Terminals. There were no survivors.[328]

Just because the military was the recipient of the benefits of Victory Bonds, that did not mean that it was immune from campaign solicitations. Ships in port at the right, or wrong, time competed with each other for the largest total sales, and the winning ship got a flag of honour while the loser·

had to fly a pennant known as the "Royal Raspberry."[329]

Print campaigns were not subtle. The 2nd War Loan told purchasers, "They Lend Their *Lives* — You Lend Your *Money*."[330] Next June, mothers, wives and sweethearts were reminded that their menfolk should be urged to buy bonds because German bombers in occupied France were less than ten hours away[331] (a little hyperbole). "God Forbid," purchasers were told in 1942, that "your Canada should ever come under the heel of a ruthless barbarism, where babies are born to be the future shock troops, or the mothers of a brutal, military race."[332]

Less intense, because it was ubiquitous, was the campaign for War Savings Stamps. These could be purchased for 25 cents each and came in eight war-or military-themed designs. Each stamp was pasted in a book holding sixteen, a total of $4.00, which was then mailed postage-free to the War Savings Committee in Ottawa. Back came a War Savings Certificate, redeemable for $5.00 in a sunlit future without Adolf Hitler. In the third week of February 1943, during one of many sales campaigns, Nova Scotians bought $21,693.50 worth of stamps.[333]

Because of their small value, stamps were, as they were intended to be, popular among school children, and also sold well in grocery stores, where customers were persuaded to take their change in stamps instead of coin. Patriotic grocers would set up competitions among cashiers of who could sell the most stamps, or shoppers who bought them could put their names in a hat for a War Savings Certificate or a $5.00 box of groceries.[334] In 1943 hairdressing and beauty salons were added to the target group. With the aid of patriotic volunteers, "Miss Canada girls" in white aprons and R.C.A.F.-style wedge caps, "an effort will be made never to allow a patron to leave the premises without buying at least one stamp." At Dartmouth High School, every class had a War Saving Stamp representative whose job was to sell as many stamps as possible to fellow students in a weekly blitz and encouraged their fellows to learn the War Savings Stamp song, to the tune of "Tramp, Tramp, Tramp":

> In the school room as I sit,
> Thinking, soldier brave, of you,
> And the thunder of the guns across the sea,

How I want to do my bit,

When my lessons all are through.

And to help you fight to keep our country free !

Chorus

Stamp, stamp, stamps that we are buying

Fill up folders one by one.

Soon we'll have enough to get

Bomb or tank or trim corvette,

And our savings will put Hitler on the run.[335]

The amounts were not insignificant. In 1944 and 1945 stamp campaigns in the Dartmouth schools raised over $20,000 in each year, enough to warrant the naming of two Harvard training aircraft "Spirit of Dartmouth" I and II.[336]

Salvage campaigns were also community focused and leaned heavily on the school system for volunteer collectors. A Salvage Committee was formed in Halifax on 6 March 1941, made up of the representatives of the city's junk dealers, the Boy Scouts and Girl Guides, the I.O.D.E., the Women's Council, and various service clubs such as Kinsmen and Lions.[337]

They began in earnest in the spring of 1941 when shortages of essential materials began to bite. Paper and metal were obvious, but bones and rags, householders were told, were also "Your War Weapons" to "clean out and clean up on Hitler!"[338] Those holding onto aluminium cookware were reminded that 7,700 pans went into each Spitfire.[339] Surplus paper was needed to wrap detonation charges in land mines, serve as wadding in cartridges, or to be turned into shipping cartons for shells, gas masks, munitions, field telephones, shell casings and so on.[340] Fat drippings from the morning's bacon or Sunday's roast, along with bones, went into the manufacture of light explosives and could be taken back to the butcher who bought them at a stated price. The patriotic individual then turned this money over to the local salvage committee or some war charity, or else gave the stuff to the salvage committee collectors in the first place. Rubber was added to the list in the spring of 1942, when Japan's seizure of Malaysia and the Dutch East Indies put rubber plantations out of reach. Before long, domed snap fasteners, easily mangled by a washing machine, unfortunately replaced elastic waistbands on underwear, and the use of an inner tube, an essential component of any day at the beach, became unpatriotic.

"Oh," said John Fisher, host of the CHNS radio show "Noontime Melodies," "if only I could look around when I come in to your home every morning on the radio, I'll bet I could make you feel very sheepish, because there must be just dozens and dozens of articles around your home that you could give to the salvage campaign."[341]

Building on that sort of daily pressure, massive campaigns were organized to galvanize the citizenry to clean out their homes. A five-day blitz in September 1943 began with a parade of army trucks and bren-gun carriers, which later helped collect the spoils. These vehicles led the scores of children who were the collectors in the campaign.[342] School children were critical to the success of these campaigns given that the classroom was a good place to mobilize their natural enthusiasm, and they were ideally placed to locate and collect salvage material from the home and nag reluctant parents into submission.

There were questions, however, as to how worthwhile much of the scrap collecting was in Nova Scotia. Because of the lack of serious war industry, the proceeds of the frequent drives were shipped on a heavily overloaded rail system to central Canada. Despite the emotional appeals, as freight it had low priority. Even the Salvage Committee had mixed feelings, wondering how much was actually useable after their overwhelmingly successful campaigns. Even with Sydney Steel so close, iron, the most obvious collectible, did not pay enough for the commercial junk men to collect, sort and ship. Many fine Victorian cast iron fences and ornamental ironwork were sacrificed and Helen Creighton speculated that much of what they went to all the trouble to collect in the end would have to be thrown away.[343]

HOSPITALITY — HOSTELS, CANTEENS AND HUTS

Citizens of the "East Coast Port" had another wartime responsibility which, to their credit, most of them embraced to a degree that was unknown and unappreciated in the rest of the country. With the beginning of the war, they began to play host to thousands of men, and later women, who passed through and stayed in the city.

DAY BY DAY

Because of the serious overcrowding in housing, restaurants and theatres, life spilled out on to the streets, where if the weather was decent, it stayed for good or for ill. For all those who could not find permanent housing, the backup was a myriad of canteens, huts or hostels sponsored by religious and social agencies, aimed principally but not entirely at the armed services and staffed largely by local volunteers. To its credit, Halifax bent over backwards to establish and staff these temporary facilities, which began to spring up almost as soon as war was declared. Here servicemen or merchant seamen got a sandwich, a cup of coffee and a piece of pie and had a chat with a member of the opposite sex who was not out to seduce or fleece him. Nearly every downtown church congregation sponsored some sort of coffee hour or hospitality after Sunday services so that servicemen could meet members of their own denomination no matter how far from home. National service organizations, such as the Red Cross, the Salvation Army, the Canadian Legion and the Knights of Columbus, dotted the harbour-side streets with their facilities.

The Dominion Government soon realized that lack of coordination and a potential for infighting could cause more harm than good and established the National War Services Advisory Board in June 1940, as an arm of the Department of National War Services. A year later, in June 1941, it took on the responsibility for ensuring that all charitable organizations registered and were working on behalf of the war effort, and assumed oversight of all other volunteer war-relief efforts.

The need for basic support was recognized as soon as naval personnel began to pour off Royal Navy ships in the autumn of 1939. A group of officers' wives coordinated by Mrs. Janet McEuan, wife of a naval medical officer, persuaded the vestry of Saint Mark's Church at Gottingen and Russell Streets to lend their church hall. Here these women set up the North End Servicemen's Canteen with naval ratings in mind. It opened on 14 October 1939, just six weeks after the war began, with a $100 advance from the R.C.N. to stock a dry canteen with chocolate bars and cigarettes. Initially, it focused on entertainment, providing billiards, cards, ping-pong and, soon, by popular request, dances, which were held on Tuesdays, Thursdays and Saturdays. Men got in free but girls paid a dime. The dances were so successful that eventually the floor collapsed under the load.

When rebuilt the tariff for the girls had gone up to a quarter, Canadian servicemen paid a dime and visiting sailors got in free.

The next request from the men was for a meal service. Once arranged, this took off dramatically and became one of the main features of the canteen. French sailors, whose pay was minimal, were subsidized and over the 1939 Christmas season 5,000 of them visited the facility. Clearly, the Saint Mark's Hall could not handle the crowds and that winter operations were moved to a larger facility on Barrington Street. From there, cook Mrs. Annie Henneberry served, in a two year period, 400,000 hot meals at 25 cents each, not including sandwiches to order, an astonishing logistical feat when one considers the vagaries of rationing and general shortages. At Christmas the dinner was free.

In 1944 the North End Canteen had 130 volunteer workers and a paid staff of eight, plus a Master at Arms, Ernest Bradfield, who kept order, though generally the men policed themselves, and from time to time a small group could be seen quietly escorting a rambunctious colleague out the door.[344]

Joyce Ripley and some of her friends, high school students, volunteered some of their free time while the boys were in cadets. They walked down from Q.E.H. after classes to work in the dining room, a big hall with long tables running the length of it, with a large kitchen along the side and a jukebox going all the time. The cooks, paid staff, produced the meals that Joyce and her friends served through wickets, mostly to naval ratings, but they never went to the dances, too "fast" no doubt for high-school girls.[345] In Dartmouth, a similar facility, sponsored by the R.C.A.F.'s Eastern Air Command, was built in the autumn of 1940 on the vacant School Board property next to the post office at King and Queen Streets. Here women volunteers of the Air Force Wives Association and the I.O.D.E. provided hospitality.[346]

The North End Servicemen's Canteen was a local effort, but most of the canteens and hostels were sponsored by national organizations with access to large reserves of capital donated by patriotic citizens across the country. The Y.M.C.A.'s Barrington Street building, which had the city's only swimming pool, had been for years perfectly adequate, like so much of the local infrastructure. With the arrival of thousands of servicemen, however, it was soon overwhelmed. Not only was the building jammed, but the R.C.A.F. frequently commandeered the pool for air-sea rescue training. Accordingly, in the fall of 1939 the Y took over the Halifax Ladies' College on Barrington Street, opposite the Y.W.C.A. building. It was remodelled and opened in December by Governor General Lord Tweedsmuir and quickly became the Y's largest Canadian operation. Staffed by a pool of 150 volunteers, it provided servicemen with a reading room, showers, accommodation, evening concerts, movies and, before gas rationing took its toll, drives to Truro, Lunenburg or the Annapolis Valley. A "Mothers' Corner" repaired clothes, sewed on badges and offered a willing ear for those who wanted one. By the summer of 1940, just six months after it opened, over 150,000 servicemen had passed through its halls.[347]

The Y also assigned supervisors to look after the harbour forts and outposts, the R.C.N. establishments at HMCS *Scotian* in the Dockyard, and, while it managed the convoys, HMS *Seaborn*. There were also branches at the R.C.A.F. embarkation depot, # 1 Y Depot (after December 1944, HMCS *Peregrine*) and at R.C.A.F. Dartmouth. It ran three summer camps for armed forces personnel at the former Y.M.C.A. "Camp Owen" in St. Margaret's Bay, the nearby "Camp Sunshine," formerly operated by the *Chronicle* for needy children, and the *Herald's* equivalent, "Rainbow Haven" at Cow Bay.[348]

In the autumn of 1940 the Canadian Legion War Services took over the Knights of Columbus hall at 65 Hollis Street and converted it into a servicemen's hostel. Shortages of matériel caused delays and, concerned by the approach of winter and the prospect of scores of shivering seamen clustered at Halifax street corners for lack of a place to go, the I.O.D.E. got involved, raised money and provided creature comforts. Despite the pressure from the I.O.D.E. to open sooner, the facility did not open until 26 March 1941 at least officially, with great ceremony as "Canadian Legion Atlantic House."[349]

Charlotte Akerlund did her first stint of volunteer work at the Salvation Army canteen at Blowers and Argyle Streets. It was a dingy sort of place at the beginning but later moved to better quarters. In those early days they served nothing but bacon, eggs and toast and the smell of grease was so pervasive that when she got home her mother would make her change her clothes before she could come inside.[350]

HOSPITALITY — THE AJAX CLUB

By 1939 the boozy free-for-all that had been nineteenth-century Halifax was a faded memory. For a time, supported by the patriotic fervour of World War I, the provincial government had flirted with total prohibition of alcohol; but as elsewhere, this course seemed to cause more problems than it solved. By 1930 alcohol could be purchased for personal consumption in stores run by the Nova Scotia Liquor Commission. This freedom was carefully hedged with regulations and restrictions intended to ensure that the consumer indulged this vice with as much guilt and inconvenience as possible. However, neither public nor police took the regulations seriously and ignored or enforced them at their convenience. Since alcohol was for private consumption only, there were no licensed establishments where one could drink in public, whether pubs, bars or restaurants. Private clubs were permitted a bar and a bartender, but could serve alcohol only to an individual and from his personal stock kept under lock and key. If you had a bottle in the car, you were required to prove, if stopped, that you were on your way directly home from the liquor store, the only place where it could be consumed. It was for your consumption only and could not be shared with anyone, not even your spouse. If the bottle in the car was open, the driver was liable to be arrested.

There was a powerful temperance lobby, which held the optimistic belief that if alcohol was not available, people would not want it. This lobby felt that even the existing regulations were licentious, and with the declaration of war urged the government to reinstate prohibition. Headed by the United Church, this lobby met the Prime Minister 12 September 1942 to press their case.[351] They rejoiced in December 1942, when the Prime Minister, who had said he supported their arguments 100 percent, announced not only a ban on liquor advertising for the duration of the war, but also a reduction in supply amounting to 10 percent for beer, 20 percent for wine and 30 percent for spirits. The alcohol content of spirits was reduced by 30 percent, and provincial governments were urged to shorten the hours during which alcohol could be sold.[352] When the Nova Scotia government ordered the closure of all liquor stores on Saturday, temperance advocates brushed aside comments that the only ones rejoicing, aside from themselves, were the bootleggers whose business would surely flourish in the drought.[353]

Once the flood of servicemen, particularly those on ships from overseas, started to arrive in the city, the restrictive liquor regulations created a huge problem. It was not so much of an issue for the officer class, who had access to wardrooms or standing invitations to the 30 private clubs in the city; but for the enlisted man, say a Royal Navy rating familiar with British pub culture or a French matelot accustomed to the fleshpots of Marseilles, Halifax was a nasty shock. They could legally buy a bottle at the liquor store, and they did; but since there was nowhere to drink it but the street, on a bench or in a doorway, they did that, too.

Charlotte Akerlund's father worked at the law courts as an interpreter for the foreign seamen who frequently found themselves before a magistrate facing liquor law charges which they found difficult to comprehend. Frequent clients were Norwegian seamen who had been arrested for public drinking. They had bought the regulation liquor permit and assumed that it was permission to drink, as well as to buy liquor, which was unfortunately, and to their bewilderment, not the case.

Dorothy Sangster, in town from "wicked" Montreal as late as the autumn of 1944, was shocked at her first sight of soldiers, sailors and airmen publicly drunk in the streets. Why, she naively asked, at first, did they not do their drinking in a hotel or a bar? Since there were none, and since it was forbidden to carry an open bottle of liquor, "the boys bought the liquor from the liquor commission, dodged into a back alley, drank the whole bottle in one gulp, and lurched out into the street again. The Halifax people to whom I spoke concerning this were indignant. 'Disgusting!' they said. But they had absolutely no understanding of the problem. Very smugly they said that 'Wicked Montreal might have its bars and taverns, but thank God we haven't sunk that low in Halifax.'"[354]

The other option, which the more opportunistic in the spirit of free enterprise were prepared to adopt, was the "speakeasy," the illegal bar, convenient for the waterfront, usually just a room or two with a few tables serving expensive and dubious booze of sometimes indeterminate origin. Along with the speakeasy went all kinds of illegal and immoral opportunities, which were exploited to the full and which provided a whole generation of transient servicemen with their only memory of Halifax.

Although everybody in law enforcement and the court system shook their heads over the liquor laws, they felt that all they could do was shrug their shoulders and soldier on. From time to time, the city police, in cooperation with the military and the R.C.M.P., would send a soldier with marked money into a known bootlegger, then when the transaction was complete, swoop down, arrest the supplier and confiscate his stock.[355] These occasional forays were necessary for the entertainment and morale of the forces of law and order, but they did little to cramp the style or the free enterprise instincts of their victims, who in all likelihood wrote it off as a necessary business expense.

When the inevitable abuses hit the streets of Halifax, the obvious solution for some was to ban the stuff entirely. Others took a more realistic view. Recognizing that reformation of the liquor laws was probably out of the question, a reasonable solution was to provide a place other than the street where a man could have a drink in a comfortable, decent environment. This was obvious enough that Mrs. Janet McEuan of the North End Canteen had no trouble galvanizing public and institutional support to provide just such a place.

Sufficient funds were raised first to rent, then buy, the vacant Odell House at the corner of Tobin and Queen Streets, a fine large mansion with a large garden, ideal for the purpose and vacant since the last member of the Odell family died in 1938. The ground was carefully prepared; the Liquor Commission was brought on side and Admiral Bonham-Carter was able to win the support of Fort Massey United Church, on the opposite corner of Tobin and Queen. Named the Ajax Club, after the Royal Navy ship which had just distinguished itself in the Battle of the River Plate, it was managed under the charter of the "Inter-Allied Hospitality and Food Fund Board." The facility was opened officially and to general acclaim on 14 December 1941 by Sir Gerald Campbell, United Kingdom High Commissioner, with a benediction by Anglican Archbishop John Hackenley. It had already provided a welcome haven for 50 of the surviving crew of HMS *Jervis Bay* and their Swedish rescuers, after their famous action in November with KM *Admiral Scheer*.

The Ajax Club was comfortably outfitted to take full advantage of the building's long history as a fine private home. Good furniture was provided by many donors and the fixtures were given by leading Canadian firms and industries. Meals were served and the bar, licensed for beer only, dispensed a maximum of five bottles at 25 cents each. Like most of the other hostels, there were facilities for reading and writing letters, and in summer the garden provided an extra attraction on nice days. The general consensus was that the Club was well and carefully run, the only untoward incident occurring when the garden wall was stormed by some Water Street prostitutes, determined to roust out "their" clientele.[356]

It was all too good to last, however. Temperance and prohibition advocates were upset at this evidence of moral decay. They had friends in high places, particularly in the offices of the Prime Minister and the Premier. The catalyst was the arrival of a new minister at Fort Massey, a man of sterner principle than his predecessor. In early 1942 the Kirk Session of the church, to the surprise and consternation of most people, including members of the congregation which included the treasurer of the Ajax Club, petitioned the Liquor Commission to cancel the Club's license on the grounds that it had become a nuisance. There was an outpouring of support for the Club. A statement by the Chief of Police declared that the only two clubs to which his men had never been called were the Halifax Club and the Ajax Club.[357] It became an uproar of national proportions. Nevertheless, the Kirk Session, sustained by the righteousness of its cause and its own significant public support, would not budge.

Supporters of the Session pointed to the conjunction of the general availability of liquor with the many allied reverses of which, in this difficult year, the newspapers were full: France had fallen, Singapore had fallen and the American fleet at Pearl Harbor had been caught napping and paid the price; it was common knowledge that these were all places where liquor was readily available. All that was required to remove the desire for alcohol was to make it unavailable and Allied victory would be assured. The argument that the Session had not protested the establishment of a flourishing brothel and speakeasy across Queen Street was of no consequence.[358]

Under heavy political pressure, the Liquor Commission refused all appeals to renew the beer license. The Club, heavily dependent on the income generated by the three cent return on empty beer bottles, closed, finally, on 23 February 1942. Not surprisingly, as temperance advocates rejoiced, so too did bootleggers and prostitutes at the prospect of the return of their old clientele.

With no other option, the somewhat disillusioned Mrs. McEuan and her colleagues fought off the Department of National War Services, which played the role of *éminence grise* to the Kirk Session in a way which did neither any credit. The department had coolly assumed that Odell House was now theirs and although they were forced to back down, they issued the final legal *coup de grâce* to close the club. McEuan, however, sold the building to the Norwegian Government-in-Exile on 1 May, and moved on to, among other things, establish the Ajax Hospitality Headquarters. The Ajax Club venture had produced a profit and at war's end Mrs. McEuan established a scholarship fund with the monies still in hand.

The Norwegian Government reopened the house as a hostel for men of the Norwegian merchant marine and in no time at all was selling schnapps to its sailors with nary a peep of opposition from across the road.

The problem of the Ajax Club and its advocates seems to have been their relative powerless status as private individuals and, it must be said, women. The fact that a few local women had established and run a successful organization on such a scale upset, it was said, some large national organizations, which felt that their jurisdictions had been invaded.[359]

The debacle was played out on a national stage with Halifax cast in the main role, either hero or hick depending upon your position on the evils of liquor. Where was wartime censorship when you really needed it? If national exposure was not enough, the 9 March 1942 issue of *Time* magazine allowed an even wider audience to smirk at the antics in an "East Coat Port." Most Haligonians kept their own counsel, but almost immediately after the war was over, new legislation permitted the establishment of taverns, suggesting that a process of rethinking had gone on beneath the surface. In the meantime, since the navy had a long collective memory, there would be a heavy price to pay when the time came.

One national organization, not necessarily a villain, stepped into the breach. The Navy League, whose members had some grasp of the reality of the situation, took over the reconstruction of the recently destroyed

Wanderers Grounds clubhouse. On 1 August 1942, just months after the closure of the Ajax Club, the new Navy League Club House, restricted to naval personnel, opened in the presence of no less a personage than Babe Ruth. Despite having two bars, one for ratings and the other for petty officers, there was not a peep about its effect on the war effort. The Navy League Club was surrounded by the open space of the Wanderers Grounds, the Public Gardens, City Field, Camp Hill Cemetery and Citadel Hill, a quarantine zone large enough to protect small children and, thereby, one supposes, mollify the guardians of the city's morals.

ALLIED SEAMAN'S CLUB

None of these clubs and related facilities was open to merchant seamen, who could be almost as numerous as their military counterparts. There was a clear division, as far as the services were concerned, between the military and civilian, and however warm and welcoming the greeting was at one of the service canteens or hostels, it did not apply to civilians of any stripe. With the institution of the convoy system, however, it was evident that even if the merchant seaman was not surrounded by the same heroic aura of his naval equivalent the need for support was as great. With great fanfare in December 1941, the Navy League of Canada opened a fine new facility on Hollis Street, the Allied Merchant Seamen's Club, a replacement for a seriously inadequate predecessor, the "Sailors' Home." Large and comfortable, the new building had reading and writing rooms, a lobby with two fireplaces, a 500-seat concert hall, a recreation room large enough for 200, as well as sleeping and eating facilities.[360] Charlotte Akerlund volunteered at the canteen. She found it very nicely fitted out and felt the quality of the food was very good. Volunteers helped out with setting tables, cleaning up, etc., but the paid staff served the food because it was felt the volunteers would be too generous with the portions. When she worked after dark, Akerlund's parents picked her up after her shift.[361]

The Club immediately became a busy and a lively place and for whitebread Halifax presented an astonishing array of nationalities: the usual assortment of Europeans, exotic enough, was spiced up with Chinese, Indians and West Indians, who came and went in numbers never seen before the war. Unless she could present seagoing credentials, no woman

other than volunteer could pass through its doors. John Fisher described it
to his national radio audience as a home for "men of many tongues and
colours; from defiant China and enslaved Greece — tousled blond
Norsemen, proud Scotsmen and men from John Bull's island. Yes, and there
are the fighting French, the Americans, the Dutch, the Poles, the
Newfoundlanders, the neutral Latins from below the Rio-Grande, the
Spaniards, the Portuguese. They all mix here in this Hostel, given to them
by the Navy League of Canada. Here in this friendly atmosphere international rivalries are forgotten."[362]

H.B. Jefferson was a little more candid in describing a typical scene:

> At the ASC quite a number of drunks were rambling
> about and "T" [Clifford Taylor, manager] says they have a
> dormitory set aside where they put these fellows at night so
> that they won't interfere with anybody but themselves. I
> was all through the kitchen, cafeteria, dormitories, writing
> rooms, reading rooms, etc., and also the bar room, in the
> basement floor where at least 400 men were gathered in a
> room as big as an average High School assembly hall, sit-
> ting around little tables, drinking beer. The bar itself is
> only about ten feet long and completely enclosed, with a
> steel grating which can be let down quickly over the serv-
> ing counter. There are no waiters or waitresses, but there
> are 4 bar tenders, 2 selling at the counter and 2 replenish-
> ing from the refrigerator, a large room where the beer is
> chilled to forty degrees. They sell all kinds that they can get
> but Labatt's appears to be the most popular as I heard two
> or three sailors taking it in preference to other brands
> although it was still warm, having just come in. T says that
> the amount of battling in the home and around the streets
> is increasing but that it shows no signs of developing to riot
> proportions. They now have 11 policemen on the premises,
> working in 3 shifts — a Chief and ten men. Most of the
> sailors sitting around the beer room today seem to be quiet,
> honest fellows, but T says the looks of some of them are

highly deceptive and that they are all better than average as fighters.[363]

The canteens and hostels fulfilled a need that was immediately obvious to citizens the moment the government began to dump thousands of servicemen into their midst without any apparent concern for the problems it would cause. It quickly became apparent that there were other gaps in the military support system where civilians could make a difference. One of these gaps was in the supply of "comforts" to servicemen in their sometimes cloistered life on duty for King and Country.

OTHER AGENCIES

Not all efforts focused on local facilities for local charity. The Atlantic War Fund Club was set up by 25 Halifax ladies who ran a "nearly new" shop out of Mills Brothers on Spring Garden Road, which raised enough money to support 17 mobile canteens in Britain.[364]

Janet McEuen, that woman of boundless energy, set about organizing the hospitable impulses of fellow citizens. In 1942, not deterred by the Ajax Club debacle, she formed the Ajax Hospitality Headquarters to look after a specific group of soldiers whose plight had caught her eye: gunners, usually British, sometimes very young, who were old enough to enlist but not thought old enough to be thrust into the maelstrom of battle. They had been assigned to man the "ack-ack" guns installed on merchant ships, the DEMS, which were spotted throughout convoys, though this posting seemed just as stressful as any of the alternatives. The gunners were, however, isolated from the formal and informal support systems of the regular army and found Halifax a lonely place. To keep them more or less "safe" she organized a network of households in Chester, Musquodoboit Harbour, Shubenacadie, Sheet Harbour, Port Williams and Hantsport to take them in while in port. Sixteen families in Hantsport alone provided a home base for 2,000 men. It was immensely successful, even if the local girls were warned not to take anything said or promised too seriously.[365]

The Central Magazine Depot was organized by another group of Halifax women soon after the war began. Its mandate was vast and all-encompassing: to distribute magazines, solicited from all over Canada, to naval ships and establishments, to army posts along the coast, in Newfoundland, Labrador and Iceland, to troop transports and merchant ships. These women built up a network of "suppliers" across Canada and the United States, who sent in used magazines: from New York, for example, the British Sailors Book and Relief Fund, the Maple Leaf Fund and the Canadian Women's Club; from Canada, service clubs such as the I.O.D.E., Kiwanis, Kinsmen, the Navy League and local groups such as the Queen Mary Club of Charlottetown and the Sailors Rifle Club of Port Colborne scoured their members and communities. The railways shipped them free to Halifax and from a freight shed on a wharf an indefatigable band of about 70 women sorted and boxed the endless piles of reading material to be sent down to HMC Dockyard and then into a lighter heading out to the anchored merchant ships in Bedford Basin, or onto the back of an army truck heading out to some coastal battery. By June 1942 they had distributed 4,000,000 magazines as well as 30,000 packs of cards and other small comforts. Next to the Red Cross, the Central Magazine Depot created and handled the largest volume of freight of any volunteer Canadian war organization.[366]

Volunteers were essential to these operations and because women were still a small part of the labour force, they were the major pool of workers. Some were single volunteers, but many were married and maintained a household as well. In Halifax, the principal service organizations were the Women's War Work and the Halifax Hospital Visiting Committees of the Red Cross Society, the International Order of Daughters of the Empire, the Women's Institutes, the Halifax Club of Business and Professional Women and the Y.W.C.A. Shift work was just as common for volunteers as for paid workers and besides working in the canteens and hostels, they knitted socks, scarves, mitts, balaclavas and sweaters by the boatload, a job that got harder as the quality of wool deteriorated. They organized canteens, arranged blood-donor drives, sold Victory Bonds and War Savings Stamps, held clothing drives and raised cash. For sailors from warmer climes, who suddenly found themselves facing the North Atlantic, they made leather vests.

The Red Cross Women's War Work Committee provided supplies for the hospital ship *Lady Nelson* and the Hospital Visiting Committee took all five military hospitals under their wing and brought in cigarettes, tobacco, fruit, ice cream and other delicacies. For their part, Dartmouth's HMS Alderney Chapter of the I.O.D.E. adopted the Marine Ward of the Halifax Infirmary and sponsored a hugely successful War Savings Stamps campaign at Findlay School and in July 1941 co-operated in opening the Dartmouth Service Centre on the site of the old Central School, next to the main post office. Here, the I.O.D.E. and servicemen's wives did their level best to create a homey atmosphere and at the regular dances held there many a Dartmouth girl met her future husband.[367] On and on it went. Because of their background, the Halifax Business and Professional Women's Club was frequently consulted by government when it sounded out public opinion. Virtually all of the organizations, comprising perhaps one third of all Canadian women, were "price watchers" for the Wartime Prices and Trade Board, noting price infractions in stores and reporting scarcities, a role, it is said, that was crucial in keeping inflation to a minimum during the war.[368]

The preponderance of women volunteers prompted the Department of National War Services to form a Women's Volunteer Service Centre in 1943, with offices in the Victory Loan headquarters on Barrington Street. The purpose was to coordinate the offers of volunteers and encourage new ones to supplement the flagging efforts of those who had been in the field since the beginning. The centre handled requests for help from the ten service clubs, provided volunteers for the Red Cross blood collection service, registered and coordinated 200 knitters, supplied typists and clerical workers where needed and co-sponsored, with the Boy Scouts, a bottle depot.[369]

Although most of these efforts met a genuine need, a few were more well-meaning than useful. In December 1940, anticipating a Christmas rush of servicemen on leave, the Canadian Legion War Services converted one half of the floor space of the Armouries on North Park into accommodation for 500 men. It shut down in mid-January after only three men had used it since it opened on 23 December.[370] In November 1940 the I.O.D.E., feeling that the needs of naval officers were being neglected, approached the Waegwoltic Club at the foot of Coburg Road, which agreed to open its clubhouse in the afternoon as a place where these men could find a "refined" place for a cup of tea, a game of cards and a chat with members of the I.O.D.E. From here, it was assumed, they would be invited into homes and introduced around. This place was however, not the cup of tea that battle-weary naval officers were looking for, and after three weeks of dismal attendance the venture was wound up.[371]

Halifax also hosted hostels sponsored by various foreign national groups for their own servicemen. The Australians and New Zealanders, for example, opened Australian and New Zealand Army Corps (ANZAC) in July 1941 at Barrington and Buckingham Streets.[372]

Although their countries were occupied, some foreign nationals maintained a distinct presence in the merchant marine and in branches of their own armed forces. That presence was large enough in August 1941 that Princess Juliana opened a hostel on Bishop Street, just an ordinary house whose downstairs middle class living and dining room became rec room, dining room and reading room, run by a Mr. and Mrs. Roda, for the men of the Netherlands navy, stationed or in transient in the city. Crown Prince Olav performed the same service for his countrymen when he re-opened the Ajax Club as a hostel for Norwegian sailors. The Norwegians also fitted up their own hospital and church.[373]

THE HALIFAX CONCERT PARTY GUILD

During the interwar years, a tradition of amateur performances developed in Halifax. It was a time when vaudeville was still a familiar, if dying, commercial enterprise but the concept carried on into the war, with many amateur groups volunteering time and talent to help fill the spare time of the garrison amateur theatricals thrived. Portia White, the internationally known contralto, got her start in the public performances that her father sponsored at the Casino Theatre to raise money for his pastoral charge, Cornwallis Street Baptist Church. Portia, whose first public recital was held in June 1939, moved onto a wider stage with the moral and financial support of the Halifax Ladies Musical Club and private individuals like Jean Mills, but before she left Halifax she made her radio debut on a 19 April 1940 broadcast from the Y.M.C.A. hostel, singing "A City Called Heaven." By the end of the year she was a regular at the weekly concerts given at the Knights of Columbus hall on Barrington Street.[374] The younger members of the family formed the White Quartette and performed regularly for the troops in Halifax.

DAY BY DAY

In 1933 Hugh Mills, owner of the Spring Garden Road department store, was a spark plug in the establishment of the Theatre Arts Guild, the standard bearer for amateur theatre in Nova Scotia. His radio voice, "Uncle Mel," was familiar to every child within range of the signal of CHNS. Mills, in partnership with his wife Jean and sister Gertrude, realized that entertainment had a role to play in maintaining morale among the masses of troops garrisoning the city's defences. They were far from alone in this belief. On the national front, so overwhelming was the desire to make some sort of contribution to entertaining troops at home and abroad that a coordinating directorate was established within the Department of National War Services before the end of 1939. When it became overburdened in 1942, it was reconstituted as the Joint Organization and Services Committee, taking in six National Services organizations (the Canadian Legion, the Y.M.C.A., the Y.W.C.A., the Salvation Army, the Knights of Columbus and the Navy League) as well as the military. Its aim was to coordinate all volunteer efforts, not just entertainment; but in the latter area it was a component of the Commonwealth Entertainments National Services Association (E.N.S.A.), whose American equivalent was the United Services Organization (U.S.O.).

Wasting no time, and with much public support, in the autumn of 1939 Hugh Mills established the Halifax Concert Party Guild (H.C.P.G), an outgrowth of an old regimental tradition of "Concert Parties" or "Smokers," with roots in the nineteenth century. Leaving the entertainment of troops overseas to national organizations, the H.C.P.G.'s focus was the troops and sailors stationed in the city, either on garrison duty or awaiting deployment either in an army camp, such as Aldershot or Debert, or in training, as in the British Commonwealth Air Training Plan establishment at Stanley, in the many isolated harbour forts or signal stations around the harbour and along the coast, or in ships of the naval or merchant navies sitting out in the stream and waiting for the signal to pass out through the gate and into the Battle of the Atlantic.

Although not unique in Canada, the Halifax Concert Party was an outstanding success due largely to the organizational abilities of the Mills family. Hugh Mills was the magnetic sort who had only to enter a room to be its focus; his gregarious personality and farflung network of contacts drew to the Concert Party a large and willing reservoir of high quality talent. The H.C.P.G. had a stable of over 700 volunteer performers, unlike E.N.S.A. and U.S.O. all volunteers,— singers, dancers, yodelers, magicians, musicians, actors, radio personalities, opera singers and more. Headliners included Abbie Lane, Charlotte Guy, Flora Montgomery, the West Sisters, Andrew Cobb, J. Frank Willis and Murray Westgate. Groups included the Dalhousie Glee Club, the Y.M.C.A. Orpheus Male Choir and the Halifax Herald Harmonica Band.[375] From time to time the local talent was supplemented by volunteers from British battleships in port who maintained shipboard entertainment troupes of professional calibre to divert the minds of their large crews from the grim reality of the Battle of the Atlantic.[376] They put on any kind of show, from a variety performance to a Chinese opera performed by Chinese seamen, to an unlikely favourite with merchant seamen, the opera Marthe by Friedrich von Flotow.

Large staged shows were organized well in advance and held on a regular basis in more or less suitable venues in the big hostels, on board ships, in service hospitals, at outposts, airforce gyms, navy canteens, army centres and every Sunday at the Allied Merchant Seamen's Club.[377] But the norm was the last minute effort, an hour-long show put together on a few hours notice for a few people and featuring, say, a singer, a dancer, an accompanist and a comedian. They were always dressed for the occasion, perhaps in their own evening clothes, perhaps in professional costumes, no matter what the conditions, and ready to belt out popular songs or leave them rolling in the aisles. This was where the Mills and their performers shone. Nothing was impossible. On one occasion for a single Norwegian seaman sick in hospital, two girl accordionists were sent to cheer him on Norway's "Constitution Day."[378] From a little back office in the Spring Garden Road store, Mills put together suitable shows for any given situation, which might be on a ship, in some barracks or the mess hall at Sandwich Battery, at an A.A. battery, at Camp Hill Hospital, Aldershot, Debert or Stanley Airport. Hugh, for all his immense ability, was "high maintenance" and not much into mundane details. His wife and soul mate, Jean "Aunt Mel," kept him organized and on track, and his sister Gertrude spent hours on the telephone dealing with all the workaday necessities that made the magic happen. They were truly the wind beneath his wings. It was Gertrude who contacted the performers, who all had "real" jobs, and made arrangements to collect them and their necessary props, costumes and musical instruments after work — and then did it all over again the next day. They might travel for an hour in one of the Guild's two donated station wagons or the back of an army truck over rutted roads, or climb into a duty boat in January, then up onto the deck of a ship in Bedford Basin on an icy ladder and in high heels. Very often, it might be to some remote outpost to perform in a stuffy room, thick with cigar smoke, where "facilities" for female performers were a problem. Charlotte Guy, always in demand on piano or accordion, recalls performing on two tables set up in the mess room at the Purcell's Cove anti-aircraft battery. A sudden air-raid drill emptied the hall of gunners in seconds, suspending the performance until the all clear sounded ten minutes later when everyone returned and the performance picked up where it left off.[379]

It was all done with élan and despatch. By July 1944 the H.C.P.G. had given over 2,300 shows to half a million men plus a weekly radio show on CHNS. In addition, they organized amateur band concerts which played to audiences totalling another million. Credit is also due to the equally busy but somewhat overshadowed Canadian Legion Theatre Group (Halifax), which put on over 780 performances. Over the same period, in Toronto's Military District 2, 22 groups put on 1,902 shows.

It did not take the Mills long to realize from their frequent contact with the services that there were other needs they were uniquely placed to fill. "Comforts" were the little things above and beyond what military stores might be expected to supply. Irrespective of nationality, Mills saw that ships and military units in transit through Halifax received things that took the hard edge off military life. This could meant curtains, furniture, radios, sewing machines, pianos, piano rolls and jigsaw puzzles. Costumes, spotlights and lighting equipment were supplied to amateur service theatrical outfits such as No. 1 R.C.A.F. Maitland, who put on an opera and minstrel show. Because of Hugh Mills, network of contacts, there was a good chance that some of the costumes were from a Broadway production of past years. Gramophones and records were particularly popular for ships because ordinary radios were not allowed at sea. In 1942, for instance, the Concert Party Guild supplied them to HMS *Manitoulin*, HMCS *Rathlin*, SS *Elm Park*, HMS

Kilhampton, and the hospital ship *Lady Nelson*.[380] Musical instruments were collected from across the country and loaned to ships or to soldiers in an outpost so that they could form a band. Often in port or when the Concert Party visited their fort, they joined in the show. Unbelievably, by the end of the war, the Halifax Concert Party had collected and distributed $11,500,000 worth of goods.

The Halifax Concert Party wound up its efforts by travelling late in 1945 to Britain and occupied Europe under the sponsorship of the Halifax newspapers, the *Herald* and the *Mail*. With the war over, thousands of troops were stuck in barracks awaiting, with varying degrees of patience, space in troopships. The entertainers did much to alleviate the boredom and make the wait more bearable. By winter 1946, when the flow of returning troops through Halifax had ended, the Guild wound down its operations. In a final goodwill gesture, its costume wardrobe was packed up and sent to Norway, recovering from five years of German occupation, where it was cut down into children's clothing.

Many individual Haligonians provided private hospitality, especially in the early years of the war when it was not difficult to do. With the beginning of rationing in 1942, however, food became scarcer. Warm meals, or even sandwiches, served to a visiting serviceman who might in a month or so give his life for King and Country cut no ice with the Rations Board, and much hospitality became a genuine sacrifice.

The Chase family offered to entertain sailors waiting for their ships to sail. Every Friday Mrs. Chase telephoned the committee set up to coordinate such visits. Sometimes as many as six sailors showed up for a hot meal, conversation, some piano and a chance to flirt with the Chase daughters while washing up after dinner. Margaret Chase recalls most of all the bad piano playing and the heady scent of heavy wool uniforms, lived in and perhaps slept in for nine days at sea in crowded quarters.[381] While the hospitality was genuine, it was understood to be "war work." In the somewhat stratified world of the Halifax Chase family, having crew members, even from HMS *Revenge*, did not mean lower standards. Chase recalls that once the weekend hospitality was over, social life returned to its normal limits.

Every family reacted in its own way. Some were never comfortable crossing class lines. Others adapted readily to the new social realities. While out hunting for fir boughs on Christmas Eve 1939, members of the Murray family came across three young Scottish ratings off the Armed Merchant Cruiser *Ascania*, six miles out of town hiking along the Waverly Road in the freezing dark just for something to do. Out of pity they picked them up, took them home, fed them, took them to church, wrote to their parents and established a fast friendship that endured throughout the war.[382]

OUTSIDE THE LOOP

For many of the Royal Navy ratings and their comrades, if truth be told, the carefully regulated hostels, the chaperoned dances, dinner with a nice family, a meal in a restaurant and a movie might be fine for a while, but something was missing.

Besides drink, a young man definitely wanted something else. If liquor was bounded by laws and regulations, it was, after a fashion, legally available. The other something definitely had no legal existence. The departure of the British army in 1906 had a sad effect on the city's prostitutes. Despite a brief revival during the excitement of World War I, merchant seamen were said to find Halifax a very dull place, the kind of dull place where the V.D. rate was unusually low.

In September 1939 that changed overnight. It was very much a free enterprise situation and much of the supply, like so many of the professional needs arising out of World War II, came from outside the community. After September, every train, it was said, had its complement of madames and girls. The Halifax police, perhaps naive, perhaps wise, perhaps just overwhelmed, could scarcely control what became, in the words of Thomas Raddall, for six years a courtesan's paradise.[383] Raids on the city's most notorious brothels rarely, if ever, uncovered girls of any sort, because they always had enough warning to slip away.

The most popular and most prominent brothel, because of its location at 51 Hollis Street just opposite Government House, was run by Germaine Pelletier: "I'm going to die at fifty-one" was a code for where a fellow could spend some free time. Stephen Kimber relates that the lineups began to form around noon and by late afternoon could stretch three blocks south to the Nova Scotian Hotel.[384]

By and large wartime practice was fairly discreet compared to the more flamboyant days of the nineteenth century. Conventions were observed for the most part, although H.B. Jefferson complained in September 1943 that hordes of sailors, soldiers, airmen and trollops were turning Hollis Street into a nightmare.[385] Still, most of the activity was out of sight, in flats and apartments comfortably furnished for the purpose. For the couple just seizing the moment, a quick cab ride to Johnson's Cabins, nestled in the woods near Timberlea on the St. Margaret's Bay Road, put a discreet distance between them and overcrowded downtown.[386]

A flurry of newspaper advertisements dramatizing in surprising detail the dangers of venereal disease, syphilis and gonorrhea. Words which had never before passed the lips of respectable citizens were there for all to see in the daily papers, and indicated the depth of a looming problem. At a 1944 conference organized by the Department of Health to discuss the rising statistics, Halifax Mayor J.E. Lloyd observed with startling candour that it was difficult to close down the city's brothels because of the contribution they made to the local economy. "You'd be surprised," he said, "at the various businesses that are tied up with it."[387] While this statement might seem germane to the conference aim of controlling the alarming spread of V.D., it was not, apparently, what the attendees wanted to hear, and after a deafening silence, debate resumed on a safer, more academic level.

Young men craved all kinds of excitement, and for some, given the infrastructure and a slim pocket book, they had to make it themselves. It was not that hard to do. The city police force was not only overwhelmed and understaffed, jurisdiction was also divided between them and the military police, who were responsible for their own men. On a warm night after a payday, the forces of law and order were almost certain to be swamped by those determined to have, once you had scoffed a liquor store or bootleg bottle of hooch, what passed for a good time on the mean streets of Halifax. The leafy suburbs of the south end and west of Robie Street were only vaguely aware of the changes after September 1939. Even on a riotous Saturday night, the civilian who minded his or her own business was unlikely to be physically bothered by merry-making servicemen or merchant seamen. Nevertheless, some of the scenes recorded by H.B. Jefferson, the city's wartime censor, make astonishing reading even for jaded later generations:

DAY BY DAY

9 April 1942 — "P" came in tonight and said that last night he went to the Capitol to see "The Fleet's In" which is one of the most amusing pictures he has seen for some time. "Ni" said that with the real fleet in, the sailors seem to have caught the spirit of the picture, as the downtown streets this afternoon were a welter of fights between U.S. sailors and U.S. marines from the USS *Philadelphia*. P. said that it started before the Yanks arrived. After coming out of the show last night he strolled down Barrington only to find the street blocked by a big mob near Buckingham, watching a fight upstairs in which the windows were kicked out of the Union Café. Naval patrols brought out two small seamen who were wrecking the place, while civil police handled a couple of civilians. One sailor thrown into the naval police wagon made a flying leap out when they opened the door for the second one and nearly got away in the crowd. Practically all of the night restaurants are now the scene of constant fighting. Particularly bad spots are the Royal, Rex, Paradise, Crown, Bon Ton, Duffy's and similar places. Kid O'Neill's Silver Slipper [formerly Gay Paree] heads the list of real tough joints.

12 July 1942 — In spite of gas rationing with the advent of warm weather Hollis Street continues to get livelier and more like its old self. In the evening thundering herds of drunks roam up and down or argue on the corners. Idle merchant seamen from the A[llied] S[eamen's] C[lub] stroll about or cluster in groups along the blocks between South and Prince. Most of them are not very noisy and I have not yet seen any interfere with passing civilians, although they often fight among themselves. One afternoon at supper time I saw a man lying on the sidewalk with a little stream of blood running down the asphalt from a wound in his head. His friends were standing around and they all seemed unconcerned including the victim, who seemed to be waiting for a taxi or ambulance.

4 August 1942 — Things are growing livelier and more congested throughout the city with considerable disorder, but nothing yet touching the riotous levels of 1917-18.... returning from the Casino the other night ran into a small riot around the Silver Slipper ... first we saw of it was when "C" had to slam his brakes on to avoid running down half a dozen civilian bums pursued by naval and military police ... they caught them all and hauled then back to Kid's where there was a sailor with his clothes torn off, teeth kicked out and other injury ... heard a constable say "If you make a move I will break your head (with this black-jack) I'll teach you to kick a man in the head when he is down." They carted off two patrol trucks full ... the city has put on 9 more policemen.

12 September 1942 — This was the first Saturday night I have been out in the early evening and was amazed at the crowded state on Barrington Street which was the most congested I have ever seen it. There were so many people that by common consent most of those going north were using the east side of the street and those going south the west side. This summer and especially within the last few weeks there has been a great change for the worst [*sic*] on city streets. On places like Hollis, Jacob, Argyle and Gottingen drunks wander in droves, sleep in doorways, bleed and puke all over the sidewalk, argue and fight.... Deadly assaults are common especially in localities like Citadel Hill, Creighton Street, etc.

15 January 1943 — It is many months since we have seen as many drunks as we encountered between the post office and the N[ova] S[cotian] H[otel] on our way home tonight. There were singing drunks, crying drunks, fighting drunks, arguing drunks, and drunks talking to themselves as they ambled along.... It must have been the warm weather and pay night combined.

12 September 1943 — At the start of the 5th year of

the war the city is changing rapidly for the worst [*sic*]. The good order that was maintained for the first 48 months is now wearing off and the city, particularly the downtown streets, are becoming as rough and tough as they were in 1917 – 18, also more crowded. Where formerly Barrington street was crowded only between Spring Garden and Buckingham Streets, the sidewalks are now full all the way from North to Inglis. The formerly quiet south end section around Atlantic Street is now alive day and night with people coming and going to the big Railway Labor Camp in that vicinity. Fights and brawls occur every few minutes and but for the naval patrols it would be unsafe to travel streets like Hollis where hordes of sailors, soldiers, airmen and trollops turn night into day and day into a nightmare.[388]

July 1942 was to have seen in Halifax the world convention of the total abstinence advocates, the Sons of Temperance. When it was cancelled because of wartime exigencies, Jefferson commented that they had missed the chance of their lives to see more horrible examples of the evils of drink in one block of Hollis Street than they would see in any ten blocks elsewhere.[389]

Given what was ahead on VE Day, these wartime paydays and fleet's-in days were like a Sunday School field day. It was, after all, not for want of trying to find alternatives that the men spent so much time on the streets, in the liquor stores, speakeasies and bordellos. There were just too many soldiers, sailors airmen and merchant seamen for the pool of motivated civilians to cope with, despite superhuman efforts, and despite the fact that their contribution was probably far greater in proportion to the size of the community than anywhere else in Canada. The Dominion Government and the armed forces by and large took no responsibility for keeping their charges occupied during their idle hours, and it showed.

CHAPTER SIX:

Scarcity Amongst Plenty

For most people memories of life in Halifax during the war are of shortages and overcrowding. For the first few brief months, it seemed that life would go on as before, and for some the war was seen to be just a blip. With the commencement of the Battle of Britain and the Battle of the Atlantic it became painfully clear that life was going to change. Except for going overseas, until the beginning of 1942 the private citizen was more or less able to come and go as he pleased, as long as he could pay for it. Advertisements appeared in the newspapers for cheap railway excursions before every holiday, and, thanks to American neutrality, a person could still escape to the United States on the 7:05 a.m. train to Yarmouth, connected with the Eastern Steamship Lines to Boston or New York.[390] The Canadian Pacific Railway, whose ocean-going steamships were already shuddering under the impact of Nazi torpedoes, still touted the joys of a Great Lakes cruise aboard the *Assiniboia*. In the autumn of 1941 the prosperous consumer was urged to buy the 1942 Pontiac, available in Fleetleader, Fleetleader Torpedo and Deluxe, combining streamlined beauty, greater length and commanding dignity.[391] The war brought a glow to the faces of automobile dealers everywhere when in May 1940 it was announced, "Automobile sales in the Dominion for the first three months of the year are 47.6 percent ahead of the same period of 1939."[392] But soon it all changed.

THE SQUEEZE BEGINS

Of late months we have had a heavy influx of visitors to
our city. Many of them come here to see us and we have
talked plainly and listened patiently. Nearly all of them
claim Halifax is dead. They say the services, generally
speaking are bad. Apartment rates are scandalously high.
They are not equipped as they should be in a modern city.
Food prices are much higher than other Canadian cities.
They cant [sic] understand why fresh fruits cost so much
more here than in inland cities. These same people com-
plain about the lack of entertainment other than theatres
and the occasional dance. They claim Halifax is the worst
city to drive in they have ever experienced. They say the
traffic moves pitifully slow. Never have they seen a city
serving a population of 100,000 without a modern traffic
light. Even large towns in central Canada and the States
have them they say. Then when it comes to the lack of
high school and library facilities — well we wont [sic]
repeat what is said. Neither will [we] about some of our
streets and the awful buildings in certain parts. Lets leave
the criticism here.[393]

Some of this criticism, voiced by John Fisher on CHNS in 1940 or
1941, was unfair. Evidently, his informants had not travelled very far
because there was in Halifax a functioning traffic light, since the spring of
1940 anyway, even if it was far out at the Arm Bridge where the Bay Road
launched forth to the South Shore. "Armdale residents," Marjorie Major
reported that August, "are watching with interest the operation of the new
traffic lights at the Arm Bridge. The police officer on duty to help adoption
of the system says left turns are the cause of much of the difficulty for
motor traffic and pedestrians alike."[394] Sometime in the 1930s a traffic light
had been installed at Spring Garden Road and South Park Street, but being
found more of a nuisance than a help, it had soon been removed. By the
autumn of 1940, however, the pressure of wartime traffic, military and

civilian, made progress of this sort inevitable. By late October 1940, a Spring Garden/South Park light was back in action and, by the following April, lights had been approved for Oxford and Quinpool, Cunard and Robie, and Agricola West and Maynard to cover the engines at the West Street fire station.[395]

The comments from these anonymous visitors had some validity. Essentially ignored by the rest of Canada since its Imperial status disappeared with the last of the British troops in 1906, Halifax had evolved a way of life that fit its slim resources. Aside from the glamorous Capitol Theatre, opened in 1930, the city's cultural infrastructure depended heavily on socializing with family and friends. With the exception of the electrical utility, public services reflected the investments made a generation or more before as the last vestiges of Victorian prosperity slipped away. Thus, when the city and the region found another Imperial role suddenly thrust upon it in September 1939, it was, not surprisingly, quite unprepared.

Over the next couple of years, into the unsuspecting city poured the men and matériel to support the war machine: a vastly expanded naval establishment; some 3,500 air force personnel in the burgeoning Dartmouth air station; a large army garrison in the city and harbour forts; several thousand civilian functionaries who manned new government bureaucracies; the expanded workforces of established industries, such as the Shipyards; and as many as 30,000 merchant seamen a month coming and going from the convoys. The city's fleshpots played temporary host to thousands on leave from garrisons, airfields and naval outposts around Nova Scotia, as well as a constant stream of civilians and service personnel en route to and from overseas assignments.[396]

Whatever its flaws and failures, the somewhat overwhelmed civic administration was understandably reluctant to expand its infrastructure to deal with the crush. Even if they had had the resources, it soon became apparent that Ottawa politicians and bureaucrats considered none of this their problem. In the end, as had happened before, in the jaundiced opinion of municipal authorities, this vast and ungrateful horde would slip away and leave Halifax to foot the bill.

HOUSING PROBLEMS

The population rose rapidly. In 1939 it was 67,872 in Halifax and 9,964 in Dartmouth. These numbers peaked in 1944 at 106,742 for Halifax and 17,277 for Dartmouth.[397] In many respects, the Government of Canada was guilty of neglect because, despite plentiful evidence that the influx was causing serious problems, its response was slow, reluctant and parsimonious.

Accommodation was the main problem. In the interwar period straitened economic times meant that the housing stock increased little. The Halifax Explosion of 1917 had resulted in the substantial and well-planned "Hydrostone" district behind Fort Needham on north Gottingen Street; but it was, and remained until well after the war, the property of the Halifax Relief Commission, whose tenants were survivors who had lost homes, breadwinners, or suffered some physical disability as a result of the disaster.

In the post-World War I euphoria, the city ventured into the social housing field, but with dismal results. The Halifax Housing Commission erected 187 dwellings between 1921 and 1923 for returning veterans. This laudable effort was doomed from the start because the houses were built at the peak of the inflationary cycle which followed the Great War. When the only boom Nova Scotians were to know until the next war collapsed, most of the owner-occupiers could no longer afford the rent of the now over-priced homes. Nor could anyone else. Only the revived housing market during World War II saved the Housing Commission from bankruptcy. No matter how desperate the need (once bit, twice shy) the wary city fathers were not inclined to pursue the chimera of public housing, not before, nor until long after the war.

Such new housing as was built was middle class, single-family dwellings in the leafy suburbs west of Robie Street. Rental accommodation remained not only static, but was often so poorly maintained that it shocked observers from away. Little provision was made for military housing before the war because the small armed forces component could be accommodated in the nineteenth-century barracks and buildings bequeathed by the departed British. Once the war began and men began to flood into the city, the Department of National Defence was reluctant to invest in new barracks on the scale their presence warranted on the grounds that expensive and extensive barracks would only be surplus at the end of the war. It was sufficient, the department argued, to pay shore-based personnel a daily housing allowance, "lodge & comp" in naval parlance, and let them find their own. In large cities such as Toronto or Montreal, this approach might have worked well enough, but for Halifax, the burgeoning military was out of all proportion to the existing population. To make matters worse, many of the 20,000 servicemen eventually stationed here, realizing they would be on their own, saw no reason why they should not share their rental accommodation with sweethearts, wives and families. Almost as soon as the war began, every train arriving at Union Station brought its complement of naive families into a city that had no room for them.

It happened very quickly. Marguerite Harding recalls that at the beginning of the war "Apartment for Rent" signs began to disappear from front windows. Within a few days, it seemed, all the signs were gone.[398] By the autumn of 1940, Clara Dennis, a well-known local author wrote to a friend, "The population of Halifax has greatly increased lately. Some say it has doubled and places to stay are difficult to get."[399] Authorities were soon issuing appeals: "Don't Hoard living Space. Make a voluntary contribution of your spare rooms to help the total war programme!"[400] Halifax homeowners did open up their homes in response. On the most basic level, many took in "P.G.s" or paying guests, usually short term and characteristically the wife of an officer in town for a few weeks while her husband was on leave, or on short term duty. Others began to divide up large rooms or take in boarders, but it was a short-term solution that often caused as many problems as it solved.

Dorothy Brackett, who moved to Halifax in the spring of 1940 to work at Moirs for $3.00 a week, rented a room on Merkel Street in the North End, which got her dinner in the evening and a bed shared with two other working girls on the same floor as the bathroom. Two men also boarded in the house, which included the family of four children.[401]

The Akerlunds, who lived on Barrington Street, more or less opposite Cornwallis Park, feeling guilty about all their space, converted two upstairs rooms into bed-sitting rooms. The tenants used the upstairs bathroom and a small bathroom was added downstairs for the family.[402] Others did not really have the space, but responded anyway to the public appeals. Donald Purchase resents to this day that when the war came so did the boarders, sometimes as many as three. He lost his bedroom and spent the rest of the war sleeping on the living-room couch or on a cot in the dining-room. He found it difficult to do homework because the house was always crowded. To add insult to injury, some of the boarders who stayed in his room cut up the felt surface of his small pool table when they sliced bread.[403] The Ripley family in Rockingham took in boarders, not because they had the room, but in response to a public appeal. The Y.M.C.A. coordinated the room allotments and in the the Ripleys' case they were inspected and approved by the Travellers' Aid, after which the boarders arrived. For Joyce Ripley, this meant that, like Don Purchase, she lost her bedroom and for the rest of the war shared with her sister. The boarders were always very nice and played games with the children. Many became good friends and when the R.C.A.F. husband of one of them was killed overseas, Mrs. Ripley kept in touch with the widow for years. More generous than the landlords who made a bad impression on so many, the Ripleys, who had an icebox with limited capacity, allowed one tenant to cool his beer under the running water from the faucet. Since the water came from a private reservoir up the hill shared by the small community, this indulgence seemed wasteful to a young Joyce, but she was told to keep her opinions to herself.[404]

The Ripleys were responsible householders trying to do their patriotic duty by responding to a wartime need. There was another kind that visitors remembered for years after the war. One landlady, Lottie Frame, was famous for evading regulations, having been in and out of court for years on charges of overcharging and failing to provide adequate heat. The messages from those who could remedy the situation were mixed. Hauled into court by the Wartime Prices and Trade Board on 11 charges of gouging, the rental authorities suggested a fine of $1,000 on each charge in view of the regular nature of her violations. In the end, however, an understanding magistrate imposed fines of only $20.00 on the first charge and $40.00 each on the rest, modest sums widely regarded by such landlords as the cost of doing business.[405]

The landlords were not the only unscrupulous ones. Sometimes opportunistic and mercenary tenants divided up big rooms and sub-let, charging what the traffic would bear. This led to tragic overcrowding, and left the occupants to cope with health hazards arising from such close proximity, limited sanitary conditions and the threat of communicable diseases such as tuberculosis and diphtheria. In 1939 Halifax had a slum area out of all proportion to the size of the city, and the rent gouging and overcrowding of World War II established slum areas throughout the city where none had been before.[406]

Dorothy Sangster, a journalist who, with her husband Sidney Katz was prominent in the post-war Canadian media, arrived in Halifax in September 1944 to produce a series of articles for the *Montreal Standard*, and spend some time with her husband, then a radar technician just returned from a remote Labrador posting. Expecting to be in Halifax for a while, they rented a room,

> It cost $16 a week, had one blanket on the bed, no heat, no
> cooking privileges, and you were forbidden to turn on the
> lights in the day time no matter how dark the day might
> be, and the days were cloudy and dark most of the time I
> was there. Besides this you were not to bring liquor into the
> room, you could not talk above a low murmur or someone
> would bang on the door, and when I politely requested per-
> mission to plug my own one-burner grill into the floor plug
> and heat water for tea once a day, the retort was,
> "Certainly not! What do you think you are getting for $16
> a week?" ... And when the landlady finally ejected us one
> day because I had turned a desk lamp on ... she did so with
> the righteous comment that, "Anyway, we Haligonians
> don't want any Germans or Jews down here!"[407]

So much for Maritime hospitality. Sangster's experience was, sadly, not untypical.

At the beginning of June 1941, there were only 57 vacant houses in Halifax and eight in Dartmouth. Of these, several were in between tenants, and others were deemed unfit for human habitation. A low-end Halifax wage earner ($1,000 per year) then paid $18.00 a month rent, although $12.25 was considered affordable. A middle-class tenant could expect to pay $26.00 a month, as compared to $22.23 elsewhere.[408] It got worse. As the demand rose, accommodation that might have cost $20.00 a month in Toronto, went for $60.00 in Halifax; if the shared bathroom was on the same floor, that sort of luxury raised the rent to $70.00.[409]

Controlling rents was very much on the mind of the Wartime Prices and Trade Board (W.P.T.B.). It had been established on 3 September 1939, even before Canada declared war, to prevent the kind of inflation that had ravaged the economy during and after World War I. On 11 September 1940, six weeks before it imposed wage controls, the Board assumed responsibility for the rent and housing prices across the country. Regulations limited rents, forbade key money or deposits and restricted the right of eviction; but in the developing maelstrom of the Halifax housing market these regulations were honoured more in the breach than in the observance. Tenants in need of a place to live were eager to pay a $50 "key deposit." Classified advertisements in the newspapers were full of appeals and suggestions of "rewards" for vacant rooms or flats. A rent might well be appropriate, but the furnishings, such as they were, would be sold or leased to the incoming tenant at an exorbitant rate.[410] The greedier landlords sometimes sold their properties in a fake transaction so that the new owner, a variation of himself, could, legally under the regulations, raise the rent.[411] And so went the imaginative circumventions, which evolved with a speed that matched the development of the accommodation shortage. When the Halifax Rentals Committee of the W.P.T.B. held its first meeting at the end of 1940, it already faced a backlog of 140 complaints. It went downhill from there.

If the effort to live on the peninsula was too much of a tiresome game, some crossed the Arm Bridge to the laissez-faire world of Halifax County. Here were acres of land, no greedy landlords and fewer W.P.T.B. busybodies. At one end of the social spectrum, shacks, which in no way met the few regulations that existed in the County, were cobbled together in the bush and rocks of Spryfield, or, if you were truly opportunistic, on the city's watershed lands. Better-quality homes found sources of otherwise unavailable building materials and went up around Chocolate Lake and along the Bay Road. Along with this unregulated overflow of houses of dubious quality came the casual siting of wells and septic tanks with its great potential for a serious public health problem, which sooner or later would have to be dealt with.[412]

HOUSING — THE CIVILIAN SOLUTION

It was clear that something had to be done to house the burgeoning civilian population. When the city suggested it would cooperate in some venture based on the 1935 National Housing Act, it was curtly rebuffed on the basis that it was too late, the Act was no longer valid and the Dominion Government would look after the problem. Given the magnitude of the problem, the city government was happy to receive the negative response. The announcement, if not the action, was not long in coming. In February 1941 the Dominion Government incorporated Wartime Housing Limited, ostensibly to supply temporary accommodation on demand for munitions workers across Canada. Virtually the first item on the agenda was Halifax, and within weeks tenders were approved for the construction of 400 houses on the Halifax peninsula, with plans for more at Tufts Cove and for workers at the Clark Ruse aircraft plant at Eastern Passage.

Even if the intent was only to house war workers and not members of the general population it seemed like a good start. However, there would be too much indecision before the first spade of soil was turned. Location was a problem. Wartime Housing preferred to use existing vacant Crown or public land. Sites later accepted, such as the former Saint Paul's glebe lands north of Duffus Street, were rejected because they were private. Some existing residents, nervous of their property values, objected to the location of some projects. Residents of Oxford Street were only mollified when promised that none of the proposed houses would come east of Connolly Street. Most nervous homeowners were soothed by the general expectation that after five years all of these houses would be removed or demolished, and the land freed up for development into high-end homes.[413]

The War Time Prices and Trade Board argued, on the basis of "If you build it, they will come," that before any emergency housing was built, Halifax should be designated a "restricted zone." Otherwise, the Board argued, "an additional number of wives and families of naval or Army personnel would move in."[414] The Board was not alone in recommending this approach, which would in effect mean that any person moving to Halifax would have to have a permit.

The City of Halifax made an attempt to snare a number of the proposed houses for what it considered its own non-military requirements and seemed to meet with some success until it became apparent that Ottawa bureaucrats had assigned them houses in what was the town of Dartmouth. Apparently the difference between the two communities could not be explained or understood and Halifax abandoned the effort.[415]

In the end, however, by 1943 the Halifax Wartime Housing project was underway. There were 17 separate components, or neighbourhoods, all for civilian war workers. At this stage all houses were rental properties. The houses, 1,546 of them, most of which stand today, were built as temporary structures, without foundations, elevated on blocks two feet above grade, with asbestos board over the crawl space and rock wool in the walls to keep out winter cold. They were located in the Saint Paul's glebe lands and nearby properties owned by the Halifax Relief Commission; the Merson Farm property bounded by Gottingen, Agricola and Duffus; Highland Park; Edgewood; Eastern Passage and Tufts Cove in the vicinity of Windmill and Albro Lake Roads.[416] Under the initial arrangements, the houses were to be demolished six months after the end of the war.[417]

The Architectural Division of Wartime Housing Limited designed four types of houses: # 1 and # 2 were one-storey, 24' x 24', with living room, kitchen, bath and two bedrooms, the one plan the mirror image of the other; # 3 was similar to # 1 and # 2, but larger; # 4 was a storey-and-a-half, 24' x 28' with a ground-floor layout similar to the others, but with two additional bedrooms above. Depending on the model, rents ranges from $25.00 to $32.00 per month.

Most of the homes were built by Brookfield Bros. Construction. The goal was eight houses a day. To speed the process up, they were bolted together from prefabricated panels made up for floors, walls and roofs, all stored in a central depot and trucked as needed to the building sites. From this construction technique they derived the name "Prefabs," which they retain to this day. An attractive feature of the "Prefabs" was the large size of their lots, encouragement for the occupants to plant a large Victory Garden to feed their families. Given the often stony soil surrounding the harbour it was an optimistic expectation, the triumph of hope over experience; but it was part of the drive to take the strain off the food-supply chain.

Posterity had judged this effort of Wartime Housing Limited to be one of the great successes of all the investments made in wartime. It could be argued that they are the most useful and permanent memorial of the conflict in Canada. Some 17,000 copies of one of the four models can be found in communities all across Canada. Elsewhere in Nova Scotia clusters can be found in Amherst, Springhill, Pictou, New Glasgow, Trenton and Yarmouth.[418]

By 1950 the "prefabs" evolved into homes and the "housing projects" into neighbourhoods. Wartime Housing's inventory of homes was transferred to Central Mortgage and Housing in 1947 and rather than removing them in favour of "superior" houses that Crown agency sold them off to municipalities, and some directly to veterans or individuals. The Halifax houses were then resold at prices ranging from $1,700 to $2,300. All purchasers agreed to construct a foundation, basement floor and permanent chimney, for which a loan of up to $2,100 was available.[419]

The Government of Canada stated firmly that once Wartime Housing had completed its approved projects, it was out of the housing market, but in the end it could not resist the pressure to provide returning veterans with a place to live. In 1948 a 274-unit project of somewhat higher-end homes, designed as permanent and complete with finished cellars and a parklike street configuration fit for the returning heroes and their young families, began to replace the barracks and vanished airfield on Chebucto Road. This project closed the books on the civic airport and the post-war dream that it could be resuscitated to serve as an "Air Taxi Service Centre," the base for an air shuttle back and forth to the commercial air component at R.C.A.F. Dartmouth.[420]

Wartime Housing Ltd. was involved in one other project that was truly temporary: the construction of barracks buildings for single workers, one of the first components of the Crown corporation's programme, complete with dining and recreational facilities. The best example was the barracks at Mulgrave Park, which in 1942 served 1,100 civilian shipyard and dock-yard workers, who paid $9.50 to $11.00 a week.[421] During the war it had the reputation of being a "little Newfoundland," and after the war, until its demolition to make way for public housing, it served Dalhousie University as quarters for married students. Associated with it was the "Manning Pool," a similar residence for merchant seamen awaiting the departing convoys.

When necessary Wartime Housing invested heavily in community infrastructure as well as housing and even maintained a "Tenants Relations Division," staffed by social workers.[422] This community involvement was not always voluntary. When 350 "prefabs" were erected in north Dartmouth it had a drastic effect on the school there, which had been designated as inadequate in 1939. The situation became desperate in 1941 and the Dartmouth School Board played hardball, stating to Wartime Housing that children "whose parents are residents of prefabricated homes erected by Wartime Housing Limited" would not be admitted to the town schools. This drastic action had the desired effect and Wartime Housing agreed that fall to build what became Notting Park School at no cost to the town.[423]

HOUSING — THE MILITARY SOLUTION

After 1943 the efforts of Wartime Housing began to address the civilian aspects of the Halifax housing crisis, but housing the military was a separate issue. Civilian government officials were worried enough to call the situation in the city "dangerous." Donald Gordon, with typical candour, laid the blame squarely on the navy. It was finally considered serious enough to occupy the Cabinet War Committee on 8 September 1943, which appointed Atlantic Ports Administrator E.L. Cousins as "emergency controller" of the Port of Halifax.[424] In his report submitted in November, surprisingly to some, Cousins did not advocate designating Halifax a "restricted" city, which many thought was the obvious answer. He proposed an extensive national campaign to discourage further movement into the city. He also advised that the R.C.A.F. vacate their Halifax facilities, "Y" Depot, in favour of the navy, a move which would provide barracks accommodation for 3,000 naval personnel and reduce the pressure on the city's rental stock by a significant degree. Although it took three years for the Government of Canada to get to this point, now that their attention was focused on the problem, it acted with commendable promptness in fully accepting the report's recommendations.

An intensive media campaign began almost immediately on the CBC, in the movie theatres and the press, warning the public against travelling to Halifax. By mid-December the R.C.A.F. began to transfer its Halifax personnel to Lachine, Que., turning over their facilities to the R.C.N. for whom they now became HMCS Peregrine, housing both men and women.

Although Cousins's suggestion of another 1,000 Wartime Housing Limited houses received short shrift from C.D. Howe, a March 1944 census, known as the "Cousins Survey," showed that the measures had eased, if not eliminated the pressure. H.B. Jefferson commented that the streets and stores were still crowded, but even before the R.C.A.F. actually began to move out, the mere prospect had the effect of easing things at Norman's Restaurant and elsewhere. He rejoiced, "since the change took place we have never had to wait for a seat."[425]

Conditions were still bad by peacetime standards. None of these measures took into account the thousands of "sweeties" still in rooming houses and flats. But before it was too late the Government of Canada had recognized that there was, perhaps, a problem.

CROWDS, CROWDS, CROWDS

Still, crowding was everywhere. Every train that came into the station was full, and the traveller's first task was to find a cab, scarce indeed. Many drivers had gone off to war and those who remained developed, deserved or not, a reputation as arrogant, insolent, rapacious profiteers.[426] The situation was bad enough that the city attempted to establish order by setting up the office of Regional Director of Transit Control and a Halifax Transit Committee which established a taxi pool and a central call office with jurisdiction over all cabs. From 15 August 1942, all taxicabs had to be licensed, not only by the municipal government but also by the Wartime Prices and Trade Board if they wanted gas coupons. The interference was fiercely resented by cabbies who, perhaps in self defense or in retaliation, formed the Halifax Wartime Taxi Association and who ignored the call office whenever they could. Calling the central office did not guarantee that the summoned cab would actually come, and the public longed for the good old days when you just called a cab company.[427]

If the traveller found a cab he almost certainly had to share it with two or three others, each of whom paid full fare. When he arrived at his hotel he had better have a reservation otherwise there was a wait of two or three days. If he was lucky, for $2.50 a night he would find a bed in a dormitory set up in a former ladies lounge.[428] The available hotel space shrank considerably during the war because the Halifax and the King Edward Hotels were commandeered by the military. The 745 rooms in Halifax and Dartmouth in 1939 shrunk to 520 rooms by 1943.[429]

All of this activity made for a lot of rubbing of shoulders, and an almighty assault on the eardrums, since war, whether on the front lines or not, is a 24-hour-a-day business. H.B. Jefferson, who, with his wife, lived in the Nova Scotian Hotel close to the action, described one foggy night in July 1943:

> For some time the harbor has been growing noisier at night and the heavy fogs of the last three weeks have increased this tendency. Last night was probably the worst since the war began. A convoy of 50 ships was crawling in all night and in addition to the usual loud blowing for the medical boat, pilot launches, coal barges, navigation signals, etc., each vessel also blew a fog warning every few yards. It was a still night, and to add to the din of customary shore fog whistles, buoys and bells, each of the ships anchored in the harbor — and there were dozens — maintained an anchor watch who vigorously rang the ship's bell every minute or so. The whole thing was a bedlam which made sleep almost impossible. Halifax has grown extremely noisy ashore as well as afloat. Nearly all the public services have become defective through heavy traffic and few repairs. Motor cycles, army and commercial trucks roar through the streets, dozens of locomotives shunt day and night with the usual bell ringing and whistling, and last but not least the street cars, now about 80 or 90 in number, pound over the dilapidated rails with a clatter that makes conversation almost impossible. At the same time, overhead there is the continuous monotonous droning of all kinds of planes. In fine weather they never let up for even one hour out of the 24.[430]

REGULATED SCARCITY — THE MOTOR CAR

Besides overcrowding, and exacerbated by it, was the gradual onset of rationing necessary on order to feed the military machine and the civilian machine dedicated to its support. Rationing was a regulated regime carefully designed to replace a free-market economy and, with the best of intentions, to spread the pain of doing so as equally as government regulation would allow. In Halifax, a thousand miles from many of the main sources of supply in Upper Canada and with burgeoning military and civilian economies and a front line ethos not found elsewhere, the machinery of regulation creaked and groaned as it struggled to cope.

The first flex of the W.P.T.B.'s muscles was a tentative effort to control the price of bread and flour before the autumn harvests of 1940, but it was rescinded that August. Nevertheless, the rise in the cost of living during the first year of the war was an obvious warning sign and the campaign began to stabilize wages and prices and prepare people for a shift from consumption to saving. At the end of 1940 the Board set the wholesale price of butter, and new taxes in May 1940 included a 20 percent surcharge on movie tickets and five percent on gasoline.

New cars were still plentiful, and at the big new garage at Sackville Street and Bell Road, there was no hint of wartime restrictions. Pretty girls had replaced men rapidly vanishing from the landscape. Motorists were directed to:

> feast your eyes on something new to Halifax. Young ladies
> all decked out in service station uniform. Your car will stop
> in front of a saluting young lady with a very ingratiating
> smile. If it is a man driving she probably wouldnt [sic] need
> to ask "shall I fill her up?" And while the Texaco is being
> pumped into your car the characteristic sweep of a femi-
> nine hand will swish across your windshield. The second
> young lady will say "Check your oil sir?" And your change
> will be returned to you by another equally delicate hand so
> dainty you'd feel like leaving the change in it & some prob-
> ably do. And when you step on the starter to go youll [sic]
> leave with a smile because youll [sic] get one as only a lady
> can give one.[431]

This motor car Shangri-la did not last. In June of 1941 production of private cars was cut by half and the number of available models reduced from 147 to 79. Those models available had limited accessories, colour and upholstery options. Dodge, for example, offered only the "Deluxe" and "Special Deluxe," and pointedly highlighted Dodge dependability, "because you may want to drive your new car many thousands of extra miles."[432]

Driving those extra miles also became increasingly difficult. By the summer of 1941 motorists were urged to cut their daily gas consumption by half by not only eliminating non-essential driving, but also by dropping from 60 mph to 40 mph on the highway. By the middle of the summer the moral, if not yet legal, pressure increased. Motorists who signed a pledge to cut gas consumption in half displayed a patriotic sticker in the window featuring the Union Jack with the superscription, "50/50 Car Pledged To Save Gasoline." New oil furnaces were banned and King Coal reigned unchallenged for a few more years. Suddenly, the allure of the pretty gas station attendants at Sackville and Bell Road became a guilty pleasure. Then the smiling face was replaced with the stern admonition that the attendant "is no longer a gasoline salesman. He is a gasoline SAVER. He will urge you to buy less, instead of more."[433] By July the stations had slipped into the orbit of the Dominion Government, which ordered them to close every night between 7 p.m. and 7 a.m., with no Sunday openings at all.

The problem was not so much a general scarcity of supply at the well head but a scarcity of tankers. At this point tankers were on the losing side of the Battle of the Atlantic and had become prime targets for the increasingly effective U-boat wolf packs, which, convoys or no, were wreaking havoc in their campaign to disrupt ocean trade. These Atlantic tankers were replaced by the coastal tankers that supplied Imperoyal from South America and the United States. As supply shrank, motorists gave up more and more of their share of the gasoline pie so that the rapidly expanding Royal Canadian Navy, the expanding British Commonwealth Air Training Plan and the massive convoys plodding their way to Britain could come and go at will. On 1 April 1942, the axe finally fell when gasoline rationing by coupon succeeded the voluntary quota system with an official limit of five gallons per week. This measure reflected a desperate shortage. U-boats were at their most effective and U-517 had even penetrated the Gulf of St.

Lawrence, causing panic there. So many tankers were sunk in May 1942 that there were no deliveries to Imperoyal for 10 days. In order to keep the R.C.N. at sea the refinery shifted its entire production to bunker oil.[434]

The situation was so desperate that, initially at least, there was a different system east of Quebec. With voluntary quotas, it was a first come, first serve system. If you arrived at the gas station first, or were a regular, you were in luck; otherwise you weren't. This system of leaving it up to the service station to ration gasoline prompted many protests. With coupon rationing fairness was countered by the reality that, since the Maritimes was supplied exclusively by vanishing tankers, the east coast had to make do with two gallons per coupon, not the five in the rest of the country. Vigorous protests were made at the highest level, but relief was a long time in coming and the provincial highways were "ghost roads."[435]

If a motorist considered all the new taxes and gasoline restrictions and still invested in a brand new 1942 automobile, which he could still do, its vaunted dependability and streamlined beauty had yet another hurdle. On 6 December 1941, Japan bombed Pearl Harbor, which precipitated the entry of a previously equivocal America into the war. With amazing speed, Japan seized British and Dutch possessions in the Pacific with most of the world's supply of rubber. By April 1942 the only available supply was existing rubber: "The shortage of rubber is so grave that any citizen hoarding rubber or using it unnecessarily is committing an act of disloyalty."[436] In May 1942 new regulations were issued by the Department of Munitions and Supply, which controlled war production, drastically limiting who could purchase not only new, but also retreaded, tires. There was even the threat that it might be necessary to strip tires off non-essential vehicles, and the responsible cottager was urged to turn in those retired inner tubes which were serving out their last days on the beach: "We can obtain substitutes for these safety devices at our beaches, but as yet we can get no substitute for rubber for our war requirements. It's up to you, 1942 vacationist."[437] The average citizen figured nowhere on the lists for gas, oil and rubber. Sunday drives to Sunnyside or Queensland Beach became an unpatriotic memory. The messages got through because by the end of the summer of 1942 it was estimated that 100,000 cars a year were taken off the road for lack of tires alone.[438] The W.P.T.B. Motor Controller official had already seized all cars in scrapyards and warned motorists that the authority existed to do the same for all civilian cars.

Pressure on motorists increased over the next two years. By 1 April 1943, the casual driver was limited to 40 "AA" gas coupons, the equivalent of 120 gallons of gas a year. The average car of the era got about 18 miles per gallon, which gave you 2,160 miles of carefree motoring at 40 miles an hour.[439] By Christmas the beleaguered leisure motorist was by now practically a suspect Nazi if he took his car out of the garage for less than two people or if he drove past a tram stop without offering someone a lift. He faced the prospect that the octane level of the little gas he had left would be cut.[440] If he still had not got the message, antifreeze disappeared that winter, so if he was determined to keep going despite all odds, he had to scrounge enough wood alcohol to fill the radiator.[441]

The screws got tighter in 1944. By then the Battle of the Atlantic had, essentially, been won and the U-boat threat controlled, if not eliminated, but the enormous buildup for the invasion of Europe sucked up virtually every spare gallon of fuel. Added to this was the innovative transatlantic flights of the R.C.A.F., the Atlantic Ferry to Britain, via Newfoundland and Labrador, and to Russia via Edmonton. Initially daring experiments, these flights were rapidly becoming routine, but were an additional drain on the nation's fuel supply. The bottomless requirements of the British Commonwealth Air Training Plan continued. The consumption of high-octane aviation fuel went from 5,453,980 gallons in 1939 to 176,298,570 gallons in 1944. By that time the R.C.N. needed 2,150,000 gallons of bunker fuel a week. Domestic use of regular gasoline shrunk hardly at all, from 882,216,930 in 1942 to 814,248,820 in 1944, but this figure includes the vast expansion of truck transport, of which the Alaska Highway service was a prime example.[442]

Scarcity was an opportunist's paradise. Motorists were advised to record the serial numbers of their tires in the event that they were stolen right off the rims.[443] Cars were being broken into and searched for ration books of any kind which might have been left in the glove compartment.[444] It is no surprise, following all of this deprivation, that the automobile became a post-war obsession.

REGULATED SCARCITY — APPLIANCES

Cars were the largest consumer item that most aspired to buy. By 1939 they had swept away the horse and buggy. But a motor car was still a luxury item, and in Halifax many middle class citizens did not feel the necessity of owning one. For them and their poorer neighbours, the greatest effect of the restrictions on private automobiles was the increasingly crowded state of the trams and trains, fuelling the post-war determination to buy a car so as to never set foot in public transit again. The same also applied to major appliances. Many a housewife did not feel the need for a vacuum cleaner or washing machine until it became clear that the post-war world was not going to include a live-in maid. In the Halifax of 1941, 98 percent of households had running water and electricity, 73 percent had baths (19 percent had nothing), and 82 percent had flush toilets. Although 71 percent had a refrigerator, only 30 percent cooked with gas or electricity. Most households sent an older child down to the corner store to get a can of stove oil. Only 17 percent had all of those luxury items which within the decade would be considered basic necessities, i.e., a radio, a vacuum cleaner, a telephone and an automobile.[445]

By 1941, 70 new corvettes were on order, and for them alone, to say nothing of growing orders for tanks, artillery and planes, the scramble to find the raw materials was intensifying. In January Prime Minister King called for more effort and more sacrifice in people's daily lives and the citizenry was urged to avoid purchasing unnecessary articles. That summer aluminum, zinc and nickel production was reserved for wartime use.[446] Despite the warnings, pleadings and taxes, people continued to flock to the stores, with the result that two years after the beginning of the war in September 1941, the Wartime Prices and Trade Board and the Wartime Industries Control Board (W.I.C.B.) took over control of consumer goods.

A month later saw an imposed reduction of 25 percent from the previous years in the manufacture of new radios, fridges, stoves, vacuum cleaners and washing machines. The use of steel in the production of "flat 50s" cigarette containers was forbidden, and, for some the most cutting of all, silk from Japan, controlled since December 1940, 85 percent of which was used for silk stockings, was banned outright.[447] "Nylons" replaced "silk stockings" and for the duration of the war, they were one of the most sought after of scarce consumer items. In summer at least, every drug store carried a tan coloured product for just this purpose, along with a sort of sandpaper mitt for removing hair. When this laborious process had been completed, the perfectionist would enlist a good friend or family member to draw an imitation seam up the back of each leg with an eyebrow pencil.[448] For the real thing, one pair per customer was the rule when they were available. A waitress at Norman's Restaurant had her own solution to that problem. Lamenting, "I could have had more stockings if I had more sailors," she gave a number of her customers a dollar bill each and sent them into a store where each bought a pair for her.[449]

In October came wage and price controls, and installment buying was heavily restricted: one-third down (50 percent for cars) and the balance within a year.[450] Despite all of this official discouragement, retail trade hit a 13-year high that December, prompting a stern warning from the powers that be, to those who were having too good a time that because of the entry of Japan into the war, the Christmas just past should be remembered as the last of the "good old days." By the next Christmas, the self-indulgent were told there would be no more ice or roller skates, tricycles, joycycles or appliances. Metal beds and furniture for home and office became scarce. Anything brass was found only in second-hand shops. Electric refrigerators, sewing machines, washing machines, vacuum cleaners, toasters, grills and scores of other appliances vanished. There would not even be Christmas trees for sale in 1943, when labour shortages ruled out commercial tree harvesting.[451] Production of radios was cut a further 50 percent[452] and within a month, even if you could find a new radio you needed a permit from the "Controller of Supplies" to buy it. By war's end, the thirst for consumer goods had become fierce. The wartime drought fuelled a post-war boom in consumer spending that has yet to slacken.

REGULATED SCARCITY — CLOTHES AND TEXTILES

With hard goods tied up tightly, the focus shifted to fabrics. Silk, as noted, was taken care of even before Pearl Harbor, but technology moved in with rayon or nylon as a good substitute. Trying to clothe a family, however, became difficult. Growing restrictions on the availability of fabric were occasioned by military necessities. One of the most obvious was the need for new uniforms for the expanding armed forces. Both the R.C.N. and the R.C.A.F. followed British patterns closely, but the army was less clearly defined. Battle dress evolved quickly from the leftover World War I uniforms handed out in September 1939. In January 1942 thousands of soldiers were issued smart new "walking out" uniforms, whose stated object was to make them the best-dressed men in the Dominion, as smart now as when they wore their best suit in civilian life.[453]

To support all this, at the beginning of September 1941, textile and clothing trades were placed under the jurisdiction of the W.P.T.B. By the beginning of 1942 a patriotic tailor was one who omitted the overlap in the jacket of a double-breasted suit and dispensed with the vest entirely. Frills and flounces disappeared from women's dresses, and by the summer of 1942 women were being advised that slacks, so recently considered "fast," were now in vogue. Hand-me-downs became the order of the day and on 10 January 1944, a touring exhibit visited Halifax to show how adult clothes could be cut down to fit children up to 14. But even this measure became more difficult with the suspension of the production of new sewing machines on 1 June 1943.[454] Expensive clothes fell under credit restrictions in July 1942, but although there were quotas, controls, and restrictions, rationing was never imposed. Underwear underwent redesign when the shortage of rubber eliminated elastic bands replaced by snap fasteners or buttons. Out went garters, corsets and rubber-soled shoes, the last of which, if you were a true patriot, you turned in in April 1942. Accessories became restricted. Umbrellas, for example, as of January 1943 were limited to three patterns, one for men and two for women.[455] Families with children who were hard on clothes and shoes and tended to too quickly outgrow them had the most to contend with. Right up to the end, childrens' underwear and shoes remained hard to get.[456] Even for children it was important to look good in public, but carefully repaired hand me downs, darned socks and sweater elbows became common. Britches were common for boys and lisle stockings for girls. In winter, lumberman rubbers were common, and in the summer, sneakers at $1.98 a pair or Sisman Scampers were the rule.[457]

REGULATED SCARCITY — FOODSTUFFS

The motor car was far from ubiquitous in 1939, but the rationing of food was something that affected everyone. Before 1939 families might have been restricted for personal economic reasons or seasonal shortages. Now, however, the W.P.T.B. led the citizenry into a whole new world. There were shortages of many things, particularly after war in the Pacific cut off sources of sugars, spices, tea and coffee; but meat and dairy rationing was driven by the need to divert production to feed Britain. Thousands of tons of food passed through the Ocean Terminals. Much of it was lost, along with the ships and men who carried it, in the desperate struggle to control the North Atlantic but enough of it made it to Liverpool and Glasgow to keep Britain fed during and well after the war.

The Nova Scotia Department of Agriculture was, first off the mark, urging farmers to greater production, encouraging youth to take up the labour slack, encouraging Nova Scotians to support the apple growers whose British markets vanished overnight, and setting out recommendations for cutting hay to the best effect. The first efforts of the W.P.T.B. were gentle, even tentative. Initially, the Board imposed a price ceiling on bread and flour in 1940, which was rescinded with the fall harvest of that year, and most of its attention was focused on industrial capacity with a wary eye on the cost of living.

During the period of the Phoney War, and for nearly another year, it was business as usual. In fact, the ordinary citizen ate better than ever. Despite wartime taxes of ten cents a pound on tea and coffee, and two cents a pound on sugar, food, generally speaking, was cheaper in 1941 than it had been 20 years earlier. Beef, for example, which had been 38.1 cents a pound in June 1921, was now 33.1 cents a pound. Flour had dropped from 4.8 cents a pound to 3.8 cents, while coffee went from 60.4 cents to 46.7 cents. Only tea was more costly, up from 70.4 cents a pound to 72.4 cents. Despite all the people flooding into Halifax the food situation seemed rosy enough, and farmers and market gardeners in Cole Harbour, Truro and the Annapolis Valley were at last reaping profits after years of hardships. Indeed, they were not producing enough and the Department of Agriculture urged urban Nova Scotians to "plant a Victory Garden," to dig up their flower beds to grow root crops, such as carrots, parsnips, onions, etc., which lent themselves to winter storage, or cucumbers and tomatoes, which could be pickled.[458] By 1941, with the disappearance of adult males, the provincial government recruited schoolboys 14 years and over for eight weeks of farm work during harvest time. The boys remained out of school until 20 October, got paid and received "special consideration" in their school work although there was no exemption from Provincial Exams. By the next year the Farm Service Force for Nova Scotia had been established to run the program, and as added incentive participants received an engraved diploma for framing and a special crest to be sewn on a jacket.[459] As a sure sign of prosperity after years of foreclosures, the banks now held high the torch of agriculture. "Always interested in the development of agriculture and practical co-operation with farmers, the Bank of Montreal is especially desirous *now* of assisting our growers of foodstuffs."[460]

This rosy outlook was an illusion for two reasons. First, there was a rapidly growing military contingent, of which Halifax was only too aware; men and women who had once fed themselves, but now had to be fed. Secondly, the country had accepted the responsibility of feeding Britain, isolated from the Continent after June 1940 and dependent on that tenuous 2,500 mile convoy link across the North Atlantic. In June 1941 the "Bacon Board" appealed to consumers to substitute fish for bacon and pork so that more of the latter could be exported to Britain,[461] and, more effectively, paid producers a premium of 25 cents a pound on pork exported to Britain.[462]

From this point on, little by little, pressure grew to change eating habits. In June the Dairy Products Board reserved all Ontario and Quebec cheddar cheese for the British market and it disappeared from grocery store shelves. Although foodstuffs remained unregulated for the rest of 1941, advertising campaigns pressured consumers to limit purchases to necessities and, in the autumn, to "serve by conserving," that is, by putting up preserves (in glass jars, not cans) to reduce winter demand and free up more food for the armed forces and for shipment to Britain. That autumn the W.P.T.B. in concert with the W.I.C.B took over the civilian economy and it was not long before the other shoe dropped.

By the end of September the entire food and clothing trade would be licensed. Wage and price controls were implemented in October. By 1 December storekeepers from Sydney to Victoria displayed the sticker authorizing them to conduct business. These were the most comprehensive set of economic controls ever applied in North America. It was not a moment too soon because the "East Coast Port" was now starting to feel the pressure.

Local farmers and market gardeners were still the source of the majority of fresh food in Nova Scotia, and with the sudden advent of thousands of military men, farmers were hard put to cope. Added to this, sudden surges in demand for foodstuffs as a convoy prepared to sail could strip Halifax wholesalers, bakeries and dairies, leaving the East Coast housewife to scrounge for basics that were plentiful even a couple of hours away in the Valley or Truro.

Ironically, Haligonians little realized that they might be awash in butter, eggs and meat as trainloads of the stuff rolled through the railyards, onto the convoys and out past Chebucto Head, while they scoured the grocery stores in vain. The agricultural abundance of central and western Canada was at the other end of that long, thin, overwhelmed rail line, and while freighters just blocks away bulged with foodstuffs that U-boat captains were planning to send to the bottom of the Atlantic, it usually took days for a couple of the boxcars to find their way on to a local siding and into the city grocery stores.

By January 1942 Donald Gordon, Chairman of the W.P.T.B., urged housewives to track prices and make sure that they remained stable, suggesting at the same time that food rationing was a possibility. Sugar was the first commodity to hit the wall and the same month as Gordon's dark hint it became the subject of a voluntary quota, limiting each household to three-quarters of a pound per person per week, and instructing hotels and restaurants to remove sugar bowls from tables and supply it only on request. At that time the public was assured that there was plenty of the stuff and that "Ration coupons *will not be used* to enforce the sugar limitations in Canada." The public was also sternly reminded that overconsumption "is not only against the law, but is also a betrayal of the war effort and consequently an offense against decency."[463]

Despite the reassurances consumers were forewarned of darker days when in May the sugar quota was reduced by a quarter of a pound, and tea and coffee were added to the quota system, not so much because of scarcity, it was said, but because "ships and lives must be conserved."[464]

Despite reassurances the promises turned out to be writ upon sand and it was certainly the epitaph for the struggling Acadia Sugar Refinery in Woodside, which closed forever in 1942. In mid-June the W.P.T.B. informed citizens that applications for temporary ration books were being mailed and should be filled out and returned immediately as coupon rationing of sugar would begin on 1 July. The turnaround time of two weeks to receive and process applications from every household in the Dominion of Canada and then return the ration books, seems astonishing to later generations, but it seems to have been considered routine at the time, even if in the final distribution volunteers were a great help.[465]

Food rationing expanded rapidly. The definition of good manners also expanded to include bringing your ration book along with your suitcase if you planned a visit of more than one or two days. The loss of a ration book was a serious issue since it involved swearing an affidavit, being issued a temporary one which was followed by a permanent replacement. One Halifax lady went through the process, then a few weeks later turned up apologetically at the Ration Board with her old one. When out shopping for a parcel to send to Britain, she mistakenly tucked it into a magazine that went into the parcel running the gauntlet of the North Atlantic. Some weeks later back it came in a letter of thanks, a round trip that many a sailor would have been happy to survive.[466] Although the temporary ration book of July 1942 was distributed through the mail, future ones were picked up at distribution centres supervised by one of twenty-eight Ration Boards in Nova Scotia.

The rationing of basic commodities became one more element families had to juggle to get through each week, a stress eased somewhat by the price control. Tea and coffee were added to the list in August, and at the beginning of September 1942 new long-term ration books were issued. Each successive one (there were five) had about six months' worth of coupons in various combinations of colours and letters. At Christmas 1942 butter was added with one half pound per person per week. The proclaimed rationale for this rationing was not scarcity, but supply management. Reflecting wartime prosperity, consumption of butter had risen by almost 11 percent and was taking up 48 percent of the milk supply. Butter rationing put a ceiling on production so as to ensure that there was plenty of milk for ordinary purposes and for cheese production destined for Britain.[467] For the same reason, the butterfat content in ice cream was restricted to 13 percent.

At the beginning of May 1943 the Board announced that meat rationing was imminent and on 27 May "spare" coupons found a use. Meat rationing was more complex because of the variety and grades of meats. There were four categories from A, worth 1/2 lb per coupon, to D, worth 1 1/4 lb per coupon. It applied to beef, veal, pork mutton and lamb. Fish, chicken, various and sundry organs and the items made from these last, such as wieners and bologna, remained unrationed. The consumer could use two coupons a week per person and was free to purchase whatever the butcher had in stock.

Rationing meant a process of re-education, and government dieticians presented the middle-class housewife with options she might not have previously or willingly considered: pot-roasted beef heart; braised calves heart; kidney creole, liver loaf, liver and spaghetti and Virginia beef tongue. Also avoiding high-end cuts but perhaps more palatable were a macaroni casserole, or a potato and cheese souffle. Once sugar rationing came in, chocolate sugarless cake, which used corn syrup, was served at the picnic which gas rationing restricted to the verandah or the back yard. A pudding made with boiled barley, eggs, milk, 1/4 cup of sugar and a little vanilla was an alternative.

Ration Book # 3, issued at the end of August, colour coded the coupons in green for tea and coffee, pink for sugar, orchid for butter and buff for meat. On 2 September 1943, its spare coupons were assigned to preserves, sweet spreads and canned fruit, with the option of using them to get more sugar.[468] The Board announced in November, in time for the Christmas season, that church or charity bazaars who applied for a permit, could sell a reasonable amount of jams and jellies without coupons.[469] They were, after all, funding huge contributions to war charities.

Although the sugar ration was not reduced, by late 1944 the public was urged to cut their consumption to make up for lower production owing to labour shortages and for increased use in the production of items such as synthetic rubber and 16-inch shells.[470] Only if she used her full ration for putting up preserves was the housewife off the hook, which was emphasized in June 1945, a month after VE Day, when, except for the preserves allowance, the sugar ration was officially reduced by five pounds over the rest of the year. This reduction was occasioned in part by bad weather and labour shortages in the West Indies, but mainly because the available supply now had to be stretched to include the liberated territories, a reason the weary consumer would hear repeated for months after the end of the war. Meat rationing, for instance, which had eased considerably after D-Day, was reintroduced to its fullest extent in the autumn of 1945, when it became clear that liberated as Europe might be, it was so devastated by war that the winter of 1945–1946 would be a grim one for friend and foe alike, even with help from North America.

Hand-in-hand with rationing went the Board's other control mechanisms. From time to time, to make a point, an example was made of some offender. Swift Canadian Company, a packing company, pleaded guilty to violating the price ceiling on beef in June 1942.[471] A Halifax grocer was fined $25 for contravening rationing regulations and a furniture dealer $257 for extending illegal credit.[472] In 1943 in an act of considerable daring, Gladys McPherson of 202 Inglis Street built with no permits whatsoever a $5,000 dwelling complete with copper down spouts and flashing. She was rewarded for her initiative with a fine of $400 and costs.[473]

Price regulation rather than prosecution was more common. Butter-fat production, for example, was subsidized by six cents a pound after July 1942. That summer the ceiling price of lamb was reduced while the wholesale price of a flat of Grade A eggs was set at 50 cents in Halifax. That same busy regulated year saw the imposition of price ceilings for potatoes and cedar shingles. The following winter of 1943–1944 brought a subsidy of a dollar a cord to combat a threatened shortage of fuel wood. During the harvest season of 1943, the Board froze the sale of tinned fruit and vegetables to force consumers to use fresh produce and save the other for winter. The autumn of 1943 brought further subsidies for the dairy industry to encourage pre-winter production, and Halifax partnered with the provincial government to build an abattoir and meat packing plant to ease the transportation bottleneck, which had as big an impact on supply as actual scarcity. Before that Christmas, chocolate bar sizes were frozen at 1941 levels, but in this one area, with a chocolate factory right downtown, Halifax had an advantage. Chocolate bars were still available for Donald Purchase to have as a fairly regular treat. Store cookies were also still found, although shortages of sugar and labour reduced their availability.[474] In 1944 ceiling prices were set for strawberries and raspberries in the Maritimes.

Rationing and controls meant a daily struggle for most Haligonians. As a girl, Marguerite Harding recalls scouring grocery stores for eggs and shortening for her mother, then checking the eggs carefully to make sure they were fresh.[475] In late 1942 finding any eggs at all was difficult. If you were not there when they were put out, priced at 56 cents a dozen, you got nothing.[476] For those so inclined, such as Mrs. Johnson of Bilby Street and Mr. Ryan of Merkel Street, you could overcome this difficulty. If the neighbours had no objections, the Superintendent of Health could be persuaded to issue permits to keep hens.[477] For those who wanted more there was, of course, always the black market where, for a price, anything was available.

On that disreputable periphery hovered the highly desirable commodity, liquor, for which a black market evolved quickly from the pre-war, prohibition tradition of bootlegging. In its simplest form, non-drinkers were often persuaded to turn over their unused booze ration, for a price, to those who would make better use of it.[478] On an edgier note, teenaged boys cruised the downtown restaurants on behalf of bootleggers, and, if asked, came up with a $4.00 bottle of whiskey for which the going price was $22.00.[479] City bootleggers rejoiced when a former rumrunner, the *Cassandra*, grounded years before at Thrum Cap, shifted in late 1942, causing 25 kegs of rum to surface and drift ashore. The R.C.M.P. got 15, but the bootleggers got the rest, which went for $125 a keg, just in time for Christmas.[480] Old rumrunners who recalled where there might be hidden caches of pre-war booze up and down the coast were in high demand. Rumrunning itself, that old Nova Scotian standby, was, despite the submarine threat, rumoured to be in fashion again because it paid so well. Even the navy, it was said, refreshed its supplies from that dubious well.[481]

Sometimes the supply was refreshed in more blatant ways. The foreman of a gang unloading whiskey from a ship at Pier 27 telephoned the police a number of times for help, then resignedly called the shipping office and told them, "Everybody on this job is now dead drunk or gone away carrying a case of whisky. I am the only one left."

The demand never slackened despite the efforts of temperance advocates. At the beginning of 1943 the Dominion government restricted the amount of alcohol available to provincial liquor commissions. This forced the Nova Scotia Liquor Commission to ration the stuff, but demand continued to rise. Reluctantly, the Liquor Commission reduced the ration still further in January 1944, once again bringing joy to the hearts of bootleggers everywhere. Each purchaser was allowed a monthly ration of one quart of spirits, two quarts of imported or four quarts of domestic wine, and 24 quarts of beer.[482]

All of these new regulations were enforced by an army of bureaucrats. Inevitably, some were swept off their feet by new-found authority. Many who had not qualified for the services found their way to employment with the Wartime Prices and Trade Board, and many were suspected of being patronage appointments. In the popular mind they were under-trained, overfed and overpaid and created great resentment when lack of common-sense carried them too far.

REGULATED SCARCITY — UNRATIONED WEALTH FROM THE SEA.

In April 1942 ships loaded with bananas arrived in port from the West Indies. The cargoes were deemed too ripe to survive the trip to central Canada, so for a few days Halifax was literally awash in the fruit. Much of the cargo was thrown overboard to float up and down the harbour until time and tide disposed of it; stevedores and dock workers staggered home under loads of them and part of the cargo was even dumped in the street. Some wheeled a mountain of bananas home on bicycles.[483] Although the steamship and importers denied it, rumour had it that they had been dumped to keep the price up.[484] This type of incident happened at least three times in 1941 and 1942. Only once did responsible officials think to donate instead of dump.[485]

Just a week later from some mysterious source came bread, floating in the harbour in such quantity that the ferry had to plow through the glutinous mass. When the *Clare Lilley* went ashore off Portuguese Cove on 1 March 1942, residents stocked up on lard, flour, bacon, biscuit and other staples.[486] When the ship finally broke up in a gale on 11 April the Dartmouth shore was strewn with groceries and tires.

On 14 January 1945, U-1232, not realizing or caring that the war was lost, attacked a convoy off the harbour mouth sinking the *British Freedom* and the *Athel Viking* and damaging the *Martin Van Buren* badly enough that the crew took to the boats. Rather than sinking as expected, the *Martin Van Buren* drifted through the foggy night to ground just offshore between Herring Cove and Sambro. The next morning an astonished fisherman saw the hulk through the mist, boarded it and found himself master of a treasure house of goods destined for American troops in Europe — tinned food, chocolates, cigarettes, plus locomotives and trucks. In no time every boat within a 50-mile radius was on its way.

Ron Buell and his buddies had built themselves a shack in the woods behind their homes. Walking along the shore on the way home from school one day they came across piles of packaged rations which they knew were from a torpedoed ship. They lugged as much as they could in their book bags to their hideaway where they snacked on the forbidden fruit for days.[487]

The sea was a source of other scarce goods. When the *Nueva Andalucia* grounded on Mars Rock in March 1942, it was loaded with aviation fuel. Enterprising Herring Covers were delighted to find that if you opened a hatch, it was there for the taking. Dipped out, or siphoned off into 45 gallon drums, it rapidly substituted for the increasingly scarce supply from the gas station. Douglas Power remembers night-time lineups along the road as people came from all over to buy unrationed gas for 25 cents a gallon. It was, however, a mixed blessing. Although free, it was heavily laced with cylinder oil, necessary for aircraft engines, but guaranteed to gum up the low-tech automobile.[488]

For weeks after one of these episodes, Halifax was awash in unrationed pleasures. Because of "connections" with family and friends along the shore, the Purchase family basement was, from time to time, full of C Rations, tins of corn and peaches, stalks of bananas, chocolate, coffee and cigarettes in packages of five. Young Donald had his first coffee and first cigarette from these stashes.[489]

Eating anything that came out of Halifax Harbour was dicey to say the least. Before the war was even a year old, the Superintendent of Health for the City of Halifax reported the bad state of Bedford Basin, "where it is known that large quantities of garbage and other materials are being dumped into the water from steamers and where there is considerable oil escaping from the boats which is practically beyond control."[490] The beaches in Africville and along the Basin shore were posted, and the superintendent hoped that meetings with the navy and port officials would resolve the problem. It did not. On 5 December 1942, boys playing by a cove in Eastern Passage, unable to resist the temptation, threw matches into the oily harbour water. The water caught fire, the west wind fanned the flames into an inferno and blew them across the road and into the village, which itself caught fire. To protect the homes and the nearby army barracks, the soldiers of the garrison, the Lanark and Renfrew Regiment, used army tractors to create a fire break by knocking down houses. In the end, one store, eight homes, ten fish houses, ten boats, part of a church and some fishing gear were lost.[491] Eight months later, in August 1943, there was so much spilled aviation fuel floating on the harbour surface that public warnings were issued against throwing matches or cigarettes into the water.[492] Gas and oil were the most visible things that went into the harbour in those environmentally unregulated days.

All of the "free" stuff came at a price. From the point of view of the authorities, this salvage was illegal on two counts. First, a ship and its cargo belonged to someone. Second, if that someone was from another country, customs duty was owed on it. These bureaucratic niceties were of little moment in the face of the age-old salvage traditions in coastal communities around the world which awarded the cargo of an abandoned ship to the finder. A ship grounded at the entrance to the harbour invariably meant a cat and mouse game between the R.C.M.P. and the salvagers, which sometimes broke out into covert and, occasionally, open warfare as each side asserted its rights, for there was no meeting of minds on this issue.

In a more innocent incident, Harold Harding and Willard Minard, stationed on McNab's Island, grew sick of canned and powdered milk. In a field across from their station, Mrs. Cleveland's cows grazed temptingly. Unable to resist, they snuck down from time to time and milked them. Years later, Harold confessed to Mrs Cleveland, who told him that she knew someone from the fort was milking his cows, but she considered it her contribution to the war effort.[493]

REGULATED SCARCITY — EPILOGUE

To the dismay of consumers the lid remained on food and consumer goods, as well as wages and prices, until 1946. There were continuing shortages owing to the need to feed Britain and Europe, and retool the economy for civilian production. There was also a justified fear of a repeat of the boom/bust which had followed the rapid deregulation after World War I, the consequences of which had gripped Halifax for 20 years. The government paid for the war not only by heavy taxation, but also by borrowing much of the surplus income its citizens had invested in War Bonds, War Savings Certificates and the like. This investment diverted the wealth created by wartime prosperity away from the temptations of the consumer goods, but with the end of the war, these millions in savings would start coming due, along with the promised bonus for demobilized service personnel.

The slow process of deregulation is considered one of the successes of the federal government's control during and after the war. On the one hand, it kept the devastated countries of Europe from starving until the 1947 Marshall Plan, initiated by the United States, started their economies on the road to recovery. And it kept the Canadian economy from overheating until it had shifted back to a peacetime footing and had time to reabsorb the returned troops.

NOVA SCOTIA LIGHT AND POWER — ELECTRICITY SUPPLY

The shortage of food and clothing was something most Canadians had to cope with, though Haligonians argued that they had to cope with it more than anyone else. But pushed to the brink were the city's public utilities, none of which had been designed to cope with the sudden load thrust upon them, and some of which were, by 1939, in serious need of capital investment, World War II or not.

Best prepared to face the onslaught were the facilities of the privately owned utility, Nova Scotia Light and Power Corporation, which provided electrical power to much of mainland Nova Scotia. As has been described above, it branched out into a war industry of its own. N.S.L.& P. also owned and operated Halifax's public transportation network, a street railway system whose 27 miles of standard-guage track covered most of the settled area of Halifax as it existed in 1939. Less known was the company's gas department, which supplied coal gas, used almost exclusively for heating and cooking, to the older areas of the city.

In the best shape of all, and in fact a wartime success story, were the N.S.L.& P.'s electrical generating facilities. Over the previous 40 years consumer electricity had developed from a novelty to a necessity and to keep up with the constantly expanding demand, equipment was regularly upgraded so that much of its generating capacity was state-of-the-art. It operated a number of corporate subsidiaries, reflecting its gradual acquisition of local systems over a period of years: The Avon River Power Co. Ltd.; Western Nova Scotia Electric Co. Ltd.; The Barrington Electric Co. Ltd.; Milton Hydro-Electric Co. Ltd.; The Chester Light and Power Co. Ltd.; and the splendidly named "The Edison Electric Light and Power Company Limited of Springhill."

In 1939 the company's Halifax and Dartmouth electrical supply came from a series of hydro generating stations at St. Margaret's Bay, the Avon River, White Rock and Black River in the Gaspereau Valley, Nictaux Falls, Bloody Creek, Fall River and Chester. A coal-fired steam-generating plant on the Halifax waterfront dated from 1912 and 1916, but was fired up only at times of peak demand or low water.[494]

Even before the war the company was in the process of expanding its generating capacity on the Black River System with two plants, one at Hollow Bridge and the other at Lumsden. Despite the disappearance somewhere in Siberia of a Swedish-built generator, completed after September 1939 and thoughtlessly sent for the sake of safety via Russia, Germany's then ally, the two plants came on line in 1940 and 1942. The timing could not have been better. HMC Dockyard and the Halifax Shipyards were on 24-hour, seven-day-a-week schedules, and in Dartmouth the new R.C.A.F. Station was, in effect, a whole new town. A new transmission line was erected to supply it and a substation and internal distribution system installed. Distribution systems were also installed to supply scattered forts and batteries. Once Wartime Housing Limited and the military began to erect "prefabs" and barracks, they too had to be supplied with power.

In this new reality, the Halifax steam plant gave up its standby role. A new boiler was added in 1941 and in August 1944 a new 12,500 kilowatt steam plant on the site came online just in time to offset the decline in hydro generation from a dry summer. There had been so little rain that to meet the demand before the new steam plant could take up the load, the Light and Power had bought the excess capacity of a local industry, suffering from shortages of material and labour. The new steam plant had a difficult birth, struggling for two-and-a-half years with red tape, priorities and shortages of materials and labour. An extra burden in construction was the decision to make it bombproof, a perfectly rational decision in 1942 when anything might be expected to come over the horizon.[495]

Throughout the war the company complained bitterly about high taxes: "The danger of the inequitable taxation policy of the Dominion Government is that it is promoting a drift to totalitarianism, which, in due course is bound to destroy initiative and enterprise." In an effort to thwart this drift it applied for and received in 1944 a reduction in power rates. This reduced its earnings, but more importantly, its taxes.[496] Nevertheless, the company prided itself, at war's end, that it had never had a shortfall of power and it had kept both industry and military operating at full capacity.

Less happy is the story of the company's tramway operation, which essentially fell apart under the strain. The tram network in Halifax, established in 1895 as the Halifax Electric Tramway Company, reflected the rebuilding of the system following the devastation wrought by the Halifax Explosion in 1917. By 1922, it was re-equipped with a short-wheelbase car known as the "Birney Safety Car." It was a compact car, designed in 1916, and particularly suited to the eighteenth-century layout of Halifax's downtown streets and their steep grades. This choice of car meant that the existing trackage could simply be rehabilitated, not reconstructed, as would have been necessary for the longer wheelbase cars then becoming standard. Further improvements in routing and equipment were made in 1926 and 1927, when the last of the old cars were retired and the Birney fleet was rounded out with a final acquisition.

A network of nine routes was established which, once the # 5 route was extended to Simpson's at the western edge of the city, remained stable until the end of electric transit in the 1960s. The original classy dark green livery of the cars, in a concession to the automobile, gave way to a highly visible yellow, prompting the wags to nickname them the "banana fleet," because they were yellow and came in bunches.

In 1939 the tram system was in pretty good shape, with 59 cars serving an annual ridership of about 9,000,000. An adult fare was a dime or three tickets for a quarter, and a transfer allowed you to travel all over the city. The management had been prescient when they saw war clouds forming and scoured North America to find extra Birneys to deal with what was optimistically seen in 1940 as a "temporary" need.[497] Twenty-three were found in Toronto, Bakersfield (California), Quebec and Sydney, just in the nick of time because not only would the other systems never have given up their cars had they known what was in store, the rapid growth in ridership threw the Halifax system into overload almost overnight. In addition, with the larger fleet of cars, the load on the electrical supply was too great and not all of the cars could be put into service. The trams used 550 volts DC generated in the company's Water Street plant, and once it became apparent that new equipment was not to be found, another continent-wide search was instituted for surplus generators found, finally, in Tennessee.[498]

The load on the system was compounded not only by the increase in population, but also by the decreased use of automobiles because of gasoline and rubber rationing. Maintenance of the trams became a problem after many experienced employees enlisted. With no hope that they, or the deteriorating parts which they had serviced, could be replaced just when they were expected to give harder service over longer hours, the clean and tidy trams began to get shabbier and shabbier. Loose bearings, worn wheels and squealing breaks gave patrons plenty of warning of an approaching train.

The condition of the tramcars was compounded by the deterioration of the trackage. Underneath the pavement the rails were fastened to wooden ties which, in the normal course of events needed gradual renewal, which was now not going to happen. With the heavier usage, especially in the heavily travelled downtown area, the pre-World War I wooden ties under the pavement "crushed and sunk from the rails [so that] their life [was] completely gone."[499] Despite long hours of overtime there was little the staff could do other than "barely ensure continued operation."[500] Since it was impossible to get new rails, in order to extend the trackage north along Gottingen Street to service the new housing, barracks and Manning Pool, the tracks that had taken summer picnickers into Point Pleasant Park were taken up and relaid at the other end of the city. Further extensions into the burgeoning west end were impossible, where barracks and housing in

Edgewood and on the civic airport lands filled up empty spaces. Workers and servicemen complained so bitterly about the long walk to the nearest tram line at Windsor and Almon that bus services were chartered from Park Transit Limited to pick them up. This service survived the war and continued until the end of the trams and the introduction of trolley coaches and new routes in 1949.[501]

Until the lid blew off on VE Day, most riders were good-natured enough, and the motormen, despite the numbers, seemed to know their passengers would wait for a bit if their regulars weren't at their stop at the regular time.[502]

By 1942 the system was carrying 100,000 passengers a day, almost the population of the city. NS.L.&P. stated publicly that owing to labour and matériel shortages it was "impossible to maintain the tramway system in satisfactory condition."[503] By war's end the fleet of 82 trams were carrying 31,540,941 passengers a year.[504] Even though the system was tired, tired, tired, it was still running, and carried on running.

Although not part of the Nova Scotia Light and Power Company system, it should be noted that there were other transit services invigorated by wartime restrictions affecting automobiles. These included the long-standing Canadian National Railways railcar service from Windsor Junction on a morning in and evening out basis; Pender's Bus, which served some of the same suburban communities along and north of Bedford Basin; and Ocean View Bus Company servicing Purcell's Cove, Herring Cove and Spryfield.[505]

When the trams were retired there was a wave of nostalgia. NS.L.&P. refused to sell the car bodies lest they suffer the indignity of ending up as chicken coops or tool sheds, and insisted on a "Viking funeral," consigning the cars to the flames. But in 1945 there was little nostalgia or gratitude. Years of overcrowding and rough rides were too fresh and the cars by then reeked of "the all-pervading smell of vomit that had accumulated through six years of transporting drunken sailors back to ship or base."[506] It is probably no coincidence that a burning tram car is still for many the symbol of the VE Day riots.

A footnote to the wartime operations of N.S.L.&P. is its almost forgotten gas department. Like the tramway system, it entered the war in relatively good shape, having devised its own system to convert Nova Scotia's high-sulphur coal to gas for heating and cooking purposes at the Water Street complex. A low-profile component of the company in 1939, it was pushed to the forefront by the shortage of oil. Within two years, the retorts, which "cooked" the coal to produce the gas, were going 24 hours a day. The demand became overwhelming when the navy installed huge gas fired ovens to supply baking and cooking needs for its burgeoning personnel, and when other city bakeries were ordered to convert to gas to save oil. Between 1942 and 1943 four new gas retorts were added. Had the war not ended when it did, these would not have been enough, because once again the plant was working 24 hours a day to keep up.[507]

As with the tram system, the war was the gas department's swansong. Despite its yeoman service for King and Country, N.S.L.& P. was committed to electrical power and had no particular interest in keeping up the gas plant, much less extending its services to the new suburbs. In January 1953 gas production ceased, the 4,041 commercial and household meters removed and those who did not convert to propane were offered credit to convert to electricity.[508]

DARTMOUTH FERRY COMMISSION

As busy as everything else, and as unprepared, was the Halifax-Dartmouth ferry owned and operated by the town of Dartmouth. The Ferry Commission operated three steam-powered vessels, *Chebucto*, *Halifax* and *Dartmouth*. The first two were Glasgow-built veterans of 1897 and 1911 respectively, while the 1934 *Dartmouth* was built in Quebec with an engine from Scotland.[509] The ferries were the only practical link between the two communities for pedestrians and automobiles alike, except for the long and tiresome drive around Bedford Basin.

The war began for the ferries in the summer of 1939 when the military ordered the *Dartmouth* to stand by for its purposes. It was soon busy ferrying A.A. guns and other military equipment to the batteries being built to protect the Bedford magazine, Imperoyal and R.C.A.F. Dartmouth.[510]

Traffic increased by leaps and bounds from September 1939. There was, of course, the new military component heading to and from the growing establishments on the eastern side of the harbour. There was the increasing effect of gas shortages and rationing, which made the drive around the Basin almost impossible. The crowds of somewhat rambunctious servicemen brought regular patrols of Military Police on board as early as 1940 and the short trip got a lot more claustrophobic after February 1941 when all the windows were blacked out.

The crowded state of the harbour meant that in these pre-radar days (it was not installed until 1973) the crews had to be constantly on the alert.[511] Because the ferries had a designated and protected route across the Harbour, marked on charts, there were only two collisions. The first was in July 1941 when the *Halifax* collided in the fog with the S.S. *Trewelland*. The following January, the two ferries collided with each other as they negotiated their way between two ships. In neither case was there serious damage, but the navy took extra precautions to keep the ferry captains aware of any ships or obstructions in the designated lanes.[512]

In the peak year of 1944 the ferries carried 6,000,000 passengers and 500,000 vehicles. To handle the load, all-night service began New Year's Eve 1942, which was a huge relief to everyone from overtime workers to movie goers to good-time Charleys. For any of these, missing the last ferry had been a huge inconvenience, and meant spending the night in a hotel or with friends. More relevant to the hordes of daytime commuters was the decision to build a new ferry. W.J. Roue of *Bluenose* fame supplied the design for a wooden vessel because steel was out of the question. No regular shipyard had the capacity, but a local builder, Hugh Weagle, was found and the community was able to watch as he built it on the shores of Dartmouth Cove. The first locally built ferry since 1864, the *Governor Cornwallis*, entered service in December 1942.

Its three vehicle lanes, rather than the two lanes of her sisters, was a godsend in dealing with wartime traffic. The new-fangled diesel-electric engines, however, gave endless mechanical trouble, and, to make matters worse, were so noisy and rough that passengers complained. Insulation, installed in an attempt to deal with some of the problems, caught fire on 22 December 1944. When the fire was discovered at 4 p.m. it had already left Halifax and during the crossing the crew struggled in desperate silence to put out the blaze and not to cause panic among the passengers. Only when the three or four hundred passengers and twenty vehicles were safely off in

Dartmouth was the fire department called. By then it was too late and soon the boat was ablaze from stem to stern. There was nothing to be done, the blazing hulk was towed to George's Island, beached and left, while the original boats picked up the slack and soldiered on for the remaining six months of the war.

The loss of the *Governor Cornwallis's* large capacity put terrific pressure on the remaining ferries. For passengers peak times meant standing room only and planning began immediately for a replacement. On 28 March 1945, a contract was awarded to Pictou Foundry and Machine Company to build a new steam-powered ferry which was launched December of that same year as the *Scotian*.[513]

THE WATERWORKS

The system that coped least satisfactorily with the demands of wartime was the municipally owned and operated water supply. It had a long and honourable history, going back to 1844 when the Halifax Water Company, the third such in Canada, was formed. It was supplied from a series of lakes in the high ground to the west of the city and was entirely dependent on precipitation and largely gravity-fed.

The weakness of the system was in its governance. The originally private operation had been bought out by the city in 1861 and, until 1872, operated by a paid commission. From then on it was operated by a Committee of the City Council. As a result, the system was badly neglected and seriously underfunded. So neglected was the system that by 1939, for example, screens over the water intakes in the lakes had long since rotted away. Since they had never been replaced, in the autumn of the year, migrating eels seeking a way to the sea, infested the pipes. Sanitation was rough and ready in its application. There was a manually operated chlorinating system, but when it did not work, which was often the case, employees resorted to throwing bags of chloride of lime into the lakes. In 1909 and 1920, water meters were installed in many houses, which brought about a dramatic reduction in consumption along with bitter complaints to aldermen. By the beginning of the war, of the 13,000 installed meters, some 7,000 were out of commission due to lack of maintenance, some had never been read, and others had not been read in years. Master meters at the intakes had also been out of action for years. Even if the infrastructure had been maintained, many of the mains were due for routine replacement, though there is no evidence of any plan to do so. When the system was finally overhauled it was found that 51 percent of the water that left the lakes was lost before it ever reached customers.

To make a bad situation worse, when the war began, illicit houses, for whose owners adequate septic systems were the last thing on their mind, were built throughout the watershed lands, with pollution of the lakes the inevitable result.

The whole ramshackle edifice teetered even further on the edge of collapse with the enlistment of staff and the transfer of others to more essential positions, leaving behind only eight harassed and demoralized employees to maintain the water supply of the port that anchored the western end of the vital supply line to Britain. After the war, the then manager of the Public Service Commission, H.W.L. Doane, consciously paraphrased Churchill's reference to the R.A.F. pilots of the Battle of Britain when he said of this beleaguered eight, "never was so much owed by so many to so few."[514]

Matters were brought to a head by the necessity and near impossibility of supplying the expanding military installations with water often on very short notice, and departing convoys and HM ships with enough fresh water for transatlantic voyages. Finally, two disastrous fires, the First Baptist Church at Spring Garden and Queen (21 March 1942) and Crane Supply (14 November 1943) on Barrington Street caused more strain.[515] Not only was there virtually no water pressure (in the first case, the *Queen Mary* taking on water at the seawall had affected the pressure; in the lattercase the fire department pumped the mains dry) so that the buildings burned to the ground in a spectacle more entertaining than edifying, but also in the aftermath the fire insurance companies threatened to raise their rates by 30 percent.[516]

Ottawa may have been indifferent to the fate of Halifax buildings, but it was not indifferent to the convoys and the navy and it finally focused its collective attention on the problem. Likewise, the citizenry, aware of the problem for years, found its attention engaged by the threat to the pocketbook by the insurance companies.

Under the aegis of the Department of Munitions and Supply, the first steps were taken in January 1942 when engineers investigated the possibility of installing extra pumping stations to boost supply.[517] This solution was like putting new wine in old bottles because when the newly installed pumps were connected to the old mains they promptly burst under the unaccustomed pressure, forcing the closure of the shipyard and a number of businesses.[518] Rumours began to spread that summer that the convoy system would abandon Halifax, where it could take three days to water a ship from a water boat, in favour of New York, where a ship could tie up at a pier, connect direct to the mains and be topped up in no time.[519]

At the insistence of the Board of Public Utilities, the Engineering Service Company (E.S.C.) was appointed to come up with recommendations. In the end, the city turned the whole mess over to them not only to investigate but also to operate. The E.S.C. operated the waterworks for a year and a half and, by undertaking simple maintenance, made dramatic improvements in the water supply. The upgrade cost some $800,000 of which the Dominion Government contributed $200,000.[520] On 1 January 1945, the Public Service Commission, an independent agency of the city, took over and continued a process of upgrading well after the war, so that by 1952, despite post-war growth, consumption had dropped from 14,000,000 gallons per day to 9,000,000.[521]

There was a gap in this success story. The city failed to act on a School Board suggestion in the summer of 1944 that the school at Africville, a community otherwise dependent upon wells, be supplied with mains water. A 6-inch main from the Quarantine Hospital on the hill above would have cost $8,000 to $13,000 and a summer-only surface pipe $1,000. After much equivocating, the City Works Committee, uncertain about the post-war future of Africville, balked at the "large expenditure for the purpose of extending sewer and water mains ... if the area is to be used for a different purpose in future. Therefore as an alternative the Committee approve of the Sanitary Engineer's recommendation that permission be granted to erect a privy."[522] There was further discussion over the next few months and the matter concluded in mid-October with a decision to set up a study to get more information about sinking a well before applying to the Public Utilities Board.[523] and there the matter seems to have rested.

CONCLUSION

If there was anything that the privations of World War II taught residents of the "East Coast Port," it was, like Scarlett O'Hara, the heroine of *Gone With The Wind* who faced the wreck of the family plantation after the Civil War, a determination never to be poor again.

Post-war prosperity, fed by the military buildup of the Cold War, assured the citizenry that they would not sink into the economic lethargy that had followed World War I. Perhaps, finally, after half a century, the ghosts of the departed and much-regretted Imperial military presence and its comfortable infusion of cash could be excised and replaced with a bene-factor based in Ottawa.

Since the perilous state of the local infrastructure had exposed the community to embarrassing national attention, to say nothing of considerable personal inconvenience, the old penny-pinching ways were replaced with a determination to build up and maintain high standards that would make the harbour communities worthy places to live and invest in without worrying about water, disease or getting from A to B.

CHAPTER SEVEN:

The End and the Beginning

For Halifax the war literally ended not with a whimper but with a bang on VE Day, 8 May 1945, when the centre of the city exploded in riots which spread across the harbour and nibbled away at Dartmouth's downtown core. Not surprisingly, this event left civilians and service personnel with a bad taste in their mouths and strained relationships. Then, in July the naval magazine in Bedford exploded in sound and fury. The heroic efforts of naval personnel from HMC ships in port prevented a devastation as bad or worse than in 1917. All that remained was to see the troops home from overseas, gather its collective wits, and set about planning to make the rest of the century worth the sacrifices that had been made.

VE DAY

In mid-1944 many people were confident that peace would arrive by Christmas. The population as a whole, civilian and military, ready and waiting for a European peace for at least two years, was getting increasingly impatient with the recalcitrant Germans who refused to admit the reality of their situation. By April 1945, however, it was certain that the end was near and the news of the final German defeat was expected almost daily.

Tensions, however, lurked beneath the surface of the "East Coast Port" that required careful and sensitive management if they were not to erupt once the lid of wartime restriction came off. Such careful and sensitive management was not to be found.

As far as the navy was concerned, tension had simmered since the Ajax Club was closed in February 1941, four years before. That grievance merged with an internal malaise arising from a sharp divide between ship and shore establishments and a suspicion that the quality, or at least the management, of recruits had declined with the arrival, after 1943, of the "Zombies," those members of the Canadian army who, as was their right until the "Conscription Crisis" of 1944, could refuse to volunteer for overseas service. Crammed into the drafting depot, HMCS *Peregrine*, the former R.C.A.F. manning depot in Windsor Park, was a large number of new recruits, along with the usual portion of misfits awaiting discharge, and others awaiting reassignment to the Pacific.[524] Those for whom Halifax was a temporary home were sick of its shabbiness, felt gouged by grasping landlords and storekeepers and resented what they saw as exorbitant restaurant prices and long lineups for indifferent service.

As far as civilians were concerned, the enthusiasm and patriotism that had prevailed for the first few years had begun to disintegrate. They were as sick of many of the same things and of the military presence taxing resources. As patience wore thin, they could hardly help but notice that most of the lineups were made up of the military. Military uniforms seemed to predominate in most of the chaos in their formerly genteel downtown. And why did servicemen, whose barracks and shipboard food was better and more plentiful than what civilians could hope for, fill up the restaurants? These matters were not helped by the minority of "Upper Canadian" snobs who did not grasp that it was amazing that the city had coped at all in the impossible situation.

Clarissa Johnston's brother, John, arrived from Ontario for a visit in September 1940 and had to find his way to their Dartmouth home: "He asked a soldier on the main street if there were any streetcars in this 'city' and the man burst out laughing, saying 'What do you mean City'? John got a big laugh out of that."[525] Civilians were tired of hearing outsiders sneer at the city's "toonerville trolleys," which, before the servicemen arrived, had been clean, tidy and perfectly adequate for their needs. They bridled at insults involving the many cobbled downtown streets which, given that horse haulage was still a factor in the freight business, provided excellent traction for shod hooves. If they hated it so much, why did they bring their wives and families into a situation where there was no room for them from the beginning?

Whatever the rights and wrongs of the civilian/serviceman points of view of each others' wartime conduct, there was no question that the community and military leadership was seriously out of touch with the pressure cooker that was Halifax in 1945. In the long-range planning for the victory celebrations, which began in August 1944, there was a sincere if naive belief that when the great day came it should not be one of riotous celebration, but of calm reflection, commemorating the sacrifices that had been made by those who had died in the struggle against fascism. Many recalled the tumultuous end to World War I and determined it should not happen again. In an editorial in the summer of 1944, the *Midland (Ontario) Free Press* had urged that when victory was proclaimed "all liquor stores and beer parlors should be closed and instead of being a day of hilarious celebration, it should be a day of Prayer and Thanksgiving."[526] This opinion made an impression at least in Lunenburg, where a public prayer service was held that September commemorating the Declaration of War. "In past years victories, Armistice and other such events were marked with hilarious celebrations, today we unite in prayer — a great change indeed. Perhaps if this way of celebrating had been used in the past this bloody war would never have taken place."[527] Such sentiments were common among well-meaning citizens, particularly those who had lost a son in the prime of his life.

The local planning committee, chaired by Director of Civil Defence, Osborne Crowell, seemed to focus as much on keeping the celebration contained as on the celebration itself. One aspect of this approach was a recommendation to close liquor stores and military canteens, with the ironic ominous forethought of protecting those places from service personnel. Official celebrations, the committee implied, were to be a civilian affair; the services could look after themselves, a strange rationale given that 90 percent of servicemen were civilians who just happened, for the time being, to be wearing a uniform.[528]

For those who chose to see, there were signs that all was not well. On 2

THE END AND THE BEGINNING

December 1944, a route #3 tram headed north along Hollis Street was loaded with about two dozen well-lubricated sailors. Scuffles broke out, two windows were smashed and the motorman, judging that none of the men planned to pay their fare (which was done on exiting, not entering), refused to stop and open the door and kept on around the corner and up Buckingham to Barrington where he was able to warn an inspector of his dangerous cargo. The sailors realized they had been shanghaied and tried to break down the doors, but they were too late because the # 3 was now next to the Police Station. Forewarned by the inspector, the car was met by a phalanx of constables. The men, compliant for now, filed off, dropping their fares in the box,[529] leaving the car to run another day and the ratings to await another opportunity.

In March 1945 the military police met to plan their VE Day strategy for Halifax. "Kid gloves" seemed to be the operative phrase, and word went out, perhaps, in retrospect, too far out, to go easy on celebrating sailors. "Apprehending a rating on this day ... may be the cause of a serious riot."[530] After all, for five years, the judicious balance between enforcement and laissez-faire, if not pretty, had worked. Some organizations were close enough to the streets to sense tension; as early as 16 April the Halifax North Civic Improvement Association warned the city that trouble was brewing.[531]

Because they, too, had ears close to the ground, or because they could not extract from the city police a promise that they would be protected, movie theatre operators placed a collective advertisement in the newspapers announcing that they would close on VE Day whenever that might be, and so they did.

It all began Monday 7 May. Despite the insane hope of the Dominion government that it could control the timing of the announcement, at about 10:30 a.m. word leaked out in Halifax that Germany had surrendered. In a timely and auspicious move, the sun came out after a cloudy start to the day and the city began to shut down, and shut down tight. The theatres kept their advertised promise; the provincial government closed the liquor stores, "until further notice," leaving the field open to delighted bootleggers, who now had Monday as an extra day to charge $15.00 for a bottle of cheap rye; virtually all of the stores closed by noon and announced that they would not be open until Wednesday the 9th; of the 55 restaurants in town, only 16 opened up on 7 May, and only 11 the following day, and most of these closed by 4:00 p.m.

At first all seemed to go well and it was announced that the following day, 8 May, was scheduled as VE Day for the official celebrations. The evening of the 7th, in what seemed like a good move, civic officials moved up by a day, part of the celebrations. South Park Street, bordering the Public Gardens between Spring Garden and Sackville, was closed off, three bandstands erected and sawdust spread on the pavement for a big street dance. David Chipman and his buddies, at 15 just the right age to enjoy the unaccustomed public blowout, mingled with the increasing crush of revellers, danced a few dances, watched the level of drunkenness escalate and thought that they had seen it all when 10 drunken sailors rolled up South Park in front of the Lord Nelson, proclaiming themselves to be the sons of the mayor and carrying between them a sign with gilded letters reading "The Law Courts," obviously liberated from above the main door of the Spring Garden Road Courthouse a few blocks away.[532] A cheerful crowd of some 15,000 watched fireworks, probably the first since September 1939, from George's Island and naval craft in the harbour, and began to disperse into the pleasant late evening air. Along with the boys, they drifted home, thinking, no doubt that the East Coast Port had said goodbye to six years of war a little raucously, perhaps, but in fine style, which a Thanksgiving Service on the Garrison Grounds the next day would bring to a fitting conclusion.

It would not be that easy. Army and R.C.A.F. personnel had been ordered to return to barracks and they did, but the navy had not been so ordered owing to a long standing "open gangway" policy of allowing men not required for duty to go ashore at will, and they did. Several thousand ratings from the ships in port and the three naval barracks were suddenly out on the streets of the town on a warm spring night free to roam at will. As the old saying goes, the devil makes work for idle hands, and what the devil focused his attention on even before all those locked but stocked liquor stores, were all those little yellow trams, which had assumed a sort of symbolic resonance in the feckless, predominantly adolescent minds of the bored ratings.

Motormen struggled to get their cars back to the car barn as groups of sailors pulled the trolleys off the overhead, and began to throw rocks through the windows. By 10:30 p.m. a frenzy erupted and tram # 126 became the sacrificial lamb for a crowd now estimated at 5,000. The car, heading south along Barrington, was seized, the motorman ejected, the fare box looted and the interior and exterior trashed by a crowd of ratings. Despite every effort the car could not be toppled over. Thus thwarted, the crowd set about its destruction by stuffing burning newspapers into the seats. The coup de grâce came when a more knowledgeable rating opened the journal boxes which held a bath of oily waste to lubricate the wheel bearings and set it alight. The other three journals were similarly lit and some of the oily waste thrown into the interior finished the job.

The police who arrived on the scene to restore order soon realized they had made a big mistake when they were overwhelmed. Their van was over-turned and the gas leaking from its tank set alight by a cigarette. Part of the fun, which involved pushing Constable Nagle back inside the burning van as he struggled to escape, was spoiled by one sailor who dragged him out. The eventual explosion was immensely satisfying and, even better, it brought firemen whose turn it now was to be harassed. After their hoses were cut and their truck threatened with the same fate as the police van they wisely retreated.[533]

Sated for the time being and clearly in control of central Halifax, atten-tion shifted to the liquor stores, another symbol of what was, in their mind, wrong with the city. There they sat in the late evening dusk, fat, juicy, vul-nerable repositories full of forbidden fruit. Starting just before midnight, the first to go, at Sackville and Granville, was soon followed by the main branch on Hollis at Salter, and then Buckingham Street. The Hollis and Buckingham Street stores got off lightly as reinforcements were able to push the looters back sooner rather than later, but it didn't really matter, there was still plenty to go round. Beer, thousands of cases of it, was the drink of choice, but cases of spirits and wine went through the windows by the hun-dreds.

To be fair to the navy, it does not appear that they struck the first spark. On the afternoon of the 7th, long before the lid blew off, a gang of boys, seized by the moment and the opportunity for license that they correctly assumed it offered, pounced on a vegetable-laden truck and distributed its cargo of bagged carrots up and down Barrington Street between the Capitol and Orpheus theatres. At the same time, another equally opportunistic group of youths, stationed at Sackville and Barrington, exercising the rights of adolescents everywhere, indulged a long suppressed urge by pulling the trolley poles of passing trams, creeping by in the holiday traffic, off the overhead which supplied their current. Great fun for the boys; for the trams, their riders and motormen, this meant a series of jack-rabbit stops and starts, and for the stalled traffic, an excuse to lay on the horn.

There it might have remained but for the many naval ratings with nothing to go back to but a stuffy fo'c'sle or crowded barrack and drifting about the city centre with everyone else, who saw this attractive tumult and thought to themselves, "surely we can do better?" Had a seed been planted that would bear fruit in only a few hours?

The riots started so late at night that many Haligonians, who depended on the newspapers for their news, remained unaware of the situation until well into the next morning, 8 May, because the papers had gone to bed before things got hot. The next morning, David Chipman got up bright and early to go sailing with friends on a 38-foot schooner. Only when they got back later that morning did they hear that all was not well, a matter of some importance to the skipper whose family store on Granville Street was right in the middle of the action. His pleasant morning on the Arm a rapidly fading memory, he headed downtown, and not far behind him was young David. Isabel MacNeill, a W.R.E.N. officer on her way to Stadacona that morning, stopped at the corner of Spring Garden and Barrington to watch the parade returning from the 10:30 a.m. Service of Thanksgiving at the Garrison Grounds. She was amazed at the sight of St. Paul's cemetery full of people sitting on tombstones drinking out of bottles, mostly civilians and navy, she recalled, with a sprinkling of army and air force. As the Parade passed the cemetery, led by the Naval Band playing "Hearts of Oak," many naval personnel, seeing the party in the cemetery, broke ranks and joined them: "The wrens, army and air force men & women continued on.... As soon as possible I continued up Barrington Street. Most of the store windows were smashed — crowds of people, mostly civilians were carrying merchandise: I recall three large ladies lugging a refrigerator through a broken window."[534]

Aware that all was not well, Admiral Leonard Murray, attending the Thanksgiving Service, ordered the 400 personnel in attendance to march through the downtown, band playing. This he expected would bring the men to their senses. If that failed, after the parade the detachment would be available to assist the Shore Patrol in picking up the troublemakers. Whatever the merits of the plan, scores of the men, estimated by Isabel MacNeill at over a hundred, joined the rioters; the orders to assist the Shore Patrol never got through so that the remainder of the detachment went back to barracks. To make matters worse, Police Chief Judson Conrod overlooked ordering his men to stay on duty until further notice, and promptly at 4 p.m., 40 men, a whole platoon, went off shift and, no doubt to their relief, straight home.[535]

The crowd that headed away from the remnants of the VE Day parade, picking its way northward through the increasing chaos of Barrington Street, felt no inhibitions about heading south to Keith's Brewery on Lower Water Street. David Chipman, only a few hours before a world away on the deck of a schooner, watched in fascination as 30 sailors picked out one from a pile of telephone poles lying along Water Street, and watched the "Battle of the Brewery" begin. He was a veteran of such great events as the 1939 Royal Visit, the Queen Hotel fire of that same year and the First Baptist Church fire of 1942, but now he found himself in the midst of an even greater show. Here Colonel Sidney Oland, having been forewarned of the chaos enveloping the centre of they city, joined his brewery workers in the warehouse, already penetrated by looters, and staved off worse destruction by handing out cases of beer. When it was evident to the looters that it was all gone, they moved on without doing any serious damage to Keith's.[536] Most of the beer was in cases of a dozen quarts and David Chipman watched happy servicemen enjoying not only the beer, but the satisfaction of smashing bottles on the curb one by one and watching the foaming beer run in rivers down the gutter. By now well lubricated, they moved on to further pillage.

Emboldened by clear evidence that the authorities could or would not do anything, attention turned once more to the Hollis Street store, virtually across the street. This time it was a case of "no more Mr. Nice Guy." The boards so hastily nailed over the windows after the previous night's more tentative assault were torn off and the store thoroughly cleaned out with an expertise born of very recent experience. David, fresh from his Keith's experience, watched the process and when it was over went inside what would normally have been forbidden territory for a 15 year old: "The store was just a shell.... It was smashed completely, full of broken window glass and bottles. And reeking of a molasses smell from all the rum that had been spilled in the pillage. No one was around anymore — the place had nothing more to offer anybody."

Impelled by the urge to complete unfinished business, one squad returned to Buckingham Street which, despite the efforts of four Mounties to persuade them out of their intent, eventually fell victim to the same fate as the others. Either another, more adventurous squad ventured far afield, or more opportunistic locals took advantage of another golden opportunity. Far from downtown the Liquor Commission had another store on Agricola near Almon. It had been boarded up and garrisoned by a couple of Mounties and a squad of military police. It was to no avail. Don Purchase, by then in high school, watched in fascination as the men from the barracks on the nearby Exhibition Grounds formed a "bucket brigade," passing cases of beer and liquor up Almon Street and over the fence into the barracks never to be seen again,[537] and civilians from the neigbourhood, scarcely believing their good luck, stocked up.

By now the revellers had accomplished more than they had ever expected or desired and simply abandoned themselves to the riotous license that generally ensues when humans are freed from normal constraints. A *Herald* reporter, with what seems to be unusual candour for the time and place, described those who, sated with their spoils, chose to withdraw from the main stage. They "swarmed away from the immediate scene and packed themselves into the Nova Scotia Light and Power Company's spare trams stored on a track just above Water Street. They drank and tossed bottles through the windows. Others with their women lurched to Cornwallis Square in front of the Nova Scotian where the scenes of debauchery were rivaled only by those on Citadel Hill and Grafton Park [the present Memorial Library]. There hundreds sat on cases and cartons drinking, singing, mingling ale with fighting and sex."[538]

For those who were still capable of action, the focus shifted back to the trams. Inhibition was completely gone; it mattered not that it was broad daylight. In the early afternoon tram # 151 on its way up Barrington Street past Stadacona had to be rescued by a phalanx of Shore Patrol after exuberant sailors climbed on the roof and snapped off the spare trolley pole. The rescue was only temporary. Some 2,000 more sailors appeared, swept away the Shore Patrol, smashed windows and lights and set the wicker seats alight, then set off, smoke pouring from the windows, at what for the Birney was high speed. At Duke Street more Shore Patrol appeared and wiser heads prevailed. The hijackers abandoned their smoking victim, but not before throwing the controller in reverse leaving the car to its fate. It soon stalled, exhausted and abandoned, until half-an-hour later when a tramway truck crept on to the scene and pushed the car along the tracks to the Water Street barn. Number 15 was not the only victim. Another Barrington Street car was seized, its hapless motorman ejected like all the others, and raced along Barrington Street until its flanges, unable to cope with the rough track and the curve at Duke Street, left the rails and ran straight into a store front where, half in and half out, it came to rest.[539]

Charlotte Akerlund worked on Sackville Street at Kelvin, Bottomley & Baird, a marine supply firm dealing in charts and navigational and scientific publications. She was responsible for the cash and when she heard that there was trouble, began to walk down Barrington Street from the family home opposite Cornwallis Park. What she saw angered rather than shocked her because of the wanton destruction and the appalling waste. At the corner of Morris and Barrington she watched ratings use a battering ram on the front door of Mackenzie & Osborne's grocery store, then drag out barrels of potatoes and apples, which were then dumped into the street. Further along, Wallace's Shoe Store had its entire inventory pulled off the shelves, dumped on the floor or thrown out on the street. The skipper of the morning's peaceful cruise on the Arm reached his Granville Street store in time to see his windows being smashed. He was not prepared to put up with such nonsense and made this very clear to the sailors who had done the damage. They in turn were not prepared to put up with him and returned with reinforcements to beat him up badly enough to put him in the hospital. Some stores, like Kelly's or Woods, by a combination of good luck and good information had had the foresight to board up their windows.[540] All around David Chipman on Barrington Street, store windows were being smashed, glass and litter carpeted the street, naval ratings and other looters carted store mannequins and merchandise about amid yelling, shouting and crowds of spectators watching the fun. And fun it seemed to be. Despite, or perhaps because of, the absence of military or civilian police, his recollection is that everyone was cheerful and in a happy mood.

Primed for six years to face an external threat, the city's civilian and military defenders were paralyzed by the threat from within, which in a way was a good thing. It was not until 8 p.m., after much argument about an obvious step, that a curfew was put into effect, backed up once the train came in, with 1,000 troops from Debert and a tour of the riot zone by a reluctant Admiral Murray in a sound truck telling his men to return to base. Fortunately for the authorities, the rioters, if not the looters, had by and large been relatively good-humoured so long as they were left to work off whatever their frustrations were. Aside from a tram car or two, and small blazes in Faders Pharmacy and People's Credit Jewellers, they had resisted the temptation to torch, as well as trash, more of the downtown. By the time the authorities worked up the courage to proclaim a curfew, the rioters were no doubt exhausted, hung over or sated, and order was restored amid the ruins with relative ease. The streets were awash in broken glass from store windows and bottles, in merchandise, clothing, stationery supplies and tins of cookies. Just about anything that was sold along the street was on it.

In the end, three people died, 211 were arrested, 564 businesses pillaged and 65,000 quarts of liquor and 8,000 cases of beer disappeared. 540 police, including R.C.M.P., city constabulary and military forces were overwhelmed in nearly 48 hours of mayhem and riot.[542]

In addition, they inspired copycat riots. In Dartmouth, across the harbour, the chief of police, who did not feel the navy's "go easy" policy applied to him, issued his men with night sticks, stopped the ferries and although the area between King and Commercial streets was busy for a while, kept a lid on the worst excesses. A riot broke out in Sydney; in New Waterford the Chief of Police was stoned by a mob of four or five hundred; and in Kentville, Yarmouth and Dominion, where little time was wasted on preliminaries, the mobs headed straight for the liquor stores and cleaned them out.[543]

The riots became a national scandal and a Royal Commission was quickly convened under the direction of Mr. Justice R.L. Kellock of Toronto. Its mandate was quick and dirty with an agenda more aimed at getting the scandal off the front pages before the national election in June than in providing any thoughtful answers.

Since the streets had been full of naval uniforms, the navy was seen to be at fault, which to a certain extent it was. To make sure the buck did not stop at too high a level, the scapegoat became the highest ranking local naval officer, Rear Admiral Leonard W. Murray, whose ground-breaking contribution to the conduct of the Battle of the Atlantic and the significance of Canada's role therein was not allowed to stand in the way. Murray appears to have been strangely unfocused during the riots and not to have grasped that, for the moment anyway, he had to shift focus to the streets of Halifax and away from the genuine possibility that rogue U-boats might be prepared to carry on the war in the North Atlantic. He never wavered in his belief, before, during and after the events, that civilians, not the navy, had been the main offenders. Civilian officials, with an eye to financial compensation from Ottawa, were not prepared to admit that blame lay other than with the navy. Whatever the rights and wrongs of the VE Day riots, much of the fault lies in the fact that the military and civilian personalities involved did not much like one another. They made no joint effort in the advance planning for VE Day, or in dealing with the riots once they began. Murray had no choice but to offer his resignation, which was accepted with alacrity and in such a manner as to imply a dismissal. No doubt to the relief of many he chose to retire in England where, to their even greater relief but to posterity's loss, he chose not to write his memoirs.

Compensation was quickly paid to the ruined businesses without the usual quibbling. Before the end of May enough glass had been received or was on the way from the United States to complete the reglazing of the downtown storefronts by the end of June.[544] Life seemed to be returning to normal.

THE MAGAZINE EXPLOSION

A definite chill had set in relationships between the civilian and military worlds. There was the empty seat beside the serviceman in the crowded tram, the restaurant that was too busy to serve a rating, the sudden difficulty of finding volunteers for the service canteens, the man on the street who spat on a sailor's shoe. Not only was it unpleasant; it was in many cases unfair, because if the city had been crowded before, it was even more so now as the harbour filled with ships returning from the North Atlantic with crews ready for a little rest and relaxation, waiting to be released from service, or on their way to the West Coast to join the Pacific war. Few of these men had any responsibility for the riots and knew little about them.

All of these returning ships proceeded in a steady stream to the Naval Magazine on the shores of Bedford Basin. The magazine, located on the eastern shore in Burnside, had been built between 1935 and 1939 to replace magazines too small, old and close to the urban centre. The new one was made of a series of small brick buildings, each surrounded by a rampart of earth and concrete. The intention was that even if one did explode, it was isolated enough from the rest that no serious damage would be done.[545] It was a good layout and in ordinary times it worked satisfactorily; but these were not ordinary times.

The "East Coast Port" had been extraordinarily fortunate over the entire period of the war; the harbour had been awash in munitions of all kinds, accidents just waiting to happen. There had been a few close calls, but no real incidents. Late in the evening of 9 April 1942, the American freighter *Trongate*, laden with ammunition and in harbour for repairs, sent out a frantic message for help by Aldis lamp as fire had broken out below decks. The timing and location could not have been worse. The port was jammed with 200 vessels, the second highest tonnage of the war, including four American army transports loaded with troops and anchored in the stream, and two British transports loading Canadian troops at the seawall. Should it explode the *Trongate* was anchored just off the Halifax ferry terminal in the best possible position to do maximum damage to the port's critical infrastructure, as well as the main business and residential areas of Halifax and Dartmouth.

An intense but silent drama ensued in the wee small hours of the morning. Not until nearly 3 a.m., when flames suddenly burst forth, was there any indication to the few watchers on the shore that anything was amiss, other than the sudden rushing about of a myriad of craft and the frenzied flash of signal lamps. The crew abandoned ship about midnight, and HMCS *Chedabucto* steamed onto the scene. Carefully circling the burning ship under the glare of a searchlight, the minesweeper surveyed the waterline. Using non-explosive practice shells, it fired a series of carefully calculated shots intended to scuttle the *Trongate* before it scuttled the port. The firing and the now spectacular flaming ship put an end to any pretense that nothing was happening, but thanks to the early morning hour and the fact that most of the city was asleep, there was no opportunity for panic to develop. H.B. Jefferson, in fact, comments on the phlegmatic detachment of those who were watching from ship or shore who could have, had the worst happened, been blown to kingdom come. By 3:30 a.m., the *Trongate* had settled softly to the harbour floor in 75 feet of water, only the tips of her mast showing and the affair settled into the obscurity of an historical footnote.[546]

Equally dangerous and dramatic, with an edge of farce, was the affair of the American munitions ship *Volunteer*, anchored in Bedford Basin waiting to join a convoy bound for the Middle East. At 5:15 a.m. a flashback from the engine room boilers ruptured the fuel lines thus pumping flaming oil into the centre of the ship. The captain and most of the officers were not only in the middle of an all-night poker game, but were also drunk and incapable of taking coordinated action. Garbled radio signals were finally interpreted, and the city fireboat *Rouille* was sent. The commander of HMC Dockyard, Struan Robertson, arrived to assess the situation. His assessment was that the situation was deadly serious. The *Volunteer's* captain, whose legal authority Robertson had no right to supersede even in this critical situation, was not drunk enough to be insensible, but drunk enough to be obstructive and he refused to allow his ship to be flooded and sunk. While the flames roared and explosions crackled below the deck, Robertson waited for the arrival of the United States naval liaison officer, the only individual authorized to divest the *Volunteer's* captain of his legal authority. That eventually accomplished, Robertson and a naval crew fought to keep the flames away from the cordite on board, eventually losing one man in the battle, Stoker George Shatford of Lunenburg. Under tow by two tugs, with the *Rouille* tied to its side still pumping in water and foam, the burning ship proceeded slowly up the harbour to Mauger's Beach on McNab's Island where, to the relief of all concerned, the seacocks were opened and it sank slowly to the harbour bottom to become, like the *Trongate*, another half-forgotten footnote.[547]

But by July 1945, even if anyone remembered the *Trongate* and the *Volunteer*, all that seemed to be moot as the war was virtually over as far as the "East Coast Port" was concerned. What could go wrong now?

At the naval magazine, because of the rush to disarm now surplus ships the individual magazines filled up rapidly and it became necessary to stack the overflow, including a large quantity of the new, highly secret and volatile explosive RDX, wherever space could be found, including outdoors and on the jetty. By 18 July the city had been sweltering for a week in a heatwave, and grass and brush everywhere was tinder dry. An ammunition barge was at the jetty at about suppertime and, speculation had it, someone flicked away a forbidden cigarette butt. Whatever the source, the barge exploded without warning, killing two men instantly and tossing a third into Bedford Basin. A huge mushroom cloud rose into the air and all over the city windows rattled and crockery shook in the cupboards — except across the basin in Rockingham, where window glass broke. People stopped in their tracks. It was just the beginning.

The first explosion scattered flaming debris all over Magazine Hill, the parched grass caught fire, which quickly spread among the caches of stacked ammunition. Outside the magazine flaming brands dropped out of the sky bringing the Dartmouth A.R.P. into action to keep a bad situation from evolving into a major forest fire. Naval Patrolman Hill, having seen the first flames in the explosive laden lighter, telephoned in the alarm from his station on the North Jetty then came to minutes later, blown 25 feet away and on the other side of a fence. Explosion succeeded explosion and each blast spread more flaming debris across the tinderbox hillside. At 9 p.m., fearing the worst if the flames reached the RDX, the Naval Headquarters contacted the still functional Civil Defence organization and advised an evacuation of the city. Trained for years for this sort of emergency, albeit with a different enemy in mind, the Civil Defence, whose head Osborne Crowell was now in his element, sprang into action with an alacrity that was a stark contrast to the stunned inaction of officials two months before.

The order was given to evacuate Halifax north of North Street, soon amended to north of Quinpool Road, tram service to that part of the city was halted and incoming trains held at Windsor Junction. All of Dartmouth, north of the Octherloney/Commercial Street intersection and as far as Bedford, was interdicted. Thus warned, Halifax residents flooded out of the city, some just as far as Point Pleasant, but many, with memories of 1917, travelled west out the Bay Road; Dartmouth residents headed out along the roads to Waverley or Eastern Passage, some on foot, some in their own cars and others in trucks sent by the R.C.N. and the R.C.A.F. Joyce Ripley and Donald Purchase were on their way into town on Pender's Bus from Rockingham to see a baseball game at the Wanderer's Grounds. When the first explosion occurred they were at Fairview and did not really think much of it. The Ripley home, however, was directly opposite the Magazine on the western shore of the basin in Rockingham. Mr. and Mrs. Ripley were immediately aware that there was a serious problem. They drove into town, found Donald and Joyce at the ball game, then went to Windsor Terrace where they picked up Donald's younger brother, Jim. Mr. Purchase, being an Air Raid Warden, was already on duty. They drove out the Bay Road with thousands of others, to Beechville, where they spent the warm, pleasant summer night in a ditch:[548]

> The stream of jostling humanity poured over the Arm
> Bridge, some in cars and some with pushcarts, prams and
> children's wagons loaded with pets and belongings. In the
> fading evening light they looked to some observers "like so
> many war-weary european [*sic*] refugees fleeing in front of
> the advancing Nazis, needing only a Messerschmitt to
> come screaming out of the blue to machinegun their
> ranks.[549]

Initially, the Murrays, who lived in Dartmouth, stayed outdoors in their yard in the warm summer evening. Pops were interspersed with louder bangs and each time a few more bricks fell from the chimneys. The air was filled with a fine debris, probably from cordite, which sifted down from the sky like snow. Eventually persuaded to leave, they settled down in a farmer's field where they finally fell asleep until "they were awakened by a brilliant light. The sky was glowing red and as they waited tensely, it came — the most ear-splitting, violent explosion of all, followed by its twin within a second or two. They were positive nothing in Halifax or Dartmouth would be left standing."[550]

Many others, determined to wring the last possible bit of drama out of their community's role in the war, braved the potential devastation and went up to the Citadel and Fort Needham to watch the show, leaving their doors and windows open (in those innocent days when all you needed to worry about were Nazis not neighbours) to save the glass from the concussions. The efficient operation of the Civil Defence organization and the military, poised for years to deal with the Wehrmacht and the Luftwaffe, inspired confidence in the population. A.R.P. Wardens went into instant action, first to carry out the evacuation, then to patrol the empty streets, while the local radio stations kept the population informed of every development. The ball game so hurriedly abandoned by Donald and Joyce was being broadcast by CHNS and the announcer, Ace Foley, interrupted his play by play from time to time to call on personnel to report to base.[551] The hospital ship *Letitia* had only just arrived in port and her crew, about to set forth on long-awaited leave, was recalled to duty, put out extra mooring lines and prepared to bring in patients. Most critical of all, Nova Scotia Light and Power, despite severe damage to critical transmission lines and transformers, kept the power flowing with only brief local outages. All of the farflung generating stations were immediately put on full alert, and since all the lines to Dartmouth had been shattered, the current in the submarine cable under the harbour linking the two communities was reversed so that the town never lost power. Radios all over the city on the air kept the citizenry informed, some giving much credit to the calm and motherly voice of Mrs. Anna Dexter of CHNS.[552] The aura of normalcy was reinforced when, at dusk, as promised years before to signal "all's well," the street lights came on as usual.[553]

On the devastated eastern shore of the Basin, two separate fires raged. The one, at the site of the original explosion, was contained and finally subdued by the efforts of the two fireboats which hovered just off shore pumping streams of water into the blaze. The other, more dangerous, was inland to the east where flaming brands had lit among the complex of magazines, setting the brush and grass ablaze. To the navy fell the dangerous, disagreeable and ultimately heroic task of reducing what could have been a disaster of epic proportions to a manageable, if major, nuisance.

The explosions went on all night with varying intensity, the last and biggest coming at about 4 a.m., impressive enough to rock buildings and smash crockery, but it was not the feared cache of RDX which might well have devastated the port. Rumbles and bangs carried on with decreasing intensity throughout the 19th until that evening when final "All Clear" was sounded.[554]

The Magazine Explosion of 1945 was a fitting conclusion to Halifax's World War II. It could have been a shocking disaster, but it was not. In some ways it was like a huge Natal Day entertainment for the amusement of the citizens of the "East Coast Port." Warm summer weather, some edgy thrills, a terrific sound and light show, and the awed and astonished eyes of the world cast their way one last time. More importantly, it reintroduced the navy to Halifax , and re-established their old relationship. The real reason the citizenry had escaped with no more than the thrills and chills of a midway ride at the Bill Lynch Shows was due to the heroic efforts of scores of naval volunteers who joined the municipal firefighters on the blazing hill-side. As freighters in the basin weighed anchor and slowly steamed through the Narrows to safety, two undermanned fireboats steamed the other way. Behind them, from the corvettes so recently returned from the North Atlantic, came scores of whalers loaded with ratings and officers. The battle with the heat and the flames was as intense as anything that might have been encountered in North Africa or Europe. The exploding ammunition, exciting from the safe distance of Halifax, threw flaming debris and shards of red-hot metal in every direction. The firefighters and volunteers who fought the inferno had no way of knowing that they would not, after surviving the war, be blown to kingdom come on a flaming Nova Scotian hillside. When it was all over, with the help of a soft rainfall, Haligonians, trudging back to their homes over broken glass to last night's supper still on the table, had reason to be grateful. And they were.

WIND UP AND WIND DOWN

The rest of the year must have been a let down, for, as Donald Purchase recalls, when the war was over, everything was all over all at once. The harbour remained busy with troop ships that up to just a year ago had taken the troops away and now brought them back. On 21 June the Canadian Parachute Battalion, the first complete unit to arrive back, marched off their ship and through the pouring rain to be cheered by thousands of Haligonians. At Eastern Passage, R.C.A.F. Lancasters arrived in groups on their way back from Britain. A huge reception awaited the West Nova Scotia Regiment on 1 October when it disembarked from the *Ile de France*. Even snowy January did not deter crowds from welcoming back the Princess Louise Fusiliers, the North Nova Scotia Highlanders and the Cape Breton Highlanders. Last, but not least of the Nova Scotia regiments to return, the Pictou Highlanders came back from garrison duty in the West Indies in April 1946.[555]

With them came boatloads of war brides, mostly British, a few Dutch, French, German, Belgian, Norwegian, Swedish and Italian, some 48,000 in all, along with 22,000 children. For most of these women, like their new husbands who had headed the other way just a couple of years before, Halifax was a barely glimpsed interval on their way to a whole new life. Princess Alice, in the official 1944 pamphlet *Welcome to War Brides*, warned newcomers that they were coming to another world, where "No amount of preparedness can begin to make one realize" the size and the distances involved. Little of this vastness was evident as the ships steamed into the harbour rimmed by granite shores and low tree-covered hills, and tied up at the wharves behind which seemed to lie a grubby collection of wooden houses and rundown buildings.

Rosalind Walsh, one of the war brides travelling on the *Ile de France* with 5,000 returning servicemen, arrived in Halifax at Pier 21 in April 1946: "Halifax in those days was drab and grey. The wooden houses resembled apple crates turned upside down. Some passengers went ashore but most stayed on board. Several came back to report that the clothing stores had out-dated styles and 'old-lady shoes.'"[556]

Controls, such a part of life since 1941 and 1942, began to ease as early as 10 May 1945. Dashing the hopes of the temperance advocates, liquor regulations eased, taxes began to disappear and, by the end of May, the gas ration was boosted from three to four gallons a coupon, entitling the motorist to a 160 gallons a year rather than the previous 140 gallons a year. Some city aldermen, fearing that the port's identity had been lost under a cloud of wartime obfuscation, urged a return to normality as early as December 1944, suggesting that it was time to drop the "East Coast Port" designation, restore the city's name to the postmark and stop censoring civilian letters.

Even though the war with Japan was still going on, it was hoped that 80 percent of wartime controls would be eliminated by mid-summer,[557] though scarcities and shortages lingered. Evelyn Fineburg, a war bride who arrived in Halifax in 1946 recalled, "everything was hard to get. You couldn't get a decent apartment because there weren't any and the houses were old and falling apart on us and you couldn't get everything you need because there was still rationing here too. You had to put your name in the furniture store and wait your turn for the furniture to come in. If you needed a bedroom suite or kitchen suite or something like that your name was taken down and you took what they got and had no choice. That was the way it was."[558]

Price controls would only gradually be eliminated in an effort to control inflation, the last of them disappearing in 1946. They had done their job. Prices had only risen 3.8 percent between October 1941 and April 1945, and the fact that inflation never got a grip on the economy is one of the success stories of the home front in Canada.

Also slow to disappear was food rationing. Rationing of meat and sugar intensified in the latter part of 1945, because Britain and Europe were so devastated that massive shipments of food basics were sent overseas for another year at least. Rationing did not finally end in Britain until 1952.

The formation in 1944 of the Department of Veteran's Affairs promised to ease the reintegration of servicemen into civilian life, and hundreds of them crowded onto Halifax university campuses practically doubling enrollment, taking advantage of government support for university tuition. The Veteran's Land Act of 1942 funded not only land, but washing machines, stoves and refrigerators. Even more significant, on 1 July 1945, the Government of Canada began to pay the family allowance, or "baby bonus," for the children in each family.[559] As early as August 1940 planning had begun for a national Unemployment Insurance Plan, coupled with a job-finding National Employment Service, which got underway 1 July 1941.[560] In February 1941 the Department of Pensions and National Health had established a Committee on Reconstruction that began to devise a post-war social safety net that would add better old-age security and health insurance to the Family Allowance package.

THE BRAVE NEW WORLD OF POST-WAR PLANNING

On 18 June 1940, on the eve of the collapse of France, Winston Churchill, speaking in the House of Commons, defined the coming darkness that would be the Battle of Britain, yet galvanized opposition to Hitler and ended with the words, "if the British Empire and its Commonwealth last a thousand years, men will still say, 'This was their finest hour.'" If Hitler was resisted, he promised, "... all Europe may be free and the life of the world may move forward into broad, sunlit uplands." By the end of 1943, even in Halifax, people were beginning to think that the dark days were past and perhaps they could see those "broad, sunlit uplands" on the distant horizon. On 1 December 1943, the province had finally proclaimed into law a 1939 Act providing for city planning, and in anticipation the Halifax City Council established what became the Civic Planning Commission on 12 November. On 20 December the Commission began its work.

If the war had done anything it had shaken the city out of lethargy and complacency. Reviled, often unfairly, in many quarters as backward and out of touch, the citizenry and their administrators were stung into a realization that when the war was over things could not be the same again and it was appropriate to establish some sort of control over the process. If nothing else, life on the home front had demonstrated the degree to which a pro-active government could control economic and social events at the national level. There seemed no logical reason why Halifax should not do the same in its own bailiwick. Clearly, it was necessary. John Marshall, dropping into the sordid reality of wartime Halifax from the rarefied atmosphere of New York's Rockefeller Foundation had, as early as 1942, found the city to be the dirtiest he had ever visited, and things had gone downhill during the subsequent three years.[561] And thanks to the tens of thousands who had passed through, and the often unflattering gaze of the national media, this state of affairs was well known.

After two years of labour, the report of the City Planning Commission was presented on 16 November 1945.[562] Previous ambitious planning efforts had gone nowhere, not only because there was no money, but because there was no public support, hence no political commitment. Hoping to avoid the fate of its predecessors, the Planning Commission did a high level consultation with a variety of groups. With the support of Colonel Oland, it was able to offer high-school students prizes for the best essays on the topic.

The "broad sunlit uplands" of Halifax's future projected a city cleansed of its "blighted areas," which were clearly identified, in case anyone had not noticed, as the 160-acre block bounded by Cogswell, North Park, Cunard, Robie and North and the waterfront, and the deteriorating 200 acres bounded by South Park, Spring Garden, Inglis and the waterfront. The good news was that these "problems" were supplemented by new neighbourhoods, already taking shape in the west end of the city, to be supplemented further when the areas of the old airport and military land were opened up. The relocation of the City Prison and Africville would see the north slope of the peninsula transformed into neighbourhood housing with streets contoured to follow the shape of the hillside and focused on a shopping and entertainment complex overlooking Bedford Basin.

To link all of this together the Commission looked to the automobile as the future of transportation. No more rattletrap trams, in fact, no mention of public transit at all; but broad roadways, many of them diagonal to ease the burden imposed by the city's steep hills, carrying cars in and out of the central business and shopping district, which remained focused on Barrington, Hollis and Granville Streets. Crossing blighted areas, a new four lane, elevated roadway, with rentable space underneath, would cut across from the intersection of Water and George to Gottingen and Cunard, then to Robie and North. It would meet another four lane road connecting the new bridge from Dartmouth, and crossing the peninsula via Chebucto. Each major intersection would feature a rotary to smooth the traffic flow. The location of a new bridge had been approved in 1933 by both the Dominion Government and the British Admiralty and seemed the most likely option; but the Commissioners realized there was an opinion in favour of a Narrows location, where a pedestrian-and-motor vehicle bridge accessed off Gottingen Street via Dartmouth Avenue could be supplemented by a railway crossing.

Access to the Ocean Terminals by a new diagonal road would take off from an intersection between Tobin and South just above Barrington and across the existing street grid to Spring Garden and South Park. It would meet a widened and improved North Park and Agricola route via another traffic circle which would connect with the crosstown route via North and Chebucto and carry on via Agricola to a boulevarded Lady Hammond Road, which would connect with a similarly improved Dartmouth and Devonshire Avenues. These last two streets would intersect with a widened and improved north Barrington Street, which would service the waterfront areas and carry along through the old Africville to link up at another traffic circle replacing the cramped underpass at Fairview and linking up with the new and improved Lady Hammond and equally improved Kempt Road.

The new western suburbs were not to be left out of this cornucopia of roadwork. Connaught Avenue would continue south and east from its terminus at Jubilee Road as a 120-foot wide boulevard swinging along Oxford and the railway cutting, meeting, along the way, the access to a new bridge across the North West Arm, then via a traffic circle, meet a continuation of Robie Street, then Young Avenue, which itself would be carried south through Point Pleasant Park to a look-off at the southern tip. Connaught would then continue east to meet an enlarged MacLean Street, which would connect with the port facilities and, via another diagonal street from the Inglis end of MacLean, connect with the Tobin/South-Barrington interchange.

Two other diagonal streets would take off from Argyle and Duke to Brunswick and Jacob, and George and Grafton to Sackville and Brunswick. The triangle thus formed, a blighted area, would be cleared and become the site of a new civic complex overlooking the harbour. To improve traffic flow further, Brunswick would be carried through Royal Artillery Park to Spring Garden from its existing terminus at Sackville.

New parks and playgrounds would be scattered through existing neighbourhoods to remedy a serious gap in the existing recreation facilities of the city, the grandest of which would be an impressive aquatic complex at the head of the North West Arm at the Arm Bridge.

To crown this reoriented post-war city would be the city's war memorial to its citizens who had served, fought and died in the conflict just ended, a new Civic Library building to replace the inadequate facilities which had served in the past. To honour its purpose, the new building should be "worthy architecturally and including within itself symbolism and dignity. The memorial part of the building should be in the nature of a shrine."

Across the harbour plans were more modest, but a surprising initiative in post-war planning had been made by the Dartmouth Ferry Commission. Flush with profits from a virtually around the clock rush hour, the commission, which had already been dispensing largesse to worthy causes, was empowered by an Act of the Legislature to beautify Lake Banook and turn it into a recreational hub for Dartmouth. Work was well under way with the acquisition of property, demolition of old ice houses, deepening the channel between Lakes Banook and MicMac, sponsoring harness racing on the ice in winter and other initiatives. It hardly got under way when work was suspended with the fiery death of the *Governor Cornwallis*, and the necessity of funding its replacement put an end to the surpluses.[563] The initiative was never forgotten and post-war planning continued to focus on not only Lake Banook, but also its nearby lakes in the Shubenacadie Canal chain. Now a venue for world-class paddling competitions, it is a fitting legacy for the now-vanished Ferry Commission.

The plan for its future direction in hand, the debate about to begin, the "East Coast Port" looked ahead to brighter days. Already the trials and tribulations of the war on the home front were fading into the background. With "Uncle Joe" Stalin rapidly transforming into a heartless tyrant threatening hard won freedoms, HMC Dockyard unexpectedly continued to hum, and war bonds, savings certificates and servicemen's separation bonuses promised a robust economy. The rest of the century looked pretty good and once the war memorials were put in place there was no point in looking back over those last six dreary years.

EPILOGUE

The long-term effect of World War II on what the rest of the country knew as an "East Coast Port" would be, for those who had lived through it, a double-edged sword.

On the one hand, although the future looked hopeful, its citizens had been shaken by the often negative publicity which their central role had brought upon them. The Ajax Club affair, tales of shabbiness, overcrowding and gouging brought home by disgruntled service personnel, VE Day riots, the near disaster of the Magazine Explosion, seemed to be the only sort of news that the rest of the country heard.

It overwhelmed the mountains of quiet selfless hospitality, volunteer services, hardships and sacrifices that the citizenry had offered and endured, far beyond what could have been reasonably expected from any community of its size. While the rest of the country digested the disparaging headlines, there was none to speak for the thousands who had laboured for a reward that, it seemed, they were going to have to find within themselves. As Colonel Edgar Mingo, the Registrar for National Selective Service, had observed as early a 1940, it was already common knowledge from what people here could see with their own eyes, that it was going to be a long haul. But not so elsewhere. He observed, "When we visited Montreal or Ottawa we found none of this war consciousness. People were going quietly about their business, making money, getting promotion and writing letters, so far removed from the actual facts that they might have originated on another planet."[564] The Halifax civilian experience was more modest than that of the citizens of London during the Blitz, celebrated, admired and commemorated still, but in the Canadian and North American context it was significant.

The East Coast Port was, it seems, prepared to accept the verdict of the rest of the country, put aside the whole messy experience and move on to a new and progressive future. Thanks to the Cold War with the Soviet Union, the military did not shut down, but continued to bring jobs and investment to the local economy. The growth of government intervention in social and economic life gave the area an increased role as a provincial and regional service centre, not only in the old areas of political responsibility, but in new ones such as health care and education. As the echoes of raucous paydays and shore leave escapades faded away, the old downtowns of Halifax and Dartmouth and their good and bad memories shrivelled. But with the automobile increasingly within reach of just about everyone, suburbs of affordable family homes filled up, then pushed beyond the Halifax peninsula, justifying Louise Clayton's vision for her acres of bush along Bedford Basin. Then when first one, then a second suspension bridge reached across the harbour, the market gardens on the Dartmouth outskirts that had fed generations of citizens were slowly overwhelmed by development.

By the year of the new millennium, there were vast new roads for battalions of new cars, the old slums had gone, along with the yellow trams, Africville, the steam automobile ferries and the throngs on the downtown streets. And gone, too, with scarcely a backward look, were most of the memories and monuments of those six busy years. Before a generation had passed, the flags, the commissioned murals, the big bronze doors and entrance lamps, the "shrine" in the "Memorial" Library, were given or hidden away behind partitions as urgent new pressures and priorities overcame them.

But for most in the old "East Coast Port", life became better and opportunities undreamed of before were now there for its citizens. If they have moved on, perhaps it is indeed into those "broad sunlit uplands" of which Churchill once spoke when he looked ahead so long ago.

We must look hard now to find memories of those turbulent six years, 1939–1945. Perhaps those which will last the longest are the thousand or so "prefabs" which confounded their designers and builders by becoming a permanent feature of the landscape and ever more highly desirable neighbourhoods. As each new generation of owners makes them their home, they take on a new life and a new existence and settle even further into the landscape. Perhaps anyone taking a walk along the beach boardwalk at Fisherman's Cove, once less elegantly known as the Crick, might reflect that it is there because sand drifting about with the tide settled around the pilings driven into the Eastern Passage channel to keep Nazi MTBs at bay.

Bibliography

NEWSPAPERS

The Chronicle, Halifax, Nova Scotia.
The Chronicle Herald, Halifax, Nova Scotia.
The Herald, Halifax, Nova Scotia.
The Mail Star, Halifax, Nova Scotia.
Progress-Enterprise, Lunenburg, Nova Scotia.
The Maritime Advocate and Busy East

INTERVIEWS

Charlotte Akerlund (Mhyre)
Dorothy Brackett (Purchase)
Hon. David R. Chipman, Q. C. Judge, Nova Scotia Court of Appeal (Ret'd.)
Charlotte Guy (Jeffries)
Joan Murray (Payzant)
Donald Purchase, R.C.N. (Ret'd.)
Joyce Ripley (Purchase)

WEBSITES

Wyatt, David A. "All-Time List Of Canadian Transit Systems" http://home.cc.umani-toba.ca/~wyatt/alltime/halifax-ns.html
Canadian War Museum - www.civilization.ca/cwm
Canadian Military Police - www.mpmuseum.org
Shearwater Aviation Museum - http://www.shearwateraviationmuseum.ns.ca
Library and Archives Canada - Online precis contain much useful and probably other-wise unavailable information on various long-defunct agencies and departments
HMC and other Ships - www.readyayeready.com
http://www.historycentral.com/NAVY/
U-boats - http://uboat.net

PRIMARY

Dalhousie University Archives, Peter B. Waite Papers, MS-2 718, A19.
Halifax Defence Complex, Parks Canada, Oral History Project, Tapes and Transcripts.
Halifax Regional Municipality, Archives, R. G. 35, files of the City Clerk.
Maritime Command Museum, Halifax, Nova Scotia.
Maritime Museum of Canada, Halifax, Marine Heritage Database.
National Archives of Canada, R. G. 24, War Diaries, copies held in the Halifax Defence Complex. (PANS):
Pier 21 Research Centre, Halifax, Nova Scotia. Oral History transcripts.
Public Archives of Nova Scotia
Places, Nova Scotia, Halifax, Militia, 1st Halifax Coast Brigade, Scrapbook, 1897 - 1956.
M. G. 1, vols. 489 - 501, H. B. Jefferson Papers.
M. G. 1, vol. 2865, Clara Dennis Papers.
M. G. 1, Nancy Forrest Papers.
M. G. 1, vol. 3587-3588 F. M. Smith Papers.
M. G. 1, vol. 3648, Isabel McNeill Papers.

BIBLIOGRAPHY

M. G. 9, Nova Scotia Light and Power.

M. G. 23, Edward Mingo Papers.

Biography, John Fisher.

Clarissa Alice "Bobbie" Johnston, "The Log of Bobbie and Jim", Diary, 7 May - 24 September 1940. Manuscript in possession of A. J. B. Johnston, Halifax, Nova Scotia.

SECONDARY

"B - H Celebrates 75th Year," *The Maritime Merchant*, vol. 59, no. 1, July 1950.

Bilson, Geoffrey. *The Guest Children*. Saskatoon: Fifth House, 1988.

Boileau, John. *Historic Eastern Passage: Images Of Our Past*. Halifax: Nimbus Publishing, 2007.

Borret, William C. *East Coast Port and Other Tales Told Under the Old Town Clock*. Halifax: Imperial Publishing Company, 1946.

Borrett, William C. *More Tales Told Under The Old Town Clock*. Halifax: Imperial Publishing Co., 1943.

Broadfoot, Barry. *Six War Years, 1939 - 1945: Memories of Canadians at Home and Abroad*. Don Mills, Ontario: Paperjacks, 1976.

Brown, Robert R. "Halifax, Birney Stronghold," *Canadian Railway Historical Association Bulletin*, number 12, April 1954.

Civic Planning Commission. The Master Plan for the City of Halifax as prepared by the Civic Planning Commission. November 16, 1945.

Contact (*pseud.*). "Halifax as a Fortress", *The Maritime Advocate and Busy East*, vol. 31, no. 7, February 1941. Sackville, N. B.: The Busy East Press Limited, 1941.

Colter, Erica, "The Home Fire Women: Organizing Volunteer Work in Halifax and Dartmouth During World War II." Thesis prepared for Honours B. A., Mount Saint Vincent University, March, 2002.

Crockett, David, and Edwin L. Dunbaugh. *Eastern Steamships*. Providence, Rhode Island: The Steamship Historical Society of America, Inc., 1997.

Draper, Alfred, *Operation Fish*. Don Mills: General Publishing Company, 1979.

Edwards, Suzanne K. Gus: *From Trapper Boy To Air Marshal; Air Marshal:Harold Edwards, Royal Canadian Air Force, A Life*. Renfrew, Ontario: General Store Publishing House, 2007.

The Elizabethan. Halifax: published by the student body of Queen Elizabeth High School, 1944, 1945.

Erickson, Paul A. *Halifax's North End: An Anthropologist looks at the city*. Hantsport, N. S.: Lancelot Press, 1986.

Farley, John. "The Halifax Diphtheria Epidemic (1940 - 1944): A Disaster Waiting to Happen or a Blessing in Disguise?" *Journal of the Royal Nova Scotia Historical Society*, volume 5, 2002, p. 44.

Fingard, Judith. *The Dark Side of Life in Victorian Halifax*. Porter's Lake, Nova Scotia: Pottersfield Press, 1989.

Fingard, Judith; Guildford, Janet and Sutherland, David. *Halifax: The first 250 Years*. Halifax: Formac Publishing, 1999.

Forbes, Ernest R., ed. *Challenging the Regional Stereotype: Essays on the 20th Century Maritimes*. Fredericton: Acadiensis Press, 1989.

Granfield, Linda. *Brass Buttons and Silver Horseshoes: Stories From Canada's War Brides*. Toronto: McLelland & Stewart, 2002.

Halifax - Dartmouth City Directories. Halifax: Might Directories Atlantic Limited, various years.

HALIFAX AT WAR

Halifax Shipyards Limited. *The Halship Saga: The War Effort of Halifax Shipyards Limited.* Halifax: Halifax Shipyards Limited, 1947.

Hanington, J. Brian. *Every Popish Person: The Story of Roman Catholicism in Nova Scotia and the Church of Halifax.* Halifax: Archdiocese of Halifax, 1984.

Harding, Marguerite, Through the Gates. Bridgewater, Nova Scotia, H. & B. Langilles Print, 1999.

Henry, Cynthia A., ed. Remembering the Halifax Capitol Theatre 1930 - 1974. Halifax: Atlantic Black Book Publishing, 2000.

Hogan, Margaret. *Esso Mariners: A History of Imperial Oil's Fleet Operations From 1899 - 1980.* Toronto: Imperial Oil Limited, 1980.

Hurst, Alan M. *The Canadian YMCA in World War II.* n. p: The National War Services Committee of the National Council of Young Men's Christian Associations of Canada, [1949?].

Imperial Oil. *Faith In the Future: The story of Imperial in the Atlantic Provinces.* n.d., n.p. [Prepared in conjunction with the unveiling of a plaque on the site of Fort Clarence on the occasion of the opening of the new refinery, 11 October 1956.]

Innes, Lorna. "And Churchill Led the Singing." *The Mail Star,* Halifax, 8 August 1968.

Innes, Lorna. "The 'Other Explosion,'" *The Nova Scotian,* p. 5. (*Halifax Chronicle Herald,* 13 July 1985).

Innes, Lorna. "When We Get Back To Port I'll See You At The North End," *Mail Star,* 23 October 1960, p. 5.

Kimber, Stephen. *Sailors, Slackers and Blind Pigs: Halifax at War.* Toronto: Doubleday Canada, 2002.

Lamb, James B. *Corvette Navy: True Stories From Canada's Atlantic War.* Toronto: MacMillan of Canada, 1988.

MacFayden, A. B., ed. *Imperial Oilways,* April 1958.

MacNeil, Robert. *Wordstruck: A Memoir.* New York: Viking Penguin Inc., 1989.

McPherson, Mary K. "Hearts of Oak", *Johns Hopkins Magazine,* August 1989.

MacVittie, John I., "A Redevelopment Study of Halifax, Nova Scotia, 1957. Supplementary Volume." Halifax: City of Halifax, 1957.

Melady, John. *Escape From Canada: The Untold Story of German POWs In Canada.* Toronto: MacMillan, 1981

Metson, Graham. *An East Coast Port: Halifax at War 1939 - 1945.* Toronto: McGraw-Hill Ryerson Limited, 1981.

Milner, Mark. *The North Atlantic Run: The Royal Canadian Navy and the Battle for the Convoys.* Toronto: University of Toronto Press, 1985.

Nicholson, (Col.) G. W. L. *The Gunners of Canada: The History of the Royal Regiment of Canadian Artillery:* Volume II, 1919 - 1967. Toronto: McLelland & Stewart Limited, 1972.

Nova Scotia Light and Power Co. *Now It Can Be Told.* Halifax: Nova Scotia Light and Power Co., May 1946. (Copy in PANS M. G. 20, vol. 206, "Nova Scotia Light and Power in W. W. II."

Nova Scotia Museum. Tracing the Built Form of HMC Dockyard (Curatorial Report Number 88). Halifax: Nova Scotia Crown Copyright, 1999.

O'Brien, Wayne D. "A History of the Armed Forces in Halifax." Typescript, Maritime Command Museum, Halifax, call # 970.627.ObT.

O'Neill, Patrick B. "The Halifax Concert Party in World War II." Theatre Research in Canada, Fall 1999, vol. 20, no. 2.

BIBLIOGRAPHY

Parker, Mike. *Fortress Halifax: Portrait of a Garrison Town*. Halifax: Nimbus, 2004.

Payzant, Joan M. & Lewis, *Like a Weaver's Shuttle: A History of the Halifax - Dartmouth Ferries*. Halifax: Nimbus Publishing, 1979.

Payzant, Joan M. *Rob and Francie. Volume II 1939 - 1945*. Privately published by the author, 2004.

Payzant, Joan M. *Second To None: A History of Public Education in Dartmouth, Nova Scotia*. Dartmouth: Dartmouth Historical Association, 1991.

Payzant, Joan M. *We Love To Ride The Ferry: 250 Years of Halifax - Dartmouth Ferry Crossings*. Halifax: Nimbus Publishing, 2002.

Porter, John E. C. "Manna From The Sea," *Atlantic Advocate*, January 1962.

Raddall, Thomas H. *Halifax: Warden of the North*. Toronto: McLelland and Stewart, 1971.

Readers' Digest, ed. *The Canadians At War*. Westmount, Quebec: Readers' Digest Association (Canada) Limited, 2nd edition, 1986.

Redman, Stanley R. *Open Gangway: An Account of the Halifax Riots*, 1945. Hantsport, Nova Scotia: Lancelot Press, 1981.

Ripley, Donald F. *The Home Front: Wartime Life at Camp Aldershot and in Kentville, Nova Scotia*. Hantsport, Nova Scotia: Lancelot Press, 1991.

Roberts, Leslie. *Canada: The Golden Hinge*. Toronto: Clarke, Irwin & Co., 1952.

"Rope Makers of Dartmouth, The," Imperial Oilways, A. B. MacFayden, ed., vol. 17, no. 2, April 1958. Toronto: Imperial Oil Limited, 1958.

Sarty, Roger and Douglas Knight. *Saint John Fortifications, 1630 - 1956, Vol. 1*. The New Brunswick Military Heritage Series. Fredericton: Goose Lane Editions and The New Brunswick Military Heritage Project, 2003.

Schmeisser, Barbara M. "Halifax Fortress Fire Command Post and Fortress Plotting Room 1942 - 1957." Halifax: unpublished report, Halifax Citadel National Historic Site, Parks Canada, 1999.

Settle, Victor L. "Halifax Shipyards, 1918 - 1978. A Historical Perspective." Thesis submitted to the Faculty of Arts, in partial fulfillment of the requirements for the Degree of Master of Arts in Atlantic Canada Studies, Saint Mary's University, Halifax, Nova Scotia. August 1994.

Shea, Iris and Heather Watts. *Deadman's: Melville Island and Its Burying Ground*. Tantallon, N. S.: Glen Margaret Publishing, 2005.

Shutlak, Gary D. "Prefabricated Houses - The Demountable House." *The Griffin*, vol. 31, no. 3, September 2006.

Smith, Marilyn Gurney. *The King's Yard: An Illustrated History of the Halifax Dockyard*. Halifax: Nimbus Publishing Limited, 1985.

Snider, D. K. *An Historical Celebration: 225 Years of Firefighting in Halifax, 1763 - 1993*. [Halifax: Halifax Fire Department, 1993].

Stacey, Charles Perry. *Arms, Men and Governments: The War Policies of Canada, 1939 - 1945*. Ottawa: Queen's Printer, 10.

Stephenson, Gordon. *A Redevelopment Study Of Halifax, Nova Scotia*. Prepared for the City Council. Halifax: Corporation of the City of Halifax, Nova Scotia, 1957.

Stowe, Leland. "The Secret Voyage of Britains's Treasure," Readers' Digest, November 1955.

Tait, Will. "Parks Canada Oral History Essay." Saint Mary's University, History 4575.0, Work Term, 9 March 2006.

Tennant, R. D., Jr., "Haligonian Street Railways." Unpublished manuscript.

Waite, Peter B. *The Lives of Dalhousie University, Volume Two, 1925 - 1980.* Kingston: McGill-Queen's University Press, 1998.

White, James F. E. "Stade im Sweiten Weltkreig - Halifax, Nova Scotia: A Canadian Staging Area". Paper Presented to the International Colloquium on Cities in the Second World War, Stuttgart, West Germany, 13 - 15 September 1989. [Copy in PANS, MG 100, vol. 91, # 6, mf. Reel 9589].

White, James F. E. " Conscripted City: Halifax and the Second World War." PhD Dissertation, McMaster University, 1994.

White, James F. E. "Pulling Teeth: Striking for the Check-Off in the Halifax Shipyards, 1944." *Workers and the State in Twentieth-Century Nova Scotia.* Michael Earle, ed. Fredericton: Gorsebrook Research Institute, 1989.

White, Jay. "The Price of Place: Working Class Housing in Halifax 1932-1945." Paper presented to the Atlantic Canada Workshop, 26 Sept. 1986 (In NSARM, MG100, Vol 77, #23).

Wilson, Dr. D. Bruce, & McIntosh, Dr. W. A. *A Survey of the Public Health Services of the City of Halifax, Nova Scotia, 1942* Halifax: King's Printer, 1942.

Wilson, Norman D. "Report on Halifax Transit," 5 September 1946. Proposal placed before Council and the citizens of Halifax by the Nova Scotia Light and Power Company Limited that it abandon tram service in Halifax and substitute trolley coach service.

Endnotes

N.B.: PANS is the Public Archives of Nova Scotia

1   The accounts of the visit of the *Hindenburg* are taken from *The Halifax Chronicle*, 6 July 1936, pp. 4, 16, and 7 July 1936, p. 1; *The Halifax Herald*, 6 July 1936, p. 14.

2   Interview with Charlotte Myhre, 2 January 2007.

3   Edwards, Suzanne K., *Gus, From Trapper Boy To Air Marshall* (Renfrew, Ontario: General Store Publishing House, 2007), p. 68. See also Phyllis Jeffrey "The German Warship in Halifax Harbour," *Halifax Chronicle Herald-The Nova Scotian*, 7 Mar. 1987, p.2.

4   *The Halifax Chronicle*, 16 August 1939, p. 1, and 22 August 1939, p. 1.

5   For a discussion of the perceived role of the raider in pre-war thinking, see Marc Milner, *North Atlantic Run. The Royal Canadian Navy and the Battle for the Convoys* (Toronto: University of Toronto Press, 1985), pp. 3 - 11.

6   NSARM, M. G. 1, vol. 489a, H. B. Jefferson Papers, file of loose typescript, date of Monday, March 24th, 1941, p. 2.

7   Robert R. Brown, "Halifax, Birney Stronghold," *Canadian Railway Historical Association Bulletin*, (Montreal, Quebec), no. 12, April 1954, p. 14. *Now it Can Be Told* (Nova Scotia Light and Power Company, Halifax, May, 1946), p. 3. This publication, based on a series of broadcasts over radio station CHNS, November 1945 - February 1946, was distributed free to the Company's 45,000 customers.

8   "Contact" (pseud.), "Halifax As A Fortress," *The Maritime Advocate and Busy East* (Sackville, N. B.: The Busy East Press Limited), vol. 31, no. 7, February 1941, p. 18. The article was reprinted from *The Halifax Chronicle*, New Year edition.

9   PANS, Places, Nova Scotia, Halifax, Militia, 1st Halifax Coast Brigade, Scrapbook, 1897 - 1956, p. 56, unidentified clipping of 5 June 1939.

10 Graham Metson, *An East Coast Port - Halifax at War, 1939 - 1945* (Toronto: McGraw-Hill Ryerson, 1981), p. 38.

11 Col. G.W.L. Nicholson, *The Gunners of Canada. The History of the Royal Regiment of Canadian Artillery: Volume II, 1919 - 1967* (Toronto: McLelland and Stewart Limited, 1972), pp. 455 - 456.

12 William C. Borrett, *East Coast Port and Other Tales Told Under the Old Town Clock* (Halifax: Imperial Publishing Company, 1946), p. 147.

13 *Lunenburg Progress-Enterprise*, 23 August 1939, p.5.

14 PANS, MG 1, vol. 3648, Isabel Macneil Papers, file 21, "Halifax in Wartime, 1939 - 1946," p. 3.

15 Brown, "Halifax, Birney Stronghold," p. 14. *The Halifax Chronicle*, 4 September 1939, p. 9.

16 Marc Milner, *The North Atlantic Run...*, p. 20.

17 Thomas Raddall, *Halifax, Warden of the North*, (Toronto; McLelland & Stewart, 1948) p. 298.

18 Thomas Raddall, *Halifax, Warden of the North*, (Toronto; McLelland & Stewart, 1948) p. 294.

19 PANS, Biography, John Fisher, Scripts, *Noontime Melodies*, 5 January 1941.

20 *Lunenburg Progress-Enterprise*, 29 July 1942, p. 2, "A Practical Wartime Budget For Working Girls."

21 *Lunenburg Progress-Enterprise*, 27 September 1939, p.8.

22 White, James F. E., "Stadte im Sweiten Welt Kreig - Halifax Nova Scotia: A

Canadian Staging Area." Paper presented to the International Colloquium on Cities in the Second World War, Stuttgart, West Germany, 13 - 15 September 1989. (PANS, M. G. 100, vol. 91, # 6, mf. Reel 9589).

23 Metson, *An East Coast Port...*, p. 48.

24 Stacey, Charles P., *Arms, Men and Governments: The War Policies of Canada, 1939 - 1945* (Ottawa: Queen's Printer, 1970), p. 35.

25 Metson, *An East Coast Port...*, p. 48.

26 A.J.B. Johnston, Halifax, Nova Scotia, Diary kept by his mother, Clarissa Alice "Bobbie" Johnston (nee Bayly), May-September 1941"The Log of Bobbie and Jim," entry for 12 May 1940.

27 *The Canadians At War* (Westmount, Quebec: Readers Digest Association [Canada] Limited, second edition, 1986), p. 29.

28 "The Log of Bobbie and Jim", entry for 26 May 1940.

29 "Annie's Columns Loved By Fleet" *The Chronicle-Herald* [World War II Commemorative Supplement], p. 19-SWW. Mrs. Coade would soon become well known for "Messdeck News," her column about naval life that appeared in *The Halifax Herald* and *The Halifax Mail* during the War.

30 *Lunenburg Progress-Enterprise*, 24 July 1940, p. 3, "National Registration Calls For 18 Questions For Men, 19 For Women;" Registration form, 31 July 1940, p. 8; Certificate, 7 August 1940, p. 8.

31 *Lunenburg Progress-Enterprise*, 9 September 1942, p. 3.

32 Information from Library and Archives Canada website, Department of Labour Fonds, R224-111-2-E. The National Selective Service Mobilization Regulations were revoked 15 August 1946 (PC 3449) and the Civilian Regulations revoked 31 March 1947 (PC 1166).

33 PANS, M. G. 23, vol. 37, # , National Selective Service, Col. Edgar W. Mingo Papers, "Summary of Operations and Recommendations Division 'G' Mobilization Section National Selective Service, Department of Labour, Col. Edgar W. Mingo, V. D., Registrar" (Halifax, Nova Scotia, 15 April 1946), pp. 2,10,19.

34 PANS, Biography, John Fisher, Scripts, "Noontime Melodies," n.d., n.p.

35 Raddall, *Warden of the North*, p. 298.

36 *Lunenburg Progress-Enterprise*, 26 June 1940, p.8

37 *Lunenburg Progress-Enterprise*, 29 October 1941, pp. 3 & 8, "Wartime Price [*sic*] and Trade Board."

38 Stacey, *Arms, Men and Governments*, p. 123.

39 Lunenburg *Progress-Enterprise*, 19 August 1942, p. 8, "Its Going To Be Tough for all of us But Not *Too* Tough".

40 *Lunenburg Progress-Enterprise*, 3 June 1942, p. 8.

41 *Lunenburg Progress-Enterprise*, 22 August 1945, p. 3, "Mackenzie Bus Lines." *The Halifax Herald*, 6 May 1943, p. 18.

42 PANS, M. G. 1, vol. 489a, H. B. Jefferson typed diary, entry for 8 August 1942.

43 *Lunenburg Progress-Enterprise*, 1 January 1941, p. 3 "Nova Scotia's Tourist Traffic." See also David Crockett and Edwin L. Dunbaugh, *Eastern Steamship* (Providence, R. I.: The Steamship Historical Society of America, Inc. 1997), chapter VII, "War and its Aftermath: 1939-1955.

44 Bobbie Johnston, "The Log of Bobbie and Jim," entry for 7 May 1940.

45 *Lunenburg Progress-Enterprise*, 18 July 1945, p. 3.

46 PANS, M.G. 1, vol. 2865, Clara Dennis Papers, file # 11, items 52 - 61, Correspondence from April 27 - November 7, letter 11-53, O. C. Lightner, *Hobbies Magazine*, to Clara Dennis, Chicago, 14 October 1940.

ENDNOTES

47 Peter B. Waite, *The Lives of Dalhousie University. Volume Two, 1925 - 1980* (Kingston: McGill-Queens University Press, 1998), p. 106.

48 Joan Payzant, *Rob and Francie, Vol. II*, 1939-1945 (Privately published by the author, 2004) p. 9.

49 Metson, *Halifax at War...*, p. 23.

50 *Lunenburg Progress-Enterprise*, 28 October 1942, p. 1, Frank Lowe, Canadian Press, "War Whisperings."

51 *Lunenburg Progress-Enterprise*, 11 November 1942, p. 3, "Wagging Tongues ...."

52 PANS, M. G. 23, vol. 37, National Selective Service, Col. Edgar W. Mingo Papers, "Summary of Operations and Recommendations Division 'G' Mobilization Section National Selective Service, Department of Labour, Col. Edgar W. Mingo, V. D., Registrar" (Halifax, Nova Scotia, 15 April 1946), p. 24.

53 Interview with Joyce (Ripley) Purchase, 5 January 2007.

54 R. Mingo Sweeny, Halifax Defence Complex, Oral History Project, Interview by Dr. James Morrison, 15 February 2001, tape 3.

55 Pier 21, Oral Histories, Colin B. Hunt, interview 14 September 2000 [no reference number].

56 Harold and Marguerite Harding, Halifax Defence Complex, Oral History Project. Interview by Dr. James Morrison, 15 March 1998, tape MIP # 1.

57 "The Journal of Bobbie and Jim," entry for 8 June 1940.

58 National Archives, R. G. 24, vol. 14344, War Diary of HQ, 1st (Halifax) Coast Brigade, R. C. A., C. A. S. F., vol. 9, Fort Sandwich, 23 July 1940.

59 These orders instituted what was called a "Precautionary Period" and arose from the disaster that befell the Russian Imperial fleet in the Russo-Japanese War of 1904 - 05. Although well aware of the crisis situation, the Russian fleet had allowed itself to be caught unprepared at its Pacific Ocean base in Port Arthur by an attacking Japanese fleet and was badly mauled. Determined that no such inattention to detail would catch the Royal Navy napping, the concept of the precautionary period was born wherein, at a certain stage in a developing crisis, military forces would be put into a state of readiness and alert. This was the case when the growing war of words between Germany and Poland following the German invasion of Czechoslovakia in the spring triggered an alarm in Whitehall.

60 Joan Payzant, *Rob and Francie, Vol. II*, pp. 5, 18 - 20.

61 PANS, M. G. 1, vol. 489a, H. B. Jefferson Papers, typed looseleaf diary, entry for 6 August 1941; Joan Payzant, *Second To None. A History of Public Education in Dartmouth, Nova Scotia* (Dartmouth, N. S.: Dartmouth Historical Association. 1991), pp. 72, 74.

62 Gordon McNeil, Halifax Defence Complex, Oral History Project, interview by Dr. James Morrison, 26 July 1978, tape COH 4.

63 PANS, W. E. Mingo Papers, file, "Misc. Letters From Ottawa." Intercepted letter, J. F. Hackett to Jerry [Hackett], d. S. S. *Waterton*, Furness Withy Lines, Halifax, N. S., 20 March 1942, undercover of "secret" letter Maj. Gen. L. R. LaFleche, ADM, Dep't. National War Services, Ottawa, to Mingo, 30 March 1942.

64 Wayne D. O'Brien, "A History of the Armed Forces in Halifax," typescript (Marcom Museum, catalogue number 970.627.0bT), p. 28.

65 William C. Borrett, *More Tales Told Under The Old Town Clock* (Halifax: Imperial Publishing Company Limited, 1943), p. 233.

66 Carl Fader, Halifax Defence Complex, Oral History Project, interview by Dr. James Morrison, 28 April 1998. Tape MIP 8.

67 O'Brien, "A History of the Armed Forces in Halifax", pp. 26, 27.

68 O'Brien, " A History of the Armed Forces in Halifax" p. 22; *Tracing the Built Form of*

HMC Dockyard (Curatorial Report Number 88, Halifax: Nova Scotia Crown Copyright, 1999), p. 26, "Map Key 1938," p. 30, "Map Key 1945."

69 Carl Fader, Halifax Defence Complex, Oral History Project. Interview by Dr. James Morrison, 28 April 1998.

70 Marguerite Harding, *Through the Gates*, Bridgewater, N.S. H&B Langilles Print, 1999 p. 159.

71 Marguerite Harding, *Through the Gates*, p. 106.

72 PANS M. G. 23, vol. 34, Col. W. E. Mingo Papers, National Selective Service Publications, "Department of National War Services, Office of the Supervisor of Recruiting, Canadian Women's Army Corps, Canadian Women's Auxiliary Air Force, Qualifications, September 1st, 1941."(Ottawa: King's Printer, 1941).

73 PANS, M.G. 23, vol. 37, W. E. Mingo Papers, "Summary of Operations and Recommendations, Division 'G', Mobilization Section, National Selective Service, Department of Labour, Col. Edgar W. Mingo, V. D., Registrar," Halifax, Nova Scotia, 15 April 1946, p. 12.

74 Barbara M. Schmeisser, "Halifax Fortress Fire Command Post and Fortress Plotting Room 1942 - 1957" (Halifax: unpublished report, Halifax Defence Complex, Parks Canada, 1999), pp. 4 - 7.

75 Marc Milner, *North Atlantic Run. The Royal Canadian Navy and the Battle for the Convoys* (Toronto: University of Toronto Press, 1985), p. 9.

76 Borrett, William C., *East Coast Port and Other Tales Told Under the Old Town Clock*. (Halifax: Imperial Publishing Company, 1946), pp. 173 - 178.

77 Evan Wainwright, Halifax Defence Complex, Oral History Project. Interview by Dr. Roger Sarty, 31 July 1979.

78 Major G. C. Callahan, RCA, Halifax Defence Complex, Oral History Project. Interview by Dr. Roger Sarty, 2 August 1979.

79 F. Jones, Halifax Defence Complex, Oral History Project. Interview by Dr. James Morrison, 25 August 1978, p. 3.

80 United Services Institute of Nova Scotia, "Military Study Group 1940," Halifax, N. S., 1940.

81 PANS, Militia, Halifax. 1st Halifax Coast Regiment, R. C. A. (Active Force). Unofficial War Diary, 1 January 1941 - 31 December 1941.

82 Brigadier G. P. Morrison, Halifax Defence Complex, Oral History Project. Interview by Dr. Roger Sarty, 02-08-1979.

83 John Boileau, *Historic Eastern Passage. Images of Our Past.* (Halifax: Nimbus Publishing, 2007) p.55.

84 Col. G. W. L. Nicholson, *The Gunners of Canada. The History of the Royal Regiment of Canadian Artillery: Volume II, 1919 - 1967* (Toronto: McLelland and Stewart Limited, 1972), pp. 453 - 454.

85 Nicholson, *The Gunners of Canada*, p. 453.

86 This and other accounts of the construction of the harbour batteries are from Major G. C. Callahan, Halifax Defence Complex, Oral History Project. Interview by Dr. Roger Sarty, 2 August 1979.

87 Nicholson, *The Gunners of Canada*, p. 453.

88 Nicholson, *The Gunners of Canada*, p. 454.

89 PANS, M. G. 1, vol. 489a, H. B. Jefferson, typed looseleaf diary, entry for 25 May 1942.

90 Borrett, W. C., *East Coast Port...*, p. 149.

91 Nicholson, *The Gunners of Canada*, p. 455.

92 R. Mingo Sweeny, Halifax Defence Complex, Oral History Project. Interview by Dr.

ENDNOTES

James Morrison, 15 February 2001, tape 3.

93 Evan Wainwright, Halifax Defence Complex, Oral History Project. Interview by Dr. Roger Sarty, 31 July 1979.

94 National Archives, R. G. 24, vol. 14344, War Diary of H. Q. 1st (Hx) Coast Brigade, RCA, CASF, 1 April 1940 - 30 April 1940, vol. 8, entry for York Redoubt, 26-4-40.

95 Major G. C. Callahan, Halifax Defence Complex, Oral History Project. Interview by Dr. Roger Sarty, 2 August 1979. F. Jones, Halifax Defence Complex, Oral History Project. Interview by Dr. James Morrison, 25 August 1978.

96 F . Jones, Halifax Defence Complex, Oral History Project. Interview by Dr. James Morrison, 25 August 1978. Transcript, p. 7.

97 Anti-aircraft Defences, Halifax Area, Jan. 10-41. HDC 108-63-1-941-0322. Department of National Defence, Record Plan S-2001-O.C. [Secret]. AA Locations, Halifax, Nova Scotia, 31 January 1944. Supercedes C-8828-2-11 of September 1942. HDC, 108-69-1-944-0285.

98 Callahan, Halifax Defence Complex, Oral History Project, Interview by Dr. Roger Sarty, 2 August 1979.

99 Robert MacNeil, *Wordstruck. A Memoir* (New York: Viking Penguin Inc., 1989), p. 41.

100 Callahan, Halifax Defence Complex, Oral History Project.

101 National Archives, R. G. 24, vol. 14344, War Diary of H. Q. 1st (Hx) Coast Brigade, RCA, CASF, 1 April 1941 - 30 April 1941, vol. 9, entry for York Shore, 15 April 1941.

102 Borrett, *East Coast Port...*, p. 154.

103 National Archives, R. G. 24, vol. 14344, War Diary of H. Q. 1st (Hx) Coast Brigade, RCA, CASF, 1 July 1940 - 31 July 1940, vol. 9, entry for Sandwich Battery, 20 July 1940.

104 Harding, Marguerite, *Through the Gates.* (Bridgewater, N. S.: H & B. Langille's Print, 1999), p. 34. Harold Harding joined up in June 1940. Because he was an electrician, he spent five years stationed on McNab's servicing the lights and was never allowed to transfer off. He was eventually told to stop asking. Information on the searchlight system is culled from his wife's book [above], his contribution to the Halifax Defence Complex, Oral History Project [interview by Dr. James Morrison, 15 March 1998] and the Halifax Defence Complex, Oral History Project interview with G. E. Avery [December 1972, January 1973] who succeeded Major Fowler as O. C. E. L. in charge of the searchlights, in 1943, until his retirement in 1944.

105 Anti-aircraft Defences, Halifax Area, Jan. 10-41. HDC 108-63-1-941-0322.

106 *Lunenburg Progress-Enterprise*, 29 July 1942, p. 1, "U-boat Shells And Sinks Nova Scotia Fishing Vessel. 4 Injured, Seven Others Escape: Entire Crew Reaches Safety After Abandoning Vessel."

107 Don Brackett, Halifax Defence Complex, Oral History Project. Interview by Dr. James Morrison, 22 February 2001.

108 National Archives, R. G. 24, vol. 14344, War Diary of H. Q. 1st (Hx) Coast Brigade, RCA, CASF, 1 May 1940 - 30 May 1940, vol. 9, entry for Fire Command Post, 5 May 1940.

109 National Archives, R. G. 24, vol. 14346, War Diary, February 1943, vol 41, 290/E, War Diary of 1st Halifax Coast Regiment from 1 February 1943 to 28 February 1943, p. 41, entry for Fire Command Post, 16 February 1943.

110 National Archives, R. G. 24, vol. 14346, War Diary, February 1943, vol 41, 290/E, War Diary of 1st Halifax Coast Regiment from 1 February 1943 to 28 February 1943, p. 41, entry for Fire Command Post, 17 February 1943.

111 National Archives, R. G. 24, vol. 14344, War Diary of H. Q. 1st (Hx) Coast Brigade,

HALIFAX AT WAR

RCA, CASF, 1 May 1940 - 30 May 1940, vol. 9, entry for York Shore, 15 & 19 May 1940.

[112] Herbert Lester Stewart, Halifax Defence Complex, Oral History Project. Interview, 18 July 2000.

[113] Major W. A. Schofield, Halifax Defence Complex, Oral History Project. Interview by Dr. James Morrison, 20 July 1978.

[114] Nicholson, *The Gunners of Canada*, p. 454.

[115] Maritime Museum of the Atlantic, Marine Heritage Database, www.readyayeready.com " HMCS Ypres" 2 August 1979. National Archives, R. G. 24, vol. 14344, War Diary of H. Q. 1st (Hx) Coast Brigade, RCA, CASF, 1 May 1940 - 31 May1940, vol. 9, entry for York Shore Battery, 12 & 13 May 1940.

[116] *Lunenburg Progress-Enterprise*, 6 October 1943, p. 2, "Germany Brings War To Halifax Harbor."

[117] Borrett, *East Coast Port...*, pp. 213 - 218.

[118] Stephen Kimber, *Sailors, Slackers and Blind Pigs. Halifax at War* (Toronto: Doubleday Canada, 2002), pp. 243 - 244.

[119] http://uboat.net/history/u190.htm

[120] National Archives, R. G. 24, vol. 14344, War Diary of H. Q. 1st (Hx) Coast Brigade, RCA, CASF, 1 June1940 - 30 June1940, vol. 9, entry for York Shore Battery, 1, 5 & 6 June 1940.

[121] Kimber, *Sailors, Slackers and Blind Pigs ...*, pp. 225, 235, 243.

[122] PANS, M. G. 1, vol. 489a, H. B. Jefferson, typed looseleaf diary, entry for 9 April 1942.

[123] Borrett, *East Coast Port...*, pp. 151, 158.

[124] Harding, Marguerite, *Through the Gates*. (Bridgewater, N. S.: H & B. Langille's Print, 1999), p. 34. Halifax Defence Complex, Oral History Project [interview by Dr. James Morrison, 15 March 1998].

[125] R. Mingo Sweeny, Halifax Defence Complex, Oral History Project. Interview by Dr. James Morrison, 15 February 2001, tape 3.

[126] F. Jones, Halifax Defence Complex Oral History Project, Interview 25 August 1978, by Dr. James Morrison.

[127] National Archives, R. G. 24, vol. 14344, War Diary of H. Q. 1st (Hx) Coast Brigade, RCA, CASF, 1 October 1940 - 31 October 1940, vol. 9, entry for Fort McNab, 1 October 1940.

[128] National Archives, R. G. 24, vol. 14344, War Diary of H. Q. 1st (Hx) Coast Brigade, RCA, CASF, 1 July 1940 - 31 July 1940, vol. 9, entry for Sandwich Battery, 23 July 1940.

[129] National Archives, R. G. 24, vol. 14344, War Diary of H. Q. 1st (Hx) Coast Brigade, RCA, CASF, 1 October 1940 - 31 October1940, vol. 9, entry for Sandwich Battery, 6 October & 23 October 1940.

[130] National Archives, R. G. 24, vol. 14344, War Diary of H. Q. 1st (Hx) Coast Brigade, RCA, CASF, 1 October 1940 - 31 October1940, vol. 9, entry for Fort McNab, 15, 23 & 26 October 1940.

[131] See the Canadian Military Police website: www.mpmuseum.org.

[132] National Archives, R. G. 24, vol. 14346, War Diary January 1943, vol. 41, 290/E, War Diary of 1st Halifax Coast Regiment, 1 January 1943 - 31 January 1943, vol. 41, Regimental Daily Order # 9, 29 January 1943.

[133] Halifax Regional Municipality Archives, R. G. 35-102, series 5A, City Clerk, vol. 6, file 352, J. W. Grant, Governor, City Prison to Health and Welfare Committee, 9 September 1940.

ENDNOTES

134 Carl Fader, Halifax Defence Complex, Oral History Project. Interview by Dr. James Morrison, 28 April 1998, tape MIP8.

135 F. Jones, Halifax Defence Complex, Oral History Project. Interview by Dr. James Morrison, 25 August 1978.

136 Shea, Iris & Heather Watts, *Deadman's: Melville Island and Its Burying Ground* (Tantallon: Glen Margaret Publishing, 2005), p. 58.

137 National Archives, R. G. 24, vol. 14346, War Diary January 1943, vol. 41, 290/E, War Diary of 1st Halifax Coast Regiment, 1 January 1943 - 31 January 1943, vol. 41, Regimental Daily Order # 9, 29 January 1943.

138 Much has been written and on many levels about convoys in World War II, scholarly histories and reminiscences, fond or otherwise. For accounts combining the best elements of the two the reader can do no better than Marc Milner's *North Atlantic Run: The Royal Canadian Navy and the Battle for the Convoys*, and Lieut. Commander James Lamb's *The Corvette Navy*.

139 *Lunenburg Progress-Enterprise*, 15 October 1941, p. 3. "Canada At War. 'The Navy,'" by B. M. P.

140 "Days of Endeavour. Selected excerpts from the memoirs of Captain Godfrey H. 'Skinny' Hays, RCN," Part Two - The Pre-war Years. *Starshell* [National Publication of The Naval Officers Association of Canada], vol. VII Number 41, Winter 2007 - 2008, p.19.

141 Milner, Marc, *The North Atlantic Run ...*, p. 54.

142 Milner, p.56.

143 Lamb, James B., *The Corvette Navy: True Stories From Canada's Atlantic War*. (Toronto: Macmillan of Canada, 1988), pp. 126, 127, 131.

144 PANS, M. G. 1, vol. 489a, H. B. Jefferson Papers, diary in loose leaf binder, entry for 27 April 1942.

145 *Lunenburg Progress-Enterprise*, 15 October, p. 3. "Canada At War. 'The Navy'" , by B. M. P.

146 Information on buildings in HMC Dockyard and HMCS *Stadacona* is extracted from various locations in the text of O'Brien.

147 Smith, Marilyn Gurney, *The King's Yard: An Illustrated History of the Halifax Dockyard* (Halifax: Nimbus Publishing Limited, 1985), pp. 47 - 52.

148 http://www.shearwateraviationmuseum.ns.ca/history/rcaf.htm

149 Borrett, *East Coast Port...*, pp. 200 - 205. www.shearwateraviationmuseum.ca.

150 http://www.shearwateraviationmuseum.ns.ca/history/rcaf.htm

151 F. Jones, Halifax Defence Complex, Oral History Project. Interview by Dr. James Morrison, 25 August 1978. Transcript, p.7.

152 Borrett, *East Coast Port...*, pp. 200 - 205. www.shearwateraviationmuseum.ca.

153 http://www.shearwateraviationmuseum.ns.ca/aircraft/index.htm

154 Payzant, Joan M., *Rob and Francie. Volume II, 1939 - 1945* (privately published by the author, 2003), p. 89.

155 http://www.shearwateraviationmuseum.ns.ca/history/rcaf.htm

156 Raddall, *Halifax, Warden of the North*, p. 318.

157 PANS, Biography, John Fisher, Radio Script, *Noontime Melodies*, n. d.

158 Borrett, *East Coast Port ...*, pp. 161 - 165.

159 Donald F. Ripley, *The Home Front: Wartime Life at Camp Aldershot and in Kentville, Nova Scotia* (Hantsport, N. S.: Lancelot Press, 1991). p. 11.

160 Pier 21, Halifax, Oral Histories, Keith Craig, interview 26 July 2001 (ref. 01.07.26 KC).

161 Marguerite Harding, *Through the Gates*, p. 76, quoting Bernie Churchill, a CNR night

clerk at the roundhouse.

[162] Pier 21, Oral Histories, Craig interview.

[163] PANS, M. G. 1, vol 489a, H. B. Jefferson, typed looseleaf diary, entries for 9 April and 17 May 1942.

[164] PANS, M. G. 1, vol 489a, H. B. Jefferson Papers, diary, entries for Wednesday, 5 November 1941 to 10 November 1941.

[165] Pier 21, Oral Histories, Victor Gray, interview 10 July 2001 (ref. 10.07.01vg).

[166] Jean M. Payzant, *Rob and Francie* Vol. II, p. 33, quoting Winston S. Churchill, the *Second World War Vol. II Their Finest Hour p. 646, in a letter to the home secretary dated 18 July 1940.*

[167] *Lunenburg Progress-Enterprise*, 14 July 1943, p. 2, and 30 August 1944, p. 3.

[168] PANS, M. G. 1, vol 489a, H. B. Jefferson Papers, loose leaf diary, entry 15 February 1944.

[169] Geoffrey Bilson, *The Guest Children* (Saskatoon: Fifth House, 1988), p. 18.

[170] PANS, M. G. 1, vol. 501, Jefferson Papers, clipping of 6 January 1942.

[171] Graham Metson, *An East Coast Port*, p. 26. *The Halifax Mail*, 21 August 1940, p. 3 "Need More Applications For Children," and 22 August 1940, p. 3, "86 Children From Britain Going To Homes In Nova Scotia."

[172] *The Halifax Herald*, 4 October 1940, p. 3.

[173] PANS, M. G. 1, vol. 489a, Jefferson Papers, loose typescript diary, p. 6, entry for Wednesday, January 22nd, 1941.

[174] PANS, M. G. 1, vol. 489a, loose typescript diary, p. 10, entry for Thursday, January 23rd, 1941.

[175] *The Halifax Herald*, 24 January 1941 p. 3.

[176] John Melady, *Escape from Canada: The Untold Story of German POWs in Canada, 1939 - 1945* (Toronto: Macmillan, 1981), p. 23.

[177] PANS, M. G. 1, vol. 489a, Jefferson Papers, typed looseleaf diary, entry for 1 January, 6 April and 7 April 1942.

[178] Pier 21, Oral Histories, transcript, Victor Gray, ref. 10.07.01.vg., interview 10 July 2001.

[179] PANS, M. G. 1, vol. 489a, H. B. Jefferson Papers, typed looseleaf diary, entry for 25 April 1943.

[180] PANS, M. G. 1, vol. 489a, H. B. Jefferson Papers, typed looseleaf diary, entry for 12 September 1943.

[181] *The Halifax Herald*, 15 April 1943, p. 20.

[182] *The Halifax Herald*, 24 April 1943, p. 24, and 26 April 1943, p. 2, "Erection of Bunkhouses in South End Protested By Citizens."

[183] http://www.historycentral.com/NAVY/ap/Wakefield.html; Carl Fader, Halifax Defence Complex, Oral History Project, summary of interview by Dr. James Morrison, 28 April 1998.

[184] James F. E. White, "Stadte im Sweiten WeltKreig - Halifax, Nova Scotia: A Canadian Staging Area." (A Paper presented to the International Colloquium on Cities in the Second World War, Stuttgart, West Germany, 13-15 September 1989) p. 4. Progress Enterprise, 28 August 1940, p. 1. As a sort of sidebar to the Norwegian presence, during the invasion of their homeland, Norwegians had managed to capture a German freighter, the *Moselyn* which, through one of the ironies that only war could bring, was under charter to a Halifax shipping company by the end of 1940.

[185] John Farley, "The Halifax Diphtheria Epidemic (1940 to 1944): A Disaster Waiting to Happen or a Blessing in Disguise?" *Journal of the Royal Nova Scotia Historical Society (Volume 5, 2002)*, pp. 51 - 52.

ENDNOTES

186 Dr. D. Bruce Wilson, Dr. W. A. McIntosh, *A Survey of the Public Health Services of the City of Halifax, Nova Scotia* (Halifax: King's Printer, 1942), p. 27.

187 HRM Archives, R. G. 35-102, Series 5A, Correspondence of the City Clerk, vol. 6, Public Health Committee, file 353, C. E. Dowden, President, Gorsebrook Golf Club, to Dr. Allan R. Morton, Commissioner of Health, City of Halifax, 6 May 1941; Dr. Morton to Public Health Committee, 7 August 1941.

188 HRM Archives, R. G. 33 - 102, Series 5A, vol. 6 file 353, "Public Health and Welfare Committee," Dr. A. R. Morton, Commissioner of Public Health, to Committee, 9 March 1942, Report on Activities of Field Nurses in February 1942, Nursing District # 7.

189 John Farley, "The Halifax Diphtheria Epidemic (1940 to 1944)..., pp. 49 - 50.

190 *Lunenburg Progress-Enterprise*, 23 May 1945, p. 4.

191 Alfred Draper, *Operation Fish* (Don Mills, Ontario: General Publishing Company, 1979), pp. 15, 171.

192 PANS, M. G. 1, F. M. Smith Papers, vol. 3588, file 50, memo, [F. M. Smith] Superintendent, to W. E. Barnes, d. at Moncton 18 July 1940.

193 PANS, M. G. 1, Smith Papers, vol. 3588, file 57, F. M. Smith, Moncton, to R. A. Gordon, Saint John, memo d. 8 March 1940.

194 PANS, M. G. 1, Smith Papers, vol. 3588, file 42.

195 PANS, M. G. 1, Smith Papers, vol. 3587, file 6, Memo, General Superintendent Sleeping and Dining Car Services, Montreal, 24 October 1939, re movement of Canadian National Express Department Employees, Montreal - Halifax - Ottawa.

196 PANS, M. G. 1, Smith Papers, vol. 3587, file 29, memo, V. P. & General Manager, d. at Moncton, 26 march 1940.

197 PANS, M. G. 1, Smith Papers, vol. 3587, Superintendent, Moncton, to G. E. Bellerose, Montreal, memo, 6 December 1939.

198 PANS, M. G. 1, Smith Papers, vol.3599, file 56, General Manager to G. A. Godfrey, Auditor of Revenue, d. at Montreal, 8 December 1939.

199 PANS, M. G. 1, Smith Papers, vol. 3588, file 56, Smith to F. N. Wiggins, Montreal, d. at Moncton, 28 November 1939.

200 Leland Stowe, "The Secret Voyage of Britain's Treasure," *Readers Digest*, November 1955, p. 37.

201 Stowe, "The Secret Voyage of Britain's Treasure" p. 37.

202 PANS, M. G. 1, Smith Papers, vol. 3588, file 46 & 47.

203 Draper, *Operation Fish*, p. 175.

204 PANS, M. G. 1, Smith Papers, vol. 3588, file 38, newspaper clippings of 9 July and 8 August [1940], both probably the Halifax *Morning Chronicle*.

205 PANS, M. G. 1, Smith Papers, vol. 3588, file 38, M. Jean Poissonier, to F. M. Smith, undated but envelope postmarked Ottawa, 15 June 1940.

206 PANS, M. G. 1, Smith Papers, vol. 3588, file 38,, M. Jean Poissonier, to F. M. Smith, 11 June 1940.

207 PANS, M. G. 1, Smith Papers, vol. 3588, file 60, "*Emile Bertin* file," memo to file, 24 June 1940.

208 PANS, M. G. 1, Smith Papers, vol. 3588, file 62.

209 PANS, M. G. 1, Smith Papers, vol. 3588, file 60, unidentified, undated magazine article, probably *Life*, also Frank Gervais, "Our Designs on Martinique," *Colliers*, 11 January 1941, p. 43, Stephen Trumbull, "Caribbean Powder Keg," *The Standard*, Montreal, 18 January 1941.

210 NAC, R. G. 24, vol. 14344, War Diary, First Halifax Coast Brigade, vol. 9, Fire Command Post, entry for 15 July 1940.

211 PANS, M. G. 1, Smith Papers, vol. 3587, file 34, unidentified and undated newspaper clipping, but probably Saint John, N. B.

212 Lorna Innes, "And Churchill Led the Singing," *Mail Star*, Halifax, 8 August 1968, p. 4.

213 Kimber, Stephen, *Sailors, Slackers and Blind Pigs* ..., p. 190.

214 PANS, M. G. 1, vol. 501, Jefferson Papers, clipping of 26 January 1942.

215 PANS, M. G. 1, vol. 501, Jefferson Papers, clipping scrapbook, clipping of 6 February 1942.

216 *The Halifax Chronicle*, 12 June 1940, p. 1, "Princess Juliana Arrives in N. S."

217 "The Log of Bobbie and Jim", entry for 13 June 1940.

218 PANS, M. G. 1, Jefferson Papers, vol 489a, typed looseleaf diary, entry for 21 August 1941.

219 PANS, M. G. 1, Jefferson Papers, vol. 489a, typed looseleaf diary, entry for 31 August 1941.

220 PANS, M. G. 1, Jefferson Papers, vol.151, clipping files, unidentified newspaper, 17 April 1942.

221 PANS, M. G. 1, Jefferson Papers, vol. 489a, typed looseleaf diary, entry for 8 August 1942.

222 PANS, Nova Scotia, Militia, Halifax, 1st Halifax Coast Regiment, R. C. A. (Active Force), Unofficial War Diary, 1 January 1941 - 31 December 1941, entry for 4 September.

223 Jay White, "Stade im Sweiten Weltkreig - Halifax, Nova Scotia, A Canadian Staging Area," p. 7.

224 *Mail Star*, 2 December 1967, p. 5.

225 John Boileau, *Historic Eastern Passage: Images Of Our Past* (Halifax: Nimbus Publishing, 2007), p. 42.

226 Notably Ernest R. Forbes, "Consolidating Disparity: The Maritimes and the Industrialization of Canada during the Second World War." *Challenging the Regional Stereotype: Essays on the 20th Century Maritimes*, Ernest R. Forbes, ed., Fredericton, N. B.: Acadiensis Press, 1989.

227 PANS, M. G. 1, vol.489a, H. B. Jefferson Papers, typed looseleaf diary, entry for 16 December 1943.

228 *Lunenburg Progress-Enterprise*, 6 January 1943, p. 3.

229 Victor L. Settle, " Halifax Shipyards, 1887 - 1978. A Historical Perspective." Thesis submitted in partial fulfillment of the requirements for the degree of Master of Arts, St. Mary's University, Halifax, 1994. Page 62.

230 Milner, Mark, *The North Atlantic Run*..., p. 217.

231 George Evans, interview of 04-19-02, by Steve Schwinghamer, Pier 21, Oral History transcripts.

232 Graham Metson, *An East Coast Port*..., pp. 75, 79.

233 PANS, M. G. 1, vol. H. B. Jefferson typed diary, entry for 1 March 1942.

234 Raddall, *Halifax, Warden of the North*, p. 304.

235 Imperial Oil, *Faith In the Future; The story of Imperial in the Atlantic Provinces*. n.d., n.p. [Prepared in conjunction with the unveiling of a plaque on the site of Fort Clarence on the occasion of the opening of the new refinery, 11 October 1956.], p. 16.

236 *Now It Can Be Told*, Halifax: Nova Scotia Light and Power, May 1946, p. 23. Copy in PANS, M. G. 20, vol. 206, "Nova Scotia Light and Power in World War II."

237 PANS, M. G. 1, vol. 489a, H. B. Jefferson typed diary, entry for 13 August 1943.

238 Lunenburg *Progress-Enterprise*, 20 January 1943, p. 6.

239 Milner, *North Atlantic Run*..., p. 218.

240 PANS, M. G. 1, vol. 489a, H. B. Jefferson typed diary, entry for 30 January 1944.

ENDNOTES

241 Settle, "Halifax Shipyards...", p. 63.
242 Donald Purchase, interview by the author.
243 *Halifax - Dartmouth City Directories*. Halifax: Might Directories Atlantic Limited, (years 1939 - 1945). Entries under "Boiler Makers," "Marine Engineers," "Foundrys," "Machinery," "Machinists," "Marine Engine Repairs," "Ship Repairers."
244 *The Halship Saga. The War Effort of Halifax Shipyards Limited*, Halifax: Halifax Shipyards Limited 1947, unpaginated.
245 Settle "Halifax Shipyards...," p. 75.
246 Milner, *North Atlantic Run...*, pp. 216 - 217.
247 Milner, *North Atlantic Run...*, p. 217.
248 Settle, "Halifax Shipyards...," p. 78.
249 Settle, "Halifax Shipyards...," pp. 80 - 81, 85.
250 PANS, Biography, John Fisher, radio script, n. p., n.d.
251 Joan Payzant, *Rob and Francie, Volume II*, p. 123.
252 Settle, "Halifax Shipyards...," pp. 144, 152, 160, 165.
253 *Now It Can Be Told*, p. 15.
254 Raddall, *Halifax, Warden of the North*, pp. 307 - 308.
255 Nova Scotia Light and Power Co. *Now It Can Be Told*, p. 23.
256 Hogan, Margaret. *Esso Mariners: A History of Imperial Oil's Fleet Operations From 1899 - 1980*. (Toronto: Imperial Oil Limited, 1980), pp. 44-45.
257 PANS, M. G. 1, vol. 489a, H. B. Jefferson Papers, typed diary, entry for 27 January 1942.
258 PANS, M. G. 1, vol. 489a, H. B. Jefferson, typed diary, entry for 12 May 1942.
259 Jay White, "Halifax, Nova Scotia: A Canadian Staging Area...," p. 5
260 Imperial Oil, *Faith In the Future: The story of Imperial in the Atlantic Provinces*. n.d., n.p. [Prepared in conjunction with the unveiling of a plaque on the site of Fort Clarence on the occasion of the opening of the new refinery, 11 October 1956.], pp. 16 - 17.
261 Hogan, Margaret. *Esso Mariners*, p. 48.
262 PANS, M. G. 3, vol. 1872, file folder "Histories of Company prepared for CHNS & Halifax Herald," typescript, "Moirs, Limited - Confectioners and Bakery Products, Halifax, N. S.", d.31 March 1941.
263 *Lunenburg Progress-Enterprise*, "Sugar Reduction Hits Candy Track," 9 December 1942, p. 8.
264 PANS, M. G. 1, vol. 489a, H. B. Jefferson, typed diary, entry for 24 November 1943.
265 Dorothy Purchase, nee Brackett, interview, 11 November 2007.
266 *The Maritime Merchant*, vol. 59, no. 1, July 1950, p. 41.
267 Smith, Harry D., *Through Dirty Windows*, Windsor, Nova Scotia: Lancelot Press, 1976, p. 29.
268 Information from Mary Guildford, Curator, Nova Scotia Museum of Industry, Stellarton, Nova Scotia.
269 Jay White, "Halifax, Nova Scotia: A Canadian Staging Area," p. 8.
270 "Rope Makers of Dartmouth, The", *Imperial Oilways*, A. B. MacFayden, ed., vol. 17, no. 2, April 1958, (Toronto: Imperial Oil Limited, 1958.), p. 4
271 *Halifax - Dartmouth City Directories*, 1939, p. 7; 1942, p. 6; 1943, p. 6.
272 Interview with Charlotte Guy Jeffries, 11 March 2008.
273 *The Elizabethan* [published by the student body], December 1944, p. 13; Year book version, 1945, p. 37; Joan Payzant, *Second To None. A History of Public Education in Dartmouth, Nova Scotia* (Dartmouth, N. S.: Dartmouth Historical Association. 1991), p. 76.
274 Don Munro, "Cadets in Training", *The Elizabethan*, Year Book version, 1945, p. 37.
275 *Lunenburg Progress-Enterprise*, 20 January 1943, p. 5, and 26 May 1943.

276 *Lunenburg Progress-Enterprise*, 8 September 1943, p. 8.

277 Marguerite Harding, *Through the Gates*, p. 27.

278 Joyce Ripley, interview by author, 5 January 2007.

279 Joyce Ripley, interview by author, 5 January 2007.

280 Joan Payzant, *Second To None*, p. 77.

281 Joan Payzant, *Second To None*, p. 73.

282 Joan Payzant, *Second To None*, p. 73.

283 Donald F. Ripley, *The Home Front: Wartime Life at Camp Aldershot and in Kentville, N. S.* (Kentville, Nova Scotia: Lancelot Press, 1991), pp. 92 - 93.

284 *The Elizabethan*, December 1944, p. 9.

285 Dan Munroe, A3, "Halifax to Kentville," *The Elizabethan*, Yearbook, 1945, p. 68.

286 Joe Levison, B6, "Flying High in the Rec Room or Grab a Foxhole They're Jitterbugging", *The Elizabethan*, Yearbook, 1945, p. 67.

287 J. Brian Hanington, *Every Popish Person: The Story of Roman Catholicism in Nova Scotia and the Church of Halifax*. (Halifax: Archdiocese of Halifax, 1984), pp. 201 - 202, 212.

288 Dalhousie University Archives, Peter B. Waite Papers, MS-2 718, A 19, *Dalhousie Gazette*, vol. LXIII, # 1, 30 September 1940, and # 10, 12 January 1945. Extracts compiled in the preparation for *Lives of Dalhousie University*.

289 References to Dalhousie University where not otherwise credited are from Peter B. Waite, *Lives of Dalhousie University, Volume Two, 1925 - 1980* (Kingston: McGill-Queens University Press, 1998), pp. 104, 105, 106 107, 113, 115, 123, 140.

290 *Halifax - Dartmouth City Directories*, 1939, p. 7.

291 Cynthia A. Henry, ed., *Remembering The Halifax Capitol Theatre 1930 - 1974* (Halifax: Atlantic Black Book Publishing, 2000), p. 2.

292 PANS, M. G. 1, vol. 489a, H. B. Jefferson Papers, typed looseleaf diary, entry for 1 November 1943.

293 PANS, Biography, John fisher, Radio Scripts, "Noon Time Melodies," 8 March & 5 February 1941.

294 PANS, Biography, John Fisher, Radio Scripts, "Noontime Melodies", 8 March 1941.

295 PANS, M. G. 1, vol. 316, Nancy Forrest Papers, file 15 h, W. C. Borrett, Managing Director, CHNS to John L. Redmond, Accountant, Maritime Broadcasting Company, 2 January 1942.

296 Donald F. Ripley, *The Home Front...*, pp. 101 - 102.

297 William C. Borrett, *More Tales Told Under The Old Town Clock*, (Halifax: Imperial Publishing Company Limited, 1943), "Radio Yesterday and Today 1925 - 1943), pp. 135 - 137.

298 Marguerite Harding, *Through the Gates*, pp. 117 - 118.

299 *The Halifax Herald*, 3 April 1943, p. 18.

300 Granham Metson, *An East Coast Port...*, p. 35, interview with Hal Brown.

301 Graham Metson, An East Coast Port..., p. 120, interview with Marjorie Whitelaw. p.148, Might's Halifax City Directories, 1941, 1942, 1943

302 Graham Metson, *An East Coast Port* ..., p. 35, interview with Hal Brown.

303 PANS M. G. 1, vol. 489a, H. B. Jefferson Papers, typed looseleaf diary, entry for 14 September 1942.

304 Graham Metson, *An East Coast Port* ..., p. 111, interview with Helen Creighton.

305 Linda Granfield, *Brass Buttons and Silver Horseshoes: Stories From Canada's War Brides* (Toronto: McLelland & Stewart, 2002), pp. 50 & 51.

306 PANS, Biography, John Fisher, Memo, n.d., from 'George' to John Fisher, Make Believe Ball Room.

307 PANS, V/F v. 94, # 19, *What To Do — And How To Do It In The Advent of and*

ENDNOTES

Emergency, side 2.

308 William Coates Borrett, *East Coast Port and Other Tales Told Under the Old Town Clock*. (Halifax: Imperial Publishing Company, 1946), p. 156.

309 H. R. M. Archives, R. G. 35-102, series 5A, correspondence of the Health and Welfare Committee, File 353, R. V. Harris, St. John Ambulance to A. R. Morton, Commissioner of Health, 4 February 1942.

310 Joan Payzant, *Second To None*, pp. 73 - 74.

311 PANS, M. G. 1, vol. 501, H. B. Jefferson Papers, clipping scrap book, no paper, but dated 15 April 1942.

312 *Lunenburg Progress-Enterprise*, 19 May 1943, p. 2.

313 Robert MacNeil, *Wordstruck*, pp. 41- 42.

314 *The Halifax Mail*, 14 December 1944, p. 13.

315 *The Halifax Herald*, 20 September 1939, p. 1.

316 *Lunenburg Progress-Enterprise*, 18 February 1942, p. 8.

317 *Lunenburg Progress-Enterprise*, 4 February 1942, p. 8.

318 PANS, M. G. 1, vol. 489a, H. B. Jefferson Papers, typed looseleaf diary, entry for 16 July 1942.

319 Graham Metson, *An East Coast Port* ..., p. 31, quoting Eric Hutton.

320 PANS, M. G. 1, vol. 501, H. B. Jefferson Papers, clipping scrap book, no paper, but dated 12 May 1942.

321 PANS, M. G. 1, vol. 501, H. B. Jefferson Papers, clipping scrap book, no paper, but dated 26 January 1942.

322 PANS, M. G. 1, vol. 501, H. B. Jefferson Papers, clipping scrap book, no paper, but dated 12 May 1942

323 PANS, M. G. 1, vol. 489a, H. B. Jefferson Papers, typed loose leaf diary, entry for 10 July 1942.

324 *Lunenburg Progress-Enterprise*, 20 December 1944, p. 8.

325 *Lunenburg Progress-Enterprise*, 19 August 1942, "It's Going To Be Tough for all of us But Not Too Tough."

326 *Lunenburg Progress-Enterprise*, 28 April 1943, p. 7.

327 Graham Metson, *An East Coast Port* ..., p. 118, quoting Helen Creighton.

328 Joan M. Payzant, *Rob and Francie, Volume II*, p. 110.

329 Graham Metson, *An East Coast Port* ..., p. 118, quoting Helen Creighton.

330 *Lunenburg Progress-Enterprise*,, 4 September 1940, p. 8.

331 *Lunenburg Progress-Enterprise*, 18 June 1941, p. 2.

332 *Lunenburg Progress-Enterprise*, 18 February 1942, p. 3.

333 *Lunenburg Progress-Enterprise*, 3 March 1943, p. 6.

334 Graham Metson, *An East Coast Port* ..., p. 119, quoting Helen Creighton.

335 *Lunenburg Progress-Enterprise*, 13 May 1942, p. 3, "Savings Stamp Song For School Children".

336 *Lunenburg Progress-Enterprise*, 27 January 1943, p. 3; Joan Payzant, *Second To None*, p. 76.

337 HRM Archives, R. G. 35-102, Series 5A, Correspondence, City Clerk's Office, vol. 6, file 360, "Salvage Committee."

338 *Lunenburg Progress-Enterprise*, 23 April 1941, p. 2.

339 *Lunenburg Progress-Enterprise*, 3 September 1941, p. 7.

340 *Lunenburg Progress-Enterprise*, 21 January 1942, p. 7.

341 PANS, Biography, John Fisher, Radio Script, "Noontime Melodies," 26 March 1941.

342 PANS, Places, Halifax, Nova Scotia Militia, 1st Halifax Coast Brigade Scrapbook, 1897 - 1956, p. 64, Halifax *Mail*, 14 September 1943.

343 Graham Metson, *An East Coast Port* ..., p. 108, quoting Helen Creighton.

344 Lorna Innes, "When We Get Back To Port I'll See You At The North End," *Mail Star*, 23 October 1960, p. 5.

345 Interview with Joyce Purchase, 5 January 2007, at 300 Ross Road, Dartmouth, Nova Scotia.

346 Joan Payzant, *Second To None*, pp. 73 - 74.

347 *The Halifax Mail*, 21 August 1940, p. 3.

348 Alan M.Hurst, *The Canadian YMCA in World War II*.(No place: The National War Services Committee of the National Council of Young Men's Christian Associations of Canada, n. d.), pp. 131 - 135.

349 PANS, M. G. 1, vol. 3648, Isabel MacNeil Papers, file 14, Ajax Club, Jay White, "Citizens and Sailors, Halifax and the Ajax Club, 1940 - 1942. Chapter Two." Unpublished mss., Department of History, Dalhousie University, 18 January 1984. Page 10. PANS, Nova Scotia, Militia, Halifax, 1st Halifax Coast Regiment, R. C. A. (Active), Unofficial War Diary, 1 January 1941 - December 1941, entry for 26 March.

350 Interview with Charlotte Myhre, 2 January 2007.

351 *Lunenburg Progress-Enterprise*, 30 September 1942, p. 1.

352 *Lunenburg Progress-Enterprise*, 30 December 1942, p. 7.

353 Editorial, *The Maritime Advocate and Busy East*, vol. 31, # 8, March 1941, (Sackville, N. B.: The Busy East Press, 1941), p. 4.

354 National Archives, William Lyon Mackenzie King Papers, item 279, p. 34456, Dorothy Sangster (Mrs. Sidney Katz) "To Whom It May Concern," d. Montreal, 9 May 1945.

355 Stephen Kimber, *Sailors, Slackers and Blind Pigs* ..., p. 117.

356 PANS, M. G. 1, vol. 3648, Isabel MacNeil Papers, file 14, Ajax Club; Jay White, "Citizens and Sailors, Halifax and the Ajax Club, 1940 - 1942. Chapter Two," p. 15.

357 PANS, M. G. 1, vol. 3648, Isabel MacNeil Papers, file 14, Ajax Club, monograph, Isabel MacNeill, "Halifax in Wartime, 1939 - 46", p. 7.

358 Jay White, *Citizens and Sailors*..., pp. 21, 24.

359 PANS, M. G. 1, vol. 3648, Isabel MacNeil Papers, file 21, "Halifax in Wartime, 1939 - 1946," p. 7.

360 *Lunenburg Progress-Enterprise*, 10 December 1941, p. 7.

361 Interview by author with Charlotte Myrhe, 2 January 2007.

362 PANS, Biography, John Fisher, CBC Radio Script, "This is Canada Too," 20 December 1942.

363 PANS, M. G. 1, vol. 489a, H. B. Jefferson Papers, typed looseleaf diary, entry for 28 April 1942.

364 Graham Metson, *An East Coast Port* ..., p. 107, narrative by Nancy Oland.

365 Graham Metson, *An East Coast Port* ..., p. 112, narrative by Norman Creighton.

366 PANS, Biography, John Fisher, CBC Talks Archives, "East Coast Reports," Thursday 25 June 1942.

367 Joan M. Payzant, *Rob and Francie, Volume II*, p. 62.

368 Erica Colter, "The Home Fire Women: Organized Volunteer Work in Halifax and Dartmouth During World War II" (Thesis Prepared for Honours B. A., Mount Saint Vincent University, Halifax, March 2002), pp. 3, 23, 28, 29, 31 - 34, 38, 43; Margurite Harding, *Through The Gates*..., pp. 120 - 121.

369 PANS, M. G. 1, vol. 3648, Isabel Macneil Papers, file 21, undated newspaper clippings.

370 PANS, Nova Scotia, Militia, Halifax, 1st Halifax Coast Regiment, R. C. A. (Active), Unofficial War Diary, 1 September 1940 - 28 December 1940, entry for 23

December.

371 PANS, M. G. 1, vol. 3648, Isabel MacNeil Papers, file 14, Ajax Club, Jay White, "Citizens and Sailors, Halifax and the Ajax Club, 1940 - 1942. Chapter Two," pp. 11 - 12.

372 Kimber, *Sailors, Slackers and Blind Pigs...*, p. 118.

373 Kimber, *Sailors, Slackers and Blind Pigs...*, p. 118 and interview by author with Charlotte Guy Jeffries, 20 March 2008.

374 Fingard, Guildford, Sutherland, *Halifax the First 250 Years*, Formac Publishing, 1999. p. 154.

375 Patrick B. O'Neil, "The Halifax Concert Party in WWII," from *Theatre Research in Canada*, fall 1999, Vol. 20, no. 2.

376 Interview by author with Charlotte Guy Jeffries, 11 March 2008.

377 PANS, Biography, John Fisher, Radio Scripts, "East Coast Reporter," CBC Network, Thursday June 4th, Interview with H. O. Mills, Concert Parties Guild, p. 3.

378 PANS, Biography, H. O. Mills, undated newspaper clippings, quoting an article in the *Montreal Standard* by Lawrence Earl.

379 Charlotte Guy Jeffries, interviewed by author 11 March, 2008.

380 PANS, Biography, H. O. Mills, Gifts file, 1942.

381 Granfield, *Brass Buttons and Silver Horseshoes*, pp. 49 - 50, "Memories of Margaret Chase Huxford."

382 Joan M. Payzant, *Rob and Francie, Volume II: 1939 - 1945*, p. 13.

383 Thomas Raddall, *Halifax, Warden of the North*, p. 319.

384 Kimber, *Sailors, Slackers and Blind Pigs ...*, pp. 5, 52, 117.

385 PANS, M.G. 1, vol. 489a, H. B. Jefferson papers, typed looseleaf diary, entry for 12 September 1943.

386 Kimber, *Sailors, Slackers and Blind Pigs ...*, p. 91

387 Kimber, *Sailors, Slackers and Blind Pigs ...*, p. 219.

388 PANS, M. G. 1, vol. 489a, H. B. Jefferson Papers, typed looseleaf diary, entries for dates indicated.

389 PANS, M. G. 1, vol. 489a, H. B. Jefferson Papers, typed looseleaf diary, entry for 16 July 1942.

390 *Lunenburg Progress-Enterprise*, 12 June 1940, p. 8, "Changes In South Shore Train Schedules."

391 *Lunenburg Progress-Enterprise*, 10 December 1941, p.7.

392 *Lunenburg Progress-Enterprise*, 22 May 1940, p. 6.

393 PANS, Biography, John Fisher, Scripts, "Noon Time Melodies," n. d. (but sometime in 1940/41), n. p.

394 *The Halifax Mail*, 22 August 1940, p. 5.

395 Halifax Regional Municipality Archives, R. G. 35 - 102, Series 5 A, vol. 6, file 357, Safety Committee. W. P. Publicover, City Clerk, to Committee on Works, 13 May 1940; H. W. Johnson, Commissioner of Works to Mayor, 23 October 1940; T. J. Moore, Clerk of the Works to Safety Committee, 30 October 1940; J. T. Conrad, Chief of Police to Safety Committee, 9 April 1941.

396 John E. C. Porter, "Manna From The Sea," *Atlantic Advocate*, January 1962, p. 59.

397 *Halifax - Dartmouth City Directory, 1939*, p. 7; *1944*, p. 6.

398 Marguerite Harding, *Through the Gates*, p. 126.

399 PANS M. G. 1, vol. 2865, Clara Dennis Papers, file 11, # 49, Clara Dennis to Cora Hind, d. @ Halifax, 7 November 1940.

400 *Lunenburg Progress-Enterprise*, 11 November 1942, p. 7.

401 Dorothy Purchase, interview, 11 November 2007.

[402] Interview with Charlotte Myrhe, 5 January 2007, p. 1.

[403] Interview with Donald Purchase, 24 May 2006 and 7 January 2007, p.5-6.

[404] Interview with Joyce Purchase, 7 January 2007, pp. 2-3.

[405] Kimber, *Sailors, Slackers and Blind Pigs* ..., p. 206.

[406] Dr. D. Bruce Wilson, Dr. W. A. McIntosh, *A Survey of the Public Health Services of the City of Halifax, Nova Scotia, 1942* (Halifax: King's Printer, 1942), p. 58.

[407] National Archives, William Lyon Mackenzie King Papers, item 279, p. 244545, Margaret Sangster to "To Whom It May Concern, Dominion Government."

[408] *Halifax Housing Atlas*, (Published by Authority of the Hon. James A. MacKinnon, M.P., Minister of Trade and Commerce, Ottawa, 1944), p. 3. Copy in PANS, M. G. 23, Edward W. Mingo Papers, vol. 37, file 8.

[409] Graham Metson, *An East Coast Port*, p. 29. Narrative by Eric Hutton.

[410] *Lunenburg Progress-Enterprise*, 22 December 1944, p. 2, "Rental Rules Tightened."

[411] Metson, *An East Coast Port*, p. 29. Narrative by Eric Hutton.

[412] PANS, M.G. 1, vol. 489a, H. B. Jefferson Papers, typed looseleaf diary, entry for 25 July 1943.

[413] *The Halifax Chronicle*, 24 July 1942, p. 20.

[414] Jay White, "The Price of Place...," pp. 18 - 19.

[415] H. R. M. Archives, R. G. 35-102, 5 A-6, Correspondence, City Clerk's Office, File 353, "Public Health and Welfare Committee." W.P. Publicover, City Clerk, to Victor Goggin, General Manager, Wartime Housing Ltd., 24 March 1942. Jay White " The Price of Place...," pp. 15 - 16.

[416] Gary D. Shutlak, "Prefabricated Houses," *The Griffin*, September 2006 (Halifax: Heritage Trust of Nova Scotia, 2006), p. 11.

[417] Dr. D. Bruce Wilson, Dr. W. A. McIntosh, *A Survey of the Public Health Services of the City of Halifax, Nova Scotia, 1942* (Halifax: King's Printer, 1942), p. 60.

[418] Shutlak, "Prefabricated Houses," p. 10.

[419] John I. McVittie, "A Redevelopment Study of Halifax, Nova Scotian, 1957. Supplementary volume," Dalhousie University, The Institute of Public Affairs (Halifax: City of Halifax, 1957), p. 9.

[420] *Halifax Chronicle*, 29 May 1945, p.12.

[421] Wilson & McIntosh, *A Survey of the Public Health Services* ..., p. 60.

[422] National Archives website, Wartime Housing Limited funds, Administrative History.

[423] Joan Payzant, *Second To None: A History of Public Education in Dartmouth, Nova Scotia* (Dartmouth, N. S.:Dartmouth Historical Association. 1991), pp. 74 - 75.

[424] Jay White, "The Price of Place: Working Class Housing in Halifax, 1932-1935." Paper presented to the Atlantic Canada Workshop, 26 September, 1986. pp. 19 - 20.

[425] PANS, M. G. 1, vol. 489a, H. B. Jefferson Papers, typed looseleaf diary, entry for 31 December 1943.

[426] Raddall, *Halifax, Warden of the North*, p. 32.

[427] PANS, M. G. 1, vol. 489a, H. B. Jefferson Papers, typed looseleaf diary, entry for 30 October 1943.

[428] Graham Metson, *An East Coast Port...*, pp. 28 - 29, narrative by Eric Hutton.

[429] *Halifax - Dartmouth City Directories*, 1939, p. 7; 1943, p. 6.

[430] PANS, M. G. 1, vol. 489a, H. B. Jefferson Papers, typed looseleaf diary, entry for 29 July 1943.

[431] John Fisher, scripts, *Noontime Melodies*, n.d., n.p.

[432] *Lunenburg Progress-Enterprise*, 5 November 1941, p. 8, "*See* and *Drive* this new Dodge !"

[433] *Lunenburg Progress-Enterprise*, 6 August 1941, p. 2. "Sign The Pledge To Save Gasoline."

ENDNOTES

434 *Lunenburg Progress-Enterprise,* 20 May 1942, p. 1, "Gives Reason For Gas Cut."

435 John Fisher, Scripts, *East Coast Reporter,* CBC, 21 May 1942.

436 *Lunenburg Progress-Enterprise,* 29 April 1942, p. 3, "Your Scrap Rubber is now a vital war material."

437 *Lunenburg Progress-Enterprise,* 12 August 1942, p. 2.

438 *Lunenburg Progress-Enterprise,* 26 August 1942, p. 3, "Tires Thinning, Steel Scarce, Pleasure Cars Soon Extinct ?"

439 *Lunenburg Progress-Enterprise,* 17 February 1943, p. 1.

440 *Lunenburg Progress-Enterprise,* 29 December 1943, p. 1.

441 *Lunenburg Progress-Enterprise,* 27 October 1943, p. 1.

442 *Lunenburg Progress-Enterprise,* 2 August 1944, p. 6.

443 *Lunenburg Progress-Enterprise,* 12 August 1942, p. 7, "Watch Your Tires."

444 *LP3-E,* 8 April 1942, p. 7, "Don't Leave Ration Books in Your Car."

445 PANS, Edward Mingo papers, M. G. 23, vol. 37, file # 8, *Halifax Housing Atlas* (Ottawa, King's Printer, 1944), p. 2.

446 *Lunenburg Progress-Enterprise,* 3 September 1941, p. 1, "Canada's War Effort."

447 *Lunenburg Progress-Enterprise,* 17 September 1941, p. 2, 8 October 1941, "Canada's War Effort."

448 Joan M. Payzant, *Rob and Francie, Volume II,* p. 161.

449 PANS, M. G. 1, vol. 489a, H. B. Jefferson, typed looseleaf diary, entry for 18 January 1944.

450 *Lunenburg Progress-Enterprise,* 22 October, 1941, p. 4, "Canada's War Effort."

451 *Lunenburg Progress-Enterprise,* 23 November 1943, p. 3.

452 *Lunenburg Progress-Enterprise,* 7 January 1942, p. 3, "War in the East...."

453 *Lunenburg Progress-Enterprise,* 14 January 1942, p. 4, "Walking Out Unifoms."

454 *Lunenburg Progress-Enterprise,* 25 August 1943, p. 7, "No Sewing Machines."

455 *Lunenburg Progress-Enterprise,* 13 January 1943, "Who's umbrella is yours."

456 *Lunenburg Progress-Enterprise,* 13 September 1944, p. 8, "The Story of Childrens' Underwear"; 22 November 1944, p. 6, "Kids are Tough on Shoes."

457 Ripley, *The Home Front,* p. 31.

458 *Lunenburg Progress-Enterprise,* 22 August 1942, p. 4, "Plant a Victory Garden."

459 *Lunenburg Progress-Enterprise,* 30 July 1941, p. 1; 6 May 1942, p. 7, " To Release Pupils for War Work."

460 *Lunenburg Progress-Enterprise,* 15 October 1941, p. 7, "Farmers As Important As Armourers."

461 *Lunenburg Progress-Enterprise,* 2 July 1941, p. 1.

462 *Lunenburg Progress-Enterprise,* 9 July 1941, p. 2.

463 *Lunenburg Progress-Enterprise,* 4 February 1942, pp. 4 & 8.

464 *Lunenburg Progress-Enterprise,* 27 May 1942, p. 8.

465 *Lunenburg Progress-Enterprise,* 17 June 1942, p. 8, "Application Cards for Coupon Rationing..."; 24 June 1942, p. 6, "Warning ... *Mail* Your Application Card ... AT ONCE !"; 1 July 1942, p. 8, "Sugar Rationing by coupon Is Now In Effect."

466 *Lunenburg Progress-Enterprise,* 3 March 1943, p. 8, "Wartime Prices and Trade Board News."

467 *Lunenburg Progress-Enterprise,* 6 September 1944, p. 8, "Milk is Not Elastic."

468 *Lunenburg Progress-Enterprise,* 1 September 1943, p. 6, "Effective September 2nd Preserves and Sweet Spreads Are Rationed By Coupon."

469 *Lunenburg Progress-Enterprise,* 23 November 1943, p. 3.

470 *Lunenburg Progress-Enterprise,* 27 September 1944, p. 8, "The Sugar Situation is Not Sweet."

[471] *Lunenburg Progress-Enterprise*, 15 July 1942, p. 6.

[472] *Lunenburg Progress-Enterprise*, 18 November 1942, p. 1, "Fines for Infringements ...."

[473] *Lunenburg Progress-Enterprise*, 23 November 1943, p. 3.

[474] *Lunenburg Progress-Enterprise*, 16 December 1942, p. 8, "Brown-Holder, Maritime Maid Biscuits."

[475] Marguerite Harding, *Through The Gates*, p. 129.

[476] PANS, M. G. 1, vol. 489a, H. B. Jefferson papers, typed looseleaf diary, entry for 15 December 1942.

[477] HRM Archives, R. G. 35-102, Series 5A, Correspondence of the City Clerk, vol. 6, file 352, Health and Welfare Committee.

[478] Thomas Raddall, *Halifax, Warden of the North*, p. 318.

[479] PANS, M. G. 1, vol. 489a, H. B. Jefferson papers, typed looseleaf diary, entry for 12 September 1943.

[480] PANS, M. G. 1, vol. 489a, H. B. Jefferson papers, typed looseleaf diary, entry for 12 January 1943.

[481] PANS, M. G. 1, vol. 489a, H. B. Jefferson papers, typed looseleaf diary, entry for 6 September 1943.

[482] *Lunenburg Progress-Enterprise*, 2 February 1944, p. 8, "Wartime Conditions Require Public co-operation."

[483] John Fisher, Scripts, CBC, *East Coast Reporter*, 14 May 1942.

[484] PANS, M. G. 1, vol. 489a, H. B. Jefferson papers, typed looseleaf diary, entry for 21 April 1942.

[485] PANS, M. G. 1, vol. 501, H. B. Jefferson Papers, clippings binder, 14 March 1942 and 19 April 1942.

[486] PANS, M. G. 1, vol. 489a, H. B. Jefferson papers, typed looseleaf diary, entry for 19 March 1942.

[487] Marguerite Harding, *Through The Gates*, p. 117, quoting Ron Buell.

[488] PANS, M. G. 1, vol. 489a, H. B. Jefferson papers, typed looseleaf diary, entry for 24 June 1942 and 12 December 1943.

[489] Don Purchase, interview by author, 5 January 2007.

[490] HRM Archives, R. G. 35-102, Series 5A, Correspondence of the City Clerk, vol. 6, file 352, Health and Welfare Committee, report of Arthur C. Pettipas, Superintendent of Health, to Committee, 8 July 1940.

[491] PANS, M. G. 1, vol. 489a, H. B. Jefferson papers, typed looseleaf diary, entry for 5 December 1942.

[492] PANS, M. G. 1, vol. 489a, H. B. Jefferson papers, typed looseleaf diary, entry for 6 August 1943.

[493] Marguerite Harding, *Through the Gates*, p. 37.

[494] PANS, M. G. 9, vol 226, Nova Scotia Light and Power Scrapbooks, p. 141, "Map showing the interconnected Power Systems of the Nova Scotia Light and Power Company Limited and Subsidiary Companies," ca. 1942.

[495] PANS, M. G. 9, vol 229, Nova Scotia Light and Power, Annual Reports, 1944, p. 5.

[496] PANS, M. G. 9, vol 229, Nova Scotia Light and Power, Annual Reports, 1945, p. 5.

[497] PANS, M. G. 9, vol 229, Nova Scotia Light and Power, Annual Reports, 1940, p. 5.

[498] PANS, M. G. 20, vol. 206, "N. S. L. P. In Wartime," *Now It Can Be Told*, p. 35.

[499] Norman D. Wilson, "Report on Halifax Transit," (Proposal placed before Council and the citizens of Halifax by the Nova Scotia Light and Power Company Limited, 1946), p. 4.

[500] PANS, M. G. 9, vol 229, Nova Scotia Light and Power, Annual Reports, 1943, p. 5.

[501] http://home.cc.umanitoba.ca/~wyatt/alltime/halifax-ns.html

ENDNOTES

502 Marguerite Harding, *Through The Gates*, p. 115.

503 PANS, M. G. 9, vol 229, Nova Scotia Light and Power, Annual Reports, 1943, p. 5.

504 Norman D. Wilson, "Report on Halifax Transit," p.8.

505 http://home.cc.umanitoba.ca/~wyatt/alltime/halifax-ns.html

506 Mary K. McPherson, "Hearts of Oak," *Johns Hopkins Magazine*, August 1989, p. 24.

507 PANS, M. G. 20, vol. 206, *Now It Can Be Told*, p. 33.

508 *Halifax Chronicle Herald*, 23 January 1953, p. 1.

509 Joan Payzant, *We Love To Ride The Ferry: 250 Years of Halifax - Dartmouth Ferry Crossings* (Halifax: Nimbus Publishing, 2002), pp. 49, 55, 66.

510 Joan M. & Lewis Payzant, *Like a Weaver's Shuttle. A History of the Halifax - Dartmouth Ferries* (Halifax: Nimbus Publishing, 1979), p. 160.

511 Payzant, *We Love To Ride The Ferry*, p. 102.

512 Payzant, *Like a Weaver's Shuttle*, p. 163.

513 Payzant, *We Love To Ride The Ferry*, pp. 79 - 82.

514 PANS, M. G. 100, vol. 5, # 2, H. W. L. Doane, "Reorganization and Reconstruction of the Halifax Water System," p. 3. Paper presented to the American Waterworks Association Annual Convention, Niagara Falls, 1946.

515 D. R. Snider, "An Historical Celebration, 225 Years of Firefighting in Halifax, 1763 - 1993" [Halifax: Halifax Fire Department, 1993], p. 14.

516 Doane, "Reorganization and Reconstruction of the Halifax Water System," p. 3.

517 PANS, M. G. 1, vol. 501, H. B. Jefferson Papers, clipping file, unidentified newspaper, 10 January 1942.

518 PANS, M. G. 1, vol. 489a, H. B. Jefferson Papers, typed looseleaf diary, entry for 14 August 1942.

519 PANS, M. G. 1, vol. 489a, H. B. Jefferson Papers, typed looseleaf diary, entry for 7 August 1942.

520 Graham Metson, *An East Coast Port...*, p. 30, narrative by Eric Hutton.

521 *Mail Star*, 8 July 1961, p, 11.

522 H. R. M. Archives, R. G. 35 - 107, Series 5-A, correspondence, City Clerk's Office, file 304, "Artesian Well at Africville, 1944," clerk of Works to Deputy City Clerk, 11 August 1944.

523 H. R. M. Archives, R. G. 35 - 107, Series 5-A, correspondence, City Clerk's Office, file 304, "Artesian Well at Africville, 1944," City Solicitor to City Clerk, 12 October 1944.

524 PANS, M. G. 1, Vol. 3648, Isabel MacNeill Papers, file 21, "Halifax in Wartime, 1939 - 46," p. 9.

525 "The Log of Bobbie and Jim," entry for 7 September 1940.

526 *Lunenburg Progress-Enterprise*, 6 September 1944, p. 1.

527 *Lunenburg Progress-Enterprise*, 6 September 1944, p. 4, "Citizens Bow Heads In Prayer."

528 Stephen Kimber, *Sailors, Slackers and Blind Pigs: Halifax at War* (Toronto: Doubleday Canada, 2002), pp. 223 - 224, 241, 244.

529 Robert D. Tennant, Jr., "Haligonian Street Railways," (Unpublished manuscript, April 2007), pp. 12 - 13.

530 Kimber, *Sailors, Slackers and Blind Pigs ...*, p. 240.

531 Graham Metson, *An East Coast Port*, p. 133, quoting Hugh Garner, "The VE Day Riots that turned Halifax Topsy-Turvey."

532 Hon. David R. Chipman, Q. C., unpublished personal memoir communicated to the author, December 2007.

533 Stanley R. Redman, *Open Gangway: An Account of the Halifax Riots, 1945* (Hantsport, Nova Scotia: Lancelot Press, 1980), pp. 17 - 18.

534 PANS, M. G. 1, vol. 3648, MacNeill Papers, file 21, "Halifax in Wartime...," p. 10.
535 Kimber, *Sailors, Slackers and Blind Pigs*, p. 278.
536 Graham Metson, *An East Coast Port*, p. 131, quoting Victor Oland.
537 Donald Purchase, interview with the author, 24 May 2006 and 7 January 2007, p. 5.
538 *The Halifax Herald*, 10 May 1945, p. 3.
539 Redman, *Open Gangway...*, pp. 32 - 34.
540 Charlotte Myhre, interview with the author, 2 January 2007.
542 Graham Metson, *An East Coast City* ..., quoting Hugh Garner, "The V E Day Riots that Turned Halifax Topsy-Turvey."
543 *Halifax Chronicle*, 9 May 1945, p. 4, 10 May 1945, p. 3, 11 May 1945, pp. 1, 3.
544 *Halifax Chronicle*, 21 May 1945, p. 14.
545 Thomas Raddall, *Halifax, Warden of the North*, p. 287.
546 Graham Metson, *An East Coast Port...*, pp.104 - 106, quoting H. B. Jefferson's description of the event.
547 Metson, *An East Coast Port* ..., pp.124 - 127, Terence Robertson "The Short Heroic Cruise That Saved Halifax."
548 Joyce Purchase, interview with the author, 5 January 2007, p. 3.
549 Mary K. McPherson, "Hearts of Oak", *Johns Hopkins Magazine*, August 1989, p. 22. In PANS, M. G. 1, vol. 3648, Isabel MacNeill Papers, file 18-2.
550 Joan M. Payzant, *Rob and Francie, Volume II*, p. 208.
551 Kimber, *Sailors, Slackers and Blind Pigs* ..., p. 304.
552 PANS, M. G. 1, vol. 316, Nancy Forrest Papers, file 15F, Fred Wren, U. S. Department of Justice, Immigration and Naturalization Service, to Mrs. Anna Dexter, 20 July 1945.
553 PANS, M. G. 20, vol. 206, Nova Scotia Light and Power, "Now It Can Be Told," p. 43.
554 Thomas Raddall, *Halifax, Warden of the North*, pp. 326 - 328.
555 Thomas Raddall, *Halifax, Warden of the North*, pp. 326, 330 - 331.
556 Granfield, *Brass Buttons and Silver Horseshoes: Stories From Canada's British War Brides*, pp. 4, 133 - 134.
557 *Halifax Chronicle*, 10 May 1945, p. 2, 11 May 1945, p. 1, 22 May 1945, p. 1, 25 May 1945, p. 1.
558 Pier 21, Oral History, Evelyn Fineburg, interviewed 23 November 1998 by Shelley Miller. Ref. –095.
559 *Lunenburg Progress-Enterprise*, 21 March 1943, p. 3, "Registration Forms Will Be Mailed...."
560 *Lunenburg Progress-Enterprise*, 4 June 1941, p. 7.
561 Waite, *The Lives of Dalhousie University. Volume Two, 1925 - 1980*, p. 112.
562 Civic Planning Commission, *The Master Plan for the City of Halifax as prepared by the Civic Planning Commission*, November 16, 1945.
563 Joan Payzant, *We Love To Ride The Ferry*, p 79.
564 PANS, M. G. 23, W. E. Mingo Papers, vol. 37, "Summary of Operations and Recommendations, Division 'G', Mobilization Section, National Selective Service, Department of Labor, Col. Edgar W. Mingo, V. D., Registrar" (Halifax, Nova Scotia, 15 April 1946), p. 10.

Index

1 Y Depot, 161
18 Dartmouth Squadron Air Cadets, 139
250 Squadron Air Cadets, 139
14th A.A. Battery, 37
1st Division, 33
2nd War Loan, 156
35th High School Cadet Battalion, Royal Canadian Artillery, 138
3rd Battle Squadron, Royal Navy, 78
53rd Battery Band, 37
53rd Heavy Battery of the 1st (Halifax) Coast Regiment, 50
54th Battery of the 1st (Halifax) Coast Regiment, 49

A

A.R.P. Platoon #9, 152
A.R.P. *See* Air Raid Patrol
A23 Coast and Anti-Aircraft Artillery Training Centre, 38
Acadia Street, 54
Acadia Sugar refinery, 117, 206
Admiral Scheer, 45, 46, 164
Admiralty House, 40, 75, 76, 149
Africville, 9, 212, 222, 244, 246, 249
Agricola Street, 184, 191, 232, 246
Air Cadets, 139
Air Force Wives Association, 160
Air Raid Patrol, 137, 150 – 154, 240
Ajax Club, 21, 162 – 67, 169, 172, 225, 247
Ajax Hospitality Headquarters, 166, 169
Albro Lake Road, 191
Aldershot, 35, 84, 173, 174
Alexandria and Hillside Hall, 39
Alfreda, 40
Alice, Princess, 109, 114, 242

All Saints Cathedral, 80
Allied Merchant Seamen's Club, 114, 167, 174, 179
Almon Street, 39, 101, 217, 232
AMCs. *See* Armed Merchant Cruisers
American Consul, 150
Amherst, 192
Anderson Square, 80
Anglin-Norcross, 135
Annapolis Basin, 35, 76
Annapolis Valley, 14, 27, 161, 203, 205
anti-aircraft defences, 53 – 54
Anti-Aircraft Operations Room, 150
Anti-Submarine Net, the, 58 – 61
Antonia, 89
ANZAC. *See* Australian and New Zealand Army Corps
Argyle Street, 161, 180, 246
Ark Royal, 17
Arm Bridge, 183, 189, 246
Armdale, 14
Armed Merchant Cruisers, 121, 129
Armouries, the, 46, 171
Army Cadets, 138
Ascania, 177
ASDIC, 59, 64
Assiniboia, 182
Athel Viking, 210
Athenia, 17, 19, 46, 86
Athlone, Alexander, Earl of, 109, 114
Athos Georgios, 97
Atlantic Ferry, 199
Atlantic Street, 54, 95, 181
Atlantic War Fund Club, 169
Austen Bros., 125
Australian and New Zealand Army Corps, 172
Auxiliary Police, 153
Avalon, 53
Avon River Power Co., Ltd., 214
Avon River, 214
Axis Powers, the, 21

B

Babe Ruth, 167
Bacon Board, 204
Baker's Point, 76
Bakersfield (California), 216
Banfora, 85
Bank of Canada, 103, 106, 107
Bank of France, 107, 108, 110
Bank of France, Governor of, 103
Bank of Montreal, 204
Bank of Nova Scotia, 23
Barrington Electric Co. Ltd., 214
Barrington Street, 10, 40, 52, 54, 75, 76, 80, 83, 134, 144, 145, 148, 153, 160, 161, 171, 172, 179, 180, 221, 227, 229 – 31, 233 – 46
Batory, 104
Battet, Captain Robert, 109, 110
Battle of Britain, 91, 182, 221, 244
Battle of Jutland, 7
Battle of the Atlantic, 19, 69, 72, 128, 130, 173, 174, 182, 197, 199
Battle of the Brewery, 231
Bay Bulls, 64
Bay Road, 11, 183, 189, 239
Bayer's Road, 15
BBC, 145
B.C.A.T.P. *See* British Commonwealth Air Training Plan
Bear Cove, 99
Bearn, 64, 108, 111, 112
Beatrix, Princess, 115
Bedford Basin, 14, 20, 54, 55, 58, 64, 100, 114, 124, 142, 145, 170, 175, 211, 212, 217 – 19, 236 – 40, 244, 248
Bedford Highway, 11
Bedford magazine, 218
Bedford Row Post Office, 30
Bedford Row, 23
Bedford, 133, 224, 239
Beechville, 239

Belgium, 20
Bell Lake, 77
Bell Road, 196, 197
Belle Isle, 96
Bernhardt, Prince, 115
Beyond the Fringe, 21
Bill White and His (Coloured) Orchestra, 66
Birney Safety Car, 11, 215, 216
Bishop Street, 115, 172
Bismarck, 13, 45, 46, 79, 94, 129
Bismarck, 6
Black River, 214
Blitz, the, 87, 248
Blitzkreig, 20
Bloody Creek, 214
Bloomfield School, 9, 140
Blowers Street, 145, 161
Board of Public Utilities, 222
Bofors guns, 121
Bomber Reconnaissance Squadrons, 77
Bon Ton, 179
Bonaventure, 104
Bonham-Carter, Admiral Stuart, 14, 16, 19, 65, 71 – 72, 78, 109, 164
Bordeaux, 111, 112
Borrett, W.C., 146
Boston, 124
Boston, 27, 28, 69, 182
Boy Scouts, 157, 171
Bradfield, Ernest, 160
Bra-Kar, 107
Brandram-Henderson Limited, 134
Brest, 108, 109, 111
Brewster 339 fighter, 111
British Admiralty, 119, 120, 245
British American Ambulance Corps of New York City, 150
British Commonwealth Air Training Plan, 35, 79, 115, 173, 197, 199
British Empire Steel Corporation, 119
British Freedom, 64, 210
British Ministry of Shipping, 120
British Petroleum Board, 132
British Sailors Book and Relief Fund, 170
Brookfield Bros. Construction, 191

Brooklyn, N.Y., 78
Browning machine guns, 121
Bruckmann, Helmuth, 92, 93
Brunswick Street, 134, 172, 179, 180, 227, 229, 232, 246
Bureau of Public Information, 29
Burns & Kelleher, 125
Burnside, 46, 53, 236
Burstall, 40

C

Cabinet War Committee, 193
Callahan, Major, 50
Camp 70, 91
Camp Hill Cemetery, 167
Camp Hill Hospital, 174
Camp Owen, 161
Camp Sunshine, 161
Campbell, Sir Gerald, 164
Camperdown, 83
Can Pac, 92
Canadian Allis Chalmers, 135
Canadian Army Provost Corps, 66, 67
Canadian Army Ship # 46, 86
Canadian Grenadier Guards, 80
Canadian Legion Atlantic House, 161
Canadian Legion Theatre Group (Halifax), 175
Canadian Legion War Services, 161, 171
Canadian Legion, 22, 66, 159, 173
Canadian National Railways, 10, 11, 46, 75, 86, 95, 104, 105, 107, 109, 135, 217
Canadian Pacific Railway, 27, 115, 182
Canadian Parachute Battalion, 242
Canadian Red Cross, 115
Canadian Women's Army Corps, 39, 43, 143
Canadian Women's Club, 170
Canso flying boat, 42
Canso, 77
Cape Breton Highlanders, 242
Cape Breton, 28
Cape Town Castle, 72
Caper Club, The, 142
Capitol Theatre, 144, 145, 179, 184, 230

Capstan House, the, 41
Caradoc, 102
Caribbean, 130, 131
Caribou, 72
Casa Blanca, Morocco, 112
Casino Theatre, 145, 172
Cassandra, 209
Catalina aircraft, 77
CBA, 145
CBC, 147, 193
Censor of Publications, 30
Censorship, 29 – 32
Central Magazine Depot, 169, 170
Central Mortgage and Housing, 192
Central School, 171
Chamberlain, Neville, 20
Chebucto Airport, 39, 41
Chebucto Camp, 39
Chebucto Head, 19, 45, 48, 49, 56, 64, 65, 77
Chebucto Road, 192, 245, 246
Chebucto, 218
Chedabucto, 237
Chester Light and Power Co. Ltd., 214
Chester, 6, 169, 214
Children's Overseas Reception Board, 88, 90
CHNS, 18, 80, 145 – 47, 158, 173, 175, 183, 240
Chocolate Lake, 189
Christian Brothers of Ireland, 142, 143
Churchill, Clementine, 113
Churchill, Winston, 20, 71, 87, 113, 122, 221, 244, 249
Cinderella Dance Hall, 148
Citadel Hill, 8, 86, 167, 180, 232
Citadel, the, 6, 240
City Council, 220
City Field, 167
City Market building, 39
City of Benares, 90
City of Flint, 17
City Prison, 54, 67, 244
City Works Committee, 222
Civic Planning Commission, 244, 245
Civil Defence Directorate, 150
Civil Defence, 137, 149 – 54, 238, 240
Clare Lilley, 210

Clark Ruse, 118, 126, 127, 155, 190
Clayoquot, 64
Clayton & Sons, 134
Clayton, Louise, 134
C.N.R. *See* Canadian National Railways
Coast Defence Battalion, 38
Cobb, Andrew, 174
Coburg Road, 171
Cogswell Street, 39, 86, 148
Cole Harbour Road, 46
Cole Harbour, 6, 58, 203
Commercial Street, 234, 239
Committee on Reconstruction, 243
Commons, the, 6, 83
Commonwealth Entertainments National Services Association, 173, 174
Confessions of a Nazi Spy, 15
Connaught Avenue, 246
Connaught Battery, 48, 66
Connolly Street, 190
Conrod, Judson, 231
Conscription Crisis, 225
Controller of Ship Construction and Repairs, 120
Controller of Ship Repairs, 120
Controller of Supplies, 201
Convoy HX1, 19
Convoy HX34, 45
Convoy HX84, 94
Convoys, 19 – 20, 68 – 73
Copenhagen, 20
C.O.R.B. *See* Children's Overseas Reception Board
Corilla, 98, 122
Cornwallis Park, 233
Cornwallis Square, 232
Cornwallis Street Baptist Church, 172
Cousins Laundry and Dry-cleaning, 153
Cousins, E.L., 193, 194,
Cow Bay Road, 46
Cow Bay, 51, 161
C.P.R. *See* Canadian Pacific Railway
Craig, Colonel Charles, 52
Craig, Keith, 84, 85
Crane Supply, 221
Creighton Street, 180

Creighton, Helen, 148 – 49, 158
Crerar, Hon. T.A., 88
Crick, the, 249
Crowell, O.R., Mayor, 65
Crowell, Osborne, 226, 238
Crown Restaurant, 179
Cumberland County, 14
Cunard Street, 184, 244, 245
Curtiss "Hawk" fighter, 111
Curtiss Kittyhawk, 78
Curtiss SBC-4 dive bomber, 111
C.W.A.C. *See* Canadian Women's Army Corps
Czechoslovakia, 103, 114

D

Dairy Products Board, 204
Dalhousie Glee Club, 174
Dalhousie University, 9, 10, 29, 101, 119, 128, 143, 144, 147, 192
Dartmouth A.R.P., 238
Dartmouth Avenue, 245, 246
Dartmouth Ferry Commission, 218 – 220, 247
Dartmouth High School, 139, 140, 151, 156
Dartmouth Iron Foundry, 125
Dartmouth Marine slips, 120
Dartmouth Ropeworks, 135
Dartmouth School Board, 139, 140, 193
Dartmouth Service Centre, 171
Dartmouth, 218
Davis, Dr. F.R., 150
D-Day, 208
de B. Oland, Major Victor, 52
de Katow, Edoard, 110
Debert, 35, 173, 174, 234
Deep Brook, 76
Defence Equipped Merchant Ships, 121, 169
Degaussing, 128, 129
DEMS. *See* Defence Equipped Merchant Ships
Denmark, 20
Dennis, Clara, 29, 186
Department of Child Welfare, 89
Department of Education, 126, 154
Department of Health, 178

Department of Labour, 23
Department of Munitions and Supply, 25, 198, 221
Department of National Defence, 118, 185
Department of National War Services, 22, 23, 159, 166, 171, 173
Department of Pensions and National Health, 243
Department of Public Health, 101
Department of Veteran's Affairs, 243
Depression Position Finder, 51, 52
Devil's Battery, 45, 48, 49, 50
Devil's Island, 49
Devonshire Avenue, 246
Dexter, Mrs. Anna, 240
Digby aircraft, 77, 138
Digby, 28, 35
Diloma, 122
diphtheria, 100 – 102
Director of Civil Defence, 226
discipline, military, 66 – 68
Dixianna, 64
Doane, H.W.L., 221
Dominion Atlantic Railway, 84, 142
Dominion Bureau of Statistics, 25
Dominion Government, 8, 9, 25, 29, 159, 181, 190, 197, 215, 222, 227, 245
Dominion Steel Corporation, 119
Dominion, 234
Dorsey, Tommy, 148
Downing Street, 13
Doyle Street, 140
Duchess of York, 37, 89, 91
Duffus Street, 190, 191
Duffy's, 179
Duke Street, 10, 134, 233, 246
Dunkerque, 107
Dunkirk, 21, 108
Dutch East Indies, 157
Dutch Village Road, 11

E

Eastern Air Command, 77, 160
Eastern Military Command, 52

Eastern Passage, 8, 11, 17, 38, 40, 41, 42, 46, 53, 59, 77, 78, 126, 130, 131, 155, 190, 191, 212, 239, 242, 249
Eastern Steamship Lines, 27, 28, 182
Edgewood, 191, 217
Edison Electric Light and Power Company Limited of Springhill, 214
Edith II, 60
Edward G. Robinson, 15
Egda, 98, 122
Egg Pond, 17
El Nil, 87
Elkins Barracks, 38
Elkins, Major General W.H.P., 38, 52
Elm Park, 175
Embarkation Movement Control, 83
E.M.C. *See* Embarkation Movement Control
Emerald, 102, 129
Emile Bertin, 64, 108, 109, 110, 111, 112
Empire Theatre, 145
Empress of Australia, 89
Empress of Britain, 7, 8, 12, 37
Empress of Scotland, 84
Engineering Service Company, 222
Engineers' Yard, the, 55
E.N.S.A. *See* Commonwealth Entertainments National Services Association
Enterprise, 102
Erg, 124
E.S.C. *See* Engineering Service Company
E.S.L. *See* Eastern Steamship Lines
Esquimault, 63, 64
evacuees, 87 – 90
Exhibition Grounds, 39, 232

F

Faders Pharmacy, 234
Fairey aviation, 118
Fairview underpass, 93
Fall River, 214
Farm Service Force for Nova Scotia, 204
Farmers Dairy, 147
Federal Reserve Bank, 103, 107

Fegan, Fogarty, 45
Fields, Gracie, 149
Fifty-First Heavy Battery, R.C.A., 37
Findlay School, 139, 171
Findlay, Allan, 29, 30
Fire Command Post, 51, 52, 56
First (Halifax) Coast Brigade/Regiment, 15
First Anti-Aircraft Battery, 15, 37, 53
First Baptist Church, 221
First Field Company, Royal Canadian Engineers, 37
Fisher, John, 18, 80, 126, 146, 158, 168, 183
Fisherman's Cove, 249
Flandrum Hill, 51
Fleet Air Arm, 80
Fleming Bros., 125
Foley, Ace, 240
food shortages, 202 – 210
Forrest, Dr. William Duff, 101
Forrest, John, 101
Fort de France, 112
Fort Hugonin, 51
Fort Massey United Church, 164
Fort Massey, 165
Fort McNab, 31, 45, 48, 51, 53, 56, 59, 60, 66
Fort Needham, 20, 185
Fort Ogilvie, 51
Fort Sandwich, 37, 52, 66, 68
Fortress Commander, 150
Forum, the, 148
Foundation Franklin, 100
Foundation Maritime, 123, 154
Fourth Anti-Aircraft (A.A.) Battery, 46, 53, 66
Fourth Light A.A. Battery, 37
Foynes, 132
France, 21, 103, 108, 111, 133, 165, 244
Franche Comte, 99
Fraser, 16
Fredericton, 91
Free French Navy, 80
French Admiralty, 110
French Village, 14
Friedrichshafen, 6
fundraising, 154 – 158
Furious, 105
Furness Withy pier, 39

G

Gaiety Theatre, 145
Garrick Theatre, 34
Garrison Grounds, 228, 230
Garrison Military Police, 67
Garrison Pier, 40
Garrison Road, 68
Gaspereau Valley, 214
Gaspereau, 14
George Street, 245, 246
George VI, King, 123
George's Island, 220
Georgic, 89
Germany, 133
Gerrish Street, 101
Girl Guides, 157
Glace Bay, 27
Glasgow, 7
Glasgow, 89, 90, 113, 203
Glen Miller orchestra, 147
gold shipments, 102 – 13
Gordon, Donald, 24, 205
Gorman, T.C., 49
Gorsebrook Golf Club, 101
Gorsebrook, 143
Gottingen Street, 21, 76, 145, 159, 180, 185, 191, 216, 245
Government House, 114, 177
Governor Cornwallis, 219, 220, 247
Governor General's Foot Guards, 80
Graf Spee, 13, 45
Graf Zepplin, 5
Grafton Park, 232
Grafton Street, 246
Granville Street, 10, 229, 230, 233, 245
Great Lakes shipyards, 73
Great Lakes, 119, 182
Greene, Lorne, 20, 147
Gripsholm, 16
Grumman Goblin, 78
Guest Children, 87
Gulf of Saint Lawrence, 72, 77, 197 – 98
Guy, Charlotte, 174, 175
Guy, George V., 138

H

Haakon, King, 113
Hackenley, Archbishop John, 164
Halcrane "Lord Kitchener," 123, 124

INDEX

Halifax Academy, 140

Halifax Academy, 9, 140

Halifax Board of Health, 101

Halifax Business and
Professional Women's Club,
170

Halifax Citadel, 38

Halifax City Council, 244

Halifax Civilian Emergency
Corps, 151, 152

Halifax Club, 165

Halifax Coast Brigade, 37

Halifax Concert Party Guild,
172 – 77

Halifax Concert Party, 66, 149

Halifax Daily Star, 30

Halifax Electric Tramway
Company, 215

Halifax Explosion, 119, 185,
215

Halifax Graving Dock
Company, 119

Halifax Herald Harmonica
Band, 174

Halifax Hospital Visiting
Committees, 170

Halifax Hotel, 153, 194

Halifax Housing Commission,
185

Halifax Infirmary, 171

Halifax Ladies Musical Club,
172

Halifax Ladies' College, 9,
161

Halifax North Civic
Improvement Association, 227

Halifax Paint Factory, 134

Halifax peninsula, 54

Halifax Relief Commission,
185, 191

Halifax Rifles, 15, 38

Halifax School Board, 140,
222

Halifax Shipyards, 10, 17,
119, 120, 121, 123, 125,
126, 184, 214

Halifax Transit Committee,
194

Halifax Volunteer Battalion,
38

Halifax Wartime Taxi
Association, 194

Halifax Water Company, 220

Halifax, 218, 219

Hallman, Art, 148

Halton, Matthew, 147

Hamilton, Ont., 38

Hampton, Lionel, 148

Hantsport, 169

harbour bridges, 245, 248

harbour defences, 44 – 66

Harding, Harold, 65

Harry James orchestra, 147

Hartlen Point, 49

Harvard training aircraft, 157

Hawker Hurricane, 78

Hazelhurst Estate, 38

H.C.E.C. *See* Halifax Civilian
Emergency Corps

H.C.P.G. *See* Halifax Concert
Party Guild

Henneberry, Annie, 160

Herring Cove, 53, 58, 65, 211,
217

Highland Park, 191

Hill, Naval Patrolman, 238

Hillis & Sons, 125

Hindenburg, 5, 6, 54

Hitler, Adolf, 6, 13, 17, 19, 92,
107, 244

HMC Dockyard, 6, 10, 14,
16, 21, 35, 40, 41, 42, 67,
74, 75, 135, 145, 161, 170,
214, 237, 247

HMCS *Cornwallis*, 35, 76

HMCS Kings, 143, 145

HMCS *Nelson*, 76

HMCS Peregrine, 76, 80, 161,
193, 225

HMCS Sambro, 72

HMCS *Scotian*, 40, 161

HMCS Seaborne, 79

HMCS Shearwater, 41

HMCS Stadacona, 40, 73, 76,
138

HMS Canada, 78

HMS Saker, 78

HMS Seaborne, 41, 78, 161

Holland, 133

Hollis Street, 10, 83, 85, 161,
167, 177, 178, 179, 181,
227, 229, 231, 245

Hollow Bridge, 214

Home and School Association,
142

Home Defence Battalion, 38

Hoskins machine guns, 121

hospitality, 158 – 72

housing problems, 185 – 94

Howe, Clarence Decatur, 95,
118, 120, 194

Hudson Bomber, 77, 155

Hugh Mills Concert Party
Division, 147

Hugh Mills, 173

Hydrostone district, 185

I

Iceland, 71, 116, 170

Icolite, 132

Ile de France, 242

Ilsley, J.L., 25

Imperial Oil Refinery (*see also*
Imperoyal), 6, 11

Imperial Oil, 130 – 32

Imperoyal (*see also* Imperial Oil
Refinery), 11, 46, 53, 54,
197, 198, 218

Indian Point, 54

Industrial School farm, 15

Inglis Street, 152, 244, 246

Inneroy, 96

Inter-Allied Hospitality and
Food Fund Board, 164

Intercolonial Railway, 135

International Order of
Daughters of the Empire,
170

Iocoma, 131

I.O.D.E., 22, 157, 160, 161,
170

I.O.D.E., HMS Alderney
Chapter, 171

Ireland, 132

Irene, Princess, 115

Islander, 59

Islville Street, 142

Italy, 95

Ives Point, 40, 51, 122

J

Jacob Street, 134, 180, 246

Japan, 157, 198, 243

Jean d'Arc, 64, 108

Jeanne de Vienne, 107

Jefferson, H.B., 30, 51, 64, 85,
95, 96, 153, 168, 178, 181,
194, 195, 237

Jervis Bay, 45, 46, 121, 164

Jesuits of Upper Canada, 143

John T. Bottomley
Woodworking Company,
152

Johnson's Cabins, 178

Joint Organization and
Services Committee, 173

Jubilee Road, 246
Judy Richardson, 148
Juliana, Princess of the
 Netherlands, 111, 114, 115,
 172

K

K225, 145
Kars, 97, 98, 122
Katz, Sidney, 188
K.C.A. *See* King's County
 Academy
Kearney Lake, 133
Keith's Brewery, 231
Kellock, Mr. Justice R.L., 235
Kelly's store, 233
Kelvin, Bottomley & Baird,
 233
Kempt Road, 93, 134, 246
Kenney, Mart, 148
Kent Regiment, 38
Kent, Duke of, 115, 116
Kentville, 35, 84, 141, 142,
 234
Ketch Harbour, 97, 122
Kid O'Neill's Silver Slipper,
 179, 180
Kiel, 46
Kilhampton, 175 – 76
Kimber, Stephen, 177
King Edward Hotel, 78, 194
King Street, 160, 234
King, Mackenzie, 22, 34, 87,
 113, 120
King's College, 9
King's County Academy, 141,
 142
Kinsmen Club, 157, 170
Kirk Session, 165, 166
Kiwanis, 170
Knight Trophy, 141
Knights of Columbus hall,
 161, 172
Knights of Columbus, 22,
 159, 173
Kretschmer, Otto, 94
Kronprinzin, 121

L

Labrador, 78, 170
Lachine, Que., 80, 84, 193
Lady Hammond Road, 12,
 246
Lady Nelson, 86, 129, 170, 176

Lady Rodney, 129
LaGuardia, Mayor, 65
Lake Banook, 247
Lake MicMac, 247
Lake Superior, 91
Lanark and Renfrew
 Regiment, 212
Lancaster aircraft, 242
Lane, Abbie, 174
Lawlor's Island, 35
Lawrencetown Beach, 6, 46,
 130
Le Verdon, 108
Leed's Store, 153
Lend-Lease, 103
Lennox, 99
Letitia, 240
Letitia, 86
Liberator aircraft, 77
License Identification Card,
 25
Lions Club, 157
Liverpool, 89, 203
Lloyd, J.E., 178
Lodging and Compensation
 allowance, 41
London, 113, 115, 147, 248
Londonderry, 71
Lord Nelson Hotel, 228
Lord Tweedsmuir, 161
Lorraine, 107
Lower East Pubnico, 122
Lower Water Street, 11, 12,
 13, 231
Luftwaffe, 6, 20, 91, 92, 94,
 102
Lumsden, 214
Lunenburg, 28, 100, 113, 161,
 226

M

Macdonald Library, 144
Macdonald, Angus L., 119,
 120, 135
Mackenzie & Osborne's store,
 233
Mackenzie Bus Lines, 27
MacMechan, Archibald, 17
MACs. *See* merchant aircraft
 carriers
Magazine Explosion, the, 235
 – 41, 248
Magazine Hill, 238
Maine, 78
Maitland, 35

Malaysia, 157
Manhattan, 99
Manitoulin, 175
Manning Pool, the, 24, 39,
 192, 216
Maple Leaf Fund, 170
Marine Department
 (N.S.L&P.), 129
Marine Nationale, 21
Marion Heights, 54
Maritime Telephone and
 Telegraph Company, 30
Maritime Towing, 153
Marks and Spencer, 89
Marmon machine guns, 121
Marshall Plan, the, 213
Marshall, John, 244
Mart Kenney and the Western
 Gentlemen, 147
Martha, Princess, 113
Martin Van Buren, 64, 210, 211
Martinique, 110 – 112
Maugher's Beach, 59, 121,
 237
Maynard Street, 184
McEuan, Mrs. Janet, 159,
 164, 166, 169
McLean Street, 95, 246
McNab Battery, 15
McNab's Island, 36, 40, 42,
 51, 54 – 57, 59, 60, 65, 67,
 68, 212, 237
McNally, Archbishop John T.,
 142
McNaughton, General
 A.G.L., 34
Melville Cove, 6
Melville Island Military
 Prison, 53
Melville Island, 67, 68
Memorial Library, 249
merchant aircraft carriers, 78,
 79
Merson Farm, 191
Michaud, J.E., 95
MicMac, 120, 123
Midland (Ontario) Free Press, 226
Mid-Ocean Meeting Point, 71
Military District 6, 85
Military Police, 67, 219
Mills Brothers, 169
Mills, Gertrude, 173, 174
Mills, Hugh, 174, 175
Mills, Jean, 172 – 174
Milton Hydro-Electric Co.
 Ltd., 214

minesweepers, 61 – 64
Mingo, Colonel Edgar, 33, 248
Minister of National Defence, 34
Miss Canada girls, 156
Mitchell, Humphrey, 95
Mogull Film Studios, 28
Moirs Chocolates, 132 – 34
Monarch of Bermuda, 37, 104
Moncton, 92
Montebello, Que., 115
Montgomery, Flora, 174
Montreal Standard, 188
Montreal, 103, 105, 106, 130, 134, 163, 248
Montrolite, 131
Moreton Bay, 94
Morris Lake, 54
Morris Street, 233
Mount Saint Vincent College, 9, 144
Mulgrave Park, 24, 126, 192
Mulgrave, 60
Mumford Road, 149
Munich Accord, 7, 103
Murphy, Joseph, 134
Murphy's Limited, 134
Murray, Admiral Leonard W., 69, 72, 231, 234, 235
Murrow, Edward R., 147
Musquodoboit Harbour, 169
Musquodoboit, 46

N

N.B. Leiesten, 97
Nagle, Constable, 229
Narrows, the, 119, 245
Narvik, 87
National Council of Women, 87
National Defence Headquarters, 44
National Employment Service, 243
National Fish, 153
National Harbours Board, 75
National Housing Act, 190
National Registration, 23
National Registration. *See* National Resources Mobilization Act
National Resources Mobilization Act, 22, 34
National Selective Service Act, 126

National Selective Service Office, 44
National Selective Service, 23
National War Labour Board, 25
National War Services Advisory Board, 159
National Youth Training Plan, 125
Naval Control Service, 15
Naval Headquarters, 238
Naval Magazine, 224, 236, 239
Naval-Control-of-Shipping office, 70
Navy Island Cove, 54
Navy League Club House, 167
Navy League Forum, 148
Navy League House, 96
Navy League of Canada, 166 – 68, 170, 173
Neagle, Anna, 115
N.C.S. *See* Naval-Control-of-Shipping
Nelles, Admiral Percy W., 45
Nelson Sea Cadet Corps, Drake Division, 138
Nelson, Robert John Roddick, 120
Nemanja, 99
Netherlands, 20
New Glasgow, 192
New Waterford, 234
New York City, 65, 103,
New York, 28, 69, 70, 108, 109, 122 – 24, 147, 182
Newfoundland, 77, 132, 170
Nictaux Falls, 214
Ninth Heavy Battery, R.C.A., 37, 46
No. 1 Fortress Company, 40
No. 1 R.C.A.F. Maitland, 175
No. 5 Bomber Reconnaissance Squadron, 77
No. 6 District Depot, 39
Nolan, Captain D.N., 99
Noorduyne Aircraft, 118
Nootka, 120, 123
Norg, 124
Norma, 107
Norman's Restaurant, 194, 201
Normandie, 123
Norseman aircraft, 118
North Atlantic and West

Indies Squadron (Royal Navy), 41
North Atlantic Patrol, 77
North End Servicemen's Canteen, 21, 159, 160, 164
North Nova Scotia Highlanders, 242
North Park Street, 171, 244, 246
North Street, 76, 238, 244, 245, 246
North West Arm Patrol, 138
North West Arm, 12, 66, 143, 246
Norway, 20, 107, 176
Norwegian Government-in-Exile, 166
Notting Park School, 193
Nova Scotia Department of Agriculture, 203
Nova Scotia Light and Power, 11 – 14, 128 – 30, 213 – 18, 232, 240
Nova Scotia Liquor Commission, 162, 164, 165, 210, 232
Nova Scotia Supreme Court, 128
Nova Scotia Technical College, 54, 125, 129
Nova Scotian Hotel, 28, 148, 177, 180, 195, 232
NS.L&P. *See* Nova Scotia Light and Power
NSS. *See* National Selective Service
Nueva Andalucia, 211

O

Ocean Terminals, 8, 10, 16, 17, 36, 65, 82, 108, 115, 122, 130, 155, 203, 245
Ocean View Bus Company, 217
Ocean View Manor, 38
Ocean View School, 38
Ochterloney Street, 14, 239
Odell House, 166
Oerlikon guns, 121
Ogdensburg, New York, 92
Ogilvie Battery, 15
Oland, Colonel Sidney C., 95, 231, 245
Oland, Richard, 15
Olav, Crown Prince, 113, 114, 172

Ontario, 120
Operation Shuttle, 131, 132
Oran, 112
Oronsay, 89
Orpheus Male Choir, 174
Orpheus Theatre, 145, 230
Osborne Head, 51, 77
Ottawa, 103, 105, 107, 108, 109, 111, 114, 120, 156, 221, 248
Oxford Street, 184, 190, 246

P

Page, Major General L.F., 52
Pan American Clipper flying boats, 132
Panama Canal, 110
Paper Mill Lake, 133
Paradise, the, 179
Paris, 21, 110
Park Street School, 38
Park Transit Limited, 217
Pasteur, 108, 109, 129
Paterson, John, 120
Pay Corps, 84
Payzant, J.W., 95
Pearl Harbor, 27, 72, 165, 198
Pelletier, Germaine, 177
Pender's Bus, 140, 217
Pennant, 51
People's Credit Jewellers, 234
Petain, Marshal Henri, 21, 112
Peter Schering, 92, 93
Pettipas, Dr. Arthur, 95
Philadelphia, 179
Phoney War, the, 19, 23, 91, 108, 203
Picton, Ont., 46, 53
Pictou Foundry and Machine Company, 220
Pictou Highlanders, 242
Pictou Lodge, 115
Pictou, 192
Pier 21, 86, 91, 94, 242
Piercy's fire, the, 152
Pine Hill Divinity Hall, 152
Pine Hill, 143
Placentia, 71
Pleasant Street, 38
Plymouth Cordage Company, 135
Point Pleasant Park, 9, 20, 28, 55, 56, 155, 216, 239, 246
Poissonier, Jean, 109

Poland, 102
Port Dufferin, 77
Port of Halifax, 193
Port Williams, 169
Porters, Montreal, 135
Portuguese Cove, 210
post-war planning, 244 – 47
Predictor, 54
Prefabs, 191 – 193
Preston, 77
Prince Edward Island Highlanders, 38, 46
Prince Street, 179
Prince's Lodge, 34, 54
Princess Helene, 28
Princess Louise Fusiliers, 15, 38, 80, 242
prisoners of war, 91
Public Gardens, 148, 167, 228
Public Health Clinic, 10, 143
Public Service Commission, 221, 222
Purcell's Cove, 175, 217
Purdy Bros., 125

Q

Q.E.H. *See* Queen Elizabeth High School
Quarantine Hospital, 222
Quebec Conference, first, 113, 122
Quebec Conference, second, 113
Quebec, 34, 35, 120, 216
Queen Elizabeth High School, 9, 138 – 42
Queen Elizabeth, 36, 83, 131
Queen Mary Club of Charlottetown, 170
Queen Mary, 36, 83, 113, 114, 122, 131, 221
Queen Mary, 114
Queen Street, 160, 164, 165, 221
Quinpool Road, 6, 142, 184, 239
Quisling, Vidkun, 20

R

R.A.F. *See* Royal Air Force
Raddall, Thomas, 17, 122, 177
Raeder, Grand Admiral, 19
Railway Labor Camp, 181

Rainbow Haven, 161
Ralston, J.L., 34
Ramilies, 129
Rampura, 129, 130
Range Pier (Wreck Cove), 40
Rangitki, 94
Rathlin, 175
Rations Boards, 176, 206
Raymond, Squadron Leader Adelard, 111, 112
R.C.A. *See* Royal Canadian Artillery
R.C.A.F. Dartmouth, 28, 41, 42, 46, 53, 77, 78, 84, 85, 138, 155, 161, 214, 218, 239
R.C.A.F. Dartmouth, 76, 118, 184, 192
R.C.A.F. embarkation depot, 161
R.C.A.F. Marine Section, 77, 78
R.C.A.F. *See* Royal Canadian Air Force
R.C.A.F. Women's Division, 43
R.C.A.S.C. *See* Royal Canadian Army Service Corps
R.C.M.P. *See* Royal Canadian Mounted Police
R.C.N. *See* Royal Canadian Navy
R.C.N.V.R. *See* Royal Canadian Navy Volunteer Reserve
R.C.O.C. *See* Royal Canadian Ordnance Corps
RDX explosive, 238, 241
Red Cross Civilian Emergency Organization, 154
Red Cross, 22, 139, 143, 150, 159, 170, 171
Regina Rifles, 80
Regional Director of Transit Control, 194
Registrar for National Selective Service, 33, 248
Reid, Commodore, 110
Reo II, 60
Repulse, 35, 102
Resolution, 102
Resources Mobilization Act
Revenge, 37, 61, 89, 104, 176
Rex Café, 93
Rex, the, 179
Richmond School, 20, 138

INDEX

R.N.A.S. *See* Royal Naval Air Service

Robert Simpson department store, 15

Robertson, Angus, 49

Robertson, Struan, 237

Robie Street reservoir, 93

Robie Street, 12, 178, 184, 185, 244, 245, 246,

Rockefeller Foundation, 143, 244

Rockhead, 54

Rockingham elementary school, 140

Rockingham, 34, 142, 238

Roda, Mr. and Mrs., 172

Roman Catholic Infirmary, 10

Roosevelt, Franklin D., 8, 71, 113, 122

Roseland Dance Hall, 148

Rotterdam, 16

Rotterdam, 20

Roue, W.J., 219

Rouger, Admiral Pierre, 111

Rouille, 237

Roy Building, 153

Royal Air Force, 46, 80, 94, 221

Royal Artillery Park, 246

Royal Canadian Air Force, 8, 15, 17, 30, 35, 42, 43, 44, 66, 67, 76, 79, 80, 84, 95, 96, 111, 118, 119, 130, 131, 139, 160, 161, 193, 194, 199, 202, 225, 242

Royal Canadian Army Service Corps, 40, 83, 84

Royal Canadian Artillery, 37, 80

Royal Canadian Mounted Police, 13, 31, 66, 67, 93, 132, 164, 209, 212, 232, 234

Royal Canadian Navy Volunteer Reserve, 40

Royal Canadian Navy, 15, 16, 28, 35, 40, 41, 49, 60, 61, 62, 64, 66, 69, 70, 71, 72, 75, 80, 96, 119, 124, 130, 135, 143, 159, 161, 193, 197,198, 199, 202, 239

Royal Canadian Ordnance Corps, 39

Royal Canadian Regiment, 67

Royal Commission, 235

Royal Dutch Navy, 80

Royal Marines, 80

Royal Naval Air Section, 78

Royal Naval Air Service, 79

Royal Naval Air Station Dartmouth, 78

Royal Naval Hospital, 40

Royal Navy, 14, 16, 28, 61, 71, 72, 78, 79, 80, 90, 108, 109, 110, 112, 130, 159, 163

Royal Navy's Trade Division, 70

Royal Netherlands Navy, 114

Royal New Zealand Air Force, 80

Royal Norwegian Navy, 80, 100, 113

Royal, the, restaurant, 179

rubber, 198

Russell Lake, 54

Russell Street, 159

Russia, 122

S

Sable Island, 77

Sackville Street, 93, 196, 197, 228, 229, 230, 233, 246

Sacred Heart Convent, 9

Saguenay, 7, 16

Sailors Rifle Club of Port Colborne, 170

Saint John, 28, 48, 73

Saint Mark's Church, 21, 159, 160

Saint Mary's College, 142

Saint Mary's High School, 9

Saint Patrick's High School, 9, 138, 140

Saint Paul's, 190, 191

Salter Street, 229

salvage, 154 – 58

Salvage Committee, 157, 158

Salvation Army, 66, 85, 159, 161, 173

Sambro Lightship, 64, 77

Sambro, 211

Samuel Brookfield, 119

San Andres, 107

Sandwich Battery, 15, 31, 50, 51, 66, 116, 174

Sandwich Point, 56

Sangster, Dorothy, 188

Sarnia, 63

Saskatoon, 89

Scharnhorst, 13

Schleisen, 7

Schleswig-Holstein, 7

School Board Commissioners, 141

School for the Blind, 89

Scotian, 220

Scott, Randolph, 145

Sea cadets, 138

Seaborne, 16

Searchlights, 54 – 58

Seebach, Thile, 7

Service Police, 67

Sexton, Dr. F.H., 129

Shatford, George, 237

Shaw, Fred, 99

Sheet Harbour, 169

Shelburne, 5, 6, 73

Shirreff Hall, 143, 144

Shore Patrol, 231, 233

Shubenacadie Canal, 247

Shubenacadie, 169

Silver Slipper, 148

Singapore, 85, 100, 165

Sisters of Charity, 142

Skeena, 7, 16

Sleepy Cove, 59

Smith's Falls, Ont., 92

Sons of Temperance, 181

South Barracks, 67

South Commons, 17

South Park Street, 152, 183, 184, 228, 244, 246

South Shore, 27, 183

South Street, 39, 52, 80, 179, 245

Southampton, 7

Spion Kop, 50, 51

Spring Garden Road Courthouse, 228

Spring Garden Road, 10, 54, 80, 144, 169, 173, 174, 181, 183, 184, 221, 228, 230, 244, 246

Springhill, 192

Spryfield, 189, 217

St. Croix, 131

St. Croix, 96

St. John Ambulance, 150, 151

St. John's, 69, 72

St. Laurent, 16

St. Lawrence River, 92, 119

St. Lawrence shipyards, 73

St. Lucia, 86

St. Margaret's Bay Road, 178

St. Margaret's Bay, 161, 214

St. Mary's University, 9

St. Patrick's Home, 149

St. Paul's cemetery, 230

Stalin, Joseph, 122
Stanley Airport, 35, 174
Stanley, 173
Stanley, Carleton, 144
Starr Manufacturing, 10
Stewart, Dr. H.L., 147
Stimson trainer, 111
Stranraer 908 flying boat, 42, 64, 77
Strawberry Battery, 45, 48, 51, 55, 56
Stureholm, 46
Sun Life Building, 103
Sunderland flying boat, 116
Superintendent of Health, 209, 211
Sussex, N.B., 38
Sweeny, Mingo, 52
Swift Canadian Company, 208
Swordfish aircraft, 78, 79
Sydney Steel, 158
Sydney, 48, 70, 216, 234

T

T. Hogan & Co., 125
Taylor Shoe building, 134
Teck, Duke of, 114
Tennessee, 216
Tenth Searchlight Battery, R.C.E., 37, 55
Theatre Arts Guild, 173
There Too Go I, 115
Third Battle Squadron, 16
Third Republic, 108
Third Squadron (Royal Navy), 21
Thirlby, 96
Thrum Cap, 209
Timberlea, 178
Time magazine, 166
Tobin Street, 164, 245, 246
Toronto Star, 14
Toronto, 106, 216
Toulon, 108,
Tower Road School, 54
Tower Road, 54
Towers, Graham, 110
Tracking and Routing Section (British Admiralty), 68, 69
Trade Union Act, 1937, 127
Transit Controller, the, 27
Treatt, Major B.D., 44, 49
Trenton, 192
Trewelland, 219
Trongate, 236, 237, 238

Truro, 27, 35, 89, 161, 203, 205
Tufts Cove, 14, 120, 190, 191
Tuscaloosa, 8
Tyr, 99

U

U-119, 62
U-1232, 210
U-1232, 63
U-190, 63
U-30, 17
U-47, 17
U-517, 197
U-806, 63
Unemployment Insurance Plan, 243
Union Café, 179
Union of Marine and Shipbuilding Workers of Canada, 128
Union Station, 83
United Church, 143, 162
United Kingdom Security Deposit Agency, 103
United Services Organization, 173, 174
United States Lines, 99
United States Navy, 70, 71, 100
University of King's College, 143
Upper Canada, 126, 196
U.S. Navy. See United States Navy
U.S.O. See United Services Organization

V

Vancouver, 134
VE Day parade, 231
VE Day riots, 224 – 35, 248
VE Day, 181, 207, 217, 224 – 35
Venezuela, 19, 131
Veteran's Land Act, 243
Veterans Guard, 80
Vichy, 21, 112
Victoria General Hospital, 10, 102
Victoria School, 151
Victory Bond campaigns, 155
Victory Garden, 32, 191, 203
Victory Loan Campaigns, 147, 153, 154, 155

Victory Loan Parade, 80
Volendam, 89
Volunteer, 237, 238
Von Werra, Franz, 91, 92, 94

W

W. & A. Moir, Ltd., 125
WABC, 146
Waegwoltic Club, 138, 171
Wakefield, 100
Wallace's Shoe Store, 233
Walrus aircraft, 78, 79
Wanderers Grounds, 35, 167, 239
War Assets Disposal Corporation, 151
War Bonds, 213
War Labour Board, 128
War Measures Act, 24, 95
War Savings Certificate, 156, 213
War Savings Committee, 156
War Savings Stamps, 18, 154, 156, 171
Wartime Housing Limited, 190 – 94, 214
Wartime Industries Control Board, 25, 26, 200, 204
Wartime Information Board, 29
Wartime Prices and Trade Board, 24, 25, 26, 171, 187, 189, 190, 194 196, 200, 202 – 206, 210
Washington, D.C., 78
Water Street, 14, 83, 154, 216, 218, 232, 245
Waterton, 39
Waverley, 239
Waverly Road, 177
Way, Thomas P., 125
WEAF, 145
Weagle, Hugh, 219
Wehrmacht, 6, 20, 102
Welcome to War Brides, 242
Wellington Barracks, 21, 40, 75, 76
Wellington Street, 80, 103
West Indian squadron, 110
West Nova Scotia Regiment, 242
West Sisters, 174
West Street fire station, 184
Western Nova Scotia Electric Co. Ltd., 214
Westgate, Murray, 174

INDEX

Weygand, General, 109
Where To Stay In Nova Scotia, 28
White Quartette, 172
White Rock, 214
White, Portia, 172
Whitehead, 51
W.I.C.B. *See* Wartime Industries Control Board
Wilhelm, Kaiser, 6
Wilhelmina, Queen, 115
William Collings & Sons, 125
Willis, J. Frank, 174
Willow Park Estate, 79
Willow Park, 40
Windmill Road, 191
Windsor Junction, 217, 239
Windsor Park, 10, 76, 79, 84, 225
Windsor Street, 39, 40, 79, 135, 142
Windsor Terrace, 239
Windsor, 217
WJZ, 146
Wm. Kennedy & Sons, 125
Women's Auxiliary Air Force (*see also* Women's Division, the), 43
Women's Council, the, 157
Women's Division, the, (*see also* Women's Auxiliary Air Force), 43, 44
Women's Institutes, 170
Women's Royal Canadian Naval Service, 40, 43, 44
Women's Volunteer Service Centre, 171
Women's War Work Committee, 170
Woods store, 233
Woodside, 10, 206
WOR, 146
W.P.T.B. Motor Controller, 198
W.R.C.N.S. *See* Women's Royal Canadian Naval Service
WRENS. *See* Women's Royal Canadian Naval Service
W.T.P.B. *See* Wartime Prices and Trade Board
Wurttemburg, 114

Y

Y Depot, 79, 80, 193

Y.M.C.A., 22, 66, 160, 172, 173, 174, 187
Y.W.C.A., 54, 170, 173
Yarmouth, 28, 35, 122, 182, 192, 234
York Redoubt, 16, 36, 40, 48, 51 – 56, 59, 65
York Shore Battery, 51, 59, 60
York Shore, 45, 53, 55, 56, 59
Young Avenue, 246
Young Street, 76, 134

Z

Ypres, 60, 61
Zeeland, 115
Zombies, 34, 67, 225

Marquis Book Printing Inc.

Québec, Canada
2009